D1500100

BACKS TO THE WALL

BACKS TO THE WALL

LONDON UNDER FIRE
1939–45

LEONARD MOSLEY

WEIDENFELD & NICOLSON
5 Winsley Street London W1

SBN 297 00271 6

Printed in Great Britain by Cox & Wyman Ltd.,
London, Reading and Fakenham

TO D. WITH MY LOVE

CONTENTS

CONTENTS

ILLUSTRATIONS

FOREWORD

This book is the story of how London and its people survived the five most painful and difficult years of their existence, from 1939–1945. It is not a statistical study of how the capital faced up to five years of war. It is not even a blow-by-blow account of London in World War Two. It is, instead, an attempt to show a great city struggling to adapt to a particularly agonising and (it sometimes seemed) endless war through the experiences, the aches, the pains, the tragedies, the deprivations, the fears, the fulfilments and the joys of the people who were there. In other words, it is many kinds and conditions of London seen by many kinds and conditions of its citizens and visitors, and I hope it comes to life through their eyes as the great sprawling, palpitating, suffering but magnificent monster that it was during the dire days of World War Two.

If I have succeeded in bringing it back to life, I have many people to thank for helping me to do so.

First of all there are those who gave me precious hours of their time to talk to me and remember. They include Lord Snow, who delved back with wit and sagacity into the days when he was a denizen of the corridors of power; Lord Boothby, who recalled life at Westminster and his own heart-breaking moments there; Henry Moore, o.m., whose artistic life was catalysed in the underground railways of London; Commander Reginald K. Smith who described his experiences with the Metropolitan Police in the East End; my old friends Jack Davies and Harold Conway with their memories of the world of the London theatre; Joan St George Saunders, for not only telling me of her own experiences but finding others who could tell theirs; and a whole host of others whose anecdotes and recollections have helped to add the circumstantial details to the story. It will become apparent to those who read the narrative (particularly those sections dealing with Free French operations in London) why some of these are not specified here.

I should like to thank the British Broadcasting Corporation for allowing me to quote from two recordings in their archives dealing with the Blitz in London.

Then there are those who have lent me their diaries or responded in other ways to my inquiries. I would particularly specify Mr Donald Ketley, who spent his boyhood in wartime London and has vividly recalled it for me from his present home in Maryland; Mr David Meade, who was a policeman in Limehouse, but now teaches in Connecticut; and many scores of others, native Londoners and soldiers-in-passage, upon whom wartime London left its mark.

There is one diarist I must single out from all the others. She is Miss Vere Hodgson. A social worker in Holland Park and Notting Hill from 1940 onwards, she faithfully and spiritedly recorded the life of her community and of her beloved London all through the triumphs and disasters of the war. It is a remarkable record. I am in her debt for allowing me to use extracts from it.

Finally, and most importantly, Mr Tom Harrisson has given me access to the Mass–Observation Papers. In the 1930s Tom Harrisson pioneered a method of sounding public opinion and public feeling which went much deeper into the thoughts and ideas of the masses than any of the forms of opinion-canvassing which have since been developed. In communities all over Britain he picked observers of both sexes and from all walks of life who 'listened in' on their friends and neighbours and reported what they said, how they felt, what they liked, what they hated. But these observers were not merely reporters of how their friends felt. They were urged to express their own likes and dislikes, and to do it in the most forthright fashion, whether they were criticising governments, politicians, regulations, policies, fashions, trends, or (when it came) the war itself. It is a tribute to Tom Harrisson's guidance and the trust that his observers placed in him that they never failed to do so. At the end of this book you will find further details of how this remarkable organisation, Mass–Observation, was conceived and its life organised. Suffice to say here that through MNO a fascinating picture has been built up of life in Britain during the 1930s and World War Two, and it is a treasure trove for historians.

A sample of the gold that is there will be found in this book.*
The Papers have now been deposited with the University of
Sussex and the good news is that Tom Harrisson himself will be
working with them over the next two or three years. The books he
distils from these remarkable documents cannot fail to be absorb-
ing, exciting and invaluable. In the meantime, the extracts I have
used will, I hope, give a flavour of the riches to come.

Elsewhere will be found a full list of all those who have helped
me with facts, figures or anecdotes. They have my deep appreciation.

* To preserve the standards of Mass–Observation and the independence of its observers, the identity of all those who reported for them
throughout the war has been concealed by pseudonyms or initials but
their reports are exactly as they wrote them.

ACKNOWLEDGEMENTS

In addition to those who have been named in the Foreword, I should like to express my thanks to many people in all parts of the world who were in London during World War Two and have taken the trouble to search their memories or their records for facts, figures and anecdotes. They include the following:

Lieut. Comm. Kenneth W. Allison, USNR, Washington DC
Dr W. Babinski, Montreal
Mrs Elsie M. Banister, St Andrews, Fife
Mrs S. T. Brown, Pittsburgh, Pa.
Commander L. J. Burt, CVO, CBE, London
Richard Collier, Burgh Heath, Surrey
Col. John J. Christy, Fort Benjamin Harrison, Indiana
Mrs Rita Cheren, New York
Mrs Tania Long Daniell, Ottawa
Rodney Dennys, Steep, Sussex
B. J. Enright, MA, Librarian, University of Sussex
Mrs P. Forster, London
Major Carl R. Greenstein, Sacramento, Calif.
Irving Gerdy, Penndel, Pa.
Admiral John Godfrey, Wilmington, Sussex
Col. Gerald M. Holland, Washington DC
Mrs Leland Hayward, Connecticut
Howard W. Johnson, Brookline, Mass.
A. H. Ketley, Romford, Essex
Eric Mandell, Philadelphia, Pa.
Staff Serg. Wilford B. Marshall, San Diego, Calif.
Mrs J. Nestor, Forest Hills, N.Y.
Gen. Carl. A. Spaatz, Chevy Chase, Maryland
David A. Shephard, New York
H. S. Taylor, Pakenham, Suffolk
Mrs Joyce Webb, Hastings, Sussex
Rev. C. Williams, London

PROLOGUE

THE LAST DAYS OF PEACE

On the evening of 3 September 1939 as dusk settled over the rooftops of the great city, a strange hush fell upon London such as no man had known since the days of the Great Plague. It was as if most of the capital's seven million souls had suddenly died. An observer who strolled in the gathering dark from Hyde Park Corner to Piccadilly Circus passed only three people on his mile long journey. Even the prostitutes who plied their trade in those days along the pavements between the Park Lane Hotel and Half Moon Street had vanished, as though deciding that on this night men's preoccupations would not include sex.

In Piccadilly Circus the lights had been doused on the animated signs that made this the brightest and gayest spot in the British Empire. No flower girls sat underneath the statue of Eros at its hub, for there were no passers-by to buy favours from them. The winged figure of Eros himself had been boarded up, as if to emphasise the disappearance of love from the capital. It was so quiet that the honking of the geese on the Green Park lakes was plainly audible, though two miles away.

Further east, on the other side of the city, Police Constable David Meade walked his beat along Limehouse Causeway and reflected that he had never felt so lonely in his life. 3 September 1939 was a Sunday, and in this part of the East End Sunday night was the time when everyone came out for a beer and a sing-song. The pubs filled up with Cockney couples. Their kids played hopscotch on the pavements outside. Often there was trouble and strife as closing time approached, but there was life too. Tonight Limehouse was dead. The pubs had closed early because they hadn't got their black-out curtains fixed yet, and it was an offence to show a light. The chalk-marks on the flagstones with which the kids marked out their games were dim and smudged. The ropes they threw over the gaslamps for swings hung limp and frayed from the crossbars. David Meade suddenly realised how they must have felt in Hamelin Town after the Pied

I

Piper had passed by, for here too in London the children were gone.

As he turned down a narrow street towards the river the darkness finally closed in and no lights came on to relieve it. The men who walked the East End streets each evening at dusk, turning on the gaslamps, had put away their poles for the duration. The way ahead was suddenly the arena for a frightening game of blind man's buff, with a sandbag, a pothole, a broken kerb or a swinging door waiting to strike or bruise him every yard of the way. Meade had practised walking in the dark for several months, in preparation for this night, but he shied in alarm when a cat squawked in an alleyway and then a stream of male profanity came from behind the blacked-out window of a house just beside him.

From across the housetops of an eery, silent London locked away behind its own doors, the great bell of Big Ben began chiming 11 o'clock, and the sound was taken up by the bell towers of half a dozen churches across the blacked-out city.

Eleven o'clock on a Sunday night – and, David Meade told himself, wryly, all was not well.

For one thing, there was a war on. Twelve hours earlier Britain's ultimatum to Germany had expired, and for the people of Britain the first night of World War Two was upon them. How long would it be before the horrors that had been forecast came raining down upon their heads?

2

Only four weeks earlier it had still been possible to hope that war could be avoided. At the beginning of August the nation's spirits had risen at the news that Parliament was adjourning for the summer recess and would not be back on their benches until October 3. If MPs could go away for that long, surely things couldn't be as bad as they seemed.

True, many Members on both sides of the House of Commons (Tory supporters of the Government as well as Labour Party opponents) had pleaded or exhorted the Prime Minister, Neville Chamberlain, to keep the summer session going, or curtail the recess to two or three weeks. The times were too dangerous for holidays, said one MP, a back-bencher named Winston Churchill. In Germany the Nazi dictator, Adolf Hitler, was mobilising the German armed forces and getting ready to march upon Poland,

Britain's ally in Eastern Europe. The Government was pledged to come to Poland's aid in the event of an attack. The German dictator had a habit of grabbing countries while the democracies were holidaying. Was this the time for the nation's watchdogs to disperse?

With the bland superiority which infuriated his opponents, Neville Chamberlain had brushed all the objections aside. The destinies of Britain could safely be left in his hands, he told them. One of his most fervent supporters, Henry ('Chips') Channon, had rushed out to the library while Churchill was speaking to check on some dates. He now pushed a note across to his premier who read it, smiled at him in thanks, and then pointed out that Hitler had invaded Austria while the House was sitting, had occupied Prague while the House was sitting, while his fellow-dictator, Benito Mussolini, had taken over Albania only a few hours after Parliament had risen. So, apparently, the dictators did not seem to worry whether the Commons was on holiday or not. MPs could rest assured that the situation was in good hands, and neither they nor the country at large must allow themselves to be panicked by the alarmist speeches of some of his friends behind him. 'Chips' Channon swung round and grinned in triumph at Churchill and his friends, bunched on the benches behind him. He called them the Glamour Boys, and loathed every one of them: Churchill himself, 'always howling for war,' the wild young Scot, Robert Boothby, and the equally wild, red-headed Irishman, Brendan Bracken, his faithful henchman; and all the other opponents of Chamberlain's policies – Anthony Eden, Leopold Amery, Harold Nicolson, Alfred Duff Cooper – who were trying to drag the country into what Channon believed was a quite unnecessary war. He was delighted at their discomfiture.

'The PM used [my] notes with devastating effect,' he wrote in his diary later.* 'By the very brilliance of his performance, and it was his third in one week, he infuriated the House, as everyone hates the truth about himself. When he sat down there were roars of delight and approval, but also some of rage.' From the Glamour Boys, of course.

The House stood adjourned until October 3, but would be recalled, the premier said silkily, 'should the need arise.'

If many an MP walked home from the House that night with

* Chips Channon, *Diaries*, Weidenfeld and Nicolson, London 1967.

fear in his heart for what lay ahead, most Londoners heard the news with joy and relief. It might not happen after all. In which case they could get back to what every decent Cockney was concerned with in August, planning where to go and what to do over the Bank Holiday weekend.

3

'Parliament is taking a holiday – why not you?' said an advertisement in the *Daily Express* that weekend. 'Visit the Belgian Coast, where everyone is happy, peaceful and smiling.'

The Harriman family did not go anything like so far afield, but the fact that they went anywhere at all was an indication of the way fortunes had changed for them in 1939. For the past four years, ever since the clothing factory in Aldgate had closed down, Bill Harriman had been out of a job, and no amount of queuing at the employment exchange or hanging around factory gates had found him another. The Harrimans hadn't been too surprised about that. In their Canning Town street of forty-four small houses, eighteen men, fourteen youths and twelve women had been out of work for more than two years. Two million workless were living on the dole in Britain.

Whenever she went up to the West End of London and looked at the fashionable shops, saw all the smart women and shiny cars, and heard money clinking in people's pockets, Eileen Harriman used to wonder bitterly whether they realised how the other half was living. This was a different world, a world where they had Empire Shopping Weeks in Bond Street and banners saying 'Be Proud of our Glorious Empire'. Did anyone in Bond Street guess that in Canning Town – and that was part of the glorious Empire, wasn't it? – the Harriman family of four people were living on thirty-four shillings a week and existing on a diet of mainly bread, potatoes and scrag ends of meat? Did they know what slum houses were like, with the rats and beetles from next door and holes in the roof? Did they know that the Harriman children, John and Linda, though they were bathed from head to foot twice a week in the kitchen, brought nits back in their hair from school that Eileen had to comb out with a dog-comb? Did they know about the Means Test, and the snoopers who came round to keep an eye on you and see that you didn't take a job on the side and

4

not report it? Eileen Harriman had taken a job, just the same – as a charwoman in a bank two hours' journey away in the West End. That distance away, no one knew you, and she didn't have to declare the ten shillings a week; ten shillings with which she could get the kids' shoes mended, buy them the clothes they were always wearing out or growing out of, and give Bill the odd shilling for a pint of beer and a bit of company at the pub. But she had to get up at four o'clock every morning, it took eight hours out of her life every day, and she was always dog tired. For four years Eileen Harriman hadn't had a drink, a new dress, or been to a film. She was twenty-nine years old.

But now, suddenly, things were better. There was a war coming, and it had changed their lives. The Government had voted for conscription and all the young men were being called up. That meant uniforms. The factory in Aldgate had reopened and Bill was back in his old job. There were still rats scrabbling about in the back lavatory, the landlord wouldn't mend the roof even though they had paid the rent, and the kids still came home with nits in their hair. But the hire purchase on the furniture was paid up. New shoes for the kids. A pair of flannels and a jacket for Bill, and a frock for herself. She had even been to the cinema to see Gracie Fields in *Shipyard Sally*.

'You can thank old 'Itler for it,' Bill said, as they bussed back from the Granada in the Mile End Road.

'Bill,' Eileen said, 'd'you think there'll be a war?'

'What's it matter, so long as I'm working?' said Bill. 'And what can *we* do about it, anyway?'

'Dad, where are we going for Bank Holiday?' asked his nine year old daughter, Linda.

There were plenty of choices, and a record number of Londoners set off to enjoy them: a track meet at the White City, cricket at Lords and the Oval, the great fair on Hampstead Heath, Tyrone Power making a personal appearance at a cinema in Leicester Square, a parade of Empire troops in Hyde Park. But in the end, like a quarter of a million other Cockneys, the Harrimans had gone fifteen miles down the river to Southend, London's very own seaside resort.

They had lunched outside a pub on the promenade on stewed eels, fish and chips, and stout (with lemonade for the kids). Afterwards, as Bill and Eileen were dozing in deck-chairs and watching the ships plough their way out to sea from the Thames Estuary, the thud of guns had suddenly shaken the sultry heat of the afternoon. The coastal batteries at Shoeburyness, just round the corner of the estuary, were starting their regular practice firing. Eileen Harriman shivered.

'D'you think 'Itler'll bomb us if there's a war?' she asked.

Before Bill could answer, a man in the next deck chair thrust a newspaper towards her.

'Look, missus,' he said, 'we're on 'oliday 'ere. D'you mind not bringing up unpleasant subjects? 'Ere, read this!'

It was an editorial in a morning paper, and the Harrimans read it together.

'Don't let Hitler spoil your holiday,' it said. 'Don't talk about crisis news. Change the subject if others bring it up. Don't brood. Take plenty of exercise. Slack livers cause most of the world's gloom.'

Eileen Harriman angrily handed the newspaper back. 'Cheek!' she said.

' 'E's right, love,' Bill Harriman said. 'Come on, let's forget about it.'

They picked up the kids from the coconut shies and rode to the end of the pier. First they watched the ships going by, so close you could almost touch them, for Southend boasted the longest pier in the world. Then Bill took Eileen on to the open-air dance floor and finally coaxed her into trying a brand new dance called 'Boomps a'Daisy,' in which partners banged their buttocks together. Eileen secretly thought it was even more vulgar than 'Knees up Mother Brown,' that other cockney stand-by. But she got a lot of laughs from the community singing which followed, especially when a compère got them singing a new hit called 'Boop Boop Dittem Dottem Whattem CHOO!'

It was midnight when they got home, tired but happy. There was an envelope lying on the mat, with the West Ham Council stamp outside. Inside was a mimeographed form saying:

EVACUATION

'In the event of an Emergency, arrangements have been made to evacuate school children from the London area to safe places in the country. It is hoped that your child/children will participate in this scheme. On receipt of further instructions, he/

6

she/they should report to Star Road School bringing with him/her/them hat, raincoat, haversack containing night-clothes, towel, soap, tooth brush and toothpaste, and he/she/they should wear a card round his/her/their neck(s) giving his/her/their full name(s), age(s), School, home address and names of next of kin.'

Eileen Harriman found it hard to sleep that night, but she told herself that she was simply over-tired from such a lovely day's outing.

4

It so happened that the MP for Southend-on-Sea was Chamberlain's fervid admirer and supporter, Henry ('Chips') Channon, and a more unlikely representative of that gamey cockney seaside resort could hardly have been found. For 'Chips' was considered by most of fashionable London to be the biggest snob of them all, and it was a title he would not have thought of repudiating. He was proud to be a snob. He had inherited his Southend seat in Parliament from his rich in-laws (who controlled the local Tory Party), and he had proved to be a conscientious MP to whom no constituent in trouble ever appealed for help in vain.

But that did not mean that he wanted to mix with them, and even less with the crude characters who swarmed in from the East End every weekend to gorge themselves on beer and fish-and-chips. Henry Channon was quite content to accept England as it was in 1939, a land divided into Them and Us, the ruled and those who had been chosen to rule them. He was a firm believer in the right of breeding, background and money. He considered London the centre of the earth. 'One of those London days,' he once wrote, 'when one's blood surges within one, and one is madly desperately happy, when one is tempted to spend a quarter's income on flowers, and something puckish impels one to a thousand capers. Oh, this London!' For him, the British Empire was the greatest institution in the history of man, and he could find no fault with it. One of his great fears was that if war came class barriers would crash down in London and the Empire would break up. The egalitarian society would be upon him, and equality was the last thing he wished to see in England.

Ironically enough, 'Chips' Channon was an American.* It was to get away from egalitarianism that he had given up his US citizenship in the 1920s and become a naturalised Englishman, since which time he had been elected to Parliament, made secretary to R. A. Butler at the Foreign Office,† married into the aristocracy, and become indistinguishable from the princes, dukes, duchesses and powerful Tory businessmen and politicians in whose circles he now moved. 'Oh, land of freedom,' he wrote of England, 'where women are all sirens and men are all gods!' He meant upper class women and men, of course.

After Parliament went into recess that August, 'Chips' had refused an invitation from friends of Neville Chamberlain to go North to the Scottish grouse moors, and he had retired instead to Kelvedon Hall, the estate in Essex which he shared with his wife, Honor, daughter of Lord Iveagh. Honor Channon was heiress to the millions her family made from Guinness stout, the favourite tipple of 'Chips's' Southend constituents.

'I woke up at six, got up and went for a long walk in the woods with Bundi,' he wrote in his diary on 6 August. 'There were yokels working, clearing out the debris, and the Essex sun shone through the trees. The noise of chopping and of boughs dragged over the turf was like a Grimm fairy story . . . We lazed all day . . . Honor and I intend to spend the rest of the month quietly here, if events in the outside world will let us.'

Three days later, however, the telephone rang and summoned him back to London. His boss, R. A. Butler, was already there and so was Neville Chamberlain. The Foreign Office had secret information that Hitler was planning a 'spectacular move' on 15 August, but Channon was warned not to let a word of it get out either to his fellow MPs or the public. 'I am genuinely apprehensive,' he wrote that night at his huge house in Belgrave Square. But he was 'quite childish in my fanatical worship of the PM,' and he was sure he would save them yet.

So was the British public. A group of London holidaymakers at Margate were asked, in a snap poll, whether they thought that Hitler would get from Poland the territorial demands he was

---

* Born in Chicago on 7 March, 1897, only son of a rich Middle West business man, he came to Europe in World War One and never went back, except for visits.

† Butler was Under Secretary of State for Foreign Affairs.

threatening to take – the Free City of Danzig and the Polish Corridor. Five replied Yes, six No, and four were undecided.

'Do you think we should go to war to defend Danzig?' they were asked. Seven said Yes, four No, and three were undecided. 'Do you think there will be a war?' Eight said No, four Yes, and three were undecided. 'Do you think Hitler wants war – or is he bluffing?' All fifteen answered No, he's bluffing.

George Bernard Shaw, the Irish playwright and the public's favourite gadfly, didn't think there would be a war, either. 'The Jews will be Hitler's ruin in the long run,' he said, 'even if they perish with him, especially if enough perish with him. Has war become more imminent? No, the peace at present is maintained by funk. Anything that intensifies funk makes for peace ... A lasting peace is a dream, but any statesman who is not desperately afraid of starting a cannonade should be sent to a mental hospital.'

On the night of 9–10 August there was a practice black-out in London. Superintendent Reginald K. Smith of Scotland Yard, in charge of K Division, which covered the West End of London, climbed to the top of Marble Arch to look at the result and afterwards remarked that 'London looked like a Gruyère cheese with a candle behind it,' there were so many lights showing. A number of drunks gathered in Trafalgar Square to splash in the fountains and sing 'Show me the Way to Go Home.'

That night George Hitchin, a London bus driver, came back red-eyed to his council apartment in Hammersmith and said to his wife:

'Blimey, if that's what driving in the black-out's going to be like, I'd be better joining up and driving a tank.'

There had been traffic tie-ups all over London as cars, buses and lorries tried to pick their way through the streets on their side lights.

Flo Hitchin shook her head. 'You stick to your bus, love,' she said. 'At least they won't be firing things at your bus, even if there is a war.'

Thirteen months later, she and her husband were to learn how wrong she was.

5

But by mid-August, even the most optimistic ostriches in London were beginning to take their heads out of the sand. And when they did so, they could see great lolloping, elephantine shapes ringing London. The barrage balloons that would, it was hoped, scare away low-flying raiders were being tried out. Many of the crews were inexperienced, and the balloons were apt to behave like unruly bulls in changing temperature or high winds. A number broke loose and went nodding off across the North Sea. 'It's not like flying a kite,' said one disconsolate balloon commander.

The Home Secretary, Sir Samuel Hoare, was forced to reassure the public on the BBC about the efficacy of the street bomb-shelters which were now being erected around London. One of them (in South Wales) had been hit by lightning in a storm and five people sheltering inside had been killed. This, said Sir Samuel, was just a fluke. People were sceptical, and quietly made up their minds to avoid street shelters if and when air raids came. As it turned out, they were quite right.

For the superstitious there was more bad news a few days later. In the middle of August, the Minister for Air, Sir Kingsley Wood, left a Cabinet meeting to fly to Belfast to launch a new 23,000 ton aircraft carrier, *Formidable*. His wife went with him. Lady Wood stood talking to the other guests on the launching platform, her hand resting on the bottle of Empire wine she was to smash across *Formidable*'s bows, when a massive groan made her turn around. At the same moment the bottle was gently pulled out of her hand and bounced, unbroken, against the aircraft carrier's side. Underneath, where spectators were gathered along the slipway, the cry arose: 'She's moving!' There was half an hour still to go before the official launching but the big ship had decided not to wait.

Hastily, someone handed Lady Wood another bottle and, mumbling a blessing, she hurled it desperately towards the moving ship. It was a hit and the bottle smashed. But the cheers which greeted her marksmanship were soon stilled by the screams coming from below. As *Formidable* lumbered down towards the water, she was scattering struts and planks in all directions. One of them hit a woman and killed her. Others broke limbs among the crowd struggling to get out of the way. Slowly, the great carrier groaned her way to the end of the slips and sidled into the water. And now another crisis arose: would the tugs, still thinking they had half an hour to wait, make it in time to the hulk's side and halt her before she crashed into the opposite bank. They managed it. Britain's newest and biggest carrier was afloat, but behind her she left a trail of death, injury and debris. Dire prophecies, too, that *Formidable* was bound to be a ship with a jinx.*

The call-up of reservists and members of the Territorial Army had been going on quietly ever since the middle of the month. The newspapers made light of it by concentrating attention on the female volunteers who had signed up in the ATS (the Auxiliary Territorial Service) the previous autumn, during the Munich crisis, and were now being summoned for training.

> 'Rock-a-bye baby, or Daddy will spank,
>   Mother's at Aldershot, driving a tank.
> When the Camp's over, Mum will return
>   And oh! what a lot of new words you will
>   learn!'

So wrote one newspaper columnist. And an alarmed magistrate wrote to *The Times* to hope that 'the girls now going into the Forces will not be encouraged to wear masculine trappings like trousers on active service.'

There were pictures of pretty girls smiling and waving. But there were others. Jimmy Thomas, an ex-driver in the Royal Army Service Corps, got back from the garage in Pimlico where he was now working on the night of 18 August and found a letter from the War Office which told him to report to Chelsea Barracks twenty-four hours later. The day after that his wife, Sally, saw him off on a train for Southampton and a troopship for the Mediterranean. She was twenty-seven years old, the mother of three small children, and the Army would pay her an allowance of thirty-eight shillings a week while Jimmy was away. In fact, she was not to see him again for five years, in 1944.

6

London in 1939 was, unlike the Government (which was Tory controlled), in the hands of the Labour Party, and its leader was a fiery little one-eyed Socialist from the East End called Herbert Morrison. ' 'Erbie', as his Tory opponents never failed to remind

---

* In fact, the carrier emerged from the war unscathed after operations in the Mediterranean and Pacific.

him, had been a conscientious objector in World War One; he had, in fact, gone to jail for his beliefs. His attitude was different now, and he believed that Britain should stand up to Hitler even if it meant war. But that August, 1939, his main concern was not what Britain should do to Hitler but what Germany might do to London. As he repeatedly told his permanent officials at County Hall: 'You see before you a frightened man. Frightened at what's going to happen to this capital if we aren't ready in time to face up to what they will do to us.'

He had a report always in front of him on his desk at County Hall. It had been prepared for the Government by the Imperial Defence Committee, and it was a terrifying document. It purported to give considered estimations of what the Germans could do to Britain, and what they almost certainly would do, once war began. It began by insisting that Germany was overwhelmingly superior in bomber and fighter planes, enough to make them masters of the sky. Once war was declared (the Defence Committee maintained) these formidable fleets of planes would sweep across the North Sea and rain down their fire and high explosive bombs upon London, and they would continue to do so for sixty days and nights. The Committee estimated that, no matter what planes and anti-aircraft fire were turned against the German bomber fleets, they would get through. And 600,000 people would die, at least three quarters of them Londoners, and the capital would die with them. There would, moreover, be more than a million wounded people in the ruins, in need of hospitalisation. But the hospitals would have been hit too.

Herbert Morrison believed every word of this terrifying report. He had to. It would have been criminal folly to ignore it. For the past months, ever since the Munich scare of 1938, he had been hurrying his officials to make preparations for a great rain of death. He had worked in close co-operation with the Home Office and its experts on Air Raid Precautions. Now, as the crisis grew worse through the sunny August days, he could persuade himself that he had done almost all that was humanly possible to prepare for the horrors to come. All over London emergency first-aid and ambulance stations had been organised. Auxiliary fire service men had been called up to strengthen the London fire brigade. Air raid wardens walked the streets. There were water tanks ready for fire hoses in every district. Hospitals had raid-proof wards and operating theatres. There were blood banks and medical flying squads to take them where they were needed. To cater for the half a million dead that London could expect from the raids, he had requisitioned vast numbers of papier maché coffins. Swimming baths were closed 'for repairs'; in fact to store the papier mâché coffins. And all around the city great holes were being dug for the mass graves into which the victims would be heaped.

But it was London's children that haunted Herbert Morrison. There were a million of them, and he vowed that they should not be among those who would be killed or maimed when the bombs started to fall. The LCC's evacuation scheme had already been drawn up, trains and buses and lorries requisitioned, ready to take the children off to the country, away from the terror of the bombs.

In his opinion, they should have been sent away in mid-August, when the situation began to get really serious. 'So long as the children remain in London,' he kept saying, 'so long can Hitler blackmail us by threatening them. Let's get them out of the way, to places of safety, so we can stand up to the Nazis without worrying about what will happen to our tots.'

The only trouble was, the Government would not let the children go. Morrison was MP for an East End constituency whose children would be most vulnerable, for it was near the docks; and each time he went across Westminster Bridge to Whitehall from County Hall he would call in at 10, Downing Street and say to Sir Horace Wilson, Neville Chamberlain's aide: 'Let the people go.'

'My dear fellow,' Sir Horace would reply, with all the smoothness of his master, 'surely that would be a policy of panic, wouldn't it? Think what Mr Hitler would say if we did a thing like that? No, the PM is against all such panic measures as evacuating the children. For the moment, anyway.'

'I wouldn't like to have your conscience,' Morrison said, 'if you leave it too late.'

7

Not even when it was announced from Moscow and Berlin on August 22 that Russia and Germany were concluding a non-aggression Pact did 'Chips' Channon entirely give up hope that peace might still be snatched from the fire. The Pact meant that Germany no longer had to worry about a Russian attack from the rear, and could go ahead with her plans to invade Poland. 'Chips' shared Neville Chamberlain's loathing for the Russians, and his indignation against them boiled up. 'The Russians have double crossed us,' he wrote. 'They are the foulest people on earth.' He added: 'Perhaps we have a few more days, even weeks, of peace, but a partition of Poland seems inevitable. For if Poland resists we automatically go to war. But I cannot bear to think that our world is crumbling to ruins. I refuse to admit it … Everyone secretly or openly, whatever they may say, hopes that the Poles will climb down.'

The Poles were in no mood for that.

On the morning of 1 September, 1939 shortly after the BBC announcement that the German Armies had invaded Poland, Herbert Morrison burst into Sir Horace Wilson's office at 10, Downing Street.

'I know,' said Sir Horace. 'You want the children out of London. But we're not at war yet, and we wouldn't want to do anything to upset delicate negotiations, would we?'

'Look, 'Orace,' said Morrison, 'go in there and tell Neville this from me. If I don't get the order to evacuate the children from London this morning, I'm going to give it myself – *and* tell the papers why I'm doing it. 'Ow will 'is nibs like that?'

Half an hour later he was on his way back to County Hall with the necessary permission.

That day the Great Evacuation began.

For the next twenty-four hours, all over London, people turned to watch the long processions of children making their way to the railway and bus stations. Most of them had handed their haversacks over to their teachers, but each one carried a small square cardboard box around his or her neck with a gas mask in it. They had cards with their names on pinned to their lapels, and brothers and sisters clung to each other's hands like grim death, and refused to be parted.

Eileen Harriman had given both Linda and John a bath in the

kitchen that morning, after the message came around that they were wanted, and at two o'clock in the afternoon she took them round to Elm Road School. Most of the children were laughing and playing, as if it were a great adventure; but some looked frightened and some were crying, and so were a lot of their mothers. Linda and John said nothing, but just held each other's hands and looked up reproachfully at their mother.

'Why can't you come with us, Mum?' Linda said, at last.

'I just can't, love,' Eileen Harriman said. 'Who'd look after your father? You know he can't even boil an egg. It won't be long, anyway. We'll soon polish off Hitler, and then you can come home again.'

She made sure that they each had the half crown she had sewn into the linings of their raincoat pockets, and told them to keep together, whatever they did. Then the teacher called them together, formed them into a long crocodile, and then they were off, down the road to the buses that were to take them to Suffolk.

In all, a million children and two hundred thousand mothers left London in the great evacuation. After they had gone, the capital was suddenly a very empty place. There were no more nursemaids and prams in the parks, no more shouts and screams from the playgrounds, no more small boats on the ponds in Hyde Park and on Hampstead Heath. In the East End, particularly, something seemed suddenly to be wrong with the acoustics of the streets, and people seemed to be cocking their ears for a missing sound. No one talked about it much, but everyone noticed it, and was sad.

8

While the poor people's children poured out of London to the reception areas in Norfolk, Suffolk and the Midlands, many better-off parents were sending their offspring further afield. 'Chips' Channon was still hoping against hope for a last-minute 'arrangement' that would bring the engines of war to a grinding halt, and he resisted friends who urged him to send his son and heir, Paul* to the safety of relatives in the United States. He knew that those doing so were being bitterly attacked in the columns of the *Daily Worker*,

* Now, like his father before him, MP for Southend-on-Sea.

the Communist organ, for 'using their wealth to buy funk-holes for their pampered offspring.' In fact, no one blamed any parent for using what money they could scrape together to send their children to safety, and many middle-class parents sacrificed their savings to send them overseas. It was the flight of the well-to-do grown-ups from the capital which aroused most resentment and contempt. Shipping offices were full of people desperately trying to buy or bribe tickets out of the clerks for the United States or Canada. The roads to the West Country were already jammed with big cars packed with trunks and boxes of food. The search was on among the panic-stricken rich for what came soon to be known as 'safe hotels', where they proposed to stay for the duration. Many were in for painful shocks. What seemed to be peaceful havens in 1939 became prime targets in 1941 and 1944, as the fortunes and orientations of the war fluctuated.

By the night of 2 September the German Army had already been fighting inside Poland for thirty-six hours and its bombers were raiding Warsaw, Gdynia and Lwow, but still Britain – pledged to come to Poland's aid – had not declared war on Germany. Neville Chamberlain was waiting to concert his ultimatum with that of Britain's main ally, France, and they were dithering in Paris and pleading for time.

A restive House of Commons received Chamberlain's explanation of his procrastination with such hostility that he was white in the face when he sat down, and old hands whispered that he would have been voted out of office had it come to a vote. Even his Cabinet were in revolt against him. When he got back to 10 Downing Street at the end of the night's session he found them waiting for him around the table. They were not going to move, they told him, until he sent an ultimatum to Germany.

Chamberlain finally nodded his head. 'Right, gentlemen,' he said, 'this means war.'

When the news reached the House of Commons, 'Chips' Channon rushed up to a fellow MP Alec Dunglass.* 'Are we all mad?' he asked.

He turned to David Margesson, the Government Chief Whip, and urged him to wait for a few hours more. Margesson shook his head.

* Now Sir Alec Douglas-Home.

16

'It must be war, Chips, old boy,' he said. 'There's no other way out.'

It was raining in London that night. As a precaution, all street lights and public signs had been turned off.

'I creep carefully,' Harold Nicolson, MP wrote in his diary*, of his journey home. He foresaw a recrudescence in London of footpads and highway robbery.

9

At 11.15 a.m. on 3 September 1939, Neville Chamberlain informed the nation over the BBC that there had been no reply to the Government's ultimatum, and that Britain and Germany were now at war. Twenty minutes later the air raid sirens sounded over London.

There had been no cheering, only a sad, silent acceptance, of the state of war, and there was no panic as the sirens wailed the warning that bombers were approaching. The crowds outside 10 Downing Street and the Houses of Parliament walked swiftly, pretending not to hurry, to the nearest place of shelter, some to the underground urinals by the river, others to the cloisters of Westminster Abbey, but most to the street shelters in Whitehall. Further east, in St Paul's Cathedral, the unusually large congregation had just finished singing:

'O God of love, O King of Peace,
Make wars throughout the world to cease!'

when the warning came, and the Bishop of Willesden led the worshippers down to the crypt. The people of the East End were to know that crypt very well indeed in the months to come.

There was very little panic anywhere. There was hardly time, for the sirens sounded the All-Clear a quarter of an hour later. It had been a false alarm, and people emerged into the Sunday morning sunshine, looking sheepish.

10

But that night it was different. The sirens sounded again at two o'clock on the morning of 4 September stopping Police Constable

* Harold Nicolson, *Diaries*, Collins, London 1966.

David Meade in his tracks as he marched down Limehouse Causeway. When the final wails had died down, it seemed to him as if all London was holding its breath and listening for a sound in the sky. He felt the skin crawling on the back of his neck.

Then the sounds came. Shouts, screams, moans, cries of: 'Jim, oh Jim!' and 'Oh, for God's sake shut up, Maggie, and get dressed!' Then doors began to open and there were people in the streets, muttering and sobbing and cursing as they hurried towards the shelters.

People were frightened, and David Meade did not blame them. He was frightened himself. Had they not been told that from now on, death from the sky would come raining down upon them? He did not believe that anyone could not be frightened.

But then, he did not know 'Chips' Channon. Now that his world was about to collapse in ruins, 'Chips' had become fatalistic. And of that terrifying two a.m. alarm, all he wrote was:

'In the night there was another air raid alarm but I did not awake until called by the butler. Then I joined the servants in the cellar, where I found everyone good-tempered and funny. The Duke of Kent sent me a message asking me to go to his shelter next door, but I was too sleepy, and declined.'

It turned out that this was a false alarm too. World War Two had begun for London with a wail and a whimper. But ordeals were to come that would change the face of London and the nature of the world.

PART ONE

THE RUDE AWAKENING

I

THE PHONEY WAR

I

Mr and Mrs Arthur Ketley and their son Donald lived in a small terrace house on a dead-end street in Chadwell Heath, on the fringe of the East End of London. On that first day of war, since it was a Sunday, Mr Ketley was not working at the docks, where he had a job as an overseer in the office, but for once he was not pottering with his plants in the back garden, either. When Donald, who was playing in the yard, came in for a glass of water he found his parents sitting around the radio, listening to Neville Chamberlain telling them that the war had begun.

Donald noticed that his father and mother looked strained and worried. His mother glanced up when the boy came in and said: 'Is it all right for him to be outside?'

'Don't be silly,' Mr Ketley said.

So Donald went back into the yard, and twenty minutes later, when the siren sounded, his mother erupted out of the door and bustled him inside. They all climbed into a cupboard under the stairs, where, normally, brooms and the like were kept. Mr Ketley had read in the papers that in Spain, when buildings collapsed under bombing, the stairs nearly always remained standing. So he had converted the closet into a temporary shelter: cushions on the floor, candles, and a bottle of 100 proof rum from the docks.

Donald watched his father pour out glasses of rum for himself and Mrs Ketley and saw that his hand was shaking so much that the bottle rattled on the edge of the glass. He knew then that both his parents were frightened.

'We should have sent him away,' Mrs Ketley kept saying.

'No we shouldn't,' Arthur Ketley said firmly. 'He's better here – with us.'

When the all-clear sounded, Donald saw that his parents were both surprised and baffled, even a little disappointed that nothing had happened. Presently they all went out into the backyard and talked over the fences to their neighbours, wondering what had happened.

Donald Ketley was eight years old at the time, and he never forgot the first morning of the war.

'It was all a wonderful adventure,' he recalled later, 'a sudden release from boredom.'

He remembered it mostly, however, because his father had been frightened, and he had never seen him frightened before.

He was carried downstairs still asleep for the second raid, and didn't know anything about it until it was over. He was disappointed, and kept saying to his mother:

'Why didn't you wake me, Mum? I missed it, I missed it!'

It was especially annoying because there were no more air raid warnings after that, and what came to be known as the Phoney War began.

2

It was not, of course, a phoney war so far as the Poles were concerned. Their country was bombed and ravaged, and then divided up between Germany and Russia, and the Poles themselves turned into a nation of slaves. Nor was it phoney for the Royal Navy.

3

Their pride had been considerably dented in the first few weeks of war by a daring Nazi submarine raid on the Royal Navy base at Scapa Flow, which cost them the battleship *Royal Oak*. That humiliation was alleviated when the German pocket battleship *Graf Spee* was trapped off the coast of Uruguay and put out of action for good. After that the Royal Navy was engaged throughout the north and south Atlantic in a bitter war with German U-boats which now lay athwart all shipping lanes leading to Britain.

In the spring of 1940 the Germans invaded Denmark and Norway, at a moment when Neville Chamberlain was boasting that 'Hitler has missed the bus'. Subsequent Ministerial statements were of such fatuous optimism that the British public cheered the dispatch of a British Expeditionary Force to Norway and waited confidently for the Germans to be thrown back into the sea. But by the end of April not all the optimistic statements emanating from the government could conceal the fact that the Norwegian campaign was going badly and that defeat was looming.

The vague uneasiness which more percipient people had felt during the idle days of the phoney war now spread to the masses. As British troops in Norway began to die in the snow or retreat towards the sea, a hitherto complacent Parliament at last turned upon the Prime Minister and his administration and demanded an explanation. Shortly afterwards, Parliament assembled in London for a debate on the situation in Norway. The date was 7 May 1940. Even while they were debating, the Germans were making new plans. Three days later they attacked in the West and the phoney war ended.

The people of London were very soon to learn just what that would mean for them . . .

2

THE BUDS OF MAY

I

At 9.45 a.m. on 7 May 1940 the policeman on duty at the main gate of Buckingham Palace marched out into the road and raised his arm to halt the thin stream of London's mid-morning traffic. Out into the Mall from the palace yard clip-clopped a gleaming black horse drawing behind it a small, elegant, maroon-red brougham of the kind once used by Victorian dandies for discreet assignations with their ladies. But this one's doors were outlined in gilt and emblazoned with a small royal cipher, and two grooms in royal livery sat side by side on the outside perch. Inside the coach a young man in Army uniform leaned back against the leather, staring vacantly out at the pale blue sky. 'No one I know,' commented a taxi-driver to his passenger. One of the grooms flourished and cracked his whip. The black horse broke into a smart trot and the brougham moved smoothly down the Mall in the direction of Trafalgar Square, an exotic anachronism from the pre-petroleum era.

Among the curious pedestrians and motorists who saw it, probably only one of them could have said where the brougham was going and what was the nature of its errand. Robert Boothby had decided that this was no morning to ride to the House of Commons, for he had much on his mind and he wanted time to think; he was in a bitterly angry mood, and the fact that it was a lovely May morning and the tulips splashed colour over the flower beds in front of Buckingham Palace did nothing to soften his feelings. He stared at the high-stepping horse and the maroon-red brougham and reflected that if anything mirrored Britain's attitude towards the war which the nation was now waging against Germany, there it was. It was seven months since Britain had declared war on Germany, and how did His Majesty George the Sixth, King of England, Emperor of India, crowned head of the greatest Empire the world had ever known, get the dispatches from the heads of his armed forces which told him how the war was going? Why, he sent a horse and brougham to fetch them from military headquarters down the road.* Dammit, Boothby muttered to himself, they might at least have rushed them to him by dispatch rider and an armed escort. The way things were going in Norway at the moment, the British Army would be on its way home while the King was still reading about their arrival!

Robert Boothby, forty years old in 1940, had come up to London from Scotland at the age of twenty-four to become the youngest Member of Parliament in the House of Commons. Though a member of the Tory party, and therefore expected to toe the party line, he had been fighting authority ever since his arrival – and no one had he fought more fiercely than the Prime Minister, Neville Chamberlain, when he tried to appease the Germany of Adolf Hitler and the Nazis through the humiliating months of 1938 and 1939. When Neville Chamberlain at last declared war on Germany on 3 September 1939, Robert Boothby had come back into the Tory party fold. Like that other rebel against appeasement, Winston Churchill (who had joined the government as First Lord of the Admiralty at the outbreak of war) he had let Chamberlain know that henceforth he would be his loyal supporter.

He had been regretting it ever since.

As a war leader, Chamberlain was proving even more inept than he had been as a man of peace. Everything was going wrong. Disaster was threatening, and he did not seem to realise it. As for his administration, with the exception of Churchill, to Boothby they seemed boobies and incompetents. Boothby winced as he remembered the telephone call he had received that morning from Leslie Burgin of the Ministry of Supply. A week earlier Boothby had been in Holland and Belgium on a mission for the government, buying up rifles which the British Army desperately needed. He had obtained firm offers of 20,000 rifles for immediate delivery, provided the British were prepared to pay in dollars. And what had Burgin said?

'My dear Boothby, we are most grateful for your efforts, but I have to tell you that the Cabinet Committee has decided that the rifles are not, after all, required. In any case, the Treasury has categorically refused to pay for them in dollars.'

The infuriating thing was that Boothby knew in his bones a great crisis was coming, and soon every rifle that Britain could

* And he continued to do so for the rest of the war.

get hold of would be vital for the safety of the country. As he marched on through Green Park towards Whitehall and the Houses of Parliament, he could feel in his pocket the letter he had written to Churchill that morning.

'I was sent over to Belgium,' he had written, 'at the shortest notice and as a matter of the greatest urgency, ten days ago, in order (in Burgin's written words) to "find and secure rifles". I found them. This morning I was told by Burgin that no rifles are required; and that, even if they were, the Treasury would not pay for them. It would be incredible if it were not true.'

He found it hard to believe he was walking through a London already seven months at war. The roads were still busy with private cars (there had been traffic jams on all roads leading out of London that Easter), rationing hardly mattered and every restaurant in London was booming; you were safe from a call-up into the forces provided you were a gardener, a greensman, a jockey, or a chauffeur; office blocks and cinemas were still being built in the capital, and in one of the newspapers that morning the following advertisement appeared.

Wanted. By gentleman (titled), handyman about house, London, S.W.1. Wages £90 and uniform. Twelve servants, three pantry, kept.

There were plenty of other advertisements like it offering utterly unnecessary and out-of-date jobs. It was as if the war had never happened and life in England persisted along its old, class-conscious way. Meanwhile, in Norway, British soldiers and sailors were dying and the Expeditionary Force sent to save Scandinavia from Nazi occupation was being forced back into the sea by an enemy better equipped, better led and ruthlessly determined to win the war.

Boothby's stride quickened as he approached the House of Commons. So far as he and his friends were concerned, there was only one thing to do: get rid of Chamberlain and his inept hangers-on before they lost Britain the war. There was no time to waste. Today was the day to do it.

There was a long queue outside the public entrance to the House of Commons. The debate that day was to be on the military situation, and the crowds had come to see the political fireworks. Some of them raised a small cheer for Boothby when they saw

him and a man shouted: 'Gi' it 'em guid and hot, Bob,' in a strong
Scots accent. He raised his hand in greeting and hurried inside.

2

Miss Vere Hodgson had had a busy day at her office in Holland
Park, but the prospect of going to the theatre that evening of
7 May 1940 revived her spirits and refreshed her, even though
there was no time to go home to wash and change. The curtain
rose at six o'clock in London now, and that meant she had to rush
straight from the office to the show. But oh, she decided, as the
house lights went down, it was worth it, and how it was worth it,
just to be transported out of herself for a little while.

She felt slightly guilty nowadays when she confessed that so
far she had found the war disappointing. ('As if wars are run for
your entertainment. You ought to be ashamed of yourself, Vere
Hodgson!') But she nevertheless could not suppress the thought
that for some time now the war had both bored and depressed her.
Worried her too – a nagging sort of anxiety that something was
wrong, that this wasn't the way a war should be run if things were
to come out all right in the end.

Vere Hodgson was a brisk, good-looking woman in her middle
thirties of an English type no one (except official registrars) would
ever call a spinster even though she was unmarried. She had left
university in her early twenties and gone to Italy to teach English
to young ladies a year or two her junior (among them Mussolini's
daughter, Edda) and one got the feeling that that was where she
had left her love, if not the whole of her heart. She had been a
teacher in Birmingham, her home town, until shortly before the
outbreak of war, and had then decided to go into welfare work in
London. She had been secretary, consultant and general dogsbody
ever since at the Sanctuary in Holland Park Road, not far from
Notting Hill Gate in West London. The Sanctuary was the
headquarters of the Greater World Federation, a philosophical and
charitable trust, and it gave shelter, money, food and general
advice to the poor of Notting Hill and North Kensington, as well
as running a mission for the needy in the East End.

But how little seven months of war had changed the nature of
her work. She remembered that first night of war in September
1939, when the air raid warnings had sounded at two in the

morning over London. For months the people had been told that once war began death would rain down upon them from the skies.

On the day war was declared, the Sanctuary in Holland Park Road had filled with groups of anxious people: old age pensioners, lonely spinsters, service-men's wives, all come to ask whether it was true that London now was become one vast charnel-house. Vere Hodgson's boss, Miss Moyes, a vigorous and practical Christian, had told them to 'scrub your floors and ask God to keep them away. There's nothing like honest sweat and prayer for holding back the forces of evil'.

Cowed, but unconvinced by her breezy insistence that God would protect hard-working Britons, they had crept back to their homes to await their fate. The wail of the siren in the early hours of September 4 signalled that death was on its way.

But then nothing had happened. For two hours Vere Hodgson, like seven million other Londoners. had crouched under the stairs of her rooming house in Lancaster Gate and waited, with a group of white-faced fellow tenants for the inevitable. She did not mind confessing later that she had been terrified and she believed that anyone in London that night who was not was an unimaginative dolt. But death had not come. It was too busy on the other side of Europe helping the German air force to slaughter the Poles. The sounding of the London sirens had been a false alarm. Somehow, ever since, Vere Hodgson had felt cheated, and the feeling of anti-climax had persisted all through the winter. Poland was battered into defeat and occupied by the Germans and the Russians, while the British and French armies stayed safe in their defences behind the Maginot line and stared at the Germans on the other side of the Rhine, but made no effort to engage them.

That morning three young women had come to see Vere Hodgson at the Sanctuary; they were all young, with young children, and all of them foolish, she knew that. At the outbreak of war they had been evacuated from London, along with half a million other young mothers, to escape the slaughter that the government feared was coming. When it didn't come they had drifted back to 'the Smoke' because they hated the loneliness of country life, the unfamiliarity of green fields, the inhospitality of the unwilling hosts upon whom they had been billeted, and because they missed the warm friendliness on London's back

THE BUDS OF MAY

streets. Now they were in trouble. Their husbands had been conscripted into the Forces, and the women had to live on Army pay allotments. Vere Hodgson seethed with indignation when she thought of what that meant to these three young wives. In London they had about twenty-eight shillings* a week to keep themselves and their children fed, clothed and the rent paid. Their husbands were either in France or Norway or in the north of England in training camps, called up for the duration. They were pressed for money and bored with their own company and that of their children; and all around there were temptations, for there were plenty of free-spending troops in London, even if they were not their husbands. Why not go out and have a good time and perhaps pick up a bit of money. 'After all,' one of them had said, 'there's a war on, isn't there?'

The only thing you could do in their case was tell them to think of their husbands and their children, slip them clothes for the kids and a few shillings for a cake or an extra bit of food or a cinema, and hope for the best. Though Vere Hodgson feared that in at least one case, the prettiest and most resentful one, it would be for the worst. What right had the government to call men into the army and pay them such appalling wages for giving their services to the country? What need was there for soldiers' wives to be faced with poverty or temptation, when every day the fashionable restaurants were full, chauffeur-driven cars were still to be seen, and some people were obviously still making their fortune? The Americans were right when they called it the 'phoney war'. There was something wrong, something false about it; she had a sneaking feeling that the government was not really taking the war seriously.

The curtain rose and she forgot her uneasiness and settled back to enjoy the show. She and her office friend had chosen to see a revue called 'New Faces', and it was typical of London entertainment that spring. No one seemed to want anything serious, particularly anything that reminded them of the war. Cinemas had strap-line announcements across their posters informing the public that 'this is not a war film'. The biggest hits in town were Flanagan and Allen and the Crazy Gang at the Palladium, in a series of slapstick gags and a line of chorus girls; a Cockney revue called 'Me And My Gal' in which the big number involved the

* The average bus driver's weekly wage was about ninety-five shillings.

whole company singing and dancing a number called 'Doing the
Lambeth Walk', a sort of Cockney conga; a nude revue at the
Windmill Theatre in which showgirls on pedestals were allowed
by the Lord Chamberlain, the official censor, to bare their breasts
and pose in G-strings so long as they kept perfectly still ('If it
moves it's rude', was the current gag about the show); and the
already mentioned 'New Faces', which had been running since
late 1939. The big moment of the evening came when a tall
brunette named Judy Campbell strolled onto the stage and, against
a background of London's West End, sang a haunting song called
'A Nightingale Sang in Berkeley Square'. Vere Hodgson had been
told that there was something so nostalgic about the song, something so strongly recalling the good old days of peace, that every
night you could see members of the audience weeping. It was true.
She found the tears welling in her own eyes as she listened, and
was ashamed of herself. Why should she weep over a love song
about peace-time London? What was there to lament about a city
so full of slums and inequalities and poverty and unemployment?
Yet she wept.

The mood changed almost immediately as a slim redhead with
marvellous legs bounced on to sing a song called 'I'm a Fallen
Angel'. This was the other great discovery of the show, a 17-year-
old named Zoe Gail, who looked like a saucy virgin and sang
songs suggesting that she wished she weren't. She had been put
into the show by the producers because, though lacking in
experience, they believed she would prove to be 'the midship-
man's delight'. She was to become more than the Navy's favourite
as the war progressed. Tonight the males in the audience loved
every moment of her.

The lights faded as she took her final bow, and then the
spotlight picked out the compère as he walked to the footlights.

'Ladies and gentlemen,' he announced. 'During rehearsals,
authors were constantly sending in sketches. Unfortunately, most
of them turned out to be *war* sketches – and we did feel that
audiences nowadays are getting just about enough about war.
However, it was suggested that for patriotic reasons, we should
have at least one war sketch. So here it is, presented with due
apologies to our good friends in His Majesty's Forces!'

The sketch was called 'Awfully Quiet on the Western Front' and
it was set in a gun battery somewhere in France. A dart board

hung from the barrel of one of the guns and some washing from the others. Downstage there was a table at which three British soldiers were sitting. One of the soldiers was knitting; the other two were having afternoon tea. There was a silver teapot and milk jug, and platefuls of pastries and sandwiches. The opening lines of the sketch were:

FIRST SOLDIER: One or two lumps, Foulkes-Foulkes? I never can remember.

SECOND SOLDIER: Two please, thenk you!

THIRD SOLDIER: Knit one, purl one, knit three, drop three.

FIRST SOLDIER: Look here, Harrington, I do think you might stop knitting while we're having tea. After all, you've been at it all day.

THIRD SOLDIER: I know, I know. But you seem to forget there's a war on. Back home in England hundreds of poor Service girls are freezing to death. They need these little things I'm doing for them.

As usual, it was a huge success with the audience, who roared with laughter over every line. There had been too much in the newspapers about well-heated billets and home comforts for the troops in France for them not to lap up every comic jab. And when a general, on an inspection trip, asked the soldiers where the enemy was and they looked astonished and cried in unison: '*What enemy?*' the whole house burst into applause.

Vere Hodgson laughed with them. Yet when she came home from the show that night and thought about it, uneasiness crowded out her enjoyment. A month ago, perhaps, it would all have been an enjoyable skit. But that night on the midnight news there had been a report of the row in Parliament over the débâcle in Norway. There the British soldiers had known who was the enemy all right, and many had been killed, wounded and captured by him. The British Expeditionary Force was in retreat and the German conquest of Scandinavia was all but complete. Added to which there had been a small item, tucked away in one of the evening newspapers under the headline WESTERN FRONT OFFENSIVE? which read:

Neutral sources in Berlin report that the German Army is now turning its eyes westward. There are strong rumours that Hitler has made up his mind to bring Holland and Belgium, which he considers pro-Allied rather than neutral, into the Nazi orbit and will use force if necessary to do so. This could well be the first move in an offensive in the West.

In which case those British boys in France wouldn't be enjoying their creature comforts much longer, and it would have been a mockery to laugh at them as she and the audience had done that night.* She felt guilty and worried.

3

Henry Moore turned away from the man at the desk to whom he had been talking and came across the gallery floor towards his wife, Irene. She was watching a workman hammering a nail in a packing case, and she balanced a picture frame against her thigh. She was a slim shapely woman with a narrow, lively Slav face and shining eyes; there was just the slightest touch of concern intermingled with the look of affection as she saw her husband approaching her. His round face was smiling but she knew him well enough not to be deceived by that.

He said, as if in answer to an unspoken question: 'We calculate I should make about £90 out of the exhibition.' His voice had not quite lost its flat Yorkshire accent but the tone was cheerful. 'That's with commissions and expenses knocked off. It isn't too much – but then, there's a war on.'

One of the workmen was taking a poster off the door as they went through and out into Leicester Square. It read: EXHIBITION OF PAINTINGS AND SCULPTURES by HENRY MOORE. Neither Henry Moore nor his wife looked at it. Their eyes had been caught by two other posters which a newspaper seller was brandishing on the other side of Leicester Square. CHAMBERLAIN: VITAL DEBATE said one, and CHAMBERLAIN FIGHTS BACK said the other.

They climbed into the small Standard tourer which they had parked round the corner, stuffed some canvases in the back, and

---

* The sketch was, in fact, taken out of the show by its author a week later. It was written by Jack Davies, now a well-known film writer but then an officer in the RAF.

drove off through Piccadilly and up Regent Street towards Hampstead.

'It will pay the rent, at least,' Irene said.

Yes, it would do that all right, thought Henry Moore, *and* still leave us fifteen pounds over. With that and the £240 a year he was getting from teaching at the Arts School in Chelsea they could continue to go on living quite comfortably. There's nothing we really lack, he thought, nothing we can't buy with the money I'm earning. And if Barbara does have twins and goes off to Cornwall, as she threatens, she'll let us take over her studio, and then we'll really be saving. It only costs £50 a year.*

There was only one thing. What if the war hotted up, and teaching became difficult? During the previous summer, when it looked as if war was inevitable, he had had a telephone call from Kenneth Clark, Director of the National Gallery, asking him to come over for a drink. But it had turned out to be more than a social occasion. Clark had been asked by the government to draw up a panel of war artists who would move among the armed forces and visit their bases and record in sketch and painting a picture of Britain at war. Once the war came, that is.

'Henry, I want to put your name on the list,' said Clark. 'Will you join?'

It was a temptation, of course. There need be no more insecurity for the duration, no more worrying about the scarcity of buyers and commissions in wartime. Yet Moore shook his head.

'No,' he said. 'What interest could there possibly be in it for me? Drawing successions of guns and soldiers and tanks and things. I did enough of that in the last war. There's nothing new I could possibly say.'

He didn't add that he had reached a climactic moment in his development as an artist when his drawings and his sculptures were leaving subjective things behind and he was beginning to visualise everything in abstract terms. It would do too much violence to his muse if he were to go back now and start making illustrations for wartime propaganda. He just could not face it, and refused the offer.

Artistically, he had never doubted the rightness of his decision.

* He was referring to their friend and fellow sculptor, Barbara Hepworth. She had triplets, not twins, and did depart for Cornwall that summer.

But now as he read the war news, and sensed the crisis coming, he wondered whether he could go on remaining aloof. He was no pacifist, but until now he had not felt involved. Now he seemed to smell something in the air, as if the winds of war were changing.

'I think the war is starting to get serious,' Irene said.

As usual, she had been reading his thoughts.

4

By 1940 Henry 'Chips' Channon* had made it quite clear that he was heart and soul a Chamberlain man. In his view, Neville Chamberlain had saved the British nation and the world by giving in to Hitler and Mussolini at Munich. He loathed Winston Churchill and had been downcast when Chamberlain brought him into the War Cabinet as First Lord of the Admiralty at the outbreak of war. His beloved Neville could do no wrong, and it was Winston whom Channon unhesitatingly blamed for the military disaster in Norway; it was Winston too whom he now suspected of intriguing behind the scenes to saddle Chamberlain with Norway and replace him as Prime Minister. In fact Churchill was innocent of political scheming (though not so innocent of military bungling over the Norway campaign) and the events of 7 May and the next forty-eight hours were neither initiated nor encouraged by him. But Chips Channon believed otherwise.

By the time MPs had assembled in their seats in the House of Commons that afternoon, London, England and the world knew that Germany had completed the conquest of Norway and had driven the British Expeditionary Force into the sea, save for a small group of troops fighting and dying in Narvik. It had been an ineptly planned and amateurishly handled operation from which no one except the soldiers fighting on the spot had emerged with any credit, and it had demonstrated (only too ominously, in view of what was to come) how short the British armed forces were in leadership, battle know-how and equipment. But the British public and Parliament had little doubt that the guilty men so far as the debacle were concerned were not the soldiers in the

* No one knows for certain how he got his nickname. Some say that it was because he once, as a bachelor, shared rooms with a man named Fish; others that he got it because he introduced potato chips to London cocktail parties.

34

field but the government which had sent them there; and their anger was not mitigated by the sunny optimism which Government spokesmen had gone on displaying about the situation right up until the final humiliation.

7 May had been chosen for the House of Commons to debate the disastrous situation, and at Westminster that afternoon observers were sniffing the air for the smell of blood. It was an opportunity for which Chamberlain's enemies had been waiting – not merely to criticise his administration for its inefficiency in Norway, but for its war policy in general, its failure to galvanise the nation, its inability to face up to the hard facts of war and legislate accordingly. Since before dawn Londoners had been queuing up to get into the House, and now the public galleries were crowded. So were those for the peers of the realm and ambassadors from Allied, friendly and not so friendly nations. Diplomats already in their seats included US Ambassador Joseph P. Kennedy, who had only an hour earlier told Lord Halifax, the Foreign Secretary, that he was disgusted by Britain's performance so far, that the armed forces in particular and England in general were inefficient ('even degenerate') and that he and his military attachés were convinced, and had so reported to Washington, that England was going to lose the war.*

Now he listened to the opening speech of the debate by Neville Chamberlain and acknowledged to himself that he had not reported wrongly. Almost from the time he had arrived in England, Kennedy had conceived an admiration for the British premier, and for not very obscure reasons. They were both men of peace who were terrified of war and its consequences. It was with Kennedy's wholehearted support that Chamberlain had tried and failed to make a deal with Hitler that would keep Britain (and, Kennedy believed, the United States) out of war. But now that the lines had been drawn and the battles begun, sadly he had to admit that there could have scarcely been a man less fitted to lead a nation at war than his friend Neville Chamberlain. He reported later that the premier's speech in the House was 'lamentable and lacking in grip'. Chips Channon, biased though he was towards his

---

* Chips Channon's opinion of the ambassador is perhaps best summed up by his diary entry: 'I talked to Mr Kennedy the new American ambassador whose chief merit seems to be that he has nine children.'

idol and eager to colour in optimistic pink anything Chamberlain said and did, could not disagree.

'Five minutes later he was speaking,' he wrote in his diary, 'and was given a warm welcome, but he spoke haltingly and did not make a good case; in fact he fumbled his words and seemed tired and embarrassed. No wonder he is exhausted; who would not be? All day and all night he works, while the small fry criticise. I realized at once that the House was not with him, and though he warmed up a little towards the middle of his speech, the very crowded House was restive and bored and the Egyptian ambassador even slept.'

In spite of the Prime Minister's lack-lustre delivery and the coolness of his reception, no one yet imagined that there would be any really dramatic surprise at the end of the debate. The critics would make their points and some of them would be wounding, but in the end (so the old hands in the Press gallery were saying) Neville Chamberlain would emerge relatively un-scathed. He might agree to some changes in the makeup of his War Cabinet – he might even appease his critics by dumping Winston Churchill, having first blamed him for the Norway disaster – but it would all work out right for him in the end. The dissident members of the Tory party were known to number not more than thirty MPs and since two former members, Churchill and Eden, had been tempted by office into joining Chamberlain, the rebels had lost both drive and the public-stirring appeal of glamorous leadership. The present leader of the group was former Cabinet member Leopold Amery, and his chief lieutenants were Alfred Duff Cooper, Harold Nicolson and Robert Boothby, rebels all but so far content to complain about Chamberlain rather than plant a bomb underneath him powerful enough to blow him out of office.

So though Chamberlain sat down to only dutiful cheers from his most fervid supporters, he had no qualms. There was a hiss of excitement in the public galleries when into his seat clanked the Member for Portsmouth North. Clanked is the word. Portsmouth is Britain's chief naval base on the Channel, and its representative (Tory, of course) was a naval man, Admiral of the Fleet Sir Roger John Brownslow Keyes, a much decorated veteran of the First World War and still an active serving officer. He had, in fact, just returned from Norway where, at considerable personal risk, he had watched the last stages of the British defeat, and he was seething with anger at the bungling and lack of preparation he had seen there. He had decided to come to the House in the full uniform of Admiral of the Fleet, all medals up, to give weight to his indignant condemnations of the Government and the Ministers he held responsible for the débâcle. He was not an articulate man; he did not need to be. His uniform and his face spoke for him. 'Roger Keyes, an ex-hero, but a man with a grievance, was damning,' Chips Channon had to admit, though he thought that the uniform and medals were of 'questionable taste, but it lent him dignity. The atmosphere was intense. . . .'

Chamberlain was still not really worried, though his supporters were beginning to whisper. At six o'clock that evening he drove to Buckingham Palace to see the King and 'he said smilingly that he had not come to offer his resignation and that he had not yet abandoned all hope of reconstructing his Government on the basis of a national coalition in which the Labour Party would join. *

George the Sixth, who liked Chamberlain and certainly did not relish the thought of having to deal with Winston Churchill in his place, offered to call in Clement Attlee, leader of the Labour Party, and tell him that he hoped he and his Socialist colleagues 'would realise that they must pull their weight and join the Nat'l Govt'. Chamberlain did not think that his help was necessary at that stage, but thanked the King for his sympathy. 'I told the PM,' wrote George the Sixth in his diary, 'that I did not like the way in which, with all his worries and responsibilities he had to bear in the conduct of the war, he was always subject to a stab in the back from both the H. of C. and the Press.'

Chamberlain seems to have been comforted and encouraged by these words and less than ever suspicious that his control over events was steadily slackening. Had he gone straight to the Chamber of the House of Commons what was happening there might have jolted him out of his euphoria; instead he went off to dinner. But in the Chamber things were happening. Leopold Amery, the leader of the dissidents, had begun to speak. In normal circumstances, Amery spoke like a chairman of a family company reading the annual report after an unspectacular year; he was worthy but dull. Most of the House watched him rise to his feet and immediately went off for dinner, and he had rows of

* Sir John Wheeler-Bennett, *King George the Sixth*, Macmillan, 1958.

empty benches both before and behind him as he launched into his attack on Government policy. But for this supreme occasion Amery had prepared hard, rehearsed repeatedly, and was for once able to project the passion and concern he was feeling over the situation. The public gallery had remained as crowded as ever, since its occupants knew they would lose their seats if they went out to eat, and the rustling and the restlessness among them stilled to an attentive silence as the import of the words reached them. And soon word spread to the bars and the restaurant of the House that 'Amery is stirring things up' and first Labour MPs and then the Tories began to slip back into their seats. They did not, however, include the Prime Minister or any members of the Cabinet. As Amery continued to speak it soon became apparent that his strategy was to take the argument away from the immediate cause of concern – the disastrous defeat in Norway – because that involved the responsibility of Churchill for many of the most serious mistakes which had been made; and Amery wanted the nation rid of Chamberlain, not Churchill. He deployed his arguments more and more towards a general indictment of the Government's attitude and lack of resolution towards the war effort, spheres in which Churchill could not be blamed.

By the time he reached his peroration, he had a well-filled House hanging on his every word and even Tory MPs had begun to applaud some of his sallies. Then came the passage which was to make the front pages of all the newspapers in Britain the following morning. He had begun by quoting Oliver Cromwell's famous words to John Hampden: 'Your troops are most of them old, decayed serving men and tapsters and such kind of fellows,' and pointing out that it was a good description, with one or two exceptions, of Chamberlain's administration. And then he paused. Afterwards he was to say that until that moment he had not decided how he would go on. He had another quotation, a much more devastating one, also from Cromwell, marshalled in his mind, but it depended upon the mood of the House whether he would use it. If they were in the wrong temper, any sympathy they might feel for him would be turned into resentment and his arguments destroyed by antipathy. But he felt waves of sympathy washing over him from all parts of the House and they emboldened him. He took a deep breath and then went on: 'I have quoted certain words of Oliver Cromwell. I will quote certain other words. I do it with great reluctance because I am speaking of those who are old friends and associates of mine, but they are words which, I think, are applicable to the present situation. This is what Cromwell said to the Long Parliament when he thought it was no longer fit to conduct the affairs of the nation: *"You have sat too long here for any good you have been doing. Depart, I say, and let us have done with you. In the name of God, go!"* '

There was a moment's silence, and then members of the Labour Opposition took up the cry: 'In the name of God, go!' The Tories sat back in squirming, uneasy silence.

Chips Channon had not been in the House to hear the slashing attack on his beloved Prime Minister, but he was soon aware of what had happened and rushed into the smoking-room to gather up the Tories and rally them behind Chamberlain.

'I am most uneasy now about tomorrow,' he wrote in his diary, 'as it is rumoured that the Opposition will challenge the Government with a division.'

Some of his Tory friends in the lobbies of the House were already betting that, if it came to a vote, at least fifty Government supporters would vote against the régime. Chips was appalled, outraged and shattered. So long as Chamberlain remained in power he was one of the charmed circle.

He wrote:

Political life will lose much of its fascination for me if Neville goes, as I shall no longer be in the inner councils of the racket.

5

Robert Boothby had had no reply from Winston Churchill to the letter he had dropped in at his office the day before, and when he passed him in the Lobby of the House of Commons on the afternoon of 8 May the old bulldog growled an unfriendly acknowledgement to his greeting and hurried on. Boothby decided that Winston was deliberately avoiding any contact with the dissidents – of whom he was naturally one – in order not to compromise his own political position.

If the rebels could get rid of Chamberlain, the man they were intriguing to put in his place was Winston Churchill. Yet the attack on Chamberlain was being made as a result of the disaster in Norway – and Churchill's responsibility for that was at least as great as his premier's. Nor had Chamberlain, during his speech to the House the day before, made any attempt to shift the blame for the débâcle from his own shoulders on to that of the First Lord of the Admiralty. If anything, he had sheltered Churchill from blame.

In the circumstances, Churchill was in a difficult position. As a loyal member of the Government, he was bound to support Chamberlain and fight the men who were out to get for him what he dearly wanted for himself, the premiership. As Boothby ordered an after-lunch brandy at the bar of the House, he could hear the buzz of speculation all around him, and all seemed to be asking the same question: What will Winston do? His enemies in particular were enjoying the situation, for they relished the dilemma in which Churchill found himself. The better he performed in the House that afternoon, the worse it would be for his ambitions. Would he be tempted not to give of his best?

Yesterday there had been a chance that the great debate would not come to a sticking point, that the Labour Opposition would yield to pressures and not bring the issue to a vote. But Clement Attlee and Herbert Morrison, their two leaders, had finally been persuaded that even the Tories were swinging against the Chamberlain administration, and they had a good chance of winning on a vote of confidence. In a swingeing attack on the Government's weakness and lack of policy, Morrison announced that the Opposition would challenge the Government to a division. The Tory party managers, after a hurried conference, immediately dispatched a three-line whip to all their members.* That meant that all Members would be required to be in the House and to vote with the Government – or be disciplined for insubordination.

Morrison's speech had not only challenged Chamberlain to a vote but it had goaded him to anger with its sly Cockney barbs and half-humorous insults. The premier's thin face flushed with the ominous red that all Members knew was the danger signal. Boothby leaned over to Duff Cooper and whispered: 'My God, he's going to accept the challenge. What a bloody fool!'

The Prime Minister had risen and was moving to the dispatch box. The House went silent as they waited for him to speak. It

---

* The Tories, with their fringe supporters, had a clear majority of 286 votes over their Labour Party opponents.

was as if they all instinctively realised that what he said in the next few seconds would settle the issue once and for all.

He spoke slowly and precisely but the dry tones had an unusual undercurrent of anger. A man less sure of himself would have angled for the sympathy of the House, but Neville Chamberlain was not one to lose his arrogance in a moment of challenge. A Churchill would have dodged the issue and temporised, but Chamberlain was not that kind of man – he was too sure that the Tories would never let him down.

'I do not seek to evade criticism,' he said, crisply, 'but I say this to my friends in the House – and I have friends in the House. No Government can prosecute a war efficiently unless it has public and parliamentary support. I accept this challenge. I welcome it indeed. At least I shall see who is with us and who is against us, and I call on my friends to support us in the Lobby tonight.'

It was a fatal error of judgement. It was the Labour Opposition which had brought the debate down to a party political level by challenging the Government to a division, but the Tories expected better of their Prime Minister. They had expected an appeal to put politics on one side in the interests of the nation, a call for unity in the face of an outside peril, and instead they had watched Chamberlain wave his political big stick – his parliamentary majority. When he had used the words: 'I call on my friends to support us in the Lobby tonight,' his tone had made it quite clear that this was not a request but a command and that the Tories had better obey or face reprisals from the Party managers.

There was some sort of a cheer from the faithful, but the rest of the House, Tories among them, sat back in astonished silence, like schoolboys appalled at a headmaster's indiscretion. Boothby glanced across to see the reaction on Churchill's face, but his head was bowed and his face carefully hidden by his papers. Chips Channon had a premonitory shudder. He moved to sit behind his Prime Minister 'hoping to surround him with an aura of affection'.

Chamberlain had need of it as the debate reached its culmination, because there was little comfort elsewhere. Speaker after speaker turned upon the Government and rent it. Chips Channon looked up at the gallery and 'several times I caught the eye of Mrs Chamberlain, who has hardly left the House for two days: she is a loyal, good woman. . . . She looked infinitely sad as she peered down into the mad arena where the lions were out for her husband's blood.'

And still the question everyone was asking was: What would Winston do?

'Would Winston be loyal?' asked Channon. 'He finally rose and one saw at once that he was in a bellicose mood, alert and enjoying himself, relishing the ironical position in which he found himself: i.e. that of defending his enemies, and a cause in which he did not believe. He made a slashing, vigorous speech, a magnificent piece of oratory ... how much the fire was real, how much ersatz, we shall never know, but he amused and dazzled everyone with his virtuosity.'

But it was not enough. At last the vote was called and Members rose, those who supported the Government into the Aye lobby, those against into the Nay. Channon shuddered. The numbers in the Aye lobby seemed ominously thin considering that the Tories were supposed to be obeying a three-line whip.

'We watched the insurgents file out of the Opposition [Nay] lobby . . . "Quislings", we shouted at them, and "Rats", "Yesmen", they replied.'

When the figures were called, the Government had its majority but had suffered no less of a defeat. Normally, in response to a three-line whip, the Government could expect a majority of 213 votes over the Labour opposition. When the Speaker announced the figures, the House realised that the majority had dropped to 81. Forty-five members of the Government had deliberately defied their leaders and voted against the Government, and 65 had either abstained or stayed away from the House. It was a devastating slap in the face for Chamberlain. When the significance of it sank in, there were immediate shouts of 'Resign, resign!'

Channon wrote: 'That old ape Josh Wedgwood began to wave his arms about and sing "Rule Britannia", Harold Macmillan next to him joined in, but they were howled down. Neville appeared bowled over by the ominous figures, and was the first to rise. He looked grave and thoughtful and sad. ... What can Neville do now? He can reconstruct his Government or he can resign; but there is no doubt that the Government is seriously jarred and all confidence in it is gone. ... Oh, the cruelty of the pack in pursuit ... shall I too crash when the Chamberlain edifice crumbles?'

Chips survived. He was of the type that always does. But, after forty-eight hours of haggling and false hope, Neville Chamberlain resigned. On the evening of 10 May 1940, the announcement was made to the nation that a National Government of all parties had been formed, and that Winston Churchill was its Prime Minister. The Government was at last facing up to the problems and the perils of war.

It was not before time. Since dawn that morning the German armies had been on the march and the German Luftwaffe was in the air. Nazi troops had crossed the frontiers of neutral Holland and Belgium. BRUSSELS BOMBED and LILLE BOMBED said the newspaper placards in Piccadilly Circus. The Phoney war had ended not with a whimper but with a bang. The Blitzkrieg that was to make Germany masters of Europe in little over a month had begun.

All over London the personalities of the day were busy writing up their diaries with prophecies of doom. 'This is the final fight,' wrote Harold Nicolson. 'I go to bed and shall, I hope, sleep. We shall be attacked from the air tonight in all probability.'

For Chips Channon it was 'perhaps the darkest day in English history ... Another of Hitler's brilliantly conceived coups, and of course he seized on the psychological moment when England is politically divided, and the ruling caste riddled with dissension and anger.'

He added: 'Will it be our turn next?'

On 17 June, Marshal Philippe Pétain, the eighty-four-years-old veteran of the First World War, announced that he was taking over the reins of the French Government, and promptly ordered the French Army to lay down its arms. In the five weeks since Churchill had taken office, the German armies had conquered Holland, Belgium and were masters of France. 250,000 British and 50,000 French troops had escaped to Britain via Dunkirk, but they had come back without their arms and downcast in spirits. Most of the watching world believed that the war was all but over.

Not, however, the British. On the night that Pétain announced France's capitulation, Winston Churchill addressed the British people. He said:

'The news from France is very bad, and I grieve for the gallant French people who have fallen into this terrible misfortune. Nothing will alter our feelings towards them, nor our faith that the genius of France will rise again.

'What happened to France makes no difference to British faith and purpose! We have become sole champions now in arms to defend the world cause. We shall do our best to be worthy of that high honour. We shall defend our island, and, with the British Empire around us, we shall fight on unconquerable until the curse of Hitler is lifted from the brows of men.

'We are sure that in the end all will be well.'

The British people agreed with him, but the rest of the world thought he and they were mad.

3

ALONE

Early on the morning of 19 June 1940, two young Frenchmen walked across Hyde Park in the direction of Stanhope Gate. One of them, Pierre Maillaud, was the acting chief of the London bureau of Havas, the French semi-official news agency. The other had, until two days before, been an attaché at the French Embassy in Albert Gate, London, but he had resigned the moment he heard Marshal Pétain announce the capitulation of France to the Germans. His name was Robert Mengin. Both young men had been appalled at what had happened to their country over the past few weeks, but it was Mengin who was sickened as well as heartbroken, for in the Embassy he had been living in a France in miniature and he had seen there the extent to which the rot had set in among his countrymen; they had been defeatists from the start, and most of them antipathetic towards the British. What had particularly nauseated him had been the remark of one senior official when the news reached the Embassy that France had accepted defeat.

'Now the British are on their own,' he had said. 'Good! They'll get what they deserve. They have it coming to them.'

It was in something amounting to despair that Mengin spent the day after his resignation. What would he do? His young wife was fretting over the small baby which had been left behind in France. He had made it plain to his diplomatic colleagues that he would have nothing to do with the Pétainist régime in France, already beginning to crawl to the German conquerors. That meant danger for him if he returned to France. But what was there for him in England? How could he serve without betraying his own country?

It was then that he turned on the radio to listen to an appeal from Charles de Gaulle. Mengin had seen de Gaulle in the French Embassy in London a couple of weeks earlier, when he had flown to England on a mission for Paul Reynaud, at that time still Premier of France. He asked his colleagues about this bony tall

officer in khaki and *képi* who stared through you when you saluted
him and had been told that de Gaulle was one of the few officers on
the front who had fought with success against the invading
Germans.* He had been promoted in the field from colonel to
brigadier, and then called to Paris to advise the Government. Now
he had come to London to ask Churchill for troops to back up
the French Army and fighter planes to operate with the French
troops fighting south of the Loire. Mengin watched him driving
away from Albert Gate with the Ambassador, Charles Corbin, for
his rendezvous with Churchill at 10 Downing Street, and he had
heard later that the British Premier, won over by his sincerity, had
promised to send troops but reluctantly denied him the planes.
De Gaulle flew back to France and that, Mengin thought, was the
last he would ever see of him.

But on 16 June he was back in London, and this time with a
different mission: to promote himself as the incarnation of a still
resistant France. He had talked with Churchill again and this time
had been invited to stay for lunch; this time his mission was not to
persuade the British leader to send troops or planes, nor to give any
further support to the politicians in France. For them de Gaulle
now exhibited such contempt that his long nose wrinkled as if
under a bad smell when he talked of them. No, this time he asked
to be accepted from now on as the voice of France – the voice of a
nation still at war with Germany – and he went on to ask the Prime
Minister for air-time on the British Broadcasting Corporation's
programmes to announce to Frenchmen everywhere that he was
their leader. Churchill had told him that he was being premature,
that the French really hadn't capitulated yet, that there was still
hope that the Government would fly to North Africa and carry
on. At which de Gaulle had shaken his head in imperious
disagreement.

'They will never go,' he said. 'They will stay in France and they
will truckle to the Germans. They are no longer Frenchmen.'

Churchill was impressed. De Gaulle was his complete anti-
thesis, totally lacking in humour, never for a moment relaxed or
human. Never once did a smile crack that grave face on top of the
tall eucalyptus tree of a body. But he exuded sincerity and patriot-

* He had driven a four-mile bridgehead into the German advance and
captured several hundred prisoners, but had hardly achieved the spectacular victory with which legend was later to credit him.

ism. 'The destiny of France oozes from his pores,' someone said, and that was certainly an asset in his favour at this black moment in France's history. So Churchill had told de Gaulle: 'You have my backing. I will let you have the BBC as your platform.' But he added that de Gaulle must hold his hand. He must do nothing to widen the gulf between Britain and France at a moment when the French Government might still decide to fly to North Africa to fight or might order its great fleet to sail to British ports. 'Hold your hand,' he said. 'Your time will come.'

The time had come, de Gaulle decided, when Marshal Pétain instructed the troops of France to throw down their arms. He called in a young French typist, Elizabeth de Miribel, and dictated a message to her, and on 18 June he sent it round to 10 Downing Street for Winston Churchill's approval.

Did Churchill read it before he gave his consent to its broadcast? It seems doubtful. That day he was immersed in domestic matters, and had an all-important speech to make on the war situation to the House of Commons. Otherwise, as he read the message through, he might have hesitated. He still wanted the French Fleet on Britain's side, and he still wanted the political and military leaders of France, especially in the French Empire, to rally to Britain and fight on in the war. But would they do so if a French officer of whom few had heard, who was considerably their junior in rank, chose to come forward and speak for them? But chance was working in de Gaulle's favour, and permission to broadcast came through.

'We must listen tonight at six o'clock,' Mengin's wife had told Robert. 'Elizabeth is thrilled with the speech. She has telephoned all her friends to tell them they must listen.'

They had turned on the radio, and at six o'clock they had heard the announcer say: '*Ici Londres*,' and then the voice that was to become so familiar the whole world over came into their ears and, for a time at least, into Robert Mengin's heart.

'Men of France, women of France,' de Gaulle began, 'the leaders who, for many years past, have been at the head of the French Armed Forces have set up a government. Alleging the defeat of our armies, this government has entered into negotiations with the enemy with a view to bringing about a cessation of hostilities.

'It is quite true that we were, and still are, overwhelmed by enemy mechanical forces, both on the ground and in the air. It was the tanks, the planes and the tactics, far more than the fact that we were outnumbered, that forced our armies to retreat. It was the German tanks, planes and tactics that provided the element of surprise which brought our leaders to their present plight.

'But has the last word been said? Must we abandon all hope? Is our defeat final and irremediable? To these questions I answer: NO!

'Speaking in full knowledge of the facts, I ask you to believe me when I say that the cause of France is not lost. The very factors that brought about our defeat may one day lead us to victory. For remember this: France does not stand alone. She is not isolated. Behind her is a vast Empire, and she can make common cause with the British Empire, which commands the sea and is continuing the struggle. Like England she can draw unreservedly on the immense industrial resources of the United States.

'This war is not limited to our unfortunate country. The outcome of the struggle has not been decided by the Battle of France. This is a world war. Mistakes have been made, there have been delays and untold suffering, but the fact remains that there still exists in the world everything we need to crush our enemies some day. Today we are crushed by the sheer weight of mechanized force hurled against us, but we can look to a future in which even greater mechanized force will bring us victory. The destiny of the world is at stake.

'I, General de Gaulle, now in London, call on all French officers and men who are at present on British soil, or may be in the future, with or without their arms; I call on all engineers and skilled workmen from the armament factories who are at present on British soil or may be in the future, to get in touch with me. Whatever happens, the flames of French resistance must not and shall not die.'

It was an appeal to the heart of every Frenchman, and Robert Mengin knew what he had to do. He had de Gaulle's number and address, and he called his aide-de-camp and asked for an appointment. Later he called again. His friend Pierre Maillaud had heard the speech and had been equally carried away. Yes, said the ADC, General de Gaulle would be glad to see them in the morning.

So here they were in Hyde Park walking towards Seymour Place and a meeting with the man who refused to admit that France had lost the war. It was a lovely day in early summer and the memory of it burned its way into Mengin's mind. 'The sky was of the purest blue,' he remembered, 'and the lawns were still green.'* The great capital seemed strangely silent to him that morning, and London had a purity and a freshness that overwhelmed him with a sense of transience and fragility.

He was suddenly assailed by doubts, and fears, aware, as these Londoners around him did not seem to be, that the world as they knew it was coming to an end. As he and Maillaud came into Marylebone and walked towards 8 Seymour Place, Robert Mengin later confessed that he was a frightened man. Was de Gaulle really the man for France? Could France in fact still be saved?

The apartment in Mayfair where de Gaulle had set up his headquarters in London had been lent to him by a rich French supporter and it was expansive. Mengin and Maillaud were shown into a vast room bathed in June sunlight. The general sat upright, remote and statuesque, with his back to the window, he stared coldly at the two young Frenchmen. A silence followed the introductions. Finally it was broken by Maillaud who explained that they had both heard and been much moved by the General's appeal, and that they had come to offer their services. How could they help?

De Gaulle asked him what was his profession, and he replied that he worked for the French news agency.

'*Eh bien,*' said de Gaulle, 'tell me the news.'

Maillaud reeled off the events of the past twenty-four hours, most of them depressing, in as much detail as he could remember, and then assuming his duty as a newspaperman he in turn began asking for news. What did the general have in mind? What were his plans?

'I will be speaking again tonight from the BBC,' de Gaulle said, coolly, 'this time to Frenchmen everywhere, in the Empire,

* Robert Mengin, *No Laurels for De Gaulle*, Michael Joseph, 1967.

in North Africa especially. I will tell them where their duty lies.'
He paused and then said some words which Mengin found
disturbing: 'I am conscious of the fact that I shall be speaking in
the *name of France.*'

The words jarred uncomfortably on Mengin's ear. They were
said with such confident detachment, with such lack of humility,
as if the man who was speaking had no idea of the enormous
arrogance of what he was saying. Maillaud however did not seem
to be taken aback. He was listening eagerly to what the General
was saying, while Mengin was watching the man rather than
hearing the rest of the words.

'I could only see three-quarters of his face,' he recalled; 'the
one eye visible to me somehow suggested the eye of an elephant,
quite round when the heavy lid was raised. . . . He had very little
chin, so little that I found myself wondering whether it wasn't
the result of a war wound. Yet it gave no impression of weakness,
but rather of smugness, of self-sufficiency, as did also the mouth
under the little brush of a moustache.'

He was suddenly reminded of a very tall boy scout.

Altogether, it was an unsatisfactory interview. They had not
been received with any great enthusiasm. They had merely been
told to wait. For what? De Gaulle had not said.

On the way back, Maillaud asked Mengin his impressions. He
answered that he thought de Gaulle was blown-up, inflated. Maillaud at once objected to the French word (*gonflé*), it wasn't quite
the word.

'But *I* think it is the right word,' Mengin said. 'You haven't had
to do your military service, so you have had no experience of that
kind of officer – inflated with the concept they have of themselves.
If you stuck a pin into them, you'd hear it – their idea of themselves – come out whistling like the air from an inner tube.'

'But what actually have you got against him?' Maillaud asked.

Mengin replied that he had been shocked to hear de Gaulle
saying that he would be speaking *in the name of France.* It seemed
the apex of arrogance to him that this man, who had failed to
impress him, should so calmly assume the mantle of France.

The two men walked back across the park in silence, the rap-
port between them lost. Mengin felt the gulf between them and
looked enviously at the Londoners going about their business all
around them. How lucky they were. Defeat stared them in the

face. It was the gravest moment in their history. Yet they had no doubts about themselves and what they had to do. They were united in their resolve. They were not torn, like the French. There were no divided loyalties. He was suffused by an enormous but affectionate jealousy of the English.

'They rarely said what they felt,' he mused. 'They left that to Churchill, who said things so very well. He said them with a passion that sometimes would have embarrassed most Englishmen, even though he did faithfully express what they were thinking inside themselves. It would be easy to think that this quiet determination to fight it out was due to the eloquence of Winston Churchill. As he said himself, Churchill had the privilege to roar; but he did not create the lion, that is to say the British people. When the lion is determined, then, whether it is Churchill who gives the roar, or Chamberlain who points the way with the umbrella, the lion charges.'

As for himself, who would point the way for him? General de Gaulle? He wanted passionately to go on fighting for France, but could he accept this tall, frigid boy scout as his leader?

With a premonitory *frisson*, Mengin realised that there was trouble ahead.

2

The war was being won too quickly even for Adolf Hitler, and for four weeks after the fall of France an ominous lull fell over Europe while the German armies halted to digest their conquests. Hitler himself did a sight-seeing tour of Paris and posed for pictures at the Eiffel Tower; and his companions, seeing the glint in his eye, wondered whether it was an anticipatory one as he imagined himself, striking a similar pose, perhaps even before the end of the summer, in front of Buckingham Palace in London. There was little doubt in his mind that he would soon be there; the war was finished, and even the British must now be realising it. He would give them a little time to start negotiations, and he might, even now, be lenient with them. But if they continued to be stubborn he would crush them.

Vere Hodgson remembers June, 1940, as a moment especially sweet and poignant. 'People were so nice to each other,' she recalled. She noted it among her co-workers at the Sanctuary in

Holland Park and among those who came for help from the charity fund; it seemed to her that no one grumbled or quarrelled or shouted any more. Even the shopkeepers were being polite to their customers (which was rare since rationing had begun in January) and several times she had found a couple of eggs or a small bag of sugar pushed into her shopping basket with a smile or a wink from over the counter.

But if there was much goodwill around in those days of the lull there was also a good deal of suspicion, and the activities of the Government did much to stir it up. With the end of the campaign in France and the threat of imminent invasion, a whole stream of emergency powers had been presented to Parliament and passed into law, all designed to give the authorities sweeping control over the populace. To judge by what had happened in the Low Countries and France, paratroops might descend upon Britain at any moment and find Fifth Columnists lurking in doorways (or even in high places) ready to help them. So steps must be taken to see that the invading forces would not find easy transport awaiting them; and spies and Fifth Columnists must be prevented from communicating with them. Therefore it was made a serious offence to leave a car unattended without first having its distributor arm taken away, and those motorists who failed to do so returned to find a summons on their windscreen and their tyres deflated.* Car radios had to be taken out or immobilised so that they could not be tuned to instructions from the enemy, and a number of motorists were heavily fined for taking a portable radio in a car from one house to another. For a stranger in London, driving became not only hell by night because of the blackout but hell by day because of the total elimination of all signposts and signs of identity. And if the bureaucrats had their way, no one would tell him where he was if he asked them. Even children had been taught to reply to strangers:

> If anyone stops me to ask the way,
> All I must answer is 'I can't say.'

There was an intensification of the Government campaign,

---

* Many a London policeman learned to regret taking this action. If, as happened several times, a motorist had immobilised his car by another equally effective method, he was apt to insist that the policeman reinflate his tyres for him.

started at the beginning of the war, to stop rumour-spreading. In 1939 and during the months of the phoney war it had been confined to a ban on talks about the sailing of ships or troop movements, and there had been posters plastered over London walls saying 'Tittle-tattle lost the battle'. (The war produced a whole new race of jingle writers.) But now, with Britain a beleaguered island, the public were officially encouraged to regard any kind of loose talk as dangerous to the welfare of the State. An emergency regulation passed in June, for instance, made citizens liable to a £100 fine and a term of imprisonment for spreading 'any report or statement relating to matters connected with the war which is likely to cause alarm and despondency.' As many a watchdog of the people's liberty in Parliament was quick to point out, this opened the doors to every busybody in the country, who would rush out to telephone the police the moment they heard anyone exercising the Englishman's long-cherished right to growl and grumble about the situation, the weather, the police or the Government. This campaign was backed by a series of advertisements issued in the newspapers by the Ministry of Information dedicated to the discouragement of that British national pastime, gossip. It was headed THE SILENT COLUMN and began by showing a series of drawings of people who should henceforward be regarded as 'unpatriotic citizens'. They were:

MR SECRECY HUSH-HUSH: He's always got exclusive news, very private, very confidential. He doesn't want to spread it abroad but he doesn't mind whispering it to you.

MISS LEAKY MOUTH: She simply can't stop talking and since the weather went out as conversation* she goes on like a leaky tap about the war. She doesn't know anything but her chatter can do harm. Tell her to talk about the neighbours.

MR PRIDE IN PROPHECY: Here is the marvellous fellow who knows how it is all going to turn out. Nobody else but he does. He's a fool and a mountebank.

MR KNOW ALL: He knows what the Germans are going to do and when they are going to do it. He knows where our ships

---

* Weather forecasts had been banned from publication since the outbreak of war. With the occupation of France by Germany, Britain was now allowed to read about 'weather conditions in the English Channel', but a staple ingredient of English conversation had been stifled by the war.

are and what Bomber Command is going to do. With his large talk he is playing the enemy's game.

MISS TEACUP WHISPER: She is a relative of Mr Secrecy Hush-Hush and an equal danger.

MR GLUMPOT: He is the gloom brother who is convinced that everything is going wrong and nothing can go right. He is so worried by the enemy's strength that he never thinks of ours. Tell him to cheer up and shut up.

TELL THESE PEOPLE TO JOIN BRITAIN'S SILENT COLUMN.

This was followed up by an announcement saying:

'If you know somebody who makes a habit of causing worry and anxiety by passing on rumour and who says things persistently that might help the enemy – tell the police, but only do this as a last resort.'

Since there were still plenty of active Fascists and Communists opposing the war effort – they were responsible for the anti-Jewish or anti-war posters which were pasted on the walls around London in June 1940 – one would have thought that the bulk of the public's complaints to reach the police would have concerned these two dissident elements. Instead, innocent drunks or crotchety but loyal critics of Government policy felt the sting of the new regulations. An Irishman with a skinful was reported by a girl for saying that the British Expeditionary Force in France had run away, and that all England was good for was finding jobs for Irishmen. He got a month in jail. A wine-merchant, appalled by a rise in the tax on drink, flamed out at a customer that the Government 'are a bunch of robbers, and the sooner Hitler teaches them a lesson the better', and was sent to jail for three months. A girl who had spent an adulterous night in an hotel with an Air Force officer was reported by a shocked chambermaid who heard her saying: 'Who cares if Hitler does come so long as we can have fun like this,' and she got a month for signing a false name in the hotel register. A British soldier was even arrested in a famous French pub in Soho, and hauled off to Cannon Row police station for creating alarm and despondency. A couple of French sailors at the bar had raised their glasses to him and cried:

'Vive la France! Vive l'Angleterre!'

To which he had raised his own glass in return and shouted:
'To hell with Hitler!'

A woman rushed out and brought back a policeman. It took
some time for him to convince the law that he had *not* been crying:
'Heil Hitler!' while giving the Nazi salute, and by the time he
did so tempers had become so hot that he was fined the next day,
anyway, for being drunk and disorderly.

Vere Hodgson thought of Londoners at this time as being
rather like a quarrelsome family faced by a death in the house; and
reunited by it. And in some ways it was true. Air-raid wardens on
their nightly patrols along the city streets noted that folks no
longer sniffed contemptuously at them as they passed by, as if
the realisation was beginning to sink in that they might have their
uses. Two months earlier they had been called 'a bunch of
slackers'. In April a City magistrate, told that a traffic offender
was an auxiliary fireman who had joined up at the outbreak of
war, had given him a thumping fine and asked him 'why he was
skulking in the fire service and wasting the nation's money instead
of doing a useful job.' But now even firemen were being looked at
through fresh and more understanding eyes, as people realised
that firemen too might soon be needed.

In every church hall and playing field throughout London
came the sound of drill sergeants bawling orders. The call had
gone forth for a Home Guard* of civilian volunteers to be ready
to repel the German invader, and they had swarmed to the
recruiting centres in a great and embarrassing surge of patriotism.
In Kensington and Belgravia every retired colonel rushed out to
do his duty, and there were squads recruited which had no one
in them below the rank of major. One such contained eight
generals and only one civilian. The first time they paraded the
generals all came in their uniform and, medals up, jingled marti-
ally beside their crestfallen civilian comrade, a local shop assistant,
clad in jacket and flannel trousers and feeling like a shag among
penguins. But on the next parade he no longer felt out of it. The
generals had all gone into mufti, wore jackets and flannels too,
and continued to do so until battle dress was issued for all of
them.

But it was not just in the ex-officer enclaves of the West End
of London that the Home Guard came forward. Smithfield

* Known at the time as Local Defence Volunteers.

Market, where the meat porters slung great hunks of beef, Billingsgate, where they handled the fish, and the London docks, where they unloaded the nation's food, all formed Home Guards and went on parade, drilling in preparation for the invader.

Not that there were arms for them, even if the German paratroops had landed. They drilled with broom handles instead, and the sight of it infuriated Robert Boothby as he walked back from the House of Commons and watched them. It was six weeks since he had been in Belgium and had earmarked a big consignment of small arms. If the deal had gone through, they would have arrived just in time – in time to re-equip the troops evacuated from Dunkirk, in time to give arms to the Home Guard. He groaned as he thought of those gleaming new Belgian rifles and machine-guns, all packed and ready for shipment, being parcelled out to the soldiers of the German army in Brussels and Antwerp and Liège.

These days Boothby was working at the Ministry of Food, helping his chief, Lord Woolton, to organise an equitable rationing system and build up reserves for the ordeals to come. It was a job he relished. With Woolton he found little to complain about, for here was a man after his own heart. He too hated civil servants and their careful rules and regulations. Until war began, Lord Woolton had been plain Fred Marquis, managing director of a chain of department stores in the north of England, and to the horror of the bureaucrats of Whitehall he had come into Government to run his department in the same way that he ran his stores. 'Feed the people!' was the motto on the wall of his department, and he didn't care how he went about it so long as he built up his stocks of food. If only there were other ministers of Woolton's calibre in the Government, he wouldn't be worrying so much about the war. But though Churchill was now Prime Minister, too many of the old gang were still around and they were a poor lot. He had no faith in them.

He had even less faith in them after what happened on the night of 10 June 1940.

For a Jew or for anyone who had been a prominent and vocal opponent of the Nazis, the summer of 1940 was an uneasy time in

London. They not only shared with all other citizens the menace of invasion; they knew that if it succeeded and Britain, like France, capitulated their fate would be sealed. Already stories were filtering back from across the Channel of the ugly punishments and persecutions to which anti-Nazis were being subjected in France and the Low Countries. There was little chance that things would be better for them in Britain under a Nazi occupation. So unabashed enemies of Hitler, Jews and non-Jews alike, quietly decided to end it all the moment jackboots began treading the streets of London. Some of them, like a famous anti-Nazi publisher, Victor Gollancz, went around with phials of poison in their pockets, in case they could not get home to the medicine cabinet or the gas oven. Remarkably few panicked and even less took steps to get out of the country, as if they realised that once Hitler took Britain he could take anywhere, and there was no place where they would be safe.

Robert Boothby had a friend who had little to hope for if the Nazis took London. His name was Richard Weininger and he was both a Czech and a Jew. He had got out of Prague just ahead of the Nazis in 1939 and moved his business interests to London. He and Robert Boothby had been associated in various enterprises for a long time, and Boothby had tangible as well as fraternal reasons for valuing Weininger's friendship. Once, in a time of great financial stress, when the young Scot had badly needed money quickly, Weininger had lent it him, without strings and without interest. It was paid back – but Boothby would never forget the gesture.

Now he was worried about his friend. He had already done his fighting against the Germans and was now no longer physically fit. His stepdaughter, who had been living in France, had succeeded in escaping from Paris ahead of the Germans and had reached Lisbon, in neutral Portugal.

She had cabled her father asking him what she should do next. Weininger showed his friend the cable when they met for lunch in Boothby's apartment in Pall Mall on 10 May, and the MP did not hesitate. Boothby urged him to leave. He should take himself and his elder daughter, who was with him in England, and go to Lisbon without delay, and then proceed *en famille* to the United States. What good could Weininger do here now? He couldn't fight. He and his daughter would be two unnecessary mouths to feed if the worst came. So why not get out and do what he could instead on Wall Street to get the financial backing that Britain now so urgently needed to carry on the fight.

But Weininger had no intention of leaving. He had already cabled his daughter in Lisbon, he said, and instructed her to come to Britain as soon as possible. He had made up his mind. If Britain was invaded, he would fight, unfit or not. If Britain was defeated, then what did anything matter any more.

No, he would stay.

It was shortly after lunch was over and the two men were discussing the future over coffee that the front door bell rang, and in came Boothby's secretary to tell him that two officers from Scotland Yard would like to see him. As they came in through the door, Weininger got up and made as if to go.

'Don't go, sir,' said one of the men from the Yard. 'Am I right in thinking that you are Mr Richard Weininger?' He nodded. 'Then would you mind getting your hat and coat and coming with us, sir?'

Boothby said, 'What the hell is this all about? Are you arresting Mr Weininger? If so, what's the charge?'

There was an embarrassed silence, and then the detective said, 'There is no charge, sir. All I can tell you is that I have instructions to detain this gentleman under Regulation 18b.'*

'But dammit, man, that's for suspected spies,' exploded Boothby. 'Mr Weininger is one of our most loyal friends.'

The detective flushed. 'It's not my responsibility, sir. I just obey my orders. And my orders,' he went on firmly, 'are that this gentleman is to go with me.'

Boothby got to his feet in a rage. 'It's outrageous!' he said. 'I'm going with you – they can't do this to you.'

The detective said, 'I'm afraid I can't allow you to go with us, sir.'

'Nor can I,' said Weininger. 'It'll be all right, Bob. You'll see. It's just the situation at the moment – everyone's nervy.' He turned to the detective. 'Will you allow me to do one thing. Can I telephone my secretary?'

* Regulation 18b was part of the Defence Regulations passed in 1939 and was designed 'to provide for the custody on security grounds of persons against whom it was not practicable to bring criminal proceedings'. Boothby had protested its passage at the time.

The man from Scotland Yard hesitated, and then reluctantly nodded. Weininger went to the telephone.

'Miss Frances? Weininger here. I'm afraid I have to go away suddenly and it will be impossible to go to the office before I leave. In case you need any advice, will you please get in touch with Mr Robert Boothby. As for my papers and files, Mr Boothby is to be in sole charge of them. Good-bye, Mary. I hope to see you soon.' He turned back to the detective. 'Now, sergeant, I am ready,' he said.

After he had gone, Robert Boothby, still in a fury, called in his secretary.

'I want this letter taken down and sent off at once,' he said. He paused and then began: 'Dear Prime Minister, I want to tell you about a shocking affair which happened this afternoon. . . . '

It was a letter which was to cost him his political career.

3

Vere Hodgson was proud of her fluency in foreign languages, and she had listened to General de Gaulle's appeals over the BBC and been thrilled with him. 'What a magnificent personality he sounds!' she wrote in her diary after the second broadcast. 'His voice is thrilling and his answer to Pétain made me shiver in my chair, such tragedy there was in his tones.' But her aunt, who lived in Kensington, was of another opinion and so were several of her neighbours. 'Auntie Nell is not too enthusiastic about de Gaulle. She thinks we have trusted foreigners too often.'

If there was much neighbourliness and mutual understanding among Londoners that summer of 1940, it did not always extend to anyone with a foreign accent, a foreign name or a foreign appearance. Ever since the fall of France the newspapers had been crammed with stories about how the Fifth Column there and in the Low Countries had helped, by spying, sabotage and panic-mongering, to undermine the morale of Britain's allies. Most of the refugees who had settled in Britain during the thirties had been victims of either Fascism in Spain or Hitlerism in Germany, and the flood of newly-arrived Belgians, Dutch or French were fleeing from the German armies, but the suspicion of foreigners and 'foreignness' was in the air. Most people were not prepared to differentiate between them and thought the whole lot were a potential threat to the safety of the country. Stories began to filter through London of Nazi girl spies disguised as nuns fleeing from Liège and SS men in ringleted wigs and false beards posing as Orthodox Jews from Amsterdam. Even the Jews themselves were looking with wary eyes at their fellow religionists from abroad, and in Whitechapel, London's largest Jewish colony, a tale was told about a spy found in a group of Dutch-speaking Jews from Holland. Suspecting that one of them looked too Aryan to be a member of the faith, a rabbi had asked him: 'Have you seen Chag Hamathzos (the Feast of the Passover)?' It was part of a Jewish prayer and any Jew should have recognised it, but this fellow had replied: 'Yes, I saw him in Antwerp last week,' and thus revealed himself as a spy.*

But it was not only the masses who now suspected the foreigners in their midst; so did the Government, and the Government had power in their hands to do something about it. As they soon demonstrated.

4

Tothill Mansions was a row of four-storey Victorian houses on the fringes of Westminster into which a number of Government ministries had moved shortly before the outbreak of war, and this was where Charles Percy Snow was working that summer of 1940. Until then he had spent his life in academic and scientific circles, living the easy, urbane existence of a don at Cambridge and working out the lines of a series of novels ('Strangers and Brothers') which was to become one of the literary masterpieces of our times. But now he was a civil servant charged with the task of recruiting scientific experts and setting them to work for the war effort. He was a large, untidy, kindly man with a melancholy look that may have been due to his lonely bachelor existence or to the fact that he was worried about the war. He was not at all sure that Britain was going to win it.

For the moment he was desperately short of scientists, and was combing the universities of Britain and Ireland to find more of them. They were needed urgently. If large-scale bombing did soon begin over Britain and if this was followed by an attempt at

---

* I have been through the records and can find no trace of any German (or any other) spy having been trapped in this way.

invasion by the German armies, there was one weapon which could well tip the balance in favour of the defenders of Britain: radar. It was radar which would spot and fix the enemy planes as they came in to bomb; it was radar which would sight barges even if they approached by night, through mist or smokescreen. It was Britain's all-important invention, the first secret weapon of the Second World War, and it would win the Battle of Britain when the time came. But for the moment it was still suffering from 'bugs' which only great scientific skill and application could eliminate, and to get it perfected and the system installed at RAF stations on the ground and in the aeroplanes flying from them meant that Snow must find for the project scores more top-rate boffins to work with its creator, Sir Robert Watson-Watt.

The Nazi persecution of the Jews and of German liberals had not simply caused world-famous savants of the calibre of Albert Einstein to leave Germany. There were scores of others whose names were unknown to the general public, all men of either great or rapidly developing scientific skill and vision: Peierls, Brotscher, Halban, Kowarski, Frisch, Rotblat, Kurti, Kuhn, Heitler, Fröhlich, and Fuchs, among others. They asked for nothing more than to use their brains and their knowledge against Germany, and Snow was grateful to them and eager to set them to work.

That was where the trouble began. Because if they were eager and he was eager, Security was not. When the order went out from the Home Office to round up the aliens in Britain in May and June, 1940, there was no discrimination and no selectivity shown by the police in the way in which they cast their net. Only those aged seventy years and over were spared – and they got around to some of them later on – and the rest were taken without warning from their homes. To many of them, still living the nightmare of Nazi Germany, it seemed at first as if a new Gestapo, English-speaking this time, had come to persecute them. The knock on the door came at seven in the evening instead of 4 a.m. and the manner was polite instead of brutal, but they were still wrenched away from their wives and children and were not told why they had been taken or where they were going.

For days Charles Snow had had to storm the reluctant bastions of the Home Office in search of information as to the whereabouts of his cherished scientists. He had had to threaten tight-mouthed officials with dire consequences ('If I have to go to the PM he'll have your heads') to find out where they had been incarcerated. Most of them were in Brixton Prison in London and he was to remember his visit there to get them out; he was a tender-hearted man and his heart bled at the thoughtless cruelty which had put so many sincere anti-Nazis in jail, sometimes in the same cells as jeering Nazis, simply because of a German name or a foreign accent. There were distinguished scholars, writers and savants among them as well as businessmen and craft workers, all of them capable of helping the British war effort, and Snow would have had them all out if allowed his way. He had to be content with rescuing his own refugee boffins and soothing their hurt pride with the promise that they would soon be at work and all this humiliation would be forgotten. Or so he thought. But authority had decided otherwise.

The Ministry of Aircraft Production had held a meeting and made a decision, and there would be no appeal from it. The release of the foreign scientists earmarked by Snow was confirmed, but – and it was a catastrophic but – none of them was to be allowed to work on radar developments. The ban was to extend not only to recent refugees, but also to naturalised British subjects and anyone else not having native-born British parents. Not only that: whatever work they henceforward engaged upon, they must keep in closest touch with the police; they must not possess motor cars, bicycles or maps; they must not move from one area to the other without first obtaining official permission (which meant that they could not, for instance, travel between Cambridge and Birmingham universities); and they must obey a nightly curfew and be in their homes, hotels or lodgings by ten each evening.

It was not only humiliating, it was a waste of tremendous scientific talent at a moment when it was most desperately needed. But he knew enough about the workings of the Whitehall mind to realise that, as long as the invasion scare was in the air, it was no use fighting; he would not change anyone's mind, not even if he went as high as Churchill himself.

But he was determined about one thing: he was not going to let all those brains go to waste. It was an affront to his pride to let the dust gather and despair set in among these men of such brilliance and such eagerness to serve. He must find a place for them in the war effort. But where? And then he had it.

In his dry voice he began to dictate a long memorandum to his immediate chief. He followed this with urgent letters to three close friends, a trio of the most distinguished scientists in Britain: Professors P. M. S. Blackett, George P. Thomson and John D. Cockcroft.

'Can you use my men?' was the substance of his plea to the professors. 'Will you let them work for the Maud Committee?' was his request to the power-in-Government.

It did not happen all at once, but slowly the replies came in. The professors were delighted to welcome and use the talents of the refugee scientists, and the sooner they came the better. As for the Ministry, they had given the matter their earnest consideration and had decided that since the Maud Committee was engaged on work of no immediate value to the war effort, and that matters of immediate security were not involved, they had no objection to seeing the refugee scientists employed in such experimental work. Only they must obey the regulations: no bikes, no cars, no maps, and no nights out.

It was enough and Snow was relieved. Drs Brotscher, Halban, Kowarski, Fenning, Freundlich, Kemmer were to report to the Cavendish Laboratory at Cambridge University; Drs Frisch, Rotblat, to Liverpool University; Professor Simon, and Drs Kuhn and Kurti to Oxford University; Dr Peierls to Birmingham University (where he was later joined by Dr Klaus Fuchs); and Drs Heitler and Fröhlich were to be available for consultation.

And that was how eighteen refugee German scientists who were considered too great a security risk to work on radar in Britain in 1940 went to work instead on the creation of the atom bomb.

5

Dolly James* swallowed the last mouthful of her gin-and-tonic and then took a compact out of her handbag to see how her face looked. She dabbed some powder on her nose and repaired the lipstick, and then laughed to herself. Fancy doing up your face to walk home in the black-out. She never would get used to the fact that the street lights of London had gone off for the duration.

'I'm off,' she said. 'I've got to be at the Labour Exchange first thing in the morning.'

* Fictitious name.

'Aw, just one more,' one of the musicians said, but she shook her head.

'Honestly, no more. I really have got to look my best in the morning. You know what they're like at the Labour Exchange.' Then she stopped and said bitterly: 'No, you don't know what they're like. You've never had to ask them for dole or a job. But I can tell you, if you look a bit off or cheap or anything like that, they send you off to be a waitress or a cleaner.'

It was ten in the evening, the end of a beautiful June day, and now that the blackout blinds and curtains had been fixed, the pub was stiflingly hot. Crowded, too, and very noisy. Since the end of the war in France people in London seemed to be drinking more, as if liquor plus noise and people eased the tension in the air. The pub was called The George, but most of the regulars who used it referred to it as The Gluepot, probably because once you came into it for a drink it was difficult to get away. Someone was always there to press you to another.

The Gluepot stood on Mortimer Street a few yards along from Upper Regent Street, in the West End of London, and it had long since become the 'local' for staff members of the BBC and members of the BBC Symphony Orchestra (Broadcasting House and the Queen's Hall, where the orchestra played, were just around the corner). It was a drab brown nondescript pub smelling of slopped beer and potato chips, but its customers gave it one of the most sparkling ambiences in London. Conductors like John Barbirolli, composers like Constant Lambert and Alan Rawsthorne, poets and artists like Dylan Thomas and Elizabeth Lutyens, comedians like Tommy Handley, and Fleet Street and US newspapermen were to be found there at least one evening a week, elbows on the beery counter, swopping the latest gossip about the war and the BBC.

Dolly James had known the pub since her husband took her there for a visit two years before the war, when she was a bride of twenty and new to London. She had met her husband at a concert in Birmingham and for both of them it had been (she told herself cynically) sex at first sight. He was a violinist in one of the London symphony orchestras and she was a secretary at a motor works, hating her job and hating the parents with whom she lived on the outskirts of Birmingham. Someone had taken her, on a day off, to a rehearsal of the orchestra and she and her friend had gone

off for a Dutch lunch with members of the string section afterwards. That was when she had first met her husband. Halfway
through the performance of the Sibelius No. 7 that evening she
was convinced that she was in love, and by four o'clock next
morning so was he. They were married at a registrar's office in
Marylebone in the spring of 1938, and everything had gone
downhill ever since.

That summer the orchestra left on a tour of Germany and the
Low Countries, and it was at a reception after a concert in Cologne
that Dolly met the young engineer. He was working, he said, on a
big project not far from here (he was, she subsequently discovered,
in charge of construction on one of the sections of the main
German defences in the West, the Siegfried Line). She liked him.
Their meeting came after one of the big quarrels with her husband
which were now an almost daily part of her life, and if the visit
had lasted longer she might have succumbed there and then.
Instead she went back to London, and that Christmas the young
German flew across to see her. In the spring of 1939 ('I must have
been mad; I was mad') she went out to Cologne to stay with him.

It was an idyllic spring and an ecstatic summer. 'I have never
been happier,' she was to say. She never read a newspaper, she
didn't listen to the radio, when she did have any doubts her lover
laughed and said: 'There isn't going to be any war,' and she
believed him. When it looked, towards the end of August, that
he might be wrong and she talked of going back to England, he
assured her that she didn't have to worry; even if there was a war
he would protect her; it wasn't as if she was politically minded,
he said, so there wouldn't be any trouble. She believed him because
she wanted to believe, and she needed him.

At the end of September 1939 three weeks after the outbreak
of war, the German police came for her and took her off to an
internment camp. She and her lover had spent most of the last
night weeping in each other's arms. Of course he couldn't protect
her: 'An engineer on a secret fortification with an English mistress
– he must have been mad to have thought he could get away with
it,' she said, and then added: 'Or in love, and we were in love.'

Early in 1940 she was among a group of British internees
released by the German Government in exchange for German
civilians who had been interned in Britain. The train pulled into
the little Dutch frontier station and she disembarked with the

others to have her passport checked by the police, her face pale under the tumbled mass of titian-red hair.*

She was sick on the ferry boat from the Hook of Holland to Harwich, but that didn't stop the police from questioning her for three hours after her arrival. In London there were more questions, this time from some men who said they were from Security; but they proved to be more sympathetic and they seemed to believe the innocence (the political innocence, anyway) of her story. She had found a one-roomed apartment just off the Marylebone Road, and started to look for work. At night she would go to The Gluepot, because she liked the company of the musicians and writers she found there. They all knew what had happened to her, but it seemed to draw them closer to her rather than repel them. 'Welcome to the kingdom of the lost!' said a drunken Dylan Thomas the first night she came in, folding her in his arms . . .

'You're sure you won't have another' one of the BBC men asked her, but she shook her head and said she had to go. As she walked out of the pub she glanced again at the man at the end of the counter, toying with his glass of beer. He had been watching her all evening, and she felt in her bones that it was not her looks that he was admiring.

Once she was out in the blackened street, she knew that he was following her. She turned out of Mortimer Street into Upper Regent Street and for a time she lost the feeling that he was with her. She was too busy concentrating on the blackness, getting her eyes accustomed to it, watching out for the down-pointed shafts of light from the muffled torches of the other passers-by. But once she had crossed Portland Place and picked her way across it into New Cavendish Street she was on home ground; she knew all the obstacles and he didn't, and she could hear him stubbing his shoe against the raised kerbstone on the corner of Harley Street and noticed, not without satisfaction, the grunt of pain he emitted when he caught the outjutting railing a few yards further on.

She was not afraid, as once she might have been. The past few months had changed her considerably, mentally, emotionally, and physically too. She felt she could handle anything this man might do. In any case, she was convinced that he wasn't going to attack her. He hadn't looked at her in that kind of way.

* It was here that the author first met her.

66

When she turned into the mews where she had her apartment she saw at once the dark blur of a car parked at the door. The footsteps behind her quickened; and then she heard a door open and a shape emerged from the blur and said:

'Mrs James? Mrs Dolly James?'

'That's me,' she said.

'May we come inside, please, madam? We're from the police.'

An hour later the doors had closed behind her, and she was inside Holloway Prison; and the first thing she was aware of once the policemen had departed was the pulsing noise which seemed to come from the heart of it. It was a continuing wave of sound, like the chatter and chirp of a thousand birds, and it was only later that she realised that the noise was human.

'My God, not another one!' she heard one of the wardresses saying as they brought her in. 'How many do they think we can cram in here?'

A big, bulky woman said, in a not unkindly voice: 'All right, dear, take off your clothes. We won't keep you long.'

'What here?' said Dolly.

'Yes, here,' the woman said. 'We're a bit busy tonight. Go on, dear. It won't take but a minute. We just want to see what you're wearing.'

She slipped off her clothes and stood there, naked, feeling cold (though it was in fact hot) and lonely, while they went through her garments one by one, then through the overnight bag she had brought with dressing gown and toothbrush, and finally through her handbag.

'All right, dear, you can dress again now,' the bulky woman said. 'We'll just find a place to put you for the night.'

They went through a number of doors and into the main body of the prison, and it was then that the noise hit her. It sounded like an animal house at the zoo. There were women shrieking, there were some singing, there were others shouting in unison, and amid all this the frightening sound of sobbing. The wardress walked down the row of cells, peering through the window in each, until finally she halted.

'It'll have to be this one,' she said.

She unlocked the door and at once a big, bony, red-faced woman burst out.

'You've got to take me out of here,' she cried. 'I won't be in the same cell as this scum. They're Jews, dirty, filthy Yids! I won't have it!'

The wardress said mildly: 'Now calm down. We'll see about it in the morning. It's too late to do anything.' And then to Dolly: 'In you go. You take the top bunk.'

She looked round the cell. There were three girls sitting huddled close together, on the bottom bunk, and all of them had the stains of dried tears on their faces. The big woman stood there glaring down at them, and then swung round towards Dolly.

'Are you English?' she asked.

'I am,' said Dolly.

The woman indicated the three huddled girls. 'Not foreign pigs like these Yids here. They can't even speak English.' And then to Dolly: 'You aren't Jewish, are you?'

'No,' said Dolly.

'And you aren't – they haven't brought you in here because you're a thief or a tart or something, have they?'

Dolly said: 'I don't know why they've brought me here. If I've committed any crime, then it's something I don't know about. All they said was I was being held under Regulation 18b.'

A large smile broke over the woman's face.

'You must be one of us!' she cried. Then, as if for the first time, she seemed to realise that she was looking at a very pretty girl. She came over and put her arm, as if in comradely fashion around Dolly's shoulders.

'When did you join the Party, my dear?' she asked.

'What party?' Dolly asked. 'And take your arm away, you big lunk!'

It was, she decided, wryly, going to be quite a war.

The announcement in the newspapers next day was a brief one. It read:

For reasons of national security, a number of British subjects have been taken into custody during recent days. They include Captain A. H. M. Ramsay, MP, and Sir Oswald and Lady Mosley, together with a number of others whose freedom of movement at this time would not be in the public interest. Certain non-British residents are also being temporarily deprived of their liberty of movement.

Captain Ramsay was a well-known anti-Semite and Sir Oswald Mosley was the leader of the British Union of Fascists, whose male and female members wore black shirts and marched through the East End of London baiting the Jews.

Dolly James was damned if she could see what connection there was between them and her. 'My God,' she had told the policeman, 'all I ever did was sleep with a German. What else do you think I gave him – the score of Handel's Water Music?'

Here she was in gaol, and yet she hadn't done a thing. On the other hand, neither had the three poor frightened German-Jewish girls who shared her cell.

Regulation 18b was non-discriminatory. It was pulling in Fascist and non-Fascist alike.* They were still being sorted out by officialdom when the air raid sirens sounded over London for the first time since 1939. The date was 25 June, 1940.

MEMORANDUM

To: Head Office, Mass-Observation, London
From: Mrs E. H., housewife,
London SE 3
Subject: Air Raid
Date: Monday, 25 June 1940

Listened to the midnight news on the BBC but as it went off (prob. due to enemy aircraft) I did not re-tune but came up to bed. Next thing I knew, Harry was shaking me and saying the sirens were going. I heard them but had been log-like for the first few seconds. Harry had heard them in the distance before ours began. Lately I've let the dog sleep on my bed at the foot. I leant over, grabbed his collar from the rail and put that on. Into my stockings. Out of nightie and into my other things. Skirt a bother – the old one has hooks, they get jammed. (Note. Although I hate the look of them, I must get slacks if raids continue: one garment to put on instead of knickers and skirt.) Put on glasses. Turned out my light, got behind curtains and opened the windows wide. Sirens now doing a fine concerto. Searchlights sweeping the sky in almost frenzied urgency. A

---

* Altogether 65 per cent of aliens and refugees in Britain were taken into custody under Regulation 18b in 1940. At least three-quarters of them were victims of Nazi or Fascist persecution in Germany, Italy or Spain.

bloody sort of moon showing through the clouds. A good crack of light showing from a house at the back. Funny how much one can take in at a quick glance. Dog was quite good, he'd gone downstairs without being told. I followed. Got into gumboots, unlocked the back door. Collected two gas masks, the pile of rugs I always prepare by the kitchen door each night. Came back for a torch. Remembered to turn off the gas, then turned off fridge's gas jet, remembered what happened in one of last September's warnings (false alarms) when we nearly gassed ourselves afterwards. Turned off kitchen light and went down to shelter and told Wags to go ahead. He did so and was waiting at the door for me. Sirens still going.

Flew back to house, turned on shelter light, got our axe, unlocked tool shed, got my watch from dining room, got dog's milk from fridge, took down the basket with thermos flask and various tins. Told Harry to bring deed box and stirrup pump. Sirens stopped, searchlights went out. All was still. I was trying to sort things out in the shelter. Harry got very angry with me (sure sign he was bothered and worried). Told me to shut up and settle down, how could he listen for guns. Retorted I must put things up and give Wags his bromide. My training of the last few months proved good. Several times I had taken Wags to the shelter and given him a drink of milk. Suggested it to him now. Harry said he must go on his shelf first. Put him there for me. Dog thrilled and had a good sniff for rats in holes between the posts. We have a shelf in the roof for the dog. Even smells could not prevail against a drink of milk. Lapped up his bromide and got back to work.

Down in the ground as we were we could feel deep thuds going on. Harry surmised bombs. I didn't know. I asked Harry if he had locked the back door, so he went back to do so and brought me down the bottles of water. Rushing about had given me wind, fearful of a heart attack I asked for some magnesia. Harry couldn't seem to understand where it was in the bookcase cupboard so I went in for it. Found he had left the bedroom light on. Turned that off. Got the front door key, my mags, and put a big rug round the bird cage. Not a sound outside, and dark now, more clouds. Made the shelter tidy. Frank came to the edge of the fence and wanted to know if we were there, they'd been so busy they had not heard us. David's crib would not go through the shelter door, they had to take him out and get the crib in sideways, they'd never thought to do it before.

When I made my first trip to the shelter I heard two police whistles and thought, 'Ah, W. and his neighbour.' Wondered if A.C. had heard and got up, could imagine him trundling round long after the others. On my 2nd trip I heard B. (next neighbour to the young C.s), calling out 'Are you there, Win?' They have no shelter and were apparently going into their neighbours' at the bottom of their garden. While dressing I had worried over the parents, all by themselves in a large house, would they hear? Would P. come over and give them a hand? Would it start Father wheezing again? How active one's mind is at a time like this.

In the shelter we had settled down now, half covered the light, which pointed straight at me and was glary. Harry sat in his corner with the old cape rammed behind his head. I at the end seat with the dog's bed at my back and a woolly door-mat to sit on. The plywood back rests seemed too sloping for me, could not get comfy. Gave dog 2nd bromide. It seemed to work, he settled down in a few minutes and was soon snoring. Harry said he was going to sleep. We felt some bigger thumps. Harry crawled into the shelter porch. Came back and growled because my Marks and Spencer watch ticked so loudly he could not hear if the guns were firing.

Frank came over for another chat. Said they couldn't feel the bumps in their shelter. Harry told him we would give them a cup of coffee later, I secretly hoped it would be warm enough. We settled down again and Harry went to sleep. I tried to but was not comfy enough. Thought of all kinds of things. Of course I was not frightened because it was so unreal and so far we had heard no gunfire. . . . Then I remembered I'd not paid a call before coming out. I wanted to go most badly. Woke Harry and told him so. He said 'Go in, you can dash out if you hear guns.' Went indoors and tended to myself. Washed my face too and powdered it. Got my identity card. Collected a rug and a small woolly mat. Looked at the time: 2.15. Incredible that we had been out there more than an hour. Crawled into shelter and was greeted by dog, who leant down and licked my head. Made Harry move over and let me remake his seat. Found I'd been so uncomfortable because my seat was reversed and slanting outwards. Harry said he was going to sleep again. Wished he had a sling for his head. Had also brought two hot water bottles last trip, and hugged those, but my behind was cold and wind seemed to go up my legs. Made a 2nd decision to get slacks . . .

I dozed but did not get right off, heard noises as before. Getting light outside now and wind coming in at intervals was freshening. Waited for the first bird sounds. Dorothy and Frank made several trips to their house. I was so cold, woke Harry and asked for a cup of coffee. He very stiff and also chilly. More cheerful now and thought coffee sounded good. Got it out and it was lukewarm. Drank my coffee and the All Clear sounded. Dog woke up and at once wanted to be let down. Harry lifted him down and they had a cuddle on the seat. I gathered up the rugs and deed box and paddled indoors. Threw off clothes and was getting into bed as Harry came up. Dog begged to be allowed again on bed, let him and he very determinedly crept into my arms and put his head on my shoulder, lying with his back to me. We do spoil him since the war.

More sirens went off, and dog flew off bed. I calling to Harry that they were beginning again, Harry said it was another All Clear. To make sure I looked out of window. Frank and Dorothy were also hanging out of theirs. Said they too were just in bed and not sure whether it was a warning or an All Clear. Back to bed, 4.15 a.m., lovely morning, and suddenly the birdsong began.

4

THE REHEARSAL

So far as the official records go, the first of the air raids on London was not to come for another month, but when the warning sirens sounded in the early hours of 25 June 1940, no one afterwards laughed it off as a false alarm. Bombs were dropped on a town in Kent and an airfield well away from the capital and no one was injured, but both the authorities and the public took the raid with deadly seriousness and afterwards regarded the night spent under the stairs, out in the garden shelter or in public shelter down the street as being in the nature of a dress rehearsal.

Only a few confessed next day that they had slept through the alarm, and Vere Hodgson chided one of her staff at the Sanctuary who had done so.

'A very dangerous thing to do,' she wrote in her diary that night, and then added: 'But how lovely to be killed asleep.'

In St John's Wood, Mrs Rosemary Black looked back on the disturbed night with some satisfaction. She was a young and attractive widow of 28 who had, some weeks earlier, become a regular diarist and observer for that remarkable organisation, Mass-Observation.* She described herself in her curriculum vitae for MO as : *Upper middle-class, mother of two children (girls aged 3 and 2), of independent means.* She lived in a trim three-storeyed house in a quiet street in a fashionable part of St John's Wood, a short taxi-ride from the West End, whose restaurants and theatres she knew well. She was fashionably dressed and attractive and she lacked for very little so far, as far as the practicalities of life were concerned: there was Irene, a Hungarian refugee, aged about thirty, to look after the children; Helen, a Scottish housemaid about 28, to look after herself and the house; and a daily woman to do the major chores. During the phoney war period she had, with little compunction, decided to go about and enjoy herself, but now that the war seemed to be getting serious she thought it time

* See section at the end of this book.

she found herself a worthwhile job. The raid, and the reactions of her household to it, confirmed her in her determination, because she was now certain all of them could cope.

> The maids seemed as cool as cucumbers, [she reported.] It's a great relief to know that they're not liable to become faint or hysterical. I shall not feel afraid to stay away from home for a night in future. Our drill worked well ... But we clean forgot to open the front door in case anyone in the street wanted shelter. Also we forgot to dress which was silly and wouldn't have done in winter. However, we shall know not to make these mistakes next time.

She was glad London had had such a nice, peaceful try-out, and next day, while dining at the Ivy, she was surprised to find her companion, Mrs B. so dismal. She was not a jitterer, she thought, but she really was *gloomy*. She had two favourite sayings: 'My dear, this looks like the end, doesn't it?' and 'Let us eat and drink and be merry, for tomorrow we die.' On this occasion, Mrs Black decided, Why not? She ordered caviare. She confessed afterwards that she felt 'somewhat guilty over doing so, but after all if it's still being imported that is the Government's funeral. Anyway, if as I imagine what we are being offered is part of the pre-war stock, it might just as well be eaten up.'

Every day Londoners got a new reminder that the war was coming closer to them. As June became July, the newspapers filled with accounts of the battle now starting in the English Channel. Hermann Goering had moved his Luftwaffe squadrons to their new airfields in northern France, and now the Me 109s were swarming over the 22-mile stretch of the Straits of Dover looking for trouble. Underneath their protective cover the Stuka dive bombers screamed down upon the convoys of British merchantmen on their way to London. And from dawn to dusk, up came the Hurricanes and Spitfires of the RAF to knock the enemy planes out of the sky – or send them scurrying back to France again. Those were the days when correspondents from all over the world lay in the sunshine on Shakespeare Cliffs above Dover Harbour and watched the fate of an Empire being settled by the shape of the white trails of vapour in the blue sky above their heads. As Churchill

74

had reminded the nation a couple of weeks earlier, the Battle of France being over, the Battle of Britain had now begun, and for the moment it was a handful of young fighter pilots in the air over the Channel who were fighting it.

For the people of London it was a battle they could not see. Dover was only 50 miles away, but since the fall of France all travel to the coast had been forbidden to anyone but residents and holders of special permits, which were hard to come by. But each day the newspapers covered the clash in the sky with all the verve they usually reserved for a Test Match or a soccer cup final. The headlines across the front pages carried figures which changed with each edition, like cricket scores: IT'S 65 FOR 12 was one typical headline, which told the readers that sixty-five German planes had been knocked down for the loss of twelve of our own.

It suddenly sounded like a great and exciting game. 'Jolly good!' commented Vere Hodgson. That night she tuned in to listen to a broadcast by Winston Churchill and she was inspired by him. 'He sounded as if he had got over the shocks France had given him and was in command of the situation again,' she wrote.

Her heart rose up in a splendid sense of English pride as she listened to Churchill saying:

'This is no war of chieftains or of princes, of dynasties or national ambition; it is a war of peoples and of causes. There are vast numbers not only in this island but in every land who will render faithful service in this war, but whose names will never be known, whose deeds will never be recorded.'

She approved of that. She looked out of her window in Ladbroke Grove at the barrage balloons floating in the sky over Notting Hill Gate and she felt resolute. She felt that Britain had suffered some blows that week. First there had been the rationing of tea, and then had come the announcement that butter and fats would henceforth be rationed to six ounces a week. Now there was a shortage of eggs.

That's bad, as I rely upon them. I shall have to switch over to baked beans.

And then buoyed up again by Churchill's words, she went on:

No invasion yet. I recall the man who said that every Britisher should put up a Union Jack on his chimney pot when the Germans arrived and it should not be hauled down until a Nazi had crawled up and hauled it down over the dead bodies of the household.

Those were her sentiments, too.

2

'... This is a war of the Unknown Warriors; but let all strive without failing in faith or in duty, and the dark curse of Hitler will be lifted from our age.'

The orotund phrases rolled out and finally stopped, and Winston Churchill reached for his whisky and soda and his cigar.

'You have just been listening to the Prime Minister,' said the BBC announcer and then nodded across the desk. Churchill leaned back in his chair, blew out a cloud of smoke, and said, 'Well, now.'

He reached over and pressed a button marked 'Secretary'. When she came in, Brigadier Leslie Hollis was with her. He congratulated the Prime Minister on his broadcast speech and got a grunt in return.

'Get me the President,' said Winston Churchill.

Hollis looked at the secretary and the secretary looked at him, and both knew what the other was feeling. This was always the most tricky diplomatic operation of the lot, and they knew that for the next half an hour they would be playing the 'put him on first' protocol game across the Atlantic that sometimes made them want to tear the telephone out of the wall. For both President Roosevelt and Winston Churchill were not men who liked to be kept waiting, and that meant that each one must be sure that the other was on the line when he picked up the receiver – and how could you make sure of that?

It was from the vast honeycomb of tunnels built 150 feet beneath Whitehall, the Hole in the Ground, that Churchill made his wartime broadcasts. He spoke from a room marked simply 'Prime Minister' from a wide desk upon which were two candles and some matches, in case the electricity failed while he was speaking.

Just along the corridor was another, much tinier room. It looked like a bathroom and it had, in fact, a bathroom door catch fixed to it with a slot marked 'Vacant' or 'Engaged' according to whether the occupant of the room pushed over the lock while he was inside. It was in here that the telephone had been installed with a direct connection to the White House in Washington, and Winston Churchill had been using it often in the past few days. When the US ambassador in London (Joseph P. Kennedy) was forecasting in every dispatch that Britain was all but defeated, and that her only hope was to sue for peace, Churchill had some earnest talking to do in order to convince Franklin Roosevelt that all was not yet lost.

Churchill would suddenly decide to speak to the President, regardless of what hour it might be in Washington. In his slippers with pom-poms, wearing his magnificent mandarin dressing-gown embroidered in red and gold dragons, the belt pulled tightly round him, his cigar clamped like some miniature torpedo between his teeth, he would stump along the corridor towards the telephone. Even in the unhealthy light from the electric bulbs that lit the corridor his complexion seemed cherubic and as pink as if he had just come from eight hours' sleep . . .*

'Put the President on,' he would say.

And that was where it became tricky. President Roosevelt was determined not to go to the telephone until he was absolutely sure that Winston Churchill was at the other end. On the other hand, the Prime Minister knew that someone would have to push the President in his wheelchair from wherever he was in the White House to the telephone, and he had no wish to sit around in the cramped telephone room while this operation was in progress.

It became a sort of transatlantic game to get both parties moving towards the instrument at the same time, so that they would pick it up simultaneously at each end of the connection.

'The President is just coming, sir,' his aide would say. 'He is picking up the telephone at this very moment.'

Brigadier Hollis would meantime be swearing that Churchil, was just stubbing out his cigar and reaching for the phone.

* To Sir Leslie Hollis and James Leasor, *War at the Top*, Michael Joseph, 1959.

On the night of 14 July, it was Churchill who had to wait, and the delay infuriated him. Hollis had slipped out of the room once the White House was on the phone, pushing over the catch from 'Vacant' to 'Engaged'. He then had to wait in the corridor. As soon as he saw the blue cigar smoke beginning to curl under the door, he knew that Roosevelt was keeping the Prime Minister waiting.

He could guess why. What had Winston to tell him that he did not already know from the newspapers? That the RAF had had another triumphant day battling with the Luftwaffe over the Channel? He had heard it over his own radio. That the British would fight on, whatever happened, even if London were laid in ruins and in ashes? But that also he knew about, because he had read it in the advance copy of Churchill's broadcast to his people.

What he did want to know was: Had Adolf Hitler decided to invade the British Isles, and if so when? Would the German air fleets dare to bomb London and make war against its civilian population? Only those two events would rouse the American people out of their determined isolation and throw them wholeheartedly on the side of Britain.

But Winston Churchill could not answer those questions for him, and Roosevelt knew it. So he did not hurry to the phone.

3

For the moment Adolf Hitler could not answer those questions himself. He could not make up his mind. For weeks every neutral capital in Europe had been alive with rumours that the British would like to come to an arrangement with Germany. The King of Sweden had offered to act as an intermediary. So had the Vatican. There had been mysterious talks in Madrid and since the British Ambassador there, Sir Samuel Hoare, had once been Neville Chamberlain's most fervent supporter it seemed logical to believe that he might have been sent to his post by Churchill for one purpose only, to contact the Germans and make a deal.

The sinking of the French navy at Tel el Kebir by the British Mediterranean fleet had, in truth, jolted Adolf Hitler out of his optimistic mood. He was pleased that a large part of it had been immobilised, because he had been desperately afraid that it would go over to the British and all but double her strength at sea. At Munich on 18 June he had said:

'With regard to the French fleet ... the best thing would be to have the French sink it. The worst thing would be to have the fleet unite with the British, because, in view of the large number of light French ships, the united British-French fleets could organise extensive convoys.'

The British had at least relieved him of the latter possibility, but in breaking the last tie with Pétainist France by sinking the French fleet the British had also demonstrated their determination to carry on the war; and that meant that all the sly talks in neutral capitals, all the oblique indications that they were ready to parley, had not been meant seriously. It had been a bluff to gain time. The British were not going to give in, after all.

On 16 July 1940, the Fuehrer sent for General Keitel and handed him Instruction Number 16 with orders that he circulate it among his fellow members of the German High Command:

'Since, despite its desperate military situation, Great Britain shows no sign of goodwill,' the Instruction said in part, 'I have decided that a plan of invasion will be prepared, and, if necessary, carried out.'

But the emphasis was on those hanging words, 'if necessary'; and Field Marshal Hermann Goering simultaneously reminded the commanders of his air fleets that his previous order still prevailed, *and under no circumstances would London be bombed without written permission from him and from the Fuehrer.*

It was necessary, first, to destroy the Royal Air Force.

4

Robert Boothby had been to Brixton Prison and was appalled by what he had found there. The drab old gaol in the even drabber inner London suburb was crammed with all sorts, sizes and shapes of men who shared one thing in common: they were being held without any charge having been made against them. Perhaps twenty of them knew why they were being held, and they were all British subjects. There was Sir Oswald Mosley and there were his followers in the British Union of Fascists: they had publicly proclaimed themselves against the war, which they blamed solidly on the Jews, and they did not conceal their admiration for Adolf

Hitler and Mussolini, for German National Socialism and Italian Fascism. There were some wild anti-Semites and some even wilder pro-Nazis, most of them retired Army and Navy officers, who had been put out of harm's way for the duration. But the rest were either naturalised subjects or German, Czech and Italian refugees who hated Britain's enemies even more strongly than the British did, and they were in despair because they could not see any reason why they should be in gaol.*

It was in Brixton that Boothby had found his friend, Richard Weininger, and he was shocked at the sight of him. He was a completely broken man. He had been kept in solitary confinement, and looked haggard with stubble on his chin (he was not allowed to use his own razor) and despair in his eyes.

'He sits there day and night racking his brains to discover what it is all about,' Boothby wrote to Clement Attlee later, 'with no allegations made, and nothing to answer. One of his stepdaughters, a most charming and intelligent girl whom I have known for years, and who has been working like a slave at a communal kitchen, has similarly been carted off to Holloway; the other who served with the Czech forces in France and subsequently escaped to Portugal is refused permission to enter this country.'

Weininger had asked: 'How can these things be?' and Boothby was asking that question himself as well. It was something he felt he must fight, and not just for Weininger's sake. All over Britain men and women were rotting in gaol without charge and without trial, simply because their parents had been foreigners or because they had once got too close to an enemy.

It was a battle after his own heart, and his friends encouraged him to go to it. 'For God's sake go on and fight this thing,' said one of them, Sir David Waley, a government official. 'Weininger's case is only one of many. I know of several myself. But we are helpless.' And Waley, a high civil servant at the Treasury, was not without his influence.

Boothby was quite aware of the fact that if he did fight this

---

* The bulk of the internees being held in Britain under Regulation 18b had now been shipped to the Isle of Man, where they were living in holiday camps and lodgings. Hard-core Nazis and Italian Fascists had been sent to camps in Canada. Those shipped aboard the vessel *Arandora Star*, most of them Italian, were, ironically enough, drowned when an Italian submarine torpedoed the ship.

thing he would be venturing on to dangerous ground. It was the Home Office, which controls the movement of aliens in Britain, which had ordered the detentions under Regulation 18b, and as rumours spread of the hardships they were causing there was a rising tide of indignation among more thoughtful Britons and considerable mental discomfort among the rest. It was not pleasant to realise that, in fighting for freedom against the tyranny of fascism, Britain had resorted to tyrannical methods herself.

'What have they done to our Magna Carta?' asked a speaker at Hyde Park Corner. 'Torn it to bloody pieces!'

In the face of this criticism, the Home Office was on the defensive, and among its officials none was more sensitive to it than the Home Secretary himself, Sir John Anderson. A kind-hearted and highly civilised man, he was well aware of the dangers implicit in the blind application of Regulation 18b. It was against all the principles of freedom and justice for which Britain stood. Nevertheless he was steadfast and stubborn in his contention that the round-up was necessary for the sake of national security so long as invasion threatened. He genuinely thought it preferable that 30,000 people should have their lives or their families or their beliefs broken up rather than allow one potential spy or saboteur to stay free in wartime Britain. He became blazingly angry when it was suggested to him that this was not the way to trap spies, that they had better ways of disguising themselves, and that the blanket application of Regulation 18b was cruel, expensive, time-wasting and the product of panic. He refused to believe that there was any real hardship at all in the wholesale gaoling, and sturdily maintained that any case of genuine hardship would receive his immediate personal attention. This was true to some extent. It was, in fact, through his intervention that C. P. Snow had secured the freedom of his refugee boffins, and it was Snow, too, who had given Anderson a further opportunity of demonstrating his 'liberalism'. He had introduced the scientist J. D. Bernal to the Home Secretary, pointing out that Bernal had been working on several ideas for the protection of civilians during air raids which might prove invaluable to the Home Office (which also looked after Air Raid Precautions). Bernal was a Communist, a real Party-line-toeing member, and since this was the period when Russia still adhered to the Russo-German Pact and was staying firmly out of the war, he refused to turn his brilliant talents towards helping Britain win the war; but he was not averse to helping to protect civilians. Anderson talked to him, was enthusiastic about his ideas, and took him into his department.

'But how can you do that?' his colleagues asked him. 'Bernal is a rabid Red.'

'I don't care if he is as Red as the fires of hell, he will go on working for me as long as I find him useful,' the Home Secretary had replied.

This was cited as an example of his broad-mindedness, and as proof that there was no vindictiveness, no xenophobia in his application of Regulation 18b. A man of heart.

The fact remained that 30,000 foreigners, the bulk of them anti-Nazis, stayed on in gaols and camps throughout Britain; and Richard Weininger was one of them. So far as he was concerned, the Home Office was adamant, and nothing that Boothby said or did would move them to let him out of gaol. The young Member of Parliament produced details of Weininger's record, and it included considerable services which the Czech-Jewish banker had rendered Britain at no small risk to himself. It pointed out the damage to his health which continued incarceration was causing. It strongly proclaimed Weininger's complete innocence of any wish to harm Britain, of his intense love of his adopted country and his eagerness to fight for her. (His complete innocence and intense patriotism were later to be proved.) It did no good whatsoever. On the contrary, it appeared to produce an anger all but amounting to vindictiveness at the Home Office – and the vindictiveness was directed against Boothby.

'Why did they react this way?' said Boothby, when asked about it later. 'I really don't know, except that they were suffering from a guilty conscience over the refugees and didn't like my campaign to get them out.'

Shortly after Weininger's arrest, the Czech banker's secretary, Mary Frances, telephoned Boothby. Her boss had put Boothby in charge of his private papers when he had been taken away and now the secretary wanted to know what to do with them. She explained that she had just received a call from Scotland Yard to say that they would be sending a man around, two days hence, to go through Weininger's files. What should she do?

'Are there any love letters in the files?' Boothby asked, half-jokingly.

'No,' she said.

Boothby thereupon said he would try to come around to the office and go through the files the following day. It should perhaps be repeated here that during the course of a long business and personal friendship, Weininger had once loaned Boothby money. Shortly before the German occupation of Czechoslovakia, Boothby had planned to go to Prague and get out the small fortune which Weininger had left behind when he fled from the Nazis. But the Germans got there before him. The money was in a Czech bank and it stayed there because the Germans refused to let it go. Subsequently, Boothby spoke in a debate in the House of Commons about the assets of the Czech Government and Czech civilians which were being held by the Nazis and attacked the Government (then still eager, under Chamberlain, to appease Adolf Hitler) for not insisting on the release of these funds to their rightful owners. It did not occur to him, since he believed in the principle of what he was saying, that he should have declared a 'personal interest' in the subject, or that someone finding out about the loan from Weininger and his eagerness to help his friend would add up the innocent facts and call it corruption.

He knew the letters concerning all his dealings with Weininger were in the files, but that did not bother him. 'It would have done had I known that the Home Office was gunning for me,' he said later. Shortly after Mary Frances had spoken to him, he found himself immersed in a new project at the Ministry of Food.

'I was heavily engaged at the Food Ministry,' he said, 'and in the evening I rang up Miss Frances and told her I was too busy to come round [to Weininger's office] directing her at the same time to hand over all the files to the Scotland Yard officers when they fetched up. This can hardly be described as the action of a man with a guilty conscience.'

He had also written letters to Winston Churchill and Sir John Anderson protesting in the strongest possible terms over Weininger's imprisonment. The letter to Churchill he handed on to Brendan Bracken, the Prime Minister's parliamentary private secretary, asking him to pass it along. He hoped it would get immediate action. He expected as much from Churchill, who was an old friend.

And that was when the trouble began.

Within a few hours the telephone rang. At the other end was Osbert Peake, Under-Secretary of State at the Home Office.

'Bob? This is Osbert – Osbert Peake.' The voice was smooth and friendly. 'The Home Secretary asked me to call you. You mention in your letter to him that you are also writing to Winston about the Weininger case. Dear boy, do you mind if I make a suggestion?'

'Any suggestion you like,' said Boothby, 'so long as it helps to get Dick Weininger out of gaol.'

'Well, it won't do that exactly.' Peake's voice became a little more crisp. 'But it might help you.' He paused and then went on: 'The Home Secretary asks you not, and I repeat not, to send your letter on to Winston for the time being. Hold it, dear boy.'

'Why on earth should I?' asked Boothby.

'I can't exactly go into details on the phone,' said Peake, 'but shall we just say that we have been through Weininger's papers and that we have found some interesting – some very interesting – letters. They concern you, dear boy. Please, please don't send your letter to Winston. Not, at least, until you have had a chance to look at the letters and talked to the Home Secretary. He would like to see you. Meantime, you will hold the letter?'

Boothby said: 'I'll see what I can do.'

He telephoned Brendan Bracken and asked him to hold the letter he had given him.

'Too late. I've handed it on to Winston,' said Bracken.

Ah well. Boothby shrugged his shoulders. What did it matter, anyway?

But it did. For Winston Churchill had taken action as soon as he read Boothby's letter. A swingeing message went round to Sir John Anderson, the Home Secretary. What was all this about imprisoning Weininger? Bob Boothby said he was a completely innocent man – release him at once!

'I'm damned if I will,' muttered Anderson when he read the Prime Minister's note. Weininger was going to stay in gaol along with the rest of them. He was furious with Boothby. He believed he had deliberately broken a pledge by sending his letter on while promising not to do so. For that he was going to suffer.

That afternoon certain letters which had been found in Weininger's file were sent across to 10 Downing Street for Churchill's perusal. With them went a note from the Home Secretary suggesting that Boothby was not exactly unbiased in his sponsorship of Weininger's case. He was a financial associate. He had borrowed money from him. Worse still, he had spoken in the House of

Commons on Czech financial affairs without revealing that his friend, Weininger, was closely connected with the matter. And that was – well, not exactly ethical, was it?

It was a moment when Winston Churchill was preoccupied with the battles to come, and in no mood and with no time to consider outside matters. His anger broke against Boothby for involving him. How dare he deceive him? It was insufferable that he should waste his premier's time over his personal affairs at a moment of such national crisis. Suddenly, from being Boothby's friend and sponsor, he became an angry and aggrieved antagonist. In vain did their mutual friends plead Boothby's case.

'I know that the Chancellor of the Exchequer, Sir Kingsley Wood, wrote a memorandum in which he said he could see no reason for taking action against me,' said Boothby. 'Bracken told me that at a luncheon at 10 Downing Street at which [Mrs] Clemmie Churchill, [Lord] Beaverbrook and himself were the only guests, Winston left the table in a rage because they all came out in support of me. When my father died ... he sent no line of sympathy. This was wholly out of character.'

No pleas from Boothby's supporters could persuade Churchill from now on that this was a trivial offence (or, in fact, no offence at all).* He was summoned to see the Prime Minister at 10 Downing Street and looked forward to it as the opportunity to explain, alone with his friend.

'But no. I was summoned not for a private talk but to the Cabinet room. There I found the Attorney-General at the Prime Minister's side, and a number of secretaries. There was no discussion. Churchill simply informed me that he had decided to refer my case to a Select Committee of the House of Commons. I was in no doubt then that he had turned against me.'

The men who formed the Select Committee could hardly be described as Boothby's friends. 'We were fighting a bitter war with Germany now,' he was to say later, 'but the MPs in the House of Commons in 1940, 1941 and 1942 were still the same shoddy lot who had cheered Chamberlain after he had licked

---

* It is considered a breach of privilege (and a grave offence) if an MP fails to declare an interest in a House of Commons debate which ends in a vote. In the particular debate in which Boothby had taken part on the future of Czech assets there was no vote, and he was not required to declare an interest.

Hitler's boots and screamed insults at us because we had been against appeasement.'

The Select Committee in due course found that Robert Boothby MP had indeed committed a breach of privilege (though it is now generally accepted that he had not), and duly condemned him for it. In Parliamentary eyes, he was disgraced. He resigned his post with the Ministry of Food and knew that his future prospects so far as a political career were concerned were nil. The young MP for Aberdeen, who had usually eaten joy as well as kippers for breakfast, discreetly faded out of Parliament and joined the RAF and moved to a bomber station in East Anglia.

He was not to make his mark in Parliament again until 1942, when he came back to make a remarkable fighting speech. Ironically enough, it was in defence of Winston Churchill – and it saved the Prime Minister from defeat at the worst moment of his wartime career.

In the meantime, like many another refugee, Richard Weininger stayed in gaol.

5

Both his French and his English friends in London thought that Robert Mengin was being difficult. They could not understand him. He kept saying that he wanted to fight for France and that he hated the pro-Nazi régime which had been set up in Vichy. But when they told him they were glad he was supporting de Gaulle, he confused them by saying that he did not.

'Then how can you be on our side? We are backing de Gaulle, and if you aren't for him you must be against us too!' they said.

'It isn't quite like that,' Mengin would begin, and would then attempt to explain his feelings. It was no good. They just didn't understand how he could be pro-Free French and not pro-de Gaulle. How could he persuade them that in his opinion General de Gaulle, although indubitably a patriotic Frenchman was also a man of overweening ambition and had embarked on a dangerous game, a game of which Mengin was determined to have no part?

All over London now there were posters on the wall which read:

A TOUS LES FRANÇAIS
La France a perdu une bataille!
Mais la France n'a pas perdu la guerre!

It asked them to rally to General de Gaulle and enlist in the Free French Forces. A recruiting centre had been set up at Olympia, in Hammersmith. It was here that Robert Mengin came one afternoon that summer of 1940 to sign up for the Free French Forces. He had been working at Free French headquarters in Carlton Gardens for some weeks now, helping a colonel friend who was a passionate Gaullist; and it was he who had suggested that the time had come for Mengin to get his position regularised.

'It is about time you started wearing the Cross of Lorraine on your uniform, mon ami,' the colonel had said. 'People are beginning to stare at you.'

By 'people' the colonel probably meant de Gaulle himself. The General had passed him in one of the corridors the other day and returned Mengin's salute by looking pointedly at the bare blue breast of his naval uniform. It must have been the only one which did not flaunt the two-barred Cross of Lorraine, the insignia of the Free French Forces.

Mengin was quite willing to join, and said so. 'Then get on and do it,' said his friend, shortly.

Olympia had been loaned to de Gaulle as his main military supply depot, and as a Free French barracks and recruiting centre. There were Free French sentries on the gates standing guard in front of groups of admiring London urchins. Mengin explained his mission and was directed first to a medical centre and then, after a searching examination, to a naval recruiting lieutenant seated behind a table. He looked at Mengin scornfully when he revealed that he had been in England for some time.

'Well, well,' he said, 'nobody could say you came here all out of breath to rush to answer the General's appeal! But now that you have finally made it, sign this.'

He pushed the Act of Engagement across the table, and Mengin read it through. With growing concern, he noted that General de Gaulle was cited personally as Chief of the Free French Forces, and that anyone signing the document had undertaken to serve with honour, fidelity and discipline for the duration of the war and three months after it. Therefore he would be swearing to obey the orders of General de Gaulle himself, and in peace as well as in war.

'I'm not signing,' he said.

The lieutenant looked at him in astonishment.

'But why not?' he asked.

'This is a personal oath of allegiance to General de Gaulle, cited by name – thus to him personally,' Mengin said. 'I can't sign it.'

The lieutenant's face went white with rage. 'Then what the hell do you think you're doing here?' he shouted. He pointed to the door. 'Now bugger off!'

Mengin leaned over and caught the lieutenant's gesticulating hand, and held it tight.

'You might try to learn some manners, mon gros,' he said, and shook the man hard. Then he walked out of the room.

But he was in trouble, and he knew it. As he walked back across London he envied once more the British all around him, in no doubt at all where their allegiances lay. But then, he reminded himself, they didn't have to sign a personal act of allegiance – except to a constitutional King. What was going to happen to him when he got back to Carlton Gardens?

Nothing much at first, as it turned out. They were very understanding, the Free French. Successions of friends and officers were sent to argue with him, but all the discussions ended at the same point: *he must sign on the dotted line.*

Finally, the celebrated jurist Professor René Cassin* consented to speak to the recalcitrant young man. He was one of General de Gaulle's most trusted advisers and Mengin expected to be intimidated by him. But he was amiable and understanding, so much so that Mengin plucked up courage enough to ask:

'The wording of this enlistment oath, do you approve of it, Monsieur? Was it you who drafted it?'

Cassin looked hard at him and then said: 'Look, young man, when your house is on fire, do you look to see whether the firemen are using filtered water to put out the blaze? We found ourselves in a position of some urgency. We did the best we could. You mustn't attach too much importance to unimportant things.'

'Good,' said Mengin, 'then I will not sign the paper, since you tell me it is not important.'

There was a long silence, and then Cassin said:

'The night brings counsel. Go and think things over calmly. You are young. You have let your feelings run away with you.

* Professor Cassin was awarded the Nobel Prize in 1968.

Come back and see me tomorrow. We will work it all out, and you, my boy, will remain in our ranks.'

Next day Mengin came to see him. He had thought things out.

'I will sign,' he told the professor, 'if, above my signature I can write in the formula employed in the French Navy, namely that I will undertake to obey any order given to me by General de Gaulle "for the good of the service and the success of the arms of France". That is restrictive – for if, in good conscience a man considers that an order is not "for the good of the service and the success of the arms of France" he can most certainly be put in irons, but not for breaking his oath. He can be shot, but not as . . .'

He was not allowed to finish. Professor Cassin, whose whole demeanour towards him had now changed said icily:

'*You are to sign exactly the same oath as the others, you are not to add or subtract a single word! Or you must leave us.*'

Mengin picked up his naval cap and walked out of the room. Yes, he was really in trouble. What would de Gaulle do to him – and to others who did not accept him as the all-powerful arbiter of France's destinies?*

* There were other Frenchmen in London at the time who shared Mengin's doubts about General de Gaulle, and at least two of them were his superiors in rank and experience. The French ambassador, Charles Corbin, and his Minister and Counsellor, Roger Cambon, both broke with the Pétain régime and refused to accept France's defeat. But they preferred to wreck their careers rather than join de Gaulle. For the full story of what happened to Robert Mengin, his book, *No Laurels for de Gaulle*, is strongly recommended.

5

THE FATAL ERROR

On 19 July 1940, Adolf Hitler spoke to his Party members in the Reichstag in Berlin and made what he called his 'final appeal' to the British people to start negotiations.

He said: 'At this hour I feel it is my duty to appeal, in good faith, for reason and wise counsel on the part of Great Britain as of all other countries. I consider that my position allows me to make this appeal, since I do not speak as a defeated man begging favours but as the victor speaking in the name of reason. I can really see no reason why this war should continue.'

But if it did, Hitler went on, the consequences for Britain would be dire and she would be annihilated.

Winston Churchill pondered whether to issue a reply to Hitler's threats, and then decided against it. Why tell the Germans anything? Let them stew on in ignorance of British intentions. Time was what Britain needed, time to get the defences organised, time to build more tanks and guns and aeroplanes, time to prepare the people for the rigours to come. Every day counted.

On 6 August Goering summoned a conference of his fleet commanders in Berlin, and told them that the invasion of Britain was on. It would be launched in the second week in September. But first the Luftwaffe must defeat the RAF.

'I expect to see them destroyed in fantastic numbers,' he said. 'Our Messerschmitts are much superior to the English Hurricanes and with skill they can out-fly the Spitfires. There will be casualties, but that is what our boys are flying for, to fight and die. And our numbers will tell.'

At the same time a concentrated attack would be launched on the ring of radar stations which had been built along Britain's south coast to warn of the approach of Nazi planes and ships. These stations would be eliminated by concentrated bombing. And in concert with these operations, there would be a series of heavy attacks upon the RAF's airfields designed to put them out of action, so that those British fighters which had not been shot down would have nowhere to land.

Goering gave the name Adlertag (Eagle Day) to the attack and ordered it to begin on 10 August. (In fact, owing to bad weather it did not start until 13 August.) He told his commanders to ground the planes for a few days and let the pilots and crews relax in preparation for the great onslaught.

While the Luftwaffe pilots in France went off to the towns to carouse on good food and wine, there was a lull in the battle over southern England. Air Chief Marshal Dowding guessed that it was the lull before the storm and on 8 August he issued an Order of the Day to the RAF:

'The Battle of Britain is about to begin. Members of the RAF, the fate of generations lies in your hands.'

On 13 August the battle began. But it did not go as Goering hoped. Eight days later, when the Nazi air chief visited his airfield in France, he found his pilots weary and dispirited.

At that time the Germans were flying 1,500 sorties a day against the RAF and their losses were catastrophic. But if the RAF were shooting down more German planes than they were losing themselves, they were bleeding even more badly from their losses than the Germans, for they had less aeroplanes to spare. If something were not done soon they would bleed to death. Though British aircraft factories were now working at full speed turning out planes for the battle, they could not keep up with the wastage created by such intensive fighting; nor could the training schemes cope with the demand for pilots who had been killed or burned in the battle.

The Germans were striking everywhere now where they were likely to do most harm to Britain's defences: at the RAF's airfields, at the aircraft factories, at oil storages and tank depots.

Only one place stayed remote from the battle: London. The Germans had drawn a line on the map around the outer perimeter of the great city, and there was an embargo on all targets inside it. There were raids on the great oil-stores at Thameshaven. There were lightning attacks on the RAF airfields nearest to London at Biggin Hill, Hornchurch and Croydon. But London itself was 'off limits' to the Luftwaffe.

Goering and Hitler were well aware of the propaganda effect the bombing of London would have upon the watching millions in the neutral world, particularly in the United States. They might even have heard the story that every night Winston Churchill came out into the open air and shouted up at the black sky:

'Why don't you come? Bomb us, bomb us!'

He knew, and so did Goering and Hitler, that only by reading of a London laid waste, its monuments destroyed, its citizens burned, its children wiped out, would America understand what was at stake and throw its aid wholeheartedly on Britain's side.

Hitler was not going to fall into that trap. He told Goering who told his flight commanders that the Luftwaffe must at all costs stay away from London. So every night there were raids all over England but none against London. The people of the capital slept peacefully in their beds, while the Luftwaffe got on with the job of destroying their defenders and defences.

And then, on 24 August 1940, a pilot's panic changed everything.

It was one of the nightly raids which the Luftwaffe was now making against the great fuel dumps which lay alongside the river Thames at Thameshaven, some ten or more miles downstream from London. The bombers which swept over after darkness on the night of 24 August flew through the flak and dropped their bombs, and then swung round as the flames burst up among them and raced back to the safety of their bases in France.

All except two planes. Their identity and the names of pilots and crews will never be known now, for they were expunged from the records of the Luftwaffe. They were not names that Germany would want to remember, for, in a way they lost them the Battle of Britain.

The planes had lost their flight leaders by the time they reached the Thames and already they must have been beginning to feel nervous. The flak was heavy. They could not see much of what lay below them. The time came when they must turn for home and they had not seen their target. The flak got thicker. They began to panic. Knowing there would be trouble if they returned with their bombs, they unloaded them, and turned for home. One bomb smashed down on to St Giles's Church in Cripplegate, in the heart of the City, and the blast ripped Milton's statue off its pedestal in a square nearby. Other bombs scattered death and destruction over Islington, Tottenham, Finchley, Stepney and Bethnal Green, killing customers just turned out at closing-time from the pubs and theatre-goers on their way home from the West End.

Goering, furious, dispatched a telegram to his Luftwaffe commanders:

AN IMMEDIATE REPORT IS REQUIRED IDENTIFYING THOSE CREWS WHO DROPPED BOMBS WITHIN THE PERIMETER OF LONDON. LUFTWAFFE HIGH COMMAND WILL ITSELF UNDERTAKE THE PUNISHMENT OF EACH AIRCRAFT CAPTAIN INVOLVED. THEY WILL BE POSTED TO INFANTRY REGIMENTS.

Next day, on 25 August, after a meeting of the Chiefs of Staff in the Hole in the Ground in Whitehall, the order was passed on to Bomber Command. Squadron Leader John Oxley's flight of 81 Hampden bombers which had been busy dropping leaflets over Germany over the past weeks was told to load up with bombs. That evening Oxley was given his target: Berlin. The buzz among the pilots and crews was that the decision to attack the German capital came directly from Winston Churchill. So the next week the Berlin area was raided several times. The bombs did little damage, but the raids infuriated the German leaders, for they had sworn the RAF would never get through.

On 4 September Adolf Hitler addressed a meeting in the Sport-palast in Berlin, in his most rancorous and sardonic mood. He attacked Churchill and his supporters with savage wit and soon had his audience roaring with laughter at his sallies and fervently applauding his shrill threats.

When would Britain be invaded? he asked.

In England they are filled with curiosity, and keep asking: 'Why doesn't he come?'

Hitler raised his voice to a shout:
Be calm. Be calm. He's coming, he's coming!
He passed on to the air raids on Berlin:
Mr Churchill is demonstrating his new brainchild, the night

air raid. Mr Churchill is carrying out these raids not because they promise to be highly effective, but because his air force cannot fly over German soil in daylight.

He went on to explain to his audience why there had been a pause in the operations of the German armies and why the invasion had been postponed. And then his tone changed and his voice began to rise:

For three months I did not answer because I believed that such madness [as this war] would be stopped. Mr Churchill took this for a sign of weakness. We are now answering night for night. When the British Air Force drops three or four thousand kilograms of bombs, then we will in one night drop 200, 300 or 400,000 kilograms:

His voice rose to a shriek:

When they declare that they will increase their attacks on our cities, then we will *raze* their cities to the ground. We will stop the handiwork of these night pirates, so help us God ... The hour will come when one of us will break, and it will not be National Socialist Germany!

Next day Marshal Hermann Goering's special train set out once more for France. Hitler had given his consent. London was to be bombed. And Goering had decided to be with his bomber squadrons when the great operation began. The capital of the British Empire was to be destroyed, its people panicked, its factories paralysed, and the path opened for the invading armies of the German Reich.

Two days later, he stood with his aides on the cliffs at Cap Blanc Nez and looked at England 22 miles away across the Channel. Over his head roared wave after wave of bombers, on their way to London.

It was 7 September 1940.

PART TWO

THE BATTLE
OF LONDON

6

THE BLITZ BEGINS

Police Constable David Meade glanced at his watch and then hurriedly drank off the dregs of his mug of tea. Two o'clock. He was due back on the beat again.

'I'll be off, then,' he said, to no one in particular, and waved his hand at the old girl behind the canteen bar. Then he walked quickly out of Limehouse police station into the sunshine of West India Dock Road. 7 September was a day of hazy sunshine over London and the streets of Limehouse had never looked drabber. A year of war had peeled the paint off the doorways and caked dust and cobwebs on to the blacked-out windows of the mean slum houses. Yet somehow the sight of it cheered David Meade and made him glad to be back on the beat again. He passed Charlie Brown's, the famous pub by West India Dock, just as they were turning them out after the lunchtime session, and half a dozen customers smiled or shouted a greeting as he passed them.

' 'Ow are you, then, love,' said one of them, an ageing Chinese woman, in a strong Cockney accent.

'Nicely, Mum, and I hope you are too,' he replied, and chuckled to himself. Less than a year ago, when he had first been posted to Limehouse as a brand new policeman, every Chinese he met looked sinister and threatening and every house into which they disappeared he suspected as an opium den or a centre for the white slave traffic. He had been brought up on a diet of Fu Manchu, 'Limehouse Nights' and 'Limehouse Blues', and Orientals for him were both inscrutable and wily. He had soon discovered that whether they kept laundries or restaurants or just worked as clerks and shop-assistants, they were Cockneys like all the others; and that went for the West Indians and Poles and Indians who were sprinkled around the dock area too. David Meade had learned to like and respect most of them.

Saturday in the East End of London was always the busiest day of the week for a policeman, and this was Saturday afternoon. He enjoyed it even though he knew that by closing time that evening he would be busy getting the drunks home from the pubs, peace-making between husbands and wives, breaking up the pitch-and-toss gambling gangs by the docks, and seeing that the two attractive but wayward sixteen-year-old daughters of Mrs Lee-Yong and Mrs Davies were back home and out of harm's way before black-out.

It was the day when money was flowing and the people came out to spend it, and what Meade liked about them was that they were so cheerful about it. Not like the stodgy, respectable citizens of the outer suburbs or the snooty residents of the West End, who all took their pleasures so sadly. The Cockneys of the East End wore their hearts on their sleeves and jingled the money in their pockets, the beer flowed and so did the sausage and mash and the jellied eels, and there was a tendency to break into 'The Lambeth Walk' and 'Knees up Mother Brown' and other Cockney songs as the evening came on. Constable Meade had helped just a year earlier to pile hundreds of weeping mothers and children into the evacuation buses and he could remember the wail that had come from them as they disappeared down the Old Kent Road. He knew what a wrench it must have been for them to leave their homes and their friends in the East End for the lonely wastes of brickless countryside and the frigid welcome of the hostesses upon whom they had been billeted. It was official police policy to frown on those who had come back to the East End in the past few months ('I just 'ad to come back, Constable. I couldn't get to sleep for those bleedin' cows bawling all night. It was drivin' me mad!'), but he sympathized with them. Somehow, for an East Ender, trees didn't have the same feeling as bricks and mortar.

His musings were interrupted by the sound of the air-raid siren, and he was at once aware of a sudden hush as the bright babbling voices all around him stopped in mid-word. Everyone was looking up into the sky. It was bright blue and cloud-flecked and for the moment not even a single vapour trail was scrawled across it. Meade decided at once that it was another of the raids down-river on the gasoline tanks at Thameshaven, but out of routine he called to the people pressing on the pavements:

'Now keep moving, please! There's a big warehouse shelter just down there on the dock — enough room for all of you and more. Let's get moving, shall we?'

As he was speaking he was aware of the buzzing sound in his ears, like the faint murmur of summer bees, only this noise got louder and louder until it drowned out the renewed chatter of the people all around him. Once more he was conscious of a sudden halt in the words – but not in the noise that came from up above. They were all staring at the sky again, too.

'I see them, I see them!' someone called out.

'Up there – look, two – no – three of them! By that big cloud!' cried someone else.

Meade said, 'Come on there! Let's get to the shelters, shall we?'

As crowds of them now started to run across the road, he gazed at the sky. Then drew in his breath.

'Shelters, everyone, quick!' he shouted, but urgently now.

'Gawd,' said a man, 'it's not just two or three – there must be hundreds of the buggers! Just look at them!'

As he spoke, Meade heard the sound. It was, he said afterwards, rather like a muffled scream. It was joined by others. And then it was as if a hundred trains were roaring at top speed out of a tunnel towards him.

'Down, down, down ...!' he cried out, and then suddenly even he couldn't hear the sound of his own voice any longer.

2

Lieutenant Commander Richard Fordham of the London Fire Service was soaping the last trace of oil off his body and preparing for a long wallow when there was a knock on the bathroom door.

'Can you come at once, sir,' said the voice of one of his firemen. 'You're wanted.'

'Tell them I'm in my bath,' Fordham shouted. '*And* remind them that it's my day off.'

Saturday, 7 September. A whole afternoon and evening free. After what had happened over the past forty-eight hours, he felt he had deserved it.

The fireman went away, but presently he was back again.

'I'm sorry, sir,' he called, 'but they still want you urgently. Please, sir – they seem a little upset.'

Commander Fordham sighed, slipped down in the bath until the water covered his shock of red hair, and then porpoised to the surface and rose in a gush of water. He reached for the towel.

What did they want him for? At least it couldn't be more spectacular than his experiences of the past two days, he told himself. Or more ridiculous.

It had all started on the evening of 5 September, just as he was leaving his home for dinner. The telephone rang and F. W. Jackson, deputy chief of the London fire services, was on the line.

'Dick, we are in trouble,' he said at once. 'The Jerries have bombed downriver again, and there's quite a blaze going on there. Oil *and* petrol are on fire.'

'That's not our affair,' said Fordham. 'It's out of the London area. We only go there if we're asked for help.'

That was the trouble, explained Jackson. They *had* asked for help earlier in the day, when the first bombs had been dropped. A London Fire Service officer had been sent downriver with fifty pumps to help the fire-fighters on the spot. A 2,000 ton tank of gasoline was ablaze and its flames were threatening seven other tanks close by. But the London fire officer had been reminded before he left headquarters that, under the Fires Act of 1938, he was under no circumstances to try to take charge when operating in another area, but must put himself under the command of the local officer.

'It hasn't worked out very well, I'm afraid,' said Jackson. 'The local officer wasn't – well – experienced, shall we say. A volunteer, you know. Good chap but an amateur. He told our chap that the fire was well in hand and that he wouldn't need anything like fifty pumps. He told him to send forty-five of them back to London.' He paused. 'A mistake, I'm afraid. They not only failed to put out the blaze in the tank, but it looks as if the others are now very seriously threatened.'

Fordham said: 'Then why doesn't he order the pumps back again?'

'Yes,' said Jackson, 'that is just what he should do. Only the unfortunate thing is, he isn't there any more. This local commander, I mean. About an hour ago he pointed out to our chap that he was just a volunteer and that he couldn't stay up all night fighting a fire, because he had to go to work early next morning. And so he just left.'

'My God,' said Fordham, and began to laugh.

'Yes,' said Jackson, 'it is funny, isn't it?' There was no humour in his own voice, though. 'But the trouble is, our chap can't do anything without having orders first from a local commander, and they just can't find another. He's in a bit of a bother, as you might say. Especially with all that oil running round asking to be set alight.'

Fordham said: 'So you want me to go out and look at the situation, is that it?'

'That's right, old chap. Only for God's sake don't try and take charge, will you? Remember it's out of our area. And please, be tactful to whoever they've put in command.'

By the time Richard Fordham got there he did not have to ask directions. The blaze from the burning fuel dump lit up the last two miles of his way. Another tank was on fire. The *bund* (the protective wall) enclosing the tanks was swimming feet deep in petrol and water, but the way the two tanks were blazing the flames would soon annihilate this protective channel and engulf the remaining tanks. The London fire officer was running around, grimy and distracted, unsure what to do. He was only allowed to take orders and the local man did not know how to give them.

Fordham took one look at the situation and asked where the telephone was. It was apologetically explained to him that the administration offices were locked up, but that there was a pay telephone in a kiosk at the gate of the compound. He rang up headquarters and after some delay got through.

'We are in a hell of a mess here,' he said. 'I want fifty pumps and three fire boats at once.'

It was the administration officer on the other end. 'You can't order reinforcements,' he said, crisply. 'That's for the officer in charge – and you aren't in charge.'

'Yes, I am,' said Fordham, aggressively. 'There's no one else here who knows anything. I'm taking over.'

'No.' The administration officer's voice was firm. 'That is something you will not do. It is out of our area. The 1938 Act says that when we are called into another area we . . .'

'. . . We take orders from the officer on the spot,' Fordham interrupted. 'I know all that. But it so happens that there isn't any officer on the spot. And at any moment the whole bloody place is likely to blow up and kill us all.'

'Keep calm, commander,' said the voice at the other end. 'We'll get you a local officer as soon as possible. We are contacting Sir Will Spens about it at the moment.'

'Who the hell is Sir Will Spens?' asked Fordham.

It turned out that Sir Will Spens was a Cambridge don, the Master of Corpus Christi College, who had, for some strange reason, been made Regional Fire Commissioner for the area including Thameshaven.

The administrator interrupted this explanation to say, 'And we have just had a message from him. He has nominated an officer to take charge and that officer is now on his way. So everything is in hand, you see.'

Only it wasn't. Fordham went back to the fire and the situation was grim. The flames were getting higher and the few pumps were failing to keep them down. How long would it be, Fordham wondered, before they all went up? He wished he had had time for a bite to eat before he was blown to perdition.

At this moment a small car drove up and out of it stepped a young man in a tweed suit. He had been sent to take over, he said.

'D'you know anything about oil fires?' asked Fordham.

'Not much,' said the young man. 'You see, I'm from the borough surveyor's department, really. Though,' he added, hurriedly, 'I have done a week's fire fighting course at the ARP school.'

'I see,' said Fordham, very quietly. 'I suppose you wouldn't mind me giving you advice, would you.'

'No, sir,' said the young man. 'I'd be delighted. Anything you say.'

'Right,' said Fordham. 'Then you just nip down to the phone and order up fifty pumps and three fire vessels immediately. Then come back up here and make yourself comfortable. And leave it to us.'

'At once, sir,' said the young man, rushing away.

By the time the pumps were up and the fire boats in position, the glare from the tanks could be seen twenty miles away, and the hard fight had begun. The fire boats pumped water from the Thames where it was picked up by the shore pumps and flung at the tanks. Fordham ordered his men in for 'close-fire' fighting, and led them over the wall of the bund into the trough of steaming oil and water.

From this position, close up to the burning tanks roaring away above them, they directed their leaping high-pressure jets. For some of the auxiliaries it was their first fire, at all times a terrifying experience. Not only were they up to their waists in water; at one point, where the Nazi bomb had dropped among the tanks, there was a deep crater now filled with water into which men kept dropping and disappearing into the murky slime. Their companions dragged them out and they went on fighting the flames.

But by daylight the fires had been mastered and five of the gasoline tanks saved. Fordham wiped the oil out of his eyes, emptied his soaked boots, and sloshed across to the young man in tweeds standing a few yards away.

'Fire under control, sir,' he said. 'It's all yours.'

'Thank *you*, sir,' the young man said. And then he went on, with a grin: 'I don't know what I would have done without you!'

Now Commander Fordham was back at his headquarters in London, washing off the last traces of oil, looking forward to an afternoon of sleep and relaxation. And here they were, after him again.

'Commander,' said the voice on the telephone, 'There's an urgent call out for all pumps. You're to get down to the East End at once. It looks as if Jerry is attacking us in force. May I wish you good luck at our first big test?'

'First big test?' exploded Fordham. 'What the bloody hell d'you think we've been doing downriver for the past 48 hours?'

That Saturday afternoon there was a needle match on at West Ham stadium. The local soccer team was playing Tottenham, the champions from the neighbouring borough. For football fans in the East End of London it was a game not to be missed, and there were 10,000 in the stands when the players lined up and the whistle blew for play to begin.

Bill Harriman was one of them, and so was his son, John. Bill had been working overtime for the past three months, and this was his first free week-end. Eileen Harriman decided to go off and see her sister out at Ilford. Linda would stay at home and look after Winston, the spaniel puppy her father had given her for her ninth birthday.

John was a West Ham fan, but his father favoured Tottenham. Their team hadn't lost as many players to the armed services, and it showed. They ran all around the home side. By the middle of the second half, they were leading by four goals to one.

And then the sirens sounded. The referee stopped, looked up at the sky, and then blew his whistle. The players gathered around him, and then began to walk off the field, to the sound of boos, whistles and catcalls from the fans in the stand.

'Dad, why do they have to stop the game for a silly old siren?' John asked.

'It's Government orders,' Bill said. 'Come on, we'd better get home.'

The crowds had begun to drift away. The two Harrimans were half-way back to Canning Town when they heard the noise of engines in the sky above.

3

Bentley Priory, 4 p.m. 7 September 1940.

Flight Lieutenant Robert Wright knocked on the door of his boss, Air Chief Marshal Hugh Dowding, and went inside. As usual, Fighter Command's C-in-C was bent over his desk, staring at a long list of statistics. He looked grimmer and even more remote than usual, and Wright guessed that he was pretty close to despair. German pressure on his airfields, his planes and his pilots was becoming too great to bear. They were losing too much and too many. If the pattern of the Luftwaffe's attack continued for another week like this, the RAF would crack, and then the path would be open to the invader.

Over the past four weeks the Luftwaffe had been steadily destroying Dowding's forward airfields, and pushing his squadrons inland. His pilots were tired out. Once he had told his Minister, when informed that the Germans had a superiority of five to one, 'Then our young men will have to shoot down their young men at the rate of five to one.' For weeks now, that is what they had been doing. But it couldn't go on. The end of their endurance was coming dangerously near. And probably the Germans knew it: for only this morning the Air Ministry had sent him a message containing the simple words: INVASION IMMINENT. The enemy's barges were cramming every port and lock along the French and Belgian coasts, and no amount of bombing seemed to disturb the build-up.

'Yes, Wright?' Dowding said, without looking up.

'It looks like a big one, sir. Ops say that several formations of twenty plus are building up over Calais.'

'Let's go down and have a look,' said Dowding.

They moved to the operations room of Fighter Command and leaned over the railing. Below them a great map of the English Channel was spread across an even larger table. Above it sat the RAF officers taking in the radar reports. Around the table were the girls of the WAAF, in their shirt sleeves, holding in their hands rakes of the kind croupiers use. Only the chips they were pushing across the table were not money but planes, and the stakes were not money but lives. Each block they moved nearer to the English coast represented a flight of enemy planes, and Dowding saw at once that this raid was indeed a big one – bigger perhaps than ever before. Already the blocks indicated that 100 plus Nazi bombers and 300 Nazi fighters were on their way in.

Dowding looked across the table to see what his Group Commander, Keith Park, had done with his defending Spitfires and Hurricanes. Yes, they were getting airborne already. And Dowding knew the tactics they would follow. They would wait until the big stacks of Nazi planes split up, as they always did, some to go for RAF airfields, others for factories, others for the oil-tanks on the outskirts of London. Then the RAF fighters would move in on them. Already the defending squadrons were making height and waiting for the enemy to split up.

Suddenly, as he looked down, a thought slid like ice through Dowding's mind.

What if the Luftwaffe *this time* did not split up? What if it just carried on, en masse? There would be no RAF fighters to stop them. The path into London would be open to them.

'That's funny,' said Robert Wright. 'They don't seem to be splitting up, do they?'

In the Hole in the Ground in Whitehall the Chiefs of Staff of the British Armed Forces were holding an emergency meeting. It had been called by General Sir John Dill, Chief of the Imperial General Staff, to discuss the situation Britain might face at any moment now – invasion. All their reports from their agents, all the photographs from reconnaissance, all the speeches from the Nazi leaders seemed to point to this as the week-end. Hitler was ready to strike at last. Dill had called in his defence chiefs to hear how they had made their dispositions.

The discussion had just begun when Brigadier Leslie Hollis,

the secretary, came in with a message and laid it before Dill on the table. The CIGS looked at it and then passed it round.

'Well, gentlemen,' he said, 'this may well be the opening blow.' He turned to Hollis. 'I think we should inform the Prime Minister. Will he be awake yet?'*

As he spoke, there was a heavy thud from the distance, followed by another and yet another.

'If he wasn't before, he is now,' said Hollis. 'I'll go and tell him that they're bombing London.'

On the cliffs of Cap Blanc Nez, Reich Marshal Hermann Goering was being interviewed by German war reporters. Over his head as he spoke wave after wave of bombers and their stacks of protecting fighters passed over the Channel towards England.

'I have come to take personal command of the battle,' he said. The target was London. It was to be 'a stroke straight to the enemy's heart'.

4

The first wave of German bombers came in from the east and made straight for the Thames estuary. A few dropped their bombs on Thameshaven once more and started the oil fires again, but over a hundred and fifty other Heinkels and Dorniers carried on up-river towards the East End of London and the docks. They were flying very high – between 16,000 and 20,000 feet – and Messerschmitt 109s and 110s wheeled in protective screens over and under them, glinting in the rays of the afternoon sun. Chief Superintendent Reginald Smith of the Metropolitan Police was on his way by car from his home in Ilford to his headquarters in East Ham when he saw people pointing upwards; he stopped the car and got out to look.

'They're going for us,' he said, when he saw them. He meant London, but a moment or two later he was able to be more particular. Superintendent Smith now commanded K Division of the Metropolitan Police. His bailiwick was just up the road and covered a great stretch of East London: East and West Ham,

* Winston Churchill always took an afternoon nap, no matter what the situation.

Silvertown, Barking, Plaistow and the great sprawl of locks and waterways known as the Royal Group of docks. Now he could see showers of bombs going down, flashing as they fell, and he could hear the thud as they made their impact.

'It's us, all right,' he said, and told the driver to get there fast.

All along the river now anti-aircraft fire had opened up and the path of the invading bombers was signposted by the puffs of their exploding shells. But save for a few dog-fights on the fringes, there was no opposition from the air. The Nazi bombers droned in, squadron after squadron of them, like lines of lorries, and at fixed points unloaded. The bombs fell first on the great arsenal at Woolwich, a veritable powder-keg, and on the factories around it. Then down came the bombs on the vast complex of docks strung out along both sides of the Thames, Victoria and Albert, West India, Surrey Commercial. Gouts of flame and smoke started up like lava bursts from both banks of the river, in ever increasing numbers; and now it was not just arsenals and docks and warehouses that were being hit but narrow streets and housing clusters and blocks of flats, the homes, from West Ham to Bow, from Bermondsey to Whitechapel, from Limehouse to Poplar, of the real Cockneys, the Eastenders, of London.

At the headquarters of Fighter Command they were desperately trying to recover from the errors of the day, and Air Vice Marshal Keith Park was frantically re-routing his Spitfires and Hurricanes and getting every plane he could muster up into the air. Already they were moving in to the battle, slicing through the Messerschmitt screens to get at and gouge into the bombers. But so far as the East End was concerned, it was too late. The bombers had unloaded and were turning for home. Another wave, in the meantime, had come in from the West and was dropping a second load of high explosives and incendiaries.

Now the great fires began.

Not in the mean little houses on either side of the river. There was nothing left of them to burn. In the slum areas of Canning Town, for instance, row upon row of tenements had been rushed up in the 1860s to house the inflow of workers for the new Thames Iron Works at Silvertown. They were mean, cheap, jerry-built, crammed back-to-back, noisome squalid slums built by grasping Victorian capitalism for their semi-slave labourers.

When the first bombs dropped around them on 7 September,

the tenement houses of Canning Town rocked and then collapsed into rubble, burying their occupants underneath.

Canning Town was where the Harrimans lived.

Bill Harriman and his son, John, had almost reached Upton Park Station when the first bombs dropped. His first instinct was to keep on going.

'All I wanted to do was get home,' he said, later. 'All I could think of was Linda back there, all on her own, poor kid. I didn't think it was going to be serious. Not then, I didn't. But I knew she'd be frightened out of her wits. But when we got to the station there was a barrier up, and a notice on it saying: NEAREST SHELTER RAYMOND ROAD. Just then there was a whistling and a thud that practically blew our heads off, and Johnny flung himself against me and put his arms round my legs. I decided we'd better go and find the shelter.'

It was an ordinary street shelter and it didn't look much safer than the one whose roof had caved in on the night of 25 June, but once inside the walls seemed to deaden the noise of the bombs. The shelter was crowded, mostly with locals who didn't look any too friendly when the Harrimans came in, and they made room for them on the benches only when a little man with a band round his arm came up and said: 'Come on, there, ladies and gents. Give the small boy and his Dad a little room.' Johnny had recovered his nerve and was soon tugging at Bill's sleeve and saying: 'Couldn't we go out and have a look, Dad.' Bill was sick with worry. What was happening in Canning Town? The bombs sounded as if they were dropping that way. And where was Eileen?

When the All Clear came they went back to Upton Park Station, but now there was a chalked notice on a board outside saying: LINE BLOCKED. They started to walk.

In the direction of Canning Town, great clouds of black smoke rose into the sky. The air was filled with the smell of burning. Soon they came upon their first crater, then their first row of wrecked houses, and then a great pile of rubble where a street had been. There were firemen and fire engines and a great confusion of hosepipes, men running about everywhere, whistles blowing and dust thick in the air. Suddenly Bill Harriman realised that though he was in his own district, he was lost. He didn't recognise any of it any more.

He began to be very scared now. Even John had gone silent. Several times ambulances went past them, their bells jangling. They were going along one half-wrecked street when Bill saw a body lying half in and half out of a door, and what seemed to be part of a tailor's dummy heaped on top of it; it took him a moment before he realised that it was a human trunk. He was pulling John to the other side of the road when a man in a tin helmet came running across.

'Hey, you there! Where the bloody hell d'you think you're going?' he shouted. And then, in a cry of alarm: 'Look out!'

Bill jerked to a stop, just short of the side of a house which had suddenly collapsed.

He waited for the man to come up, and saw that he was a warden.

'I'm looking for Star Road,' he said, desperately. 'Can you tell me where Star Road is?'

'What would you want to go there for?' the warden asked.

'That's where I live. And that's where my daughter Linda is.'

5

Police Constable David Meade put his hand to his head and felt for his cap, but it had gone. There was a great singing in his ears but through it he could hear the continual thud, thud, thud of bombs, and each one of them shook his body like a convulsion. He climbed unsteadily to his feet and looked around him. Although it was still early evening, everywhere seemed to have gone dark and he could hardly see across the road; and it was only slowly that he realised that the street and the sky above him were thick with dust and smoke. There was dust everywhere. He looked down at his hands. They were covered with it, black, greasy dust. He ran a dirty finger over his face and decided that it, too, must be black.

The first people he saw when he looked around him were a young man and a girl who were slowly rising to their feet, on their knees first, and then gingerly upright. He remembered seeing the couple just before the bombs began falling, a nice pair of kids, he had thought, and he glanced more than once at the girl, a very pretty blonde. He saw the back of her now and was startled because she was obviously coloured; and not only that, she was naked up to the waist, her long legs and backside distinctly brown.

But then when she straightened up and turned he realised that her hair, though streaked black and hanging every way, was still mainly blonde. She was crying, great heaving sobs, as she crossed her hands below her waist to cover herself. He started to move across but her young man suddenly seemed to realise what had happened. He slipped off his jacket and began tying it around the girl's waist by the sleeves.

It was the first freak effect of bomb-blast that David Meade had seen, but there would be others in the hours to come. The lucky ones would be those who only got their stockings or their clothes whipped off by the blast.

The first thing Superintendent Reginald Smith saw when his car rounded a bend in Canning Town was a huge sow spread-eagled across the road on the edge of a bomb crater. Its entrails were spilled across the road. On the other side of the crater two more pigs were running aimlessly around in circles, and he could hear their terrified grunts above the crash of the bombs. It was the first time he had realised that here, in the centre of one of the most populous slum areas in London, a family had been keeping a pig farm for generations. The animals had broken loose, and some were badly wounded. The first thing he did when he reached his office was order the issue of guns and a squad of men to dispatch the injured pigs. Then he asked the question uppermost in his mind:

'What about West Ham Stadium?'

'Two bombs on it, sir,' the sergeant said. 'But Jerry was too late. Everyone had gone home ten minutes earlier.'

'Where've we been hit the worst?'

The sergeant pointed at the map on the wall. 'There's two slum areas that won't need clearing after this,' he said. 'Jerry's done it for us.'

He was pointing at Silvertown and Canning Town.

'And what about casualties?' the superintendent asked.

'They're bad, sir,' the sergeant said. 'Lots of people buried, too. You know those tenements, sir. Just fell down on top of people. The rescue teams are digging them out now.'

Where the Harriman house had been there was now a mound of brick and plaster rubble, mixed up with bits of floor boards and furniture and torn rolls of linoleum, all piled up into a heap. When Bill Harriman and his son came up with the warden a stretcher bearer team was scrambling down the last slope, and the warden stopped them and then indicated to Bill that he should take a look at what they were carrying. Through the dusk that caked her face and shoulders, Bill recognised an old woman from the end of the street. He shook his head and the warden signalled the stretcher bearers to go on.

The rescue squad were working at the far end of the mound, picking their way through the rubble and filling up a series of buckets and baskets and a large, buckled tin bath.

'That's our bath, Dad,' John suddenly said.

There were a couple of official-looking men at the bottom of the rubble, and they turned and looked at the warden.

'Who are these people?' one of them asked. 'What are they doing here? This is a prohibited area, you know.'

The warden explained about Bill Harriman, and about his daughter. The official turned at once to the men on the pile and shouted:

'There's someone here says his daughter was in the house.'

A voice from someone they could not see came back:

'Ask him if he had a dog.'

John broke in: 'Yes. Winston. We left Winston behind with Linda!'

One of the men on the top of the pile looked down at the man and the small boy, and then said:

'You'd better come up here.'

They scrambled up the mountain of rubble to the top, and when they got there, the same men looked down at the boy.

'What did you say your dog's name was?'

'Winston,' said John.

'And what's your name, son?'

'John,' he said.

'Then call your dog, Johnny,' the man said.

They all waited and John began shouting, down towards the heart of the rubble:

'Winston! Come on, Winston! Good boy, Winston!'

Suddenly the man motioned him to be silent. They all stood

there on the rubble, listening. And presently, they heard from somewhere deep down a scrabbling and the broken whine of a dog.

On Saturday evening, around about six-thirty, when the All Clear sound was heard over Chadwell Heath, Arthur Ketley said to his wife:

'Let's go down to the Cooper's Arms. I could do with a drink this evening.'

Ever since tea-time they had been listening to the sounds of planes going over, and their son Donald had caught them glancing uneasily at each other each time there was a faint thud from the distance. But on this occasion at least, Chadwell Heath was not in the target area.

The Cooper's Arms was the Ketleys' local pub, and they liked it because there was a small garden outside with tables and chairs, which meant that they could take the boy with them. They walked down the road in the evening sunlight and when they got to the pub Arthur Ketley went inside for a pint of mild and bitter for himself, a shandy for Mrs Ketley and a ginger-beer for Donald. When he came out again his face was troubled.

'I hear they've caught a packet in Silvertown and Bermondsey,' he said. 'It's terrible, they say. Awful trouble. People are streaming out of the East End.' He glanced at the boy and then back to his wife. 'Lots of rumours around, too. They say Jerry may be coming at any moment now.'

'In that case, we know what we're going to do, don't we,' said Mrs Ketley, firmly. 'We're staying put.'

For the past few days there had been an advertisement in all the newspapers. It had been issued by the Ministry of Information and, as usual, was printed in space bought and donated by the Brewers' Society, and it read:

WHAT DO I DO
if I hear news
that Germans are trying to land,
or have landed?

I remember that this is the moment to act like a soldier. I do *not* get panicky. I *stay put*. I say to myself: Our chaps will deal with them. I do *not* say: 'I must get out of here.' I remember that fighting men must have clear roads. I do *not* go on to the

road on bicycle in car or on foot. Whether I am at home or at work, I just *stay put*.
CUT THIS OUT – and KEEP IT!

Mrs Ketley had kept hers and to her it seemed good advice. She was not going to make the mistake that those poor souls in France and Belgium had made. She had seen newsreels of them marching along the roads with prams and bundles, and she had seen the human debris in the ditches after German planes had been over to bomb and machine-gun them. That wasn't the way she and her family were going to die; that she was determined on. If it must be, they would die in their own homes.

The family sipped their drinks in silence. It was growing dark now, and as they looked westwards towards London they noticed the glow in the sky.

'Gosh, Dad, look at that sunset,' said Donald.

'Lovely,' said Mrs Ketley.

There was silence, no sound except for the clattering of glasses from inside the pub. Then Arthur Ketley said:

'That's no sunset.'

He was echoing words that were being said all over London at that moment. At St Paul's Cathedral the Dean, the Reverend Walter Robert Matthews was walking in the twilight across the floor under the great dome when he lifted his eyes to the stained glass windows. It was usually from the West that the luminescence came, but not this evening: it was the eastern windows which glowed with a strange red beauty. Further west, in Piccadilly and Leicester Square and in Hyde Park, pedestrians in the streets thought that something had gone wrong with the universe, for the sun was setting, it seemed, in a great red couch of flames, to the east. But of course it was not the sunset that was painting the sky red but the great fires now raging all over the East End of London.

Around nine o'clock that night the Ketleys, sitting silently in the garden of the Cooper's Arms, their glasses long since empty, heard the sirens begin again. First they wailed faintly in the distance, from the shores of the Thames Estuary in Essex and in Kent, and then, like cocks crowing to each other, nearer and nearer sirens took up the cry and passed beyond Chadwell Heath and on into the centre of London.

'Home, I think,' said Arthur Ketley.

Without too much haste, they made their way down the road back to the terraced house in the dead-end street. Just as they were turning into it from the main road, they heard a noise. Into view through the pale September night came an open cart of the kind used by Cockney junk men. An old nag was pulling it along, spurred on by a man in a cap and muffler, with a woman beside him. The cart was piled high with a table, several chairs and an assortment of carpets and junk. Three children were walking beside the cart, their hands on the rails, allowing themselves to be pulled along.

Behind them came two men pushing bicycles with sacks over their crossbars, and then more women and children, some of them pushing prams and wooden trollies, others carrying small cases and handbags stuffed with odd impedimenta. The Ketleys had stopped to watch them, and as they passed they noticed that they were most of them black with soot or oil or some sort of stain, and that their eyes looked bloodshot, and that none of them talked. Not even the babies they saw were crying.

'Where've you come from?' asked Arthur Ketley of the man on the cart.

'Silvertown,' said the man, shortly. 'It's bloody murder back there, sheer bloody murder! We've 'ad it, mate, we've really 'ad it this time.'

Mrs Ketley said, hesitantly (for tea was rationed now), 'I could give you a cup of – well, maybe some water or something? You look tired.'

'Thanks, Missus,' said one of the women, 'but we ain't stopping till we get out of this mess. I wouldn't stay 'ere either if I was you. They're going to blow this place to bloody smithereens.'

As she spoke the faint buzz in the air which had been tantalising their ears grew into an angry hum, and then the sound began to come in upon them in waves as planes in great numbers roared over them on their way to London from the east.

Now the children began to cry and so did some of the mothers, and the man on the cart tugged at the reins and urged the old nag into a canter.

The Ketleys went silently into their house and shut the door behind them. They did not attempt to put on the light. Instead, they went to the space under the stairs and crammed themselves inside the cubbyhole. Arthur Ketley took down the glasses and reached for the bottle of rum, and then they settled down for the long night.

6

At eight o'clock that Saturday night the British Government did a foolish thing. One might even say that they panicked. All through the daylight bombing of the East End Winston Churchill had been in conference in the Hole in the Ground with his Chiefs of Staff, and certainly the reports that reached them were grim. The RAF had been caught out. They had been in the wrong place when the invading bomber fleets came up the Thames, and though they had badly mauled the enemy planes on their way home most of them had succeeded in dropping their bombs just where they wanted. Moreover, anti-aircraft defences along the Thames had proved to be woefully inadequate and had hardly bothered the incoming planes. It had truly been a bad day for Britain. The targets hit were valuable and vital ones. The blow to civilian morale would be considerable.

All this, however, dire though it might be, was no justification for the action taken by the Chiefs of Staff at 8 p.m. that evening, and pending another explanation Winston Churchill must take his share of the blame, for the action was taken with his consent. The code word 'Cromwell' was sent out to the army. There is some argument still about what precisely 'Cromwell' was supposed to mean: did it mean 'invasion beginning' or 'invasion has begun'?

Whatever it was, there seems no reason why it should have been issued at all, for there was nothing to suggest that invasion was nearer at 8 that evening than it had been that morning, when the 'invasion regarded as imminent' message had been sent out from Whitehall. True, the raid on London was heavy and its results already catastrophic, and true, it could have been interpreted to Churchill by his experts as the necessary softening up that was the predictable prelude to a landing. But there was no movement in the North Sea nor in the Channel to indicate that the massed invasion barges had set out from France and Belgium to begin the assault.

What may have caused the Prime Minister and his military advisers to panic was the vast number of planes the Germans had used. Might not some of them be paratroop carriers? Was an *airborne* landing part of the operation against London?

In fact it was not, but the General Staff thought it was and Churchill went along with them. 'Cromwell' was meant to be a signal for Army eyes only, but all over the country military units now had Home Guards attached to them, and these in turn worked in close liaison with the air-raid wardens, the fire services and the police. Within an hour of the issue of the code-signal all Britain knew about it. In most places it was interpreted as an alarm call signalling that the invasion had actually begun. Church bells were rung as a warning to the populace, the Home Guards turned out with their odd rifles, shotguns and staves, the wives and children went down to the cellars, and stout civilians prepared to die in the ditches.

In the East End the confusion caused by the bombing was compounded into chaos as fire-fighters and ARP wardens were ordered, amid the flames and fumes and crashing bombs, to watch out for paratroopers and Fifth Columnists.

' 'Ow the 'ell d'you recognise friend from foe?' asked one Cockney fireman, 'when we're all covered with the same shit?'

Shortly after eight that Saturday evening the German bombers started coming in again. At his headquarters in Northern France Hermann Goering was exultant. What did it matter if forty-five planes had been lost? Most of them had dropped their bombs first, and so had the two hundred and fifty others which had returned. Every target had been hit – and London was in flames. From now on, his pilots were told, the job would be easy.

'Drop your bombs wherever you see the fires,' they were told.

By nine o'clock the rescue squad had managed to get a shaft down into the rubble, and one of the men had been lowered into it. It was too narrow for a spade or a pickaxe, so the man was working away with his hands and a small coal shovel and filling baskets with the debris, which the men up above hauled away.

Bill Harriman was working with the rescue squad, helping them to empty the baskets. They had tried to dissuade him, but after a time they seemed to realise that it helped, and they let him go on. He was covered from head to foot with fine dust, and his face was caked like a clown's except for the places where the tears had run down his cheeks. Little John had fallen asleep and been taken down to a warden's post around the corner. Every so often, the man down the shaft would gesture to the others and then, in the silence, call out: 'Winston!' and then everyone would listen. They still heard some scrabbling, but there were no whines any more.

Every so often there were articles in the baskets of debris that Bill Harriman recognised: one of the Mickey Mouse mugs they had bought for the children, a saucepan, a wedding picture of himself and Eileen off the mantel shelf, the glass still intact. About half past nine, the man in the shaft called out: 'Ask him if he recognises this.'

It was one of Linda's shoes. The man said:

'I think I'm getting close. Everybody quiet for a moment.'

They all fell quiet again. The only noise to be heard was a faint buzzing in the distance. And a rubbling sound, as the man poked and prodded, calling out: 'Winston! Winston!' in between.

The air raid siren began to sound again. They could hear one after another taking up the wail along the Thames. When it was over, the man down the shaft said:

'It's her all right. And the dog.'

You could tell by the tone of his voice that both of them were dead.

Suddenly, all of them could smell escaping gas, and the men in the rescue squad hastily put out their cigarettes.

7

For most of London's firemen the East End raid of 7 September was their baptism by flame. Four-fifths of them had had no experience of actual fire-fighting at all, for they were volunteers who had joined up as auxiliaries (some to escape call-up into the Army). They had been taught at their training lectures that a thirty-pump fire was a big one. But by midnight on 7 September there were nine fires in the East End alone needing a hundred-plus pumps to fight them, and on the operations map at London Fire Brigade Headquarters there were notices pinned to several places on the map saying: 'Fire out of hand.'

The biggest of these was in Quebec Yard, in Surrey Docks, down on the Thames, where acres of warehouses were ablaze.

The heat was so fierce that it had set alight the wooden blocks in the roadways.

A blaze covering such an area is not only worse than a smaller one in direct proportion to its area, [the London Fire Brigade's historian wrote later*], but it is harder to fight than its mere extent would suggest. The greater the cumulative heat, the fiercer the draught of cold air dragged in to feed it, and thus the quicker the movement of the fire and the greater the length of its flames. They were so long and their heat so great as to blister the paint on fireboats that tried to slip past under the lee of the opposite river bank 300 yards away. Solid embers a foot long were tossed into streets afar off to start fresh fires. Stocks of timber which the firemen had drenched began at once to steam, then to dry, then themselves to burst into flame in the intense heat radiated from nearby blazes. ... At Woolwich Arsenal men fought the flames among boxes of live ammunition and crates of nitro-glycerin, under a hail of bombs directed at London's No. 1 military target. But in the docks themselves strange things were going on.

At one blazing warehouse on Commercial Dock the firemen waded in through a fog of smoke and then staggered back, clutching their eyes; it was as if they had been attacked by a swarm of savage flies. And when they tried to breathe, the air that went into their lungs felt like liquid fire. The warehouse was a pepper store, and the pepper was afire.

There were rum fires, with torrents of blazing liquid pouring from the warehouse doors and barrels exploding like the bombs themselves. There was a paint fire, another cascade of white-hot flame, coating the pumps with varnish that could not be cleaned for weeks. A rubber fire gave forth black clouds of smoke so asphyxiating that it could only be fought from a distance, and was always threatening to choke the attackers. Sugar, it seems, burns well in liquid form as it floats on the water in dockland basins. Tea makes a blaze that is 'sweet, sickly and very intense'. One man found it odd to be pouring cold water on hot tea leaves. A grain warehouse when burning produced great clouds of black flies that settled in banks upon the walls, whence the firemen washed them off with their jets. There were rats in

* *Front Line* (H.M. Stationery Office).

their hundreds. And the residue of burned wheat was 'a sticky mess that pulls your boots off'.

The German bombers, now coming over in wave after wave, had no trouble at all. Even the Thames itself was alight along part of its length, a highway of flame pointing to the centre of the target.

All night long the burning fires in the East End had ringed off several areas so that they became, in effect, diminishing islands whose boundaries were defined by the encroaching flames, or by the Thames itself. Some of the people inside were taken off by boat, but that was not always possible. So hundreds of thousands of them waited inside the burning rings, while the firemen outside battled to hose a way through so that rescue cars and buses could come in and bring the people out. Bombs were coming down. Gas mains were going up. The houses had crumbled into dust. The heat was mounting and smoke made it hard to see and breathe. The dead and injured lay in the dust and rubble, with not even water to wash their wounds or quench their thirst.

In the circumstances panic might have been expected, but in fact there was very little of it. The bombing seemed to have stunned everyone. Mrs Nancy Spender, an ambulance worker, managed to get into East Ham after a nightmare drive past burning warehouses and over bomb-cratered roads, and eventually she reached a shelter where a bomb had struck. She reported:

We went over to the shelter and put our heads in. I suppose there were about forty people there. I said 'Anybody hurt?' and not a soul answered. So I said again 'Anybody hurt?' and still nobody answered, so I went up to one woman and tapped her and said 'Is there anybody hurt here?' and she said 'Over there there's a mother and a two-day old baby, they've both been dug out, and I think further up there's a boy with a very bad knee, he got dug out, he was buried up to his waist, but I don't know about the others.' So I went over to the mother, she didn't speak, and I wrapped her in a blanket and put her on a stretcher, and I said 'Is there a warden here?' and somebody said 'No, he was killed half an hour ago.' So I got a couple of men, anyway, to help me, and we took her back on the stretcher, put her in the ambulance, then I came back again and collected the boy, with some help, and then we got back to the ambulance with him and after that I just filled the ambulance with as many people as I could cram in, about fifteen or sixteen. Still nobody spoke, it was all the most deathly silence, and I got in beside them, not beside the driver, and drew the curtains to shut out the ghastly glare, and deafen the noise a bit, and we drove off.*

It was in an ambulance that Bill and John Harriman, with the body of Linda on the bunk beside them, arrived shortly before midnight at an emergency dressing station set up at the London Heart Hospital in the Mile End Road. The first bombs of the night raid dropped at the end of Star Road shortly after they had got Linda's body clear, and while an ambulance man was trying to revive her. She and the dog had died not from the blast of the bomb or the crush of the rubble, but from a pocket of gas escaping from the wrecked kitchen stove. They worked on the body for a long time, but everyone knew it was no good; she had been dead for hours.

They stopped when the bombs burst, and the Harrimans found themselves bundled into the ambulance and driven away. At the hospital Linda's body was taken to the mortuary, and they were given cups of tea and left in a waiting room. No one seemed to know quite what to do with them. They sat around until the All Clear went at 5 a.m. and then Bill woke John up and they went out, hand in hand, into the Mile End Road. No buses or Underground trains seemed to be running, so they began walking East, back towards Canning Town. Bill wanted to be there when Eileen got back. He didn't want anyone else to tell her that Linda was dead.

All through the night, and all the next morning, groups of East Enders from Stepney and Bermondsey and Canning Town trekked by cart or bicycle or on foot to the safety of the woodland glades of that favourite cockney playground, Epping Forest, where they just lay down and slept. But many more stayed where they were, among the bomb craters, in a coma, too exhausted, too frightened, too stunned to talk or move.

Then, being Cockneys, they recovered their spirits, if not their tempers, and they had plenty to say.

* *The Blitz*, Constantine Fitzgibbon, Wingate 1957.

Four hundred and thirty Cockneys would neither speak nor hear, for they had died in the raids. One thousand six hundred others were in hospital. But there were hundreds of thousands left who had survived, and as the hours went by their tempers rose. Their houses had been destroyed, a great many of them had nowhere to go. Yet nothing was being done about them. Why not? they asked. Why were there no shelters and food and evacuation plans to get them away? And why was it that they had been chosen, the poor people in the East End, while the bigwigs in the Government and the posh folk up West in Knightsbridge and Mayfair had slept safely in their beds? And why had the German raiders so easily got through?

In official circles there were two views of the great raids of 7 September 1940. For Air Marshal Dowding and his staff the night's attacks were a welcome change in the Luftwaffe's tactics. They hoped for more of the same. The raids on London could not have come at a better time, since they had switched the pressure from the RAF's fighter-stations just at the moment when they were all but destroyed, and given a respite to the RAF pilots dog-fighting over the Channel just when they were tired to the point of collapse.

Winston Churchill shared their satisfaction. It would do him a disservice to say that he rejoiced over the night's raids; far too many people had been killed and far too much damage had been done for that. But he was extremely conscious of the propaganda effect that the death-roll figures would have upon the neutral world, and President Franklin D. Roosevelt had already been on the private line from the White House to extend his sympathy to the British people.

The statisticians were, however, somewhat disconcerted. They had expected many, many more people to be killed. Considering the amount of bombs that had been dropped, the fires started, the houses destroyed, they had calculated that there would be thousands not hundreds waiting to be buried. It was somewhat inconvenient that there weren't. Because with so many people still alive and so many houses destroyed, that meant that there would be far more homeless than they had expected.

And they hadn't made anything like adequate arrangements to take care of them. Even the pigeons in the East End no longer had any homes to go home to; flocks of them were now flying over Bermondsey and Poplar and Bow, looking vainly through the smoke for lofts where they used to roost.

MEMORANDUM

From: Peter Donald
Age: 28
Profession: Writer. Conscientious objector.
Time: September 1940. Subject: Reaction to air raids.
Note. Peter Donald is a lodger in East London with a GPO worker and his wife, Mr and Mrs R. There is one daughter, Brenda, and one son now serving in the RAF.
Friday Brenda has gone to the pictures. Mr R. is on late duty again. Mrs R. is sitting before me knitting. Quite chatty but only about war and what we ought to do to Germany. Every few minutes she looks out of the door ostensibly to 'see the stars'. I suspect she is waiting for the searchlights to pop up and to listen to the distant drone of planes. The raids now terrify her. 9.20 p.m. Wow! Sirens! Mrs R. is off to the shelter. Slams door. This time I'm taking her impedimenta down for her. She forgot it last time. 9.30 p.m. That's that. She's got all she'll want for the night, I hope. Brenda is still out. Mr J. [the other lodger] is in and gone to bed. Now I'm going to do some writing and study. 10.30 p.m. All quiet. Still alone. Conclude Brenda returning from the pictures (if she came out) has gone down to the shelter with her mother.
10.50 p.m. Brenda returned bringing with her two friends (sisters) aged 19 and 16 (artisan class). They stayed about fifteen minutes. Most of the time they talked about knitting jumpers. After that Brenda washed and ate some biscuits and knitted until 11.35 p.m. I'm tired and so is she. Then since her father has not returned and there is no All Clear she decided to make up her bed on the floor of the front parlour. I lay down on my bed.
Saturday 12.57 a.m. I can't get to sleep so write the above notes. At the moment of writing there is heavy gunfire. A bomb. Very close. A violent thump. I go down to Brenda's room, the front room downstairs. She moans.
4.25 a.m. I stayed with Brenda most of the night. There was gunfire most of the time and an occasional distant bomb. Mr

R. did not come home and Mr J. stayed in bed. Brenda was very amorous but owing to the constant tension of circumstances and the state of nervous excitement present during a raid I found it almost impossible to pay her any attention for more than a few minutes at a time. She seemed to forget the danger we were in and couldn't understand my feelings. At any normal time I expect I should have been eager enough for her but at normal times she is almost prudish. The excitement of a raid causes her to become sexually excited. I can't fathom this at all. Must be due to some psychological or glandular change caused by fear. I don't know. (Note. This matter interests me. I wonder if other observers have met with similar cases of sexual excitement during air raids. Personally I'm just the reverse!)

Later. There was a raid from 9–10 a.m. from 1–2 p.m. and 6–6.40 p.m. Only dog fights overhead and a few bombs. We are getting used to it now. I think I am. Visiting a local baker's I questioned the young lady assistant (aged about 26).

'What do you think of these raids?'

'Oh, they don't bother me much now. I say if you are going to be killed, you are, so what? I say the chances of a direct hit are very small. I guess it's like getting a lead pencil and throwing it on the floor and chucking grains of salt on it to see how many stick on it. I'm pretty calm.'

'Do you think this war will last long?'

'No. Matter of weeks. Why, eighty million Germans can't be kept down for ever. They will be free and in fifty years all this will be history.'

8.15 p.m. Have a bath. 9.5. Sirens. Mrs R. to shelter. Mr R. still at GPO. Brenda stays at home. Nothing to report.

10.15 p.m. Mr R. returns. Came through raid from GPO. Shall now try to get some sleep.

Sunday 2.5 a.m. The last hour has been a lifetime! About 1 a.m. I was half asleep, planes overhead. Suddenly came a distant whistling which I knew to be a falling bomb. I leapt out of bed. The whistling probably lasted about two seconds. It seemed a lifetime. I wrenched open the door and then dived for the front room where Brenda lay. I yelled her name, then with a cracking crunch the bomb fell somewhere close at hand – there was no actual explosion. I grabbed hold of the girl who was asleep. She moaned and somehow I made her realise that bombs were falling. Somehow I shoved her in the cupboard under the stairs. No further explosions occurred but outside the firemen were yelling: 'We're coming, we're coming!' Mr R. who was asleep in the kitchen stirred and said: 'What's all this commotion?' I told him, but he was too sleepy to understand. I heard crackling and leaving the girl, saying 'Now you stay there' I ran outside. At first I thought that the big furniture store under which Mrs R. was sheltering was alight, but it was a photographer's and a tailor's with a block of flats above. Right next door to the depository. I suppose I was outside about two minutes after the bomb fell. I've never seen anything catch alight so rapidly. Within three minutes the roof had collapsed and flames were gushing out. The ARP services were *wonderfully efficient*. (The fire was only 25 yards from their HQ.) About a quarter of a mile away, two more fires had broken out – bigger than the ones close at hand. I ran indoors. Mr R., very white, said: 'I'm going down to the shelter.' I heard a shout from outside and thought I heard a gas warning. I grabbed my mask and yelled: 'Be prepared for gas!' I felt oddly calm, but it proved I was wrong.

Mr R. said: 'Christ! I'm going down to the shelter and Brenda is coming with me, no nonsense.'

'I'm *not* going down there,' said Brenda.

'I wouldn't go down there for a hundred thousand pounds,' I said. 'Why, man, it's the most dangerous place in the neighbourhood. Think what it would be like if all that caught alight.'

'Well, I'm going,' said Mr R. and he walked off.

Brenda and I and Mr J. watched the fire in the street until the latter thought we had better clear out in case the walls collapsed. But I didn't think there was any fear of that, it was not close enough.

'The police will turn us out if there is any danger,' I said.

'Isn't it awful,' said Brenda, as we stood watching the flames.

'Now look here,' I said. 'If you've got to get out of the house, what is it you value most to take with you?'

'My clothes, of course.'

We went back home. Presently Mr R. returned. 'No, I didn't go down the shelter.' Gives us details of fires and their location. 'Now I'm going to see how Mum is in the shelter.' He goes off.

Brenda says, 'I'd like to go and see the fires. Take me.' She slips on her coat and we go off too. She holds my arm until we get into the main street, then she drops it and holds my hand. People are running to the fire from all directions. The All Clear sounds. Brenda says, 'Let's go back, I'm a bit frightened.' (The glare from the six fires within three hundred yards was rather spectacular. Gave me an unreal sensation as if I was seeing it on the screen.)

We came back and Brenda practically collapsed on the stairs with exhaustion and reactions following excitement. I lifted her into a comfortable armchair but she would not take any of the sal volatile I offered her. Presently I made her lie down on the front room floor and covered her with rugs etc.

'You won't go out again will you in case the sirens go again?'

'No.'

By degrees we calmed down. Mr R. returned from seeing Mrs R. in the shelter (who simply refused to come to the surface) and we all fell asleep.

6.50 a.m. I rose early and surveyed the damage in the neighbourhood. Raining.

Monday 11.10 a.m. The remainder of yesterday was too strenuous for writing in this diary. Nervous exhaustion today. Don't feel capable of writing of the vast fire I viewed from a point seven miles from the City. Pepys would have given a graphic description. I can't – not now anyway. It is too ghastly, too tragic, too unnerving. I am tired. Only two hours' sleep for the past 48 hours. It seems we live for the moment. I am more strongly pacific than ever. Quietly determined as never before to work for peace when this mad war is over. Perhaps tomorrow I shall feel more like writing of personal matters but I have to make this note today to let you know my *mood*. Quiet determination that I shall do my bit to assure that *this* time we will say and *mean* 'Never again.' It rests with us.

8.5 p.m. Sirens early tonight. Everyone in this house except myself and Mr J. is irritable. Several times during the day we were on the verge of rowing.

Brenda said, 'If there was a raid and I saw *anybody* going by, I should ask them in – even dirty gipsy people.'

Said her mother, menacingly, 'You try, my lady! Asking people into my house!'

Still don't feel like writing about war. The rumours and news

I hear makes me dully antagonistic, a kind of impotent rage against the leaders, especially Chamberlain.* A friend of mine (radio dealer age 50, mid-class) expressed *my* feelings when he said:

'And old Neville came to the window and said "Peace in our time" and within a year he said "England is now at war with Germany". The double-crossin' old nitwit. Look at his speech when he came back from Munich. "When I was a lit-tel boy (said with a lisp) my muvver said ter me, hif at first you don't succeed, try, try, try a-gain." How very very very nice dear friends of dear Mr Chamberlain.'

Another friend (Baker, 42) said to me:

'Friend, keep this under your hat. We're going to lose this war. I told my brother that months ago. There's no sense in this war – just slaughter for slaughter's sake. I was in the last war and I know. It's the leaders' war. The people don't count – of course they don't.'

Later. Now I'm in a fatalistic mood. What will be will be. Mrs R. tends to give me the jitters – she's so very panicky. Mr R. reads at great length the reports of the bombing and tends to get the wind up as a consequence. He spent last night in the shelter with his missus. Brenda and I stayed behind. There was much gunfire. The noise and tension made her sexually excited (see previous remarks) and I felt in such a don't-care-what-happens-now mood that I was intimate with her but she got more kick out of it than I did. Felt fed up afterwards.

* Neville Chamberlain remained a minister in Churchill's administration until his death in 1941.

7

THE BIG RAIDS

Silvertown was one of London's worst slum areas in 1940. Most of its inhabitants lived three and four to a room in row after row of insalubrious jerry-built houses. The name came from the biggest factory in the district, Silver and Company, which employed a large force of young women in the manufacture of rubber goods and waterproofing materials. There were fertiliser and soap works nearby. The air above curdled with a mixture of appalling smells which the natives had long since ceased to notice. In addition to the factory workers, there was also a large population of seamen and dockers, for Silvertown was surrounded on all sides by the docks and wharves of the Pool of London, and these waterways cut the district off from neighbouring West Ham, to which it was administratively attached.

When Superintendent Reginald Smith had done his first tour of K Division after being posted there in the spring of 1940 his police guide had saved Silvertown for the last and told him:

'This is the place you'll have to watch out for, Reg. It's not the people. They're all right. Typical Cockneys, friendly lot. Get a bit drunk on Saturdays. Did you know there are more pubs in Silvertown than any other equivalent district in London? They use 'em, too. But they don't do any real harm. No, it's the West Ham Council. Real lot of Bolshies, if you ask me. Won't do a thing about the war.'

Superintendent Smith was to discover that his guide, though he used the language of a diehard Tory, had truth on his side. Not that the councillors of West Ham were Bolshies. A majority of them were simply stubborn and stupid old men. Their average age was over sixty and they refused to listen or to learn. West Ham was a stronghold of the Labour Party and most of the members who filled the safe seats on the council were party hacks who had slavishly followed the Party line all through the 1930s. That line was to express loathing and abhorrence of Hitler, the Nazi Party and Fascist Germany but to do nothing to rearm Britain to face up to the enemy. When the Government instructed local councils throughout Britain to start building air raid shelters for their people in 1937–39, the old men of West Ham refused. They stubbornly insisted that war was not necessary and therefore would not come; so why waste money on protecting people from it? When Whitehall pressed them they said: *We will build shelters if the Government will pay for them – but not unless.* (That will show those Tories they can't bully us, they told each other gleefully.) The trouble was, the Government didn't try to bully them. If the Socialists of West Ham wanted to leave their people unprotected, that was all right with them.

When the bombs started raining down, from the start, Silvertown seemed to get more than its share. Silver and Company was soon on fire and the black smoke from the rubber billowed up and acted as a target for the second, third and fourth waves of bombers: and down came the high explosives and incendiaries on the houses surrounding it. The trek of refugees began, fleeing with what belongings they could gather across the swing bridges to the higher ground on the other side; and police, firemen and air-raid wardens were glad to see them go, because Silvertown was no longer a place for anyone to stay in. Those who remained behind were either the dead, the sick and infirm, the wounded or those stubborn souls who refused to leave their damaged houses and their life's possessions.

In the early hours of Sunday morning, September 8, Superintendent Smith managed to get through to Silvertown from his headquarters to see the situation for himself. He does not like to talk too much about the journey. Bombs were dropping almost continuously. Roads were barred by bomb craters or collapsed buildings. Firemen were battling great fires everywhere and his car several times had to be helped over the piles of criss-crossing hosepipes leading down to the pumps on the Thames. There was too much noise from the fires and the bombs to talk to anyone, and in any case everyone was wearing a mask or had tied a handkerchief around his or her face against the fumes and the appalling stench from the wrecked fertilizer factory.

In the centre of Silvertown he found a local clergyman trying to control the situation. All the air-raid wardens were either dead or had fled with the refugees.* The Reverend Walter Paton had taken over and was trying to round up women and children from the wrecked houses and get them to some sort of shelter. His own church and home had been wrecked. There was barely a house standing in three square miles, save for one semi-bombed school into which he had crammed nearly seven hundred men, women and children. Their state was pitiful. They sat on their baggage, stunned out of their minds by continual noise and bombing, waiting to be rescued from the inferno.

'You've got to get them out, you've got to get them out!' the Reverend Paton kept saying.

Smith had vowed that he would. Somehow he had made his way to a police station that was working and had got to work on the telephone. Yes, he had been told, the situation in Silvertown was known. Yes, it was realised that the people were in a desperate situation. Yes, a convoy of buses had been sent to get the people out of the school where they were sheltering. And yes, it was realised that the school was very vulnerable not only to bombs but to blast. Later on Sunday morning he had received confirmation that a convoy of coaches was on its way to Silvertown to rescue the homeless. And somehow, after that, the multiplicity of his other tasks had made him forget those miserable, devastated people sitting on their luggage in that forlorn school, waiting in the flare of bombs to be taken away to safety. He had forgotten until Monday morning when his secretary came into him and said,

'Isn't it terrible about Silvertown, sir? They had a direct hit on a school there – four hundred and fifty people killed. A lot of women and kids among them.'

He said, 'But they shouldn't have been there! They were sending coaches for them. What happened to the coaches?'

What had happened to the coaches was that they had been told to assemble at a public house called 'The George' and then go in to collect the refugees. But the convoy leader had taken them to a pub called 'The George' on the wrong side of the river. By the time they reached the school the sirens started going again and the drivers decided that Silvertown was no place to stay while bombs were falling, and retreated back across the river. Some hours later, when they got back, the school was gone, and most of

* Like West Ham's councillors, most of the borough's air-raid wardens were over sixty.

the people in it. No wonder the people of Silvertown, the survivors, that is, were bitter. As for Superintendent Smith, he was sick at the thought of what might have been done. . . .

Now he was faced by another problem of people in shelters; and this time there were thousands, not hundreds, involved. By this time the blitz had really begun, at least on the East End of London. There were about three or four raids every day and alerts all through the night. Desperate for some place to hide, the Cockneys were searching for any place which looked deep and safe. One sanctuary they had found was an unfinished stretch of the London Underground railway just beyond Stratford Broadway station.

'You had better come and look at it,' his sergeant said. 'You won't believe your eyes, or your nose.'

When he got there it was two a.m. and there was a raid on. They stumbled over the last stretches of railway lines leading out of Stratford Broadway station until they came to a black mass ahead of them which was impossible to define as a shape but easy to identify from the great wafts of hot air and the sounds which came pulsing out of it.

'I'd put your hankie over your face if I was you, sir,' the sergeant said. Smith, who got queasy on boats, felt the blood draining out of his face.

'The first thing I heard,' he recalled, 'was the great hollow hubbub, a sort of soughing and wailing, as if there were animals down there moaning and crying. And then, as we went on, it hit me, this terrible stench. It was worse than dead bodies, hot and thick and so foetid that I gagged and then was sick. About fifty yards in I stopped. Ahead of me, I could see faces peering towards me lit by candles and lanterns, and it was like a painting of hell. There were young voices singing and old voices wailing and baby voices crying. And everywhere these faces staring out of the flickering darkness.'

His sergeant said to him, 'There's all sorts in there, I can tell you – white and black and yellow, though most of them are so filthy you can't tell the difference. Some of them haven't been out for days and they refuse to come out. Some of the old folk are dying, but we won't know when they're dead until they bring the bodies out. You can't tell from the smell. They do everything in there. No sanitation and no shame, I can tell you.'

He made as if to go on, but Smith was suddenly overwhelmed.

Four days of sleeplessness, bombing and responsibility had told at last. He started to vomit again.

'I can't go on,' he said. 'I've got to get out of here. But something's got to be done, it's got to be done.'

He turned and began to hurry towards the light at the entrance to the tunnel.*

The first night after Bill had made contact with Eileen, the Harriman family moved into the Stratford Tunnel and stayed on for the next three days. They seemed to be in a state of shock and did not notice the filth and the stench around them. Eileen stayed huddled up on a blanket, weeping and sleeping, and refusing the food that Bill and Johnny brought back for her.

But she had to come out for Linda's funeral, and when she got out into the daylight and looked at herself in her handbag mirror she took a deep breath.

'Gawd,' she said, 'I do look a mess. What must you think of me, Bill?'

They found a public bath and got themselves cleaned up, and then went to the cemetery. They had been too stunned to say anything when it was suggested that Linda be buried in a common grave with all the others, and now it was too late. But after the ceremony, Eileen Harriman wiped away the tears and with them seemed to wipe away her apathy and hopelessness, too.

'We've got to find somewhere to live, Bill,' she said. 'We can't go on staying in that stinking hole.'

'I've been working on that,' Bill Harriman said.

2

For four continuous days after 7 September 1940, it was the East End that felt the full fury of the German bombing campaign, and living on the other side of London was like being in another world. In Kensington and Hammersmith and Maida Vale and Ealing you heard the sirens and many people went to their shelters, but the

---

* Stubborn to the last, West Ham Council refused to accept responsibility for the tunnel, despite Smith's pleas. Finally the whole borough was taken over by the Government and the tunnel, among other things, cleaned up.

planes they heard overhead dropped their bombs on Plaistow and Poplar, the Mile End Road and Bow. The Cockneys did not even have the satisfaction of reading about themselves in the newspapers. The Ministry of Information saw to that. Though it was impossible to disguise East London from a reconnaissance plane, and therefore the Germans must have had a clear picture of the damage they were inflicting, all details of buildings hit and localities destroyed were deleted from both the newspapers and the reports of foreign correspondents. The result was that the people of the East End felt isolated in their suffering, and the feeling spread among them that so long as it was just the Cockneys who were getting beaten up the folks up West weren't losing too much sleep.

'What d'you think we've got down here, smallpox?' one docker asked a reporter. 'We feel as if we've been put in bloody quarantine.'

As a result of the mealy-mouthed nature of the official communiqués, rumours spread rapidly across the country about what was happening in the East End, and it was these rumours which were mainly responsible for the legend that riots and demonstrations against Government apathy started in certain dock areas in mid-September. These in fact never happened, though there was ample justification for them, for there was plenty of neglect, more than enough stupidity, and quite a lot of official indifference to individual suffering and hardship.

The rumours were such that four or five days after the bombing had reached its peak, commanding officers in army camps all over the country were beginning to report restiveness among their conscript troops, particularly among those with London associations. A Mass-Observer with a Cockney regiment reported just how his fellow soldiers were feeling:

Interest in papers and radio immediately quickened after the bombing began, and that was when they began to be delayed, arriving sometimes at lunch, sometimes at tea. Our judgement of the gravity of the situation was made more on the speed of the communication than anything else. Radio bulletins vague in their geography, measured in their admission of damage spread the alarm they were calculated to allay. 'A school in the East End of London' means nothing to a German but to an East Ender in search of information it is the school at the corner of his street. Vagueness may confuse the enemy but it diffuses anxiety through a much larger section of the public than precision.

One of the troopers attached to the regiment had left shortly after the blitz had begun to go home to Poplar on forty-eight hours' leave.

Brown did not return until Monday lunchtime, over twelve hours overdue. We'd all fantasised his death, his injury, and when he came in there was a cheer. He stood between the cots for a second, his usually pale white slum face flushed and drawn.
'East End,' he said, 'they've wiped it out.'
And then he ran to his cot and lay there, helmet and gasmask still slung, head buried in the pillow, weeping. Some had not been looking, and they called out to him, brushing their boots, getting their equipment on. I thought his wife or daughter had been killed and I shouted: 'Shut up!' Then there was silence, the unnatural, uneasy silence of a mass faced with the emotion of an individual. It became intolerable until someone shouted: 'For God's sake carry on!' So we carried on talking, sometimes casting a glance at the little man crying on his iron cot. His wife and child were not dead but a time bomb had fallen on his house, he had left his family in an air raid, had had no sleep all the time he had been in London. Emotionally expecting Armageddon, he described later destruction to fit this picture. Not the East End only but the docks, Woolwich and God knows what else were wiped out. The flames of fire against the smoke of burning buildings had coloured his whole imagination. Others coming from London filled in the panorama of misery and destruction and the fears which we had hitherto suppressed during our separation rose again like giants after their sleep.

The invasion scare was still on. Winston Churchill in his last broadcast, shortly after the start of the blitz, had warned that the Germans might be landing at any moment. Seventy-five per cent of all troops were by now confined to barracks and kept in a state of alert. The result, this soldier observer reported, was increased talk of desertion among the soldiers many of whom slipped away to see how their families were going on in London.

We queued constantly in our spare time to telephone to London to be told of infinite delay, almost no letters arrived, morale sank very low, we learned that Charing Cross, Waterloo, Vauxhall Bridge had been bombed, no ships floated in the Port of London. We feared that this was true and no news, each day no news, and when news came it was a telegram to say F's mother is dead, C's wife, H's house had been blown to bits, J's wife had been blown on top of her baby by bomb blast. We know the calculation of the enemy was to cause just such disquiet among us, but the absence of any machinery to inform us of our losses in relatives or property and the dislocation of communication depressed us. Idle in camp, waiting, we thought of our people, sleepless, huddled in shelters, the horrors we knew had happened to our comrades happened to us. Our commanding officer realised the danger. The regimental secretary was instructed to go to the East End and get news of various people but this is a clumsy machine to operate.

It was a relief to the Government when, on the night of 13 September, a German bomber strayed off course and dropped a bomb on Buckingham Palace. 'Dolts, idiots, stupid fools!' cried Winston Churchill when he heard that the censors at the Ministry of Information had deleted the location from an Associated Press flash to New York. 'Spread the news at once. Let it be broadcast everywhere. Let the humble people of London know that they are not alone, and that the King and Queen are sharing their perils with them.'*

A few days later the Queen was quoted in the newspapers as saying, 'Now I feel I can look the East End in the face.'

It seemed to have a tonic effect upon most Cockneys, and Union Jacks began to appear miraculously on burned houses all over dockland and the Royal Family got a warm welcome when they toured the bombed areas.

By that time everyone in London was in it. After 13 September the Luftwaffe's attack gradually spread across the whole spectrum

---

* In fact, though it was not revealed at the time, the King had a very narrow escape from death. Two bombs fell thirty yards away in the courtyard in front of his study. 'A very accurate piece of bombing, if I may say so,' remarked a palace constable to the Queen. Buckingham Palace was bombed several times after this, and a dashing RAF sergeant pilot named J. H. (Ginger) Lacey became a national hero when he jumped one bomber in the act and shot him down over Westminster.

of the capital, and the East End was indeed no longer alone. There were bombs upon the City, and churches, hospitals and stockbrokers' offices fell upon each other in the rubble. The bombers moved towards the West End and dropped their loads on Westminster, Chelsea and Kensington. Night after night the planes came back and it was all the same whether you were a docker in Bow or a debutante in Park Lane, you ducked for cover as the incendiaries, the high explosives and the landmines crashed down upon the Mile End Road, Ealing Broadway, Piccadilly, Leicester Square and Hampstead. Soon Mrs Rosemary Black in her fashionable house in St John's Wood was writing:

The papers now say that London has taken the worst punishment from bombing anywhere, even worse than Rotterdam. We are all delighted to hear this.

The life of London gradually changed that autumn. Dusk became the zero hour, for that was when the big formations of German bombers now came over.

'Everyone knows it, for just before dusk the streets are noisy with the chatter of those who are rushing for the public shelters,' wrote Robert Nichols, an armaments worker, who lived in Eltham, a suburb of South East London. 'They carry their suitcases with spare clothes, others carry blankets and pillows. I am told that some of them get to the shelters shortly after teatime and stake out their claims in a favourite corner by placing their gear on the seats. Then they go away like theatregoing pit-ites,* leaving their gear as evidence of priority. When the alert sounds they just walk into the shelters and claim their places. This causes hot arguments and even fights among the women. A warden of my acquaintance had a finger broken intervening in such a fight.'

Nichols preferred to sleep during the raids in the Anderson shelter which he had dug into his small back garden. The Anderson, named after the minister in charge of air raid precautions, had a steel reinforced roof which was cushioned with soil, and steel sides. It was supposedly safe from all but a direct hit and many a London householder made it snug with electric light, chairs and table and bunks. 'I feel as safe in an Anderson as

---

* Queuers for pit and balcony (non-bookable) seats at London theatres could hire a stool and leave it with their name outside the box office, claiming it just before curtain time.

anywhere,' he maintained. Yet even when the blitz on London was at its worst, a surprising number of Londoners never went out to take shelter. A poll taken at the end of September showed that during the long night air raids 44 per cent of Londoners stayed at home, 44 per cent went to shelters, and 12 per cent made other arrangements. This figure changed once the people got used to the raids, and even more people decided to risk staying at home.

It was the poorer Cockneys who continued to patronise the shelters, and this was hardly surprising. When you live in a tiny one-up-and-one-down house in a slum row, there is no room in your paved backyard for an Anderson shelter, and it is no use reinforcing a nook under the stairs if the house is so frail that it falls down at a near miss. So off they went every night to the shelters to take their chance of being killed, but at least in company.

> Different types of shelters applied to different temperaments [reported a Mass-Observation survey]. There were the Anderson shelters. There were the surface shelters in the streets. Trench shelters had been dug underground into the parks and squares. And there were the Tube shelters.

The Tube (or Underground railway) shelters had, in fact, not been included in the Government's plans when they began organising protection for London under the bombing. It was the East Enders who decided to take them over. Driven from their homes by the intensity of the Luftwaffe's attack, they simply bought tickets at the nearest Underground station and rode down the moving staircase to the platform far below. There they slung down their bedding on the platform, gathered their children around them, and refused to budge. Soon it became a nightly routine. The moment the sirens went down they came and there they stayed until the all-clear sounded.

It was there, in mid-September 1940 that the sculptor Henry Moore discovered them, and they were to change his life.

All that summer Moore had been living through what might be called a fallow period in his artistic development. The war all around him was distracting. He had turned down the offer from Sir Kenneth Clark to become a war artist because he did not want to spend his time drawing tanks and guns and searchlights for propaganda illustrations. To a certain extent he was hoping to keep aloof from the war and carry on with his own individual life:

his life as an artist, working out the new pictures and the new sculptures he was planning, pure abstract works that would take him further and further away from subjective reality.

It was, of course, impossible to ignore the war, even before the blitz began. It meant that no commissions were forthcoming, that no exhibitions were possible, that material for his sculptures was hard to get and hard to move. He paid the rent by continuing teaching at the Chelsea School of Art, and he and his wife Irene lived on in the studio they had taken over from Barbara Hepworth in Hampstead.

'We had been to Chelsea for the evening, with some friends, I expect,' he said, 'and we were on our way back to Hampstead. We could no longer use the car because petrol rationing was now strict, and, in any case, it was difficult travelling across London in the black-out, especially now the raids had begun. All the same, I think it was the first time Irene and I had used the Underground for a long time. I remember that we changed trains at Leicester Square Station and that was the first time I saw the Tube shelterers. I remember stepping over them as we got out of the train from South Kensington and wondering about what sort of conditions they must have been enduring to bring them down to sleeping on a railway platform, but the impact was blunted for the moment, possibly because we were in a hurry to catch our connection.'

When their train reached Hampstead Station and the automatic doors opened the Moores found that they could hardly step onto the platform for bodies. They were lying everywhere. What they did not know at the time was that Hampstead is one of the deepest Underground stations in London, and that its reputation for safety had already spread across the capital. From miles away whole families had begun trekking in daily to take up their nightly abode deep down in the warm womb of the station, where they could hear neither the sound of bombs nor guns, and where they could sleep in ostrich-like security, cut off from the war and the death and destruction going on above them.

'It so happened that there was a raid going on by the time we reached Hampstead,' Moore said, 'and they wouldn't let us go up to the surface. Bombs were dropping too close, they said. They had stopped the lifts and everyone would have to wait until the raiders moved away or the all-clear sounded. It was only then that

I began to look around me. And suddenly I was excited by what I saw.' He smiled. 'You could say that in every direction I looked I could see what have since been called Henry Moore reclining figures. I just stood there, watching them – the lonely old men and women, the family groups, the chatterers and the withdrawn. When they announced that the all-clear had sounded and we could go up to the surface, I went reluctantly. That night and all next day I worked on a sketch. But when the evening came, I stopped and put some notebooks in my pocket and set off for the Underground. I stayed there for several hours, making myself inconspicuous and drawing figures and groups.'

It was two or three days later that Sir Kenneth Clark telephoned Henry Moore and asked him once more whether he would enrol as a war artist.

'Now the situation had changed and we were all in it,' Moore said, 'and now I knew it wouldn't just be soldiers in uniform and tanks and guns, I said yes. I told him about my Underground sketches and what I wanted to do. So I was made a war artist and they gave me a pass which allowed me to go where I wanted and move about during the raids.'

His experiences in the Underground shelters changed the whole direction of Henry Moore's artistic drive. His ideas had been moving more and more towards abstract shapes in both his drawings and his sculptures, but the Cockneys sprawled across the platforms of Piccadilly, Hampstead, Bayswater Road and Liverpool Street drew him back to the human shape and the human predicament.

Talking to Henry Moore about his experiences in London in 1940 and 1941 is a curious experience compared with the recollections of most others who went through the horrors of the blitz. It is as if his artistic compulsion kept him aloof from the battle raging all around him. He was one of those who was never once afraid, and as he talks the impression grows that he was somehow never involved in the human sense, and that the people he transferred so strikingly from the Underground platforms to his famous series of blitz drawings were truly, as he said, nothing more than Henry Moore Reclining Figures to him.

'From September 1940 onwards,' he said, 'I went about London all the time the night raids were on. I bought myself some sketch books and I would spend the evenings going from shelter to shelter.

I didn't talk to many people, and I tried not to let them see what I was doing. I would go down the moving staircase and tuck myself away in the corner of an exit and survey the people sleeping on the platform from there. It wasn't so easy when the trains were still running, because the place would be full of people stepping over the bodies and milling around. But when the trains stopped and quietness came I would settle down to serious work. I took care not to let them see me sketching. That would have been much too rude. People were trying to get a little privacy, even down there. They were undressing. They were snuggling down onto the platform, often two under the same blanket. Children were being put on their little pots. There wasn't any real order down there at that time – people had just come down to escape the raids spontaneously – and in some ways it was a quite extraordinary mess and chaos.'

He went on, emphatically: 'But that was just what I wanted. The unexpected, the unorganised. The impact made by the whole improvised succession of scenes down there in the Underground was quite important for me. It humanised everything I had been doing. I knew at the time that what I was sketching represented an artistic turning point for me, though I didn't realise then that it was a professional turning point too. You see, I wasn't really well known at that time. I certainly wasn't making much money. But I handed my first book of sketches to Kenneth Clark and he showed them to everybody, and then the Ministry of Information started to distribute the others. And once the drawings were seen. . . .'

As the weeks went by, the authorities gave up all hope of persuading Londoners to abandon the Underground shelters for the official refuges they had organised in the streets and parks. The Cockneys didn't trust them. They preferred to be deep down in the earth where they could not hear bombs or guns, and there would have been a revolt if the Government had tried to move them. So having failed to persuade them, they joined them. Wardens and welfare workers moved in and the job began of organising the platforms for the thousands of nightly tenants.

'Later, they began to clean things up,' said Moore. 'They brought down canteens and served teas and organised latrines and things like that, and then it ceased to be interesting for me. But before! I would get behind a pillar and sketch a head or a hand.

What I was trying to portray in my groups was the profound depth of this place where these people were talking and sleeping, the distance they were away from the war that was raging above their heads, but of their awareness of it in their faces, in their attitudes, in the stale air around them. I was both excited and engaged by everything I saw around me – until it got organised and then it was no longer interesting for me.'

For the sake of his wife, Irene, who liked neither the raids nor crowds, Henry Moore found half of a farmhouse which he rented at Perry Green, on the Hertfordshire-Essex borders, some twenty-five miles from London.* But each afternoon he and a friend pooled their petrol coupons and drove into London, where he stayed until dawn, wandering from shelter to shelter. He discovered the unfinished Underground railway tunnel beyond Stratford Broadway, in East London, whose conditions had so nauseated Superintendent Reginald Smith. Henry Moore spent hours there, sketching in the gloom, seemingly unaware of the stench and only conscious of the sights and sounds all around him.

'Then there was a great old warehouse of a shelter at Tilbury,' he said. 'It can't have been safe at all and thousands would have been killed if it had been hit. It was full of great bales and tins and packing cases. It was quite theatrical. I loved being there and watching the people.† It was a fascinating time. You could come up into the streets and see the fires and the gaps in the buildings and the patterns of the twisted tramlines and tangled overhead wires. I found it continuously exciting and I worked like a glutton. I loved the fires particularly. That autumn we decided that my mother, who had been living on the South Coast, should go to live with my sister in Manchester, where we thought she would be safe from raids. She was an old lady and she had never been to Manchester before, but it was arranged that she would be met at the station. Anyway, when we got to St Pancras Station in London and I was saying goodbye to my mother I suddenly

* He and his wife now live in the whole farmhouse, which he bought after the war.

† Moore was unaware that this shelter was one of the great scandals of the winter of 1940. It was a food warehouse containing rations for half of London. The warehouse had been taken over spontaneously by the local people and was soon swimming in filth, most of which was contaminating the bales of food all around the shelterers. It was some time before it could be cleared and cleaned up.

decided on an impulse to go with her. It was just as well I did.
When we got to Manchester there was absolute chaos. The city
had been bombed. There was a milling crowd at the station and
in the blackout you couldn't see or find anything or anyone. Even
if my sister had come to collect my mother she wouldn't have
found her, especially since we were abominably late.'

They set off in the blackout through the unknown city to find
his sister. It took them hours.

'In the meantime,' said Moore, 'I hadn't told Irene where I was,
so she must have been a bit worried by this time. Next day the
telephones didn't seem to be working. But that afternoon I set
off back to the station in Manchester to catch the evening train
back to London, and just as I reached Piccadilly [Manchester
has a Piccadilly too] the air raid started, a heavy one. I just stood
there watching it. I got so fascinated that I missed the train. I just
stood there all night watching the bombs crashing down and the
buildings crumbling. It was marvellous.'

From these experiences in the blitz came the series of drawings
that made the name of Henry Moore known all over the world.
And like Churchill, he enjoyed every moment of the blitz.

3

Mrs Rosemary Black was enjoying it too, though she felt a little
guilty about admitting it, even to herself. As the bombs dropped
nearer and nearer to her house in St John's Wood that autumn of
1940 she found life in London had suddenly taken on a new
flavour. She wrote in her diary:

Thinking it over, though, I've come to the conclusion that I am
enjoying *all this* in so far as it has not yet affected me personally.
Doubtless I should sing a very different tune if a bomb wrecked
my house or maimed me and my children, but it's no use worrying about such things. I do get such a kick out of finding myself
comparatively fearless and also self-controlled and calm with
regard to dealing with others, and remaining immune from their
fright. I who have always considered myself the world's most
arrant coward – I used to feel physically sick at the thought of
being woken in the night by a siren – to pass through an ordeal
such as even the comparatively safe civilian must endure these
days in London gives me a new self-respect and certainty. I

believe I shall feel prouder and stronger all my life for having been so tested.

And of the bombing itself, she added:

It's like mountain air. It seems to make one tireless and wide awake and vital. Boredom, the biggest enemy of modern man's soul, has indefinitely disappeared.

Six months ago she had been a bored, rich young widow with two children, wondering every morning what to do with her day. Some extracts from her diary illustrate the change in her outlook and attitude, the growing awareness of an upper middle-class Englishwoman of the people and conditions around her which had previously been beyond her ken, of the poor and the under-privileged who were her neighbours though she had ignored them before, of the stirring feeling that something ought to be done. In September 1940 she was still looking for a wartime job and had been going the rounds of the service bureaus, and the time had not yet come when she would start working to ameliorate the misery around her. But war and the bombing was opening her eyes, and she was learning. . . .

Every night from mid-September onwards the Luftwaffe came over regularly, and seven million Londoners prepared, according to their facilities, temperaments and location, for the nightly ordeal. The Black family (Rosemary and her two baby daughters, the Hungarian nurse, the Scottish maid and Joy Bone, a volunteer ambulance worker) retired to the reinforced air-raid shelter which Mrs Black had had built into her larder, next door to the kitchen in the basement of her house. For the moment it was still a class-conscious English household in which the servants were expected to remember their place. On 16 September she wrote:

The blitz came most uncomfortably close tonight. There was the usual violent barrage after the evening siren. Then about 9.30 just as I was crawling into my bed in the dugout there was a violent bomb explosion which sounded as if it were in the next street. Anyway it was close enough to rock the house on its foundations. It really seemed to me that the beams and walls of the dugout were rocking from side to side like those of a ship in a heavy storm. . . . Joy who had been standing beside me turned as white as lard and nearly fell down. I thought she was going to fall against one of the upright supports and cut her head open. Then she caught hold of it. I felt pleased with myself because I never moved a muscle except for my lower jaw which I must admit slowly dropped further and further. Joy said slowly, 'It's not that I'm frightened, it's just that terrible noise.' What a fool remark. Of course it's the noise that one's frightened of. There were several more explosions though not so near and the planes sounded extremely loud, so I called the maids into the shelter and we sat about rather uncomfortably while the children slept on like the dead. Marvellous. I felt most uncomfortable about sleeping in the shelter myself and leaving the maids always in the kitchen – not that one can't reach the shelter from the kitchen in half a split second, but the shelter's far quieter and one's bound to feel rather more confident in it. I should like to take turns about with them since it would really be hopeless for us to sleep in the shelter together in any comfort, but the trouble is that Mrs B. refuses to have 'a great smelly maid six inches from her. She couldn't sleep a wink.' I suppose it wouldn't be very nice for the maids either. It's obviously nicer for them to sleep separately and, so to speak, unchaperoned. . . .

In any case, it was Mrs Bone who had to be thought of first. 'On account of her hard and dangerous war work, for the sake of us, she is the one who must receive first consideration.' Mrs Bone did not fail to keep her informed of all that was going on during the bombing, and some of it was alarming.

The interesting thing she said is that her ambulance station is a hotbed of fear, [reported Mrs Black]. She said they're all working each other up into a state of nerves in which they can think and talk of nothing but how frightened they are. Fear of course is very infectious and the fearful ones spread their fright among the others. They've gone into a state of real jitters, jump at every bang, shriek when there is a loud crash and when the lights go out, start brooding on the terror of the ten-minute walk home through the night barrage almost as soon as they arrive in the afternoon.* Some of the girls prefer to spend the

---

* By this time the anti-aircraft barrage in London was so intense that there was often a greater danger in the streets of getting killed by shrapnel than by bombs.

night in deckchairs in the stuffy smoky noisy canteen rather than brave the short walk home. These of course haven't had their clothes off for a week on end and are rapidly becoming nervous wrecks. All the more honour to these people for carrying on while they're so mortally afraid, but it seems imbecile that such a state of affairs should have come about. Surely the shift leaders who at present do nothing but rotas and permits should have been given as their first and foremost function the maintenance of morale and the prevention of fear talk. Games, good example, ask people not to talk about their fears, etc. Then too Mrs Bone says all the other business is so badly organised. For example, gasmasks broken through being stuffed up with cigarettes, makeup, etc., nearly everyone ignorant of their own first-aid kits, and the use of the tourniquet apparatus with which they had been supplied which was different from the one on which they'd learned and practised. Above all, no hurricane lights or torches until lights had been off twice. Now wouldn't one think the veriest village idiot would have had more sense than not to have seen to such a thing from the first. Strangely enough, Mrs Bone says that the men, and more particularly the older men, many of them ex-Service, are far worse about fright and panic than the women. 'My dear, whenever there's a detonation anywhere they rush about pell mell and fling themselves flat on the floor. Very odd.'

Mrs Black was very conscious that even though Britain's situation was now dire indeed, and that all over the land men, women and children were dying or suffering acutely, there was still a lack of urgency in the way the nation was facing up to the emergency, and everywhere she went she saw the muddling amateur or the soulless bureaucrat at work. She was young and strong and willing. She typed, she spoke languages, she was an expert car-driver and she had taken a course in first-aid, but finding a job even as a chauffeur was proving difficult.

On 17 September, she wrote:

I need hardly say I got no results from the WVS [Women's Voluntary Service] as regards driving. Fool ever to have imagined it. The branch's head had not turned up, and it was 10.45 a.m. and none of the other members of the branch were capable of dealing with her business. One of them seemed to be

spending her whole time tidying up some tea things in a corner.
Two women who said they had been asked to come in and help
by the head were sitting gloomily on hard chairs awaiting her
return, as no one else had any idea of giving them anything to
do. After explaining myself to a scatty looking underling who
took down my name and address on an odd corner of paper
which would obviously lose itself, I said I really must go. She
said the head would ring me up as soon as she had a spare
moment to do so. Quite certain she will never do any such
thing. What a fight it is even to find out how to apply as a
volunteer for anything, no matter how badly the need for help
is proclaimed.

She went on to the local town hall to sign up for ARP and found
the same apathy and indifference there.

Every department seemed to be full to bursting with pathetic
people who'd lost their homes and were waiting for emergency
food cards, compensation application forms, travel vouchers,
instructions. They were standing and sitting everywhere,
jammed together like sardines, silent for the most part in dumb,
apathetic resignation. Many people wandered unhappily about
not knowing where to go or where to get what they wanted. The
doorman was in the midst of an endless flow of inquirers. I
gather that hundreds had come here by mistake thinking to find
the food office, which is in Praed Street. Others had gone to the
food office only to be sent here for emergency cards. . . . Some
seemed to have spent the whole morning being shunted from
pillar to post. . . . A black-haired slum woman with only one
tooth was very angry. She made the doorman a scene and he
was rude and harsh. Oh God, the inefficiency and muddle
everywhere. Why not clear and definite directions in clear
letters as to what to do in an emergency and where to go to do
it placarded at street corners, in post-offices and phone boxes
and in every ARP and WVS? This after a year of war! Oh, the
utterly futile, maddening chaos in this *something* country with
its wholly damnable local governments and the filthy rudeness
with which they treat their tragic, homeless poor. Came out
hopelessly depressed and disgusted, and feeling that if we ever do
win this war it will be entirely due to good luck and in no smallest
degree to good management, and that we damn well deserve to

be thoroughly beaten. Muddle and inefficiency are quite bad enough but the cruelty of petty officials to the wretched victims of war is something quite else.

In the next three weeks the people of St John's Wood (and the rest of London, for that matter) heard the air-raid siren between seven and eight times every day, and bombs dropped within sight or sound two or three times. But this seemed to stimulate most people.

A young architect's assistant named Paula Shepherd wrote:

Decided to buy a winter outfit. If we are all dead it won't matter, if we are all alive there won't be the stuff to buy by the end of the month. It's a most wonderful moonlight night, searchlights going up for miles among the stars. Perfect night for a raid.

Rosemary Black's home had suffered several more near-misses, but this seemed to encourage rather than depress her. Early in October she wrote:

Mrs Bone just came in with the exciting news that a policeman who came into their ambulance station says that apart from the East End, which is beyond all comparison, our part of the world has had the worst damage and the heaviest casualties. We feel thrilled. The morale around the tenement [a block of working class houses bombed the night before] is now quite magnificent. The weaklings had left for the safer places and those remaining, those around the tenement whose houses have been smashed up, are flatly refusing to leave there, so that the London County Council has eventually given in and arranged for reglazing and general repairs to begin at once. Those whose homes have gone, far from wishing to leave the district, are being accommodated with neighbours right on the spot.

And still the bombs edged ever closer to the Black house. On October 12, amid a giant's hail-storm of heavy and light and quick-firing anti-aircraft guns, there came the noise that the Black family was learning to live with and dread.

About a minute afterwards there was a horrifyingly loud scream and by the time it was halfway through I was thinking that it was about the longest drawn out I had ever heard. But it kept getting louder and louder and louder – hateful! – and after the

146

usual horrid pause there was a long drawn out crashing. The house didn't swing slowly and regularly as with a concussion bomb but shook sharply like a dog coming out of water. The curtains flew inwards. It seemed as though the walls were thinking of doing the same. One really felt as if we might see the nose of a bomb peering into the room. While this was going on Stan and Mabel (Stan is an airman from a nearby barrage balloon sight; Mabel the maid) both got up or rather slid off their chairs still half crouching. Mabel had her hands round her head somewhere and I, immovable as usual, went on just sitting where I was and I remember distinctly thinking while the crashing was thundering to its climax: 'How comic their blank faces look.' Then as the house shook there was a jingling of broken glass, part of it obviously from the window of the room in which we all were. I all at once, in a frightful rage, leaped to my feet gesticulating wildly and crying: 'Hell and dammit, now they've got my glass. Oh blast, it just would go in this room!' I was thinking of how chilly the autumn mornings were going to be in a room with panes missing from its windows. Stan said: 'That's right, you give it 'em, Mrs Black!' We all began to laugh.

But next day as more bombs came down it was no longer a laughing matter, and it was a small child who made the first crack in her façade of fearless superiority.

God almighty, what a day, [she wrote on 14 October]. I went up to get my bath over before Mrs Bone arrived from the ambulance station. She arrived home just as I was dressing. The first I heard of her was a weary hollow voice calling out that she had brought a child with her and was it all right. I said that yes, of course it was, and finished dressing in a fumble of haste to hear about this mystery.

She came down to find the child, pale, exhausted and snively, wrapped up in an eiderdown in an armchair in front of the fire. Mrs Bone took her on one side and explained that the child, Ann, was suffering from shock. The previous night's bombs had fallen only 40 yards away from the Black house and right on top of a block of flats at the end of the road. The child, eight years old, had been on a visit with her mother and elder sisters to their paternal uncle, who was head porter at the flats. The family had all been together in the porter's lodge when the bomb fell (except for the father, who was at home in Fulham). There had been at least a hundred casualties and at least a dozen deaths in the flats, and in the porter's lodge the child's mother, sister, uncle and cousin had all been badly wounded and were now in hospital, in a serious condition. The aunt had died in the ambulance on the way to hospital, and no one had yet succeeded in finding the child's father in Fulham.

Rosemary Black wrote:

The poor wretched child, miraculously unhurt in all this carnage, had been brought into the ambulance station in a hysterical condition. That was hardly surprising. She was crying out that she wanted her Mummy with her, why had they taken her Mummy away – there had been a terrible crash and then she had screamed and then they had come and taken her away from her Mummy. She wanted to go back to her, why didn't they bring her Mummy? Her Mummy's face had been all covered with beetroot, wasn't it funny? She had eventually been more or less calmed down and spent the night on a couch at the ambulance station sleeping in between bouts of sobbing. In the morning she was still too shaken and upset to be sent home to Fulham, particularly since no one knew whether the father was at home. She started crying hysterically again at the prospect of staying on at the ambulance station, and Mrs Bone had taken the law into her own hands and brought her round here.

The trembling child was taken upstairs to be bathed and put to bed. It had been quite a night in London and there was heavy damage everywhere, and Mrs Bone poured out the story of Maida Vale and Paddington's sufferings in a gush of gory detail.

I felt sick with horror [wrote Mrs Black], at the realisation that while we had been ragging and laughing about that bomb, all this death and destruction had taken place only a stone's throw away.

Mrs Bone had been on the run all night, for Edgware Road and Marble Arch had been bombed as well as Paddington and St John's Wood, and bread-baskets of incendiary bombs had been showered all over Marylebone. Gas mains and water mains had gone, and there had been an endless inflow into the station, blood everywhere, people having hysterics, 'particularly two servant girls who shrieked and wept and laughed insanely every time bombs or barrage became noisy, driving everyone nearly as crazy as themselves.'

At one moment in the early hours of the morning Mrs Bone had asked permission to come round to the Black home to borrow Dettol and Milton and bandages, for they were running short. She had also asked if she could bring Rosemary Black and one of the maids back to act as casual labour. 'We could have helped to deal with lost children, hystericals and so on or at least done the donkey work of scrubbing away blood, boiling water for sterilisation, making cups of tea for shock cases and so on. But the answer was a lemon, needless to say.' Mrs Bone was informed that she could not be permitted to procure either help or supplies from an unofficial source, and even if the rules were waived because of the condition of acute emergency it would be impossible for her to leave her post without an official permit, which no one had the time to deal with. Rosemary Black was 'almost speechless with fury. To be kept away from such an opportunity to be really helpful and useful and valuable at such a critical time, and by what? By nothing but the everlasting barbed wire entanglements of red tape which frustrate everyone day in and day out.'

Joy Bone sighed, and cried: 'Oh, if only you knew how I was aching to have you! Oh, to have someone sensible to help!'

She went on with her tale of the night's disasters and the all-pervading disorganisation and confusion. Her fellow ambulance driver, Lennie, had rushed away from a bombed site with a badly injured girl who had died on the way to the hospital. The hospital authorities had refused to take in the body.

'She said it was impossible for her to drive about with a corpse in her ambulance,' said Mrs Bone. 'She needed the four bunks for other casualties. She said if the hospital authorities tried to put the body back in the ambulance she was just going to drive off. "Throw it in the gutter if that's the best you can do," she said, and drove away, back to where she was needed.'

But they were all feeling the strain, said Mrs Bone. So many bombs. So many sleepless nights. So much blood and suffering. Her own shift-leader, a middle-aged volunteer, was losing his voice through nerves.

Even Lennie, who is ever calm and philosophical and brave as a lion and the last hysterical person it would be possible to find, who is cool and calm and upon whom even her seniors rely, flew into a passion and cried out that she couldn't stand this sort of thing any longer and that she was going to leave the bloody ambulance station – they were risking their lives every hour of the night, and for what? They were doing hardly any good, everything was red tape and muddle, and she was going to get out of it for good and go into munitions where at least, if one risked one's life, one knew it was for some purpose.

Mrs Bone began to weep from sheer nerves and exhaustion, and was taken upstairs in her turn to be bathed and put to bed.

It was a time when nerves were fraying everywhere, and when thousands came close to despair, wondering how long they could stand the bombs and the shrapnel, not to mention the red tape. But it was a time too when many a Cockney realised what ambulance workers, air raid wardens, policemen and fire watchers were doing for them, and on the walls of many a wrecked house graffiti began to appear. But it was no longer DOWN WITH THE JEWS or THIS IS THE BOSSES' WAR or HAIL MOSLEY as it had been during the phoney war. Instead they scrawled OUR ARP WORKERS ARE WONDERFUL or OUR THANKS TO THE AFS [Auxiliary Fire Service].

One afternoon in mid-October Rosemary Black walked around the bombed streets of Maida Vale and Paddington to see what the Luftwaffe had done to it. Afterwards she wrote:

This part of the world is certainly a mess. Quite apart from the wrecked block of flats, which was the actual site of the bomb's fall, the houses between there and our house are all more or less progressively damaged. ... Everywhere doors are askew and iron railings broken and contorted, pavement stones uprooted, copings fallen away, tiles missing from roofs. Edgware Road has a huge crater only forty yards from the previous one made in it. Everything around is not only twisted and scarred but also blackened by fire. Nothing is left of the windows of the shops there but huge jagged splinters sticking out of the framework. Inside are wrecked beams and remnants of furniture ... it is a chilly scene of desolation.

And then she added:

> Yet from many broken windows and in many half-wrecked, abandoned or broken buildings and from sticks planted in bomb-craters, waved Union Jacks. The sight of the national flag flying over the ruins is for me the most moving thing of the whole war. I never felt so humbly and proudly thankful to be English as just then. How fine it is that after watching one's country gradually degenerating slowly but surely into the ranks of the second rate, to see it glorious again and to feel whole-hearted pride and joy in it. I was very nearly undone by the sight of a nine-inch square of faded tattered paper, obviously the smallest and cheapest flag available, fluttering from the gaping, twisted window of a burned-out tenement. For an awful moment I thought I was going to burst out crying in the middle of the public highway – what was left of it, that is.

On the way home she stopped at a wrecked shop which was still open for business, and there she bought a couple of Union Jacks.

> I feel I am entitled to fly a flag now that the house has sustained a slight amount of damage.

4

When the air-raid sirens first started wailing over London and news reached Holloway Prison that the East End was the principal target, most of the Fascist detainees raised a cheer and went around with smiles of triumph on their faces.

'That's right, blow the dirty Yids out of their rat-holes!' they cried, and when they could get an unfortunate refugee into a quiet corner they would dance around her, shouting: 'The Yids, the Yids, we're going to get rid of the Yids!'

But as the pattern of the blitz moved across London and the bombs began crumping down uncomfortably close to Holloway's high brick walls, the vindictive cries were heard less and less. Dolly James was scared to death whenever a raid was in progress, but she took comfort from the fact that she was not half as frightened as some of the pro-Hitler bully-girls who were sharing her incarceration. Sometimes, in the hush between the crump of the bombs, she could hear the muffled sobs from neighbouring cells where the wives of the Fascist leaders had now been gathered together.

'Don't worry, dear,' she heard one of them saying. 'He knows where we are. He'll see we don't come to any harm. He'll be needing us soon.'

By this time no one in Holloway really knew what to do about Dolly James. She had made it clear to the female Fascists that she resented their approaches, both political and amatory. On the other hand, she couldn't put up with the whining and snivelling that went on among the refugees.

'It isn't fair,' they kept saying. 'Why have they put us in here? Don't they know that we've been persecuted? Must they make us suffer more?'

All right, it wasn't fair. It wasn't fair for them and it wasn't fair for her, but what was the use of going on with it night and day? Where did it get you, except a bawling out from the wardresses and the furtive but painful kick or kneeing from the real old lags, who were exasperated by the noise and by the overcrowding which the influx of all these 'bloody traitors' had caused.

Two weeks after her arrival in prison she had been told that her appeal was to be heard by the tribunal, but a fat lot of good that did her. They listened like a trio of nervous hens to her story, but she knew from the look in the eyes of the woman member that she hadn't got a chance. When she told them of her love affair, the look on the face plainly said, 'But this woman is nothing but a common adulteress. And preferring to give her body to an enemy when she's already married to an Englishman! It is not to be endured! Lock her up and throw the key away!'

They didn't say anything of that sort to her face, of course. In fact the chairman of the tribunal, a kindly-looking lawyer whose face she had seen more than once in the newspapers, treated her quite gently. But he pointed out, mildly, that her – ahem – lover was now quite an important man in the Nazi Party, and so long as there was a danger of invasion it might not be wise, etcetera, etcetera. But he did assure her that her case would be kept under constant consideration, and in the meantime she must realise the difficult circumstances and thank her lucky stars she wasn't a German girl in Berlin facing a Nazi tribunal. Why, they would have shot her over there.

'I'm not sure I wouldn't prefer it,' she had said.

The woman member looked at her as if she ought to have her head shaved.

When she got back to Holloway she found that she had been moved out of her cell with the two German refugee girls (the big Fascist lunk had already gone off to join her ideological sisters). She was glad of that. Their constant weeping got on her nerves. Instead, although it was supposed to be against regulations, she was put in a cell with a couple of 'ordinary' prisoners. After a worrying week in which they pushed her around and jeered at her for 'getting soppy over a Jerry', they seemed to accept her. One was a thief in her middle thirties who made a speciality of walking out of stores with fur-coats under her clothes. The other was a junoesque Negro tart from Soho who was in for knifing a sailor who had tried to cheat her.

They knew the facts of prison life and they had learned how to make it bearable. They took her to the baths and rid her of the bugs she had picked up in the other cell. They had somehow got hold of extra blankets for their beds. They were allowed out at special times to empty their slops, so that their pots never overflowed and covered the floor of the cell with filth, as it had done in the other. They gave her cigarettes, of which they seemed to have plenty.

They made the terrifying nights of that autumn and winter of 1940 bearable for Dolly James, and she was grateful to them.

One night, during a week of extremely heavy raids, when it seemed almost certain that they would get a bomb on them, Dolly James' nerve went. She was lonely and despairing and, as she told herself, she had made a real bugger of her life. What hope was there for her? She began to sob.

Presently there was a movement from one of the other beds. It was the black girl. She slipped in beside her, took her in her arms, and rocked her gently, stroking the misery away.

It got her through the night, and finally she slept. But oh dear, she told herself next morning, it certainly wasn't like being comforted by a man.

5

There was a new craftsman in London now, and he worked with his nose. Some called him the 'body sniffer'. He could smell blood, and he could tell you whether it was the blood of a live or a dead Englishman.

He would wander among the rubble of a wrecked house, picking his way among the split beams, the broken furniture, the piles of bricks and the sad domestic debris of someone's home and he would snuffle like a dog. All around him wardens and rescue workers would be waiting for his signal. They knew that underneath the pile, somewhere, was a human being, trapped. For hours they had been digging their way downwards, stopping now and then to listen in the silence between the bombs for some sort of sound: a moan, heavy breathing, the knock of a fist or the scrabble of agonised fingers. And then, when no more sounds came, the 'body sniffer' would take over.

How he did it no one knew. There was enough smell around a bomb incident, heaven knows, to make it seem impossible to detect a specific odour. The bomb smell was a raw mixture of powdered brick dust, gas, sewers and smoke that got in everyone's throat and nostrils. But the 'body sniffer' would snuffle in the rubble and then whisper: 'Blood down here.'

He would press his head closer and closer into the detritus, and then he would either shake his head and say: 'Stale. It's a stiff,' or he would get very excited and shout: 'Fresh blood down here, and still flowing.'

The rescue men would move in and start the tricky work of digging down until a finger, a leg, a hand or a head would reveal the trapped soul for whom they were searching.

All over London now the rescue squads were hard at work digging, digging, for the trapped citizens of London. Though they got used to the bombing as the weeks went by, this was one fear that never left Londoners as they crouched under the stairs or lay in their shelters – the fear of being buried in the rubble and left there to die, slowly, unheard for the noise of the battle above. To most Cockneys the men of the rescue squads became some sort of super-beings, ears always cocked for the moan or the groan beneath the rubble, never willing to give up the search so long as there was the remotest chance that the body lying deep down in the cratered earth was still breathing.

In fact, they were men merely doing a job, difficult and dangerous though it may have been; and once they got used to the blitz, and to what it could do to a house and the people buried beneath it, it was a job like any other for which they would knock off work at the end of their shifts, and expect overtime if they were told to carry on. It is hardly surprising that they soon became hardened and, on the surface, at least, unfeeling, about the people they were trying to rescue.

'Shut up, you old bitch!' they would cry out in exasperation at a wretched old woman whining continuously underneath the rubble.

'All right, boys, everyone knock off. Nothing but stiffs down here!' a foreman would cry, while relatives huddled dumbly in the gloom.

John Strachey, who was an air raid warden in Chelsea, describes one incident where the rescue squads had laboured for hours to get at some victims trapped under the wreckage of a house, but the beams were too heavy and the jacks failed to move them. Each time the floor they were trying to raise would rise an inch or so, only to fall again. Strachey wrote:

> The rescue men began to feel baffled. The soaking rain was turning the rubble into a disgusting gritty paste which covered them from head to foot. The droning overhead never ceased. One of the rescue men said:
> 'Can't do nothing here – let's go'
> Another said:
> 'Shut up, you bastard, they'll hear you.'
> In this case they carried on. In some cases, when it really seemed hopeless, when the bombs began coming too close, the rescue squads moved away. But one sort of incident would keep them at work no matter what the time or the conditions overhead, and that was when they knew a child was buried beneath a building. Then they would work desperately and continuously, and if, at the end of their labours, the child was brought out dead, then their anguish was very real.*

Sometimes the digging beneath the soil of London was not for bodies but for bombs. In one of the great mid-September raids a high-explosive bomb fell very close to the south-west tower of St Paul's Cathedral. It missed the tower by a few feet and plunged through the soft sub-soil into the road outside and ended up in the clay beside the foundations of the cathedral.

Word spread through the capital from mouth to mouth (for the

* John Strachey, *Post D.*, Gollancz.

news was censored from the newspapers) that London's own beloved church, the jewel in her crown, the great Christopher Wren dome towering over the Thames and the City, was threatened. Underneath her ticked a bomb powerful enough to blow her to perdition and change the face and the skyline of London.

All through the blitz St Paul's had stayed open for the people to come in and worship, and by night and by day there had been no lack of Londoners praying beneath the dome as the bombers droned overhead. No lights could be lit in the great cathedral save for a small night-light placed on the floor immediately under the dome and from which those who walked the great spaces got their bearings. Up above a relay of vergers and choir-singers and deans walked the famous Whispering Gallery or patrolled high up in the dizzy heights of the dome itself, ready with stirrup pumps and sand-buckets to douse the incendiary bombs which were now raining down on London. Up there the view of the blitz was an awe-inspiring sight, the sky fretworked with searchlight beams, the river glinting from the fires, the earth palpitating as bombs burst and guns fired. The great dome acted as an echo chamber and the noise was like the crack of doom.

Now save for the Dean and a number of volunteers, the great cathedral was closed to all visitors. 'It has always been my great regret,' said the Dean, the Very Reverend W. R. Matthews, later, 'that we had to break our record, and that, unlike a certain famous theatre with its naked ladies, we could not claim "We never closed."'*

The bomb disposal squad, commanded by a mild looking lieutenant of the Royal Engineers named James Davies, arrived at St Paul's less than a hour after the bomb had dropped. Police had cordoned off all approaches to the cathedral and were slowing down traffic for half a mile in the streets around Ludgate Circus in case the vibrations set off the bomb. Twenty minutes later Davies had lost the services of three of his men; digging into the crater they had gone straight into a jet of gas from a broken gas-main and were knocked out instantly. Gas experts, called in to plug the leak, found a creeping gas fire coming along the pipe towards the bomb and 'for perhaps a minute or two, but not more than that, a complete evacuation was contemplated, with the cathedral thus left to its fate'. Then Dean Matthews stoutly insisted that he would, if necessary, go up with the great edifice

* The Windmill Theatre.

that was St Paul's, at which point the gas experts went back to work with extinguishers and put out the flames, and the dark hole in the ground was open once more to Lieutenant Davies and his helpers.

They found the bomb 27 feet 6 inches beneath the surface, and by that time their task had only just begun. The clay soil into which the missile had plunged had put a high polish upon it, and neither human hands nor metal clamps could get a sure grip upon its surface. It took twenty hours to put steel hawsers round one end of it, and these were then passed up to ground level and run through pulleys to two trucks working in tandem. Between them they delicately hauled the bomb from its bed in the earth, and twice the watchers all but fell on their knees and prayed because twice the hawsers snapped and the bomb slipped back. At the third attempt it came out. It was eight feet long and it weighed a ton and it was very much alive. It had enough explosive in it to raze St Paul's and quite a few buildings all around.

Lieutenant Davies was asked if he planned to defuse it there and then.

'I've a feeling it isn't that kind of a bomb,' he replied. 'All the time I've been touching it, I've sort of sensed a voice inside it shrieking to get out. I don't think we're going to stop it from going off – some time – no matter what we try.'

It was then decided to get the bomb away from St Paul's as quickly as possible. A route was quickly mapped from Ludgate Circus down the Mile End Road and through the East End to Ilford and Hackney Marshes. A call was made to Superintendent Reginald Smith of K Division to clear a route through his bailiwick and evacuate every house a hundred yards deep along every foot of the way. With extra loving care, Davies and his men loaded the bomb aboard one of the lorries and packed its side with cushions, cloths and wooden blocks to stop it from rolling. Then, with a police car leading him half a mile ahead, and a trail of other cars well behind, Davies drove (solo, for he refused to take any of his men) at top speed through the streets of the East End to Hackney Marshes.

There he exploded it a few hours later. It made a crater a hundred feet across.* St Paul's Cathedral was saved for the time being.

* It formed a convenient hollow, three and a half years later, for the erection of part of the Mulberry harbours which were assembled at Hackney Marshes and used in Normandy after D–Day 1944.

5

There was another kind of bomb that was even more terrifying than the deep, penetrating HE. The people called it a land mine. It came swinging down from the skies in an uncanny silence, dangling from the end of a great parachute. When it hit, the whole of an area for half a mile around was devastated, and windows were shattered up to ten minutes' walk away.

It was, in fact, a magnetic mine of the kind invented by the Germans for sowing in waterways used by Allied ships, as the first 'secret weapon' of World War Two. But now that the Royal Navy had found ways of 'de-gaussing' vessels against the mine's magnetic pull, it had been adapted by the Luftwaffe for land bombing. It was eight feet long, two feet in diameter, two-and-a-half tons in weight and packed with explosives. On moonlight nights (and the Germans preferred to drop them by moonlight) you could see these strange messengers of death slowly falling through the sky, and the problem was which way to run in order to escape the destruction dangling from the canopy.

In the archives of the BBC is a recording of a survivor's description of what it was like to be underneath when a landmine fell. This was the one which destroyed the Langham Hotel and most of the area around Broadcasting House, at the top of Regent Street, on 8 December 1940. The narrator (he prefers to remain anonymous) had just cycled in to work at the BBC when he heard a swishing noise in the sky, which abruptly stopped, as if in mid-air.

There was an air raid on and he looked up above, expecting incendiaries, but no fires showed. Finally he walked through the blackout to the entrance to Broadcasting House and stood there, talking to the two policemen, Vaughan and Clarke, who were on duty there.

A saloon car was parked alongside the kerb, [he remembered] and I could see to the left of the car the lamp post in the middle of the road opposite the Langham Hotel. The policemen had their backs to this, so did not observe what followed. Whilst we were conversing I noticed a large, dark, shiny object approach the lamp post and then recede. I concluded that it was a taxi parking. It made no noise. The night was clear, with a few small clouds. There was moonlight from a westerly direction, but Portland Place was mainly in shadow. All three of us were wearing our steel helmets; my chinstrap was round the back of my head.

Though he didn't know it, the shiny object he had taken for a taxi was, in fact, a huge land mine swinging by the end of its parachute from the lamp post in the middle of the road. A few seconds later, the parachute slipped and lowered the canister to the ground.

At that moment there was a very loud swishing noise, as if a plane were diving with engine cut off – or like a gigantic fuse burning. . . . Even at that moment I did not imagine that there was any danger in the road, and thought that it was coming from above, up Portland Place. My head was up watching, and before I could lie down flat the thing exploded. I had a momentary glimpse of a large ball of blinding, wild, white light and two concentric rings of colour, the inner one lavender and the outer one violet, as I ducked my head. The ball seemed to be ten to twenty feet high, and was near the lamp post.

Several things happened at once. His head was jerked back and his helmet blown away, and something hit him hard on the forehead and the nose.

The explosion made an indescribable noise – something like a colossal growl – and was accompanied by a veritable tornado of air blast. I felt an excruciating pain in my ears, and all sounds were replaced by a very loud singing noise, which I was told later was when I lost my hearing and had my eardrums perforated. I felt that consciousness was slipping from me.

He rallied and forced himself into a crouching position, feet against the kerb, hands covering his face.

I remember having to move them over my ears, [he went on], because of the pain in them. . . . This seemed to ease the pain. Then I received another hit on the forehead and felt weaker. The blast seemed to come in successive waves, accompanied by vibrations from the ground. . . . Later, in our first aid post they removed what they described as a piece of bomb from the wound. Whilst in the gutter I clung onto the kerb with both hands and with my feet against it. I was again hit in the right chest, and later found that my double-breasted overcoat, my coat, leather comb-case and papers had been cut through, and the watch in the top righthand pocket of my waistcoat had the back dented in and its works broken.

The noise, the pressure and the blast seemed endless and intolerable, but just as he felt he could bear it no longer and would go mad or burst with the tension, the torment seemed to slacken.

A shower of dust, dirt and rubble swept past me. Pieces penetrated my face, some skin was blown off, and something pierced my left thumbnail and my knuckles were cut, causing me involuntarily to let go my hold on the kerb. Instantly, although the blast was dying down, I felt myself being slowly blown across the pavement towards the wall of the building.

But eventually he staggered to his feet to find a scene around him like Dante's Inferno. The front of the building was lit by a reddish yellow light; the saloon car was on fire to the left of him, and the flames from it were stretching out towards the building – not upwards.

He went on:

A few dark huddled bodies were round about, and right in front of me were two soldiers: one, some feet from a breach in the wall of the building where a fire seemed to be raging, was propped up against the wall with his arms dangling by him, like a rag doll. The other was nearer, about twelve feet from the burning car; he was sitting up with his knees drawn up and supporting himself by his arms – his trousers had been blown off him. I could see that his legs were bare and that he was wearing short grey underpants. He was alive and conscious. I told him to hang onto an upright at the entrance and to shout like hell for assistance should he see or hear anyone approaching. I went back to look at the other soldier. He was still in the same posture and I fear he was dead. I looked around. There was a long, dark body lying prone, face downwards. ... There appeared to be one or two dark, huddled bodies by the wall of the building. I had not the strength to lift any of them. I wondered where the water was coming from which I felt dripping down my face, and soon discovered that it was blood from my head wounds.

He was one of the few survivors of a land mine which had exploded so close by. He had his wounds dressed and went to work as usual at the BBC. A bomb had already dropped on Broadcasting House earlier in the evening and its explosion was heard by listeners to the 9 o'clock news, though the announcer, Bruce Belfrage, paused only briefly in his recital of the day's happenings.

About three out of every ten of the land mines which dropped on London did not explode. They hung from trees and overhead electric wires, swinging ominously just above the ground. Sometimes they came down and still failed to explode, though in theory each one was supposed to go off fifteen seconds after impact. One family heard a clattering in their backyard in Ealing and, thinking there were incendiary bombs coming down, rushed to the kitchen door with shovels and spades to deal with them. But when they pushed at the door, it would not open. They saw why when they came round from the front into the yard: a land mine was propped up against the door.

The swinging menaces and the propped-up 'duds' had to be dealt with, and quickly. So long as they were there, untreated, as many as 3,000 people at a time had to be moved out of a district and found alternative accommodation. Ordinary high explosive bombs were dealt with by Army engineers like Lieutenant Davies, who had dug out the bomb at St Paul's, but magnetic mines were much more complicated, and only the Navy knew how to deal with them.

That was where the trouble started. The Navy was used to magnetic mines dropping in the sea, and their experts were stationed in naval ports and bases. When the monsters came silently toppling down on London, there was no expert to deal with them. And that was how a Cambridge professor temporarily enrolled in the Navy, Commander Peter Danckwerts, found himself having a number of unwilling but intimate affairs with a series of magnetic mines.

Danckwerts had already seen one of the mines and had had its mechanism explained to him by an expert from the Admiralty. It seemed that when a magnetic mine fell on land the fuse inside it started buzzing for fifteen seconds, and then it went off. But

sometimes the fuse buzzed for only a few seconds and then stuck
– but would start buzzing again if you moved it around.

The important thing when dealing with these mines, [said
Danckwerts], if you had to move them at all before you took
the fuse out, was to listen very carefully all the time, and if
you heard it buzzing to run like hell, because you might have
up to fifteen seconds to get away.*

But there were other complications. The monster was full of
gadgets. It had an electric detonator at the bottom of a hole at the
side of the mine which was the devil's own job to get at. Opposite
this was another hole, and when you unscrewed this there was a
whoof and out shot a spring, a yard long – a scaring experience the
first time it happened. Then there was the top of the huge cylinder
which had to be screwed off, and underneath was a perspex cover
through which the time clock and all the connecting wires could
be seen. These had to be cut. The right ones – in the right order.

It wasn't his job at the time to worry about magnetic mines,
but Danckwerts was interested and he took one of the fuses back
with him to his headquarters in the Port of London Authority,
down on the docks. He and his torpedo officer and the third
member of his team, a petty officer in the regular Navy, studied
the fuse, took it to pieces, and put it together again.

It was just as well they did.

That night, at the height of the big raids on South London, his
telephone rang. ARP headquarters reported that three parachute
mines had dropped in their area and that the Army bomb disposal
officer had refused to touch them. They were mines, and all mines
were the Navy's affair. The ARP controller asked Danckwerts if
he would come over at once.

Danckwerts explained that mines were not his speciality, and
that experts would have to be got hold of.

'Oh, my God, who deals with mines?' asked the controller.

'I'm afraid the nearest people are down in Portsmouth,'
Danckwerts said.

'That's all very well,' replied the controller, 'but I've got several
thousand people evacuated around these mines. I can't wait for
people to come up from Portsmouth.'

* Commander Danckwerts' account is in the archives of the BBC.

Danckwerts promised to do what he could to speed things up. What he did, in fact, was ring Portsmouth and get permission to tackle the mines himself. He told the mine experts that he thought he could handle the job, and was given reluctant permission.

He went and woke his torpedo officer and his Chief Petty Officer, and they agreed at once to go with him. 'They were both very good with gadgets and getting difficult things unscrewed and so on,' he said. 'Of course we didn't have any of the proper tools for this job. One was supposed to have non-magnetic tools, quite apart from which most of the things were very hard to unscrew unless you had tools of the right shape. But we got a lot of screwdrivers and, most important of all, we took a ball of string, that is the essential thing for bomb disposal.'

It was a hell of a night at the height of the blitz, and South London, to which they drove, was a nightmare scene of roads blocked with bomb craters, wrecked trams and buses, blazing gas mains, exploding bombs and crashing anti-aircraft guns. It took them a long time to find the first landmine. Finally they saw a man walking along the street in pyjamas and dressing-gown, carrying a suitcase, and decided he might be fleeing from the mine. He was. He took them back to show them where it was, lying among some bushes in a garden, the parachute draped over the next-door wall.

We went up and had a look at it with our torch, [said Danckwerts], and we found unfortunately that the all-important fuse was underneath, so we'd have to roll it round before we could get it out. My Chief Petty Officer and I rolled it very, very cautiously indeed while the third member of the party kept his ear as close to it as he could and listened to see if it buzzed.

It didn't. So next they unscrewed the fuse. But they didn't take it out. Not yet. The Germans had started setting booby traps for bomb disposal experts, and nowadays they would place a trigger fuse under the ordinary fuse, so that when you took out the ordinary fuse the other one went off.

So, having loosened it, Danckwerts looped some of his ball of string around it and then motioned his companions to follow him over the wall into the next garden, and then round the back of the house and into the street beyond; and only after they had unreeled about a hundred yards of string, all the time keeping it just short of taut, did he pause.

Then he yanked on the string. Nothing happened, except that the string seemed to pull back and forth like elastic, without coming away. It had caught round a rose bush. He crawled back and freed it, then took up his old position – and this time the string came away. When they went back, the fuse was lying on the ground. Danckwerts picked it up, gingerly, walked a few yards and then threw it to the ground. There was a pause and then a sharp crack. The fuse was still sensitive, all right.

Then a smoke and back to the job of taking the mine's mechanism to pieces. After which (covered in soot by this time, for mines were blackened by the Germans to stop them glinting if a searchlight caught them hanging under a plane) they set off in search of the others.

It took some time in a blacked-out London lit only by bomb-fires over routes pitted with bomb craters. The second mine they eventually found standing upright in the middle of a recreation ground. They edged up to it, put down their tools while they examined it, and lost their tools. After scrambling around fumbling vainly in the grass, they left and found a bus depot and broke into the emergency toolkit there; and that mine was rendered harmless with spanners normally used to mend an ordinary London bus.

The final one was in a field just beside a gasworks. 'The sun was up by then,' said Danckwerts, 'it was a sunny morning and we had a large, interested crowd which had to be held back by volunteers while we dealt with it. So by this time we'd done three mines and we had a parachute each as a souvenir, which we were very happy about, and a lot of miscellaneous explosives. . . . We went home very pleased with ourselves.'

Danckwerts and his team were made official 'land mine disposal experts' after that. They dealt with a dozen mines before being called off.* A dozen was considered the limit a team should risk their lives to deal with. Their worst moments came when the mines buried themselves on roofs or in the upper storeys of houses, and they didn't have a chance to run if the fuse started buzzing.

His jumpiest moment came when he fitted his beloved ball of

* Commander Danckwerts was awarded a George Cross for his work.

string to a mine-fuse and then spun it out from the house where the monster was embedded across the road to the protection of a building across the way. But before he could pull the string it was yanked out of his hand.

'God, it's going off!' cried one of his team, and they flung themselves flat.

Instead there was a silence, broken by a clanking sound from the road. An air raid warden had walked past, kicked the string and pulled out the fuse, and was dragging it along behind him.

All over London now, men were tinkering with land mines and high explosive bombs which had failed to explode, but might go off at any moment. Royal Engineers were grubbing in the mud beneath Waterloo Bridge and in the noisome sewers of Stratford-atte-Bow. Naval experts had five terrifying hours standing on top of a half-filled gasometer over the lip of which a landmine hung by the fraying guidelines of a torn parachute. Two days later the War Office in Whitehall and several other Government offices had to be evacuated because a landmine had landed on Hungerford Bridge, which ran across the Thames from Charing Cross Station. Rendering it harmless was made agonisingly more difficult because the heat of an electrified line had welded the mine to the rails. Half official London held its breath while Captain Roberts from the Admiralty embarked on the long, tedious, perilous job of cutting it free.

6

By mid-September 1940, even Reich Marshal Hermann Goering accepted the fact that his Luftwaffe had failed to sweep the RAF out of the skies. Since the destruction of Britain's air defences was a prerequisite for the invasion of the United Kingdom, Adolf Hitler angrily told his generals to postpone 'Operation Sea Lion.'*

There was, however, no halt to the bombing, which continued relentlessly. The first heavy daylight raids had proved so costly that they had now been abandoned, but night attacks increased in intensity. Every part of London now wore the scars of bombs: Leicester Square, Piccadilly and Shaftesbury Avenue, Buckingham

* 'Sea Lion' was the code name for the landing in Britain.

Palace, the Houses of Parliament, 10 Downing Street, the great department stores in Oxford Street, all the main-line stations, the docks, Marble Arch and Trafalgar Square (where though Nelson still stood atop his column, one of the lions on guard at his feet had lost a nose).

Londoners who queued to shelter in the Underground stations each evening were beginning to discover why London officials had tried (but in vain) to stop their use. It was not just that they were noisome and insanitary from lack of lavatory accommodation; that many of them were soon flea-ridden and crawling with lice; that some of the deeper ones had a mosquito problem that winter because the insects, attracted by the foetid air, decided not to leave. Many of them were also downright dangerous. Lines ran under the Thames and were vulnerable to tunnel falls, and flooding. Floodgates had been installed to isolate sections of tunnelling in case of breach by water, with heavy gates operated electrically. But when bombs knocked out the electrical system, the gates would not close, and then there was disaster.

Those underground stations which were only a short distance beneath the surface of London provided only psychological protection for those who filed down to them each evening, and even that comfort was no longer available by the end of October. By that time Trafalgar Square, Bounds Green, Praed Street and Balham tube stations had all received direct hits. The worst of these was Balham.

Though the shelterers did not realise it, Balham Underground was, in fact, one of the most vulnerable spots in London. It was only some twelve yards below the surface of the street, and above it was a vast cobweb of water pipes, main sewers, electric and telephone cables and gas pipes. On the night of 14 October a bomb dropped just short of the station. Six hundred and eighty people were sheltering on the platform below.

The bomb smashed the water, the sewer and the gas pipes and first a trickle and then a flood of water and sewage began to pour in. The electric lights went out. The smell of gas was everywhere, and women and children began to scream. Soon water was welling up the emergency stairs, and the panic in the swirling stinking blackness had begun. . . .

But Londoners continued to believe in the Underground shelters, and so long as they did so it was up to the authorities to

make them safe and sanitary. So the deepest of them were reinforced and strengthened and flood gates made proof against bombs
and power failures. Lavatory systems were organised and canteens
moved in. At one of the most efficiently run, Aldwych, just off the
Strand, there was even nightly entertainment from actors working
in adjacent theatres.

One man who narrowly missed being involved in the Balham
Station incident was George Hitchin, bus driver for the London
Passenger Transport Board. These days he often remembered his
wife's remark the year before, when he told her driving a tank was
better than taking a double-decker bus out in the blackout.

'At least they won't be shooting at you while you're in a bus,'
Flo had said.

But for the past month that is just what they had been doing.
The Vauxhall route was absolute murder. You could never be
sure of the route, because it was always getting blocked by bomb
craters or collapsing buildings. You couldn't see a thing by the
slits of light from the headlamps, and there was every kind of
obstacle in the way, from beds blown out of bombed houses to
potential passengers, stepping out into the road at the last moment
and expecting you to see them. And practically every night was
bomb night on the Vauxhall route, with raids all the way and
shrapnel rattling on the roof like hailstones.

On the night of October 14 George Hitchin was taking it easy
along the Balham High Road when his new conductress, Arlene,
rang the bell and he pulled up to the kerb. Ahead of them the sky
had suddenly gone almost as bright as day. A plane overhead had
dropped a cluster of flares which hung in the sky, bathing the
black buildings in a dazzling glare.

Arlene had come through the dimmed out bus and spoke
through the communicating window.

'What do we do now?' she asked. Everybody knew enough
about bombing by now to know that flares in the sky meant that
bombs would be coming down any moment. But Arlene had been
on the buses for only a few days, and this was her first trip after
dark.

'We get on,' George said. 'We're late already.'

It was a matter of pride these days to try to keep to the time schedules laid down for the routes, despite the detours down back streets and unknown highways.

'Okay,' the girl said, brightly. One thing, George decided, she didn't sound scared. She rang the bell and they went on down the High Street.

About a quarter of a mile ahead, in the glare of the flares, he could see the red shine of another bus ahead of him, and suddenly it began to dance up and down as if somebody were manipulating it with a piece of string. The deep crash of an exploding bomb sounded ahead, and then there was an uprush of smoke and earth, and he could see the bus ahead literally bouncing. He stamped on the brakes and stopped, and sat there for a moment, wondering what to do. No further bombs fell, so he let off the brake – he had kept the engine running – and began to edge forward down the road. It was suddenly very silent.

Then it happened. The bus ahead of him had come to rest in the middle of the road, and now it suddenly began to sink into the road. It had, in fact, sunk to its rooftop into the main shaft of Balham Underground Station. . . .

That night, as he recounted the extraordinary happening to his wife, telling her how they had helped in the rescue, and what 'a plucky little kid' his new conductress, Arlene, had turned out to be, he noticed that Flo was silent and unresponsive.

'I don't think it's right,' she said, finally.

'What's not right?'

'Having girls on the buses,' Flo said. 'They can't be half as good as the men.'

'But the men have been called up, love,' he said. 'Besides, it isn't true. The girls do the job fine – and they've lots of guts. All the drivers say so.'

Flo shook her head. 'They'll cause trouble,' she said. 'You just see if they don't.'

'Nonsense,' said George, cheerfully. 'They don't make any difference at all. We treat them like mates – just as if they were men.'*

* Mates, maybe, but not quite like men. Mrs Flo Hitchin was killed in the great raid on London on 16 April, 1941. George Hitchin married his conductress the following summer.

7

One of those for whom a bomb on an underground station solved an insuperable problem was Mrs Sally Thomas.

It was now more than a year since she had seen her husband, Jimmy, off to Egypt. Quite a lot had happened to her since. For one thing, she had found she couldn't keep the kids and herself on Jimmy's Army allowance. For another, she had discovered that you could get terribly lonely when your husband was overseas – and no prospect of his return for months or even years.

That was the real cause of the trouble she was in now.

On 17 September 1940 she was walking past Lyons Corner House at Marble Arch when the anti-aircraft barrage started in Hyde Park and policemen started herding passers-by into the tube station. Sally tried to elbow her way through and walk on, but the crowd swept her down the steps and finally down to the station platform below.

She was slightly the worse for drink and didn't particularly care what happened to her. That afternoon she had been to the adoption society in the Marylebone Road and got fairly polite treatment from a woman official until it came to filling in the papers.

'Of course,' the woman had said, 'you will have to have these papers countersigned by your husband.' Seeing the expression on Sally's face, she went on: 'You just can't have your child-to-be adopted, you know, unless the father consents.'

There was a pause. The woman's manner changed.

'I see,' she said. 'Your husband isn't the father.' She sighed, heavily. 'I'm afraid his consent is still necessary, just the same, and until we get it there is nothing we can do.'

Sally had got up to go to the door.

'You've forgotten the papers,' the woman said. 'Don't you think he ought to know what you've been doing?'

She spent the rest of the week's allowance in a pub in George Street on gin and tonics and then accepted a couple of rums-and-ginger from a man at the bar; it would have been more if he hadn't suddenly caught sight of her stomach and abruptly left the pub. When she came out herself she could walk quite steadily but was no longer worrying either about the kids back home in Pimlico or the one burgeoning inside her. Everything seemed suddenly full of hope.

All right, I will send the papers to him, she told herself. *If Jimmy loves me, he'll understand. It was only one night, I was lonely, I needed a drink and I had no money, and then this fellow . . .*

' 'Ere, ducks,' said a woman on the Marble Arch station platform, 'come and sit beside me on this cushion and make yourself comfortable.'

That was the moment when the bomb hit.

The bomb on Marble Arch station on 17 September caused one of the unluckiest tragedies of the blitz. It was only a small bomb, and Marble Arch station, heavily reinforced against the enormous weight of traffic overhead, was considered one of the safest in London. But the nose cap of the bomb found a tiny hole between two girders and exploded.

The force ripped along the corridor of the station with a fantastic impact. Eighteen people were killed by blast alone. There wasn't a mark on them when the rescuers found them, but they were all stark naked. Others were killed and injured by the tiles which the force of the explosion tore off the walls and turned into sharp bullets which tore into flesh and bone.

'There were forty known casualties, of whom over twenty were dead,' wrote William Sansom in *Westminster At War**. 'The shocked amounted to many more. It was a bewildering, dreadful time; and it is remembered at the Report Centre that when one rescue leader, a strong man and a good worker, telephoned his message – through his words he was sobbing.'

Sally Thomas was among the ones who survived the blast but were wounded by the flying tiles. When she woke up in St George's Hospital the following evening she realised that she wouldn't have to worry about the adoption papers any more.

It would be untrue to say that anyone ever 'got used' to the air raids, but, as C. P. Snow put it, 'it began to seem quite minor if there were bombs in your actual neighbourhood but not on your actual house'. Nevertheless, within two months of the start of the blitz only 22 per cent of London's population were still sleeping regularly in public shelters, and Cockneys were learning to believe and be proud of the slogan now chalked on the walls: LONDON CAN TAKE IT. What was remarkable was the small amount of

* Faber, 1947.

absenteeism in workshops, offices, docks and warehouses, especially if it is borne in mind that hardly a night passed without a warning and a raid and from late evening until dawn the anti-aircraft barrage was banging away with teeth-chattering persistence.

The anti-aircraft barrage in 1940 can hardly be said to have been effective in bringing down enemy planes (it probably knocked out more civilians from falling shrapnel). Nor did it improve as the weeks went by, for so many shells were being fired that the barrels of the guns were wearing out. But Londoners liked the noise and Churchill told General Pile, who commanded the anti-aircraft defences, to 'keep on shooting away regardless'. People became worried when the guns held back to give the night fighters a chance to cut in on the Nazi formations. They preferred the noisy ineffectiveness of the guns to the fumbling operations of the RAF's night fliers,* and they refused to blot out the reassuring but deafening thunder of the barrage with earplugs now being issued free by the Government. As a result, they didn't get much sleep at nights. A poll taken at the beginning of October 1940 which asked Londoners how much sleep they had had the night before got these answers:

None	31 per cent;
Less than 4 hours	32 per cent;
4–6 hours	22 per cent;
More than 6 hours	15 per cent.

Yet next morning they were back at the bench or the typewriter, some with the marks of the bombing still on them. 'Ivy Crouch burst in with bag and baggage,' wrote Vere Hodgson, 'having been bombed out of the Three Arts Club at Marble Arch. She spent the night in a public shelter.' Yet Ivy Crouch had come to work. The big stores hit on a Friday night along Oxford Street were back in business on Monday morning lacking only those members of their staff who had been killed or wounded in the raid.

Though all London was now affected by the bombing and the Government could accurately say, 'We're all in it together, rich and poor alike,' it was still the Cockneys in the East End who were suffering the most, and it was here that there was resentment and widespread rumblings of discontent. They were the same bombs. They contained the same amount of explosives and they came

* Whose planes had not yet been fitted with radar for night interception.

down with the same terrifying swish and were aimed with the same lack of discrimination. But the fact remains that it was still better to be bombed in the West End than in the East End of London. You had a better chance of survival. And, having survived, you were better looked after.

At a moment when London was getting its worst drubbing, Henry Channon wrote in his diary (5 November 1940):

Harold [Balfour, Minister for Air] fetched me, and drove me to the Dorchester, where we dined with the Elvedens, a large party with Peggy Dunne, sweet Nell Stavordale and others. Half London seemed to be there. The [Duff and Lady Diana] Coopers were next to us, entertaining the Walter Elliots. ... Oliver Lyttleton, our new President of the Board of Trade, was throwing his weight and his wit about. He and his wife were dining with the Lloyd Georges, the Gwylyms. ... It was exhilarating. I gave Bob Boothby a champagne cocktail in the private bar, which now looks, seems and smells like the Ritz bar in Paris, rue Cambon. Our bill must have been immense for we had four magnums of champagne. London lives well; I've never seen more lavishness, more money spent, or more food consumed than tonight, and the dance floor was packed. There must have been a thousand people. Leaving, Harold and I wore our tin hats, and the cloakroom attendant said to me, without a trace of a smile, 'You have a screw loose, sir, in your hat – if you can wait I'll send for the engineer.' We left the modern wartime Babylon and got quickly into Harold's Air Force car. The contrast between the light and gaiety within, and the blackout and the roaring guns outside was terrific: but I was more than a little drunk.

This was life under the bombs in the West End. It was danger-ous and people got killed. But somehow it was different from what the mass of the people were experiencing.

In the West End the stores, the restaurants, the cafés were back in action within a few hours of the raids. Gas and water mains were reconnected and essential services resumed. The milkman did his rounds. The newspapers arrived.

But it didn't seem to happen like that in the East End, and the people there were slowly coming to the conclusion that nobody 'up West' cared a damn so long as the Cockneys stayed quiet. Districts like Stepney had become devastated areas. What houses were still standing had no gas, no light and no water. Reception shelters for the homeless were hopelessly inadequate. Cafés were shut and pubs boarded up. Schools had either been bombed out or closed. Deep shelters were non-existent. True, the tunnel whose foetid disorder had so nauseated Superintendent Reginald Smith had been cleaned up and equipped with latrines and canteens, but it could only cope with a fraction of the local population. The rest of them trekked every night with their belongings to the West End to queue for tickets to Leicester Square and Holborn and Piccadilly Underground stations, and were stared at as they waited in the rain by passing office workers with what they took to be amused contempt.

'More and more people around here are crying for peace,' wrote Robert Nichols, an armaments worker in South East London. 'They don't care what ensues so long as the bombing ceases. They've been too mollycoddled and flattered these last few years and they have no reserve of self-reliance. The limit of endurance of some women has already been reached by having to spend a night in a cold shelter.'

This was both harsh and inaccurate. To describe the average slum-dweller in Poplar or Bow or Whitechapel, often out of a job, trying to bring up children in a noisome rat-ridden house, as 'mollycoddled' was sheer fantasy. The Cockneys of East London were reacting in the same way, and showing the same guts, as anyone 'up West'. But that they were fed up with the way they were being neglected there was no doubt. The jagged wrecks whose appearance so galvanised the artistic instincts of Henry Moore were their homes, and if their condition had been miserable before it was appalling now.

In the circumstances it is amazing how few of them actually rose up in protest. In fact there was only one demonstration of any size during the whole of the blitz in London, and this happened in September 1940, in Stepney. Stepney had two Communist activists among its more prominent citizens. One was their local Member of Parliament, Phil Piratin, thin, burningly intense. The other was chairman of the Stepney Tenants' Defence League, 'Tubby' Rosen, fat and jolly, except when he was goading the capitalists. For both Piratin and Rosen this was not, of course, their war at all; not for the moment, anyway. Russia still relied upon its pact with Germany and was not yet involved in the war; and the Party line in Britain was the same as Moscow's, that the bosses rather than Germany were the enemy. The two Communists stressed at their street corner meetings that so far as the blitz was concerned, they were being treated as second-class citizens.

'Our people are dying like rats here in Stepney,' shouted Tubby Rosen at a meeting in Commercial Road, 'and why? Because the Tory bosses refused us the money that was needed to build deep shelters for our protection. So while we crawl into the surplus hen houses they call street shelters, which wouldn't even protect a rooster from the rain, up West the Government's rich friends and *their* girl friends sleep cosy in double beds, two to a compartment, in their own private deep shelters. Comrades, it's about time we took them over!'

Now it so happened that most of the big hotels in the West End of London had made arrangements to turn their basements into air-raid shelters for their customers, and none had done it more efficiently than the Savoy Hotel. Several storeys of the hotel had been dug into the ground when it was built, and these were reinforced. One portion of the River Room was kept as a restaurant and cabaret, and had quickly become one of the gayest spots in blitz-time London. The other was divided by curtains into dormitories for singles, cubicles for couples, and a separate section for snorers. Down below there were more rooms once reserved for private parties and now turned into guest-shelters. (The Abraham Lincoln Room was, for a time, kept for the Duke and Duchess of Kent, when the former came down on leave from the RAF; he was killed in 1941.)

The Savoy Hotel was therefore an obvious target for a demonstration, especially since it was the nearest big and fashionable hotel to the East End. Piratin and Rosen also knew that most US newspapers now made the Savoy their headquarters, that half the editors in Fleet Street called there at least once a day, that it was a favourite eating place for members of the Cabinet, and two of the most amusing gossips in London, Lady Asquith* and Lady

---

* Lady Asquith wore her own special form of battledress, which consisted of a floor length evening gown and train with white Russian boots underneath.

Diana Cooper, were always to be seen there. So a hundred rebels were recruited and told that the Stepney Tenants' Defence League was about to march on the Savoy.

'We'll be in all the papers tomorrow,' said Tubby, happily.

Unfortunately, they timed their protest march badly. It was not until six o'clock in the evening that the US pianist Caroll Gibbons and his orchestra began to play in the restaurant, not until eight p.m. that the cabaret began, and not until ten that US and Fleet Street correspondents gathered in the bar. And usually it was later than that when the pyjama- and battle-dressed guests went down to the cubicles below for jig-saw puzzles, crosswords, and other fun and games.

The Stepney protesters arrived shortly after noon. The Savoy Hotel's historian, whose attitude to the demonstration is not exactly sympathetic, reported what followed in this way:

> Wendell Wilkie, who had come over to observe British morale and report to his government on Lease Lend, was almost due to arrive for luncheon with Sir Harry McGowan and other business leaders when a crowd of angry women, yelling Communist slogans, marched from the forecourt into the lobby and made determinedly for the restaurant. Some opened their fur coats to reveal incongruous banners proclaiming 'Our children are Starving' and 'Ration the Rich', and a number had even arrived in taxis to storm the barricades.*

It seems hardly likely that Piratin and Rosen, both good window-dressers if not time-keepers, would have dressed their women in fur coats or brought them in taxis. Even comfortably off middle-class women possessed few fur coats in Britain in 1940. Stanley Jackson, the historian in question, seems to have been misled by the bulky appearance of the young women who led the demonstrators. Most of them were pregnant, and had been told to flaunt the fact. Porters were less likely to be rough with them. Jackson goes on:

> A warning from Hansen, the head porter, led to prompt action by 'Willy' Hifflin, the newly appointed general manager, who deployed porters to repel the invaders. Hugh Wontner [the managing director] was also quickly on the scene and ordered that the doors leading to the restaurant should be closed. Half

* Stanley Jackson, *The Savoy*, Muller, 1964.

the women were thus cut off from those who had in the meantime sat themselves down at the tables with arms folded, screaming abuse or demanding to be served with food. Others wrapped themselves round pillars, tied their scarves to chairs and clawed at waiters who asked them to leave.

It went off rather more calmly and with more English phlegm than this. True, an hotel servant panicked and sent for the police and demanded that the protesters be thrown out.

'I'm afraid I can't see my way to doing that, sir,' said the police sergeant. 'You're an hotel, you see, sir. You come under the Innkeepers' Act. If a bona fide traveller comes in and asks for a meal, and these people look like bona fide travellers to me, then they've a right to be served. Now if they're making a row, or breaking things, or doing a mischief, that kind of thing, then we'll be willing to escort them off the premises, but otherwise, so far as we are concerned, they're clients of the hotel and have a right to be treated as such.'

Piratin and Rosen had gambled on the fact that an air raid would still be in progress when they arrived at the Savoy and they had begun their march up the Strand to the hotel the moment the sirens sounded. Once inside the hotel they then had a quite justified right to be taken down to the shelters with all the debs, hostesses, Cabinet Ministers and millionaires who usually used them. Unfortunately, they hadn't realised that no one ever used the shelters during daylight alerts, which were no longer serious. Furthermore, as luck would have it, this day's daylight raid was uncommonly short and the all-clear sounded while they were still milling around the foyer.

They could only now stay on legitimately if they marched into the bar and ordered drinks or into the restaurant and ordered food. But one glance at the restaurant menus quickly told them that meals were beyond their means, and neither Piratin and Rosen were willing to use Party funds to feed them. So they filed quietly out into the Strand again and the demonstration fizzled out. It had been wrongly timed. A night demonstration and occupation of the Savoy's dormitories at the height of a big raid would have made all the difference.

British newspapers, once they learned that the protest was Communist inspired, buried the story. Most American newspapermen missed it and filed the story second hand. Only the Nazi newspapers picked it up from agency dispatches and exaggerated it into a wild workers' riot against the Government.

It was the only protest march in London during the whole of the blitz, and failed to make its legitimate point because of its political inspiration.

The demonstrators marched back to the bleak acres of Stepney and the world of boarded up cafés, beerless pubs, broken sewers and the stench of ruptured gas mains. Several weeks later people 'up West' began to take notice, and the mobile canteens, the Government-run British restaurants, and squads of dedicated women moved in and gradually turned the East End back into a civilised place.

8

A NOISY WINTER

I

For C. P. Snow 1940 was an agonising year. It so happened that he was one of those who, somewhat to his own surprise, and certainly to his discomfiture, found himself frightened by the bombing. He has written in one of his books:

> As long as I lived, I also knew a different fear, one of which I was more ashamed, a fear of being killed. When the bombs began to fall on London, I discovered that I was less brave than the average man. I was humiliated to find it so. I could just put some sort of face on it, but I dreaded the evening coming, could not sleep, was glad of an excuse to spend a night out of town. It was not always easy to accept one's nature. Somehow one expected the elementary human qualities. It was unpleasant to find them lacking.*

He sympathised with those who shared his fears and deprecated the word-of-mouth condemnation then going round London of a famous be-knighted actor who had walked off the stage in the middle of an air raid out of sheer panic.† He knew exactly what he had been feeling. Snow envied the Londoners all around him who were so much less frightened then he was.

> My landlady in Pimlico, for instance, was as brave as a lion. So were the clerks in the office, those I met in the pubs in Pimlico, and most of my friends. It made me feel worse.

The daylight bombing he had not taken seriously and he soon gave up going to the cellar shelter in his office in Tothill Street.

> It was no good at all, really. I remember an old civil servant telling me that there was a plan to evacuate certain departments

* *The Light and the Dark*, Faber, 1947.
† Though he certainly did not approve of the actor's subsequent behaviour in getting himself sent to Cairo by ENSA and making his way to the safety of South Africa.

A million mothers and children were evacuated from London when war began. Some children, suitably labelled with their names and destinations, travelled in batches with their schoolteachers.

After the fall of France a great round-up of aliens and refugees was carried out. Young women and men up to the age of 70 were taken to jail and then to camps in the Isle of Man or shipped to Canada. Some, as this picture shows, were Nazis and Fascists, but the bulk were innocent refugees from Hitler's terror, victimised by a panicky Government.

For the first year of war everyone carried gas-masks, to work, to dances, to bed. Even babies had their own special masks.

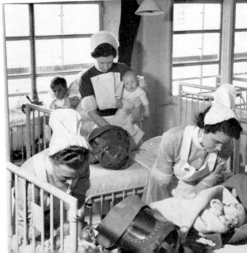

For most Londoners the worst inconvenience of the phoney war was the blackout. White-painted lamp-posts slightly mitigated the perils of after-dark navigation through the streets.

Just in case they couldn't hear the siren (deaf people, for instance), police would often cycle through the streets telling Londoners a raid was on.

TITTLE TATTLE LOST THE BATTLE

Left:

There was never a 'phoney war' at sea, where German U-boats were lying in wait for every British convoy. A huge propaganda campaign was launched against careless talk that might give away shipping movements. September 1940 was the date when the Germans were expected to invade Britain, and before that date a campaign was launched to persuade the civilian population to 'stay put' and leave the roads clear for the defending British soldiers and tanks. This was one of the many advertisements appearing in the national newspapers. A typical British touch: its cost was paid for by the makers of Britain's beer.

Right:

A barrage of balloons flew over London and other big cities to protect them from low-level raids by German planes. The great gas-filled monsters yawed and strained at the trucks to which they were anchored, sometimes broke loose in high winds or were fired by lightning during storms, but kept the enemy from machine-gunning or dive-bombing London's streets.

Below:

The tracer-pattern of shells searching the London skies for a flying bomb in 1944.

Most Londoners with a small garden erected an Anderson shelter in it, and these reinforced steel hutches (capable of sheltering six people) were extremely effective, as the picture above taken after a raid shows.

Once the big raids began, Londoners (especially East Enders who had no place to put their own shelters) flocked to the safety of the Underground stations, where they slept on the platforms.

Conditions in shelters and Underground stations were chaotic to begin with, but they were soon organised and regular places and bunks assigned to ticket-holders – providing they behaved.

WAY OUT

This ticket may be withdrawn at the Controller's discretion at any time, and will be if <u>any</u> of the following things happen :—

(a) The shelter ceases to be available ;
(b) The holder of this ticket or any member of his family commit any offence or creates any nuisance or disturbance in the shelter, or fails to do his share in keeping the shelter tidy and clean ;
(c) This ticket is produced by any one other than the registered holder ;
(d) The shelter is not used by the holder for four consecutive days without explanation to chief marshal ;
(e) The holder disregards any lawful order or request of a police officer, shelter marshal or other authorised officer ;
(f) The holder fails to remove from the shelter all bedding and personal belongings as and when required for shelter-cleansing purposes, etc.

Most of Britain's young women were
called up during the war, and the chief
attraction was the women's services. This
picture shows representatives of the ATS
(women's section of the Army), the
WRNS (Women's Royal Naval Service),
and WAAFs (Women's Air Force)
seeking recruits in a big store in London.
Also in the picture (*left*) is a representative
of the Women's Land Army, which
wasn't half so popular.

St. Paul's Cathedral and the City in the aftermath of one of the great raids.

Overleaf: The great land-mines and oil-bombs exploded and spread the fires over London. The city by night seemed as light as day.

Holborn Circus at the height of a 1941 raid.

Blasts from bombs did extraordinary things to men and, as this picture shows, to the buses in which they were travelling.

The great terror for most Londoners during the Blitz was that they might be buried under their bombed homes. Rescue squads were organised to dig them out, and they laboured on so long as they could hear a movement or a whimper underneath the rubble.

Sometimes whole areas were evacuated because of unexploded bombs, with policemen standing guard to keep out householders who might be tempted to go back for that forgotten bottle of whisky or packet of cigarettes.

Hot meals were organised for victims and rescue squads; they were rushed to the bomb sites by the vans or the WVS (Women's Voluntary Service), who stayed on the job whether raids were in progress or not.

Right:
   The Germans did not deliberately try to bomb hospitals, but practically every hospital in London was hit sooner or later.

Stations were bombed and lines torn up during the blitz, but somehow the trains still got through and the commuters from the suburbs still travelled up to their offices.

But often the city streets through which they walked from their bombed stations to their offices had changed drastically overnight.

Above:
Business went on as usual in the City. This picture was taken sixty feet underground beneath Lloyd's of London during a raid.

Right:
Until the American troops arrived in Britain, the biggest contingent of foreign troops in Britain belonged to the Polish Army-in-exile. This picture shows them on Polish National Day, 1941, celebrating mass in Westminster Cathedral.

Below:
The great gathering–place for American troops in London was Rainbow Corner, Piccadilly, where the American Red Cross had set up a club for GIs. Inside there were canteens, a theatre and stalls to which every famous name in show business came at one time or another to entertain or lend a hand; but for many a GI the chief place of entertainment was outside watching the girls go by.

London crowds awaiting the official announcement of VE Day and the long–awaited fact that the war with Germany was over. Scenes got much wilder later on, though the bulk of Londoners received the news quietly but thankfully.

The V1s or Doodlebugs (unmanned planes filled with explosives)
began falling on London in the summer of 1944, and were followed by
V2s (rockets). They were Hitler's secret weapons and although they did
not prolong the war they made the last months painfully hard for
Londoners to bear.

if the bombing got too fierce or invasion came, but, he added, your department can't be evacuated and, anyway, the PM is determined that we are all to die in the last ditch, and no one can say him nay.'

But night bombing troubled him, and his friend Professor P. M. S. Blackett, who was an expert on such things*, calculated that the safest place for Snow was the fourth floor of a block of steel and concrete buildings in Pimlico called Dolphin Square, and found him an apartment there. Dolphin Square was solidly bombed a few nights after Snow moved in (it was built beside the Thames) and got another direct hit later, but the novelist-turned-civil-servant stayed where he was, obviously not wanting to hurt Blackett's feelings.

The fear of being killed was, however, something that Snow could learn to live with. What agonised him much more was a less personal fear – he was simply afraid that Britain was going to lose the war. He envied the ordinary British citizen who could say, so proudly and confidently, 'Now that France is out and we are alone, we can get on with winning the war.' At the same time he resented this cheerful, thoughtless, invincible optimism, because he himself believed that the betting was at least 5:1 against Britain.

He would come back late at night from his office and fumble his way into his darkened apartment in Dolphin Square and watch the searchlights along the Thames vainly probing the sky for Nazi bombers droning overhead. Somewhere up there night-fighters of the RAF were searching too, and the result was almost always as futile. The bombers were having it almost all their own way, and the defenders were still flying blind. But at least he knew that up there in the hostile sky the balance would soon be changing, and soon it would be the bomber crews who would begin to tremble when they entered British air space. The radar system which had guided the RAF to their targets in the summer of 1940 and helped so much to win the Battle of Britain was in process of rapid development, and already the first prototypes were being fitted into night fighters. Soon their pilots would really

---

* He was the scientist, for example, who discovered that 'France is not quite where we thought it was' and made important changes in the plan for the Allied landing in Normandy on D-Day.

be able to 'see' their enemy targets in the dark.* Soon there would be radar sets on every searchlight and in every battery. And then the day of the invulnerable bomber fleet would be over.

But that would not win the war for Britain; it would only make it more difficult and more costly for the enemy to win it. What was needed was a miracle: the United States in the war, for example, or something even more unlikely, like a German attack upon Soviet Russia. He still could not believe that Adolf Hitler was stupid enough to provoke or promote either or both of them. In the meantime, he put his faith (what faith he had) in Britain's chances of victory on her ability to go on standing up to the punishment she was taking while science – and the new weapons it was developing – came to her aid.

And that was the trouble. Which weapons should be given priority?

Charles Snow is not a man given to toying with the *ifs* of history, but there is one if which has always tantalised him. *If Winston Churchill had come to power at the beginning of 1939, when war first began with Germany, instead of in 1940 after the debacle in France, would the Battle of Britain have been lost instead of won?* It seems a ridiculous possibility to discuss, but the facts behind it are not ridiculous. In 1939 the radar system which saved England was not ready and did not reach a workable stage, despite intensive effort, until just before the Battle of Britain began. Any delay in its development during the first crucial nine months of war would have meant that the RAF's fighter planes would not have had radar to tell them when the Nazi bomber fleets were leaving France, which direction they were taking, and where they were hiding up in the clouds. Radar enabled the RAF to substitute brains for brawn, to be guided in to battle, to strike the enemy just at the right moment. It more than made up for the RAF's numerical inferiority to the Luftwaffe.

But if Churchill had been in power, would radar have been available? In the years leading up to war, the development of radar had been strongly attacked as useless and ineffective by one man, Professor F. A. Lindemann.†

---

* Though for over a year after the radar sets were working the British public (and the enemy) were told that the RAF had trained 'cat's eyed' pilots who could see in the dark from special exercises and a diet of carrots.

† Later Lord Cherwell.

It was suspected by Snow and believed by most of his scientist friends (certainly by Watson-Watt, the inventor of radar) that Lindemann's dogged opposition to the development of the system right up until the eve of war stemmed not from his objections to its feasibility but to his hatred of one of its principal sponsors, Professor Henry Tizard. For a variety of reasons which are beyond the realm of this story, Lindemann was not only jealous of Tizard's scientific eminence but he was also dedicated to bringing about his downfall. So far as he was concerned, nothing that Tizard could do was right. If Tizard was enthusiastic for the development of radar, then Lindemann insisted that it was unworkable and not worth the money being spent on it.*

His opposition to radar reached such vehemence shortly before war began that two professors on the scientific committee of which Tizard was chairman and Lindemann a member resigned, saying that they could no longer listen to Lindemann's savage abuse of their chairman. These two professors, Blackett and A. V. Hill, were so valuable that the committee was immediately reconstituted with Lindemann replaced by another scientist.

But if Churchill had been in power when that quarrel took place, everyone knew that it was Tizard and not Lindemann who would have been replaced. For Lindemann was Churchill's friend. It was an extraordinary friendship. Lindemann was a narrow-minded ascetic of Teutonic extraction who neither drank nor smoked and lived on a diet of cheese and water-cress, and made it plain that he strongly disapproved of anyone who lived otherwise. How could he be so close to the cigar-smoking, brandy-swilling, gourmandising Winston Churchill, and why did Churchill have so much faith in him? The reasons again are too complicated to go into here. The fact remains that so far as the Prime Minister was concerned, Lindemann could do no wrong.

If Churchill had been Prime Minister in 1939 Lindemann would have been at his side. And if Lindemann had been there, Tizard would have been out and so quite probably would radar. And then what would have happened when the great Nazi bomber fleets came against England? Charles Snow was to say later:†

---

* His own pet method for stopping enemy bombers, which he seriously put forward, was a screen of balloons floating thousands of feet high from wires stretching across the path of the incoming planes.

† In his famous Harvard lecture, *Science and Government*. OUP, 1960.

We should, without any question, have been morally better prepared for war when it came. We should have been better prepared in the amount of war material. But studying the story I have just told, I find it hard to resist the possibility that, in some essential technical respects, we might have been worse prepared. If Churchill had come into office, Lindemann would have come with him. . . . Without getting the radar in time we should not have stood a good chance in the war that finally arrived. With Lindemann instead of Tizard, it seems at least likely that different technical choices would have been made. If that had been so, I still cannot for the life of me see how the radar system would have been ready in time.

Now Churchill had come into office at last, and Lindemann had come too. And what had happened? Tizard was gone, forced off his committees and out of his job within weeks of his rival's accession to power. Lindemann was quite ruthless. He made it plain that henceforth any new scientific development, any new weapon would have to be discussed with him first, and he would decide whether to recommend it to the Prime Minister. Tizard was dispatched on a mission to the United States. 'The Prof', as Lindemann was called, took over. And things changed so far as science and Government were concerned.

Changed for the worse, in Snow's view.

'This is no time for false modesty,' Lindemann had said.* 'I happen to believe that I have more brains than all these other people,' with a gesture towards Whitehall that was meant to include politicians, soldiers, civil servants and his fellow scientists. He had gone on to tell Harrod that because he had more brains he could render a unique service to Britain. For this purpose what he required was *power* – and that was to be acquired by knowing more and more about what was going on. Therefore, everything must come through him, and with the power that this knowledge gave him he would be in a better position to serve his country and Winston Churchill.

So henceforward, as Snow's friends were discovering, the only way to the Prime Minister was through Lindemann's ear. He was not receptive to many outside suggestions, particularly scientific

* In a conversation with his assistant, Roy Harrod. See R. F. Harrod, *The Prof*, Macmillan.

ones, and he did not pass them on. He knew much better himself.

'He was a dedicated gadgeteer,' said Snow 'and beware the scientist who is a gadgeteer. He was always thinking up wild schemes for confounding the Germans which he passed on to Churchill, who naturally lapped them up. He liked gadgets too. There was Habbakuk, a plan for putting floating icefields off the German coast and flying bombers off them. There was a crazy scheme for a Commando raid on the Baltic. And others.'

It was these gadgety ideas which were taking up time in 10 Downing Street while decisions of scientific importance were held up by a sneering and contemptuous Prof.

Yes, C. P. Snow was a frightened man in 1940, but the fear of being bombed was minor when compared with the fear of losing the war. And nothing that Professor Lindemann was pouring into Winston Churchill's receptive ear helped him to sleep at nights. So long as the Prof was there with Churchill, he feared that things could get worse.

2

That autumn Italy launched its troops across the Albanian frontier towards Epirus, and Britain had a new ally in the war: Greece. For days the newspapers played the story across their front pages and hailed the Greeks as gallant comrades in the fight against tyranny and dictatorship. Ordinary Londoners, however, suspected that they might prove more of a liability than an asset and were muted in their welcome of their new allies. They had grown disenchanted with foreigners and resigned to more and more enemy victories, and, in any case, they were immersed in their own affairs, for bombing was intensive at the time. There were many who thought like Paula Shepherd, the young architect's assistant, who wrote:

'Now it's Greece! If Athens and the Acropolis are bombed and the treasures of the Greek islands, I'll admit that this generation of fools and madmen is not worth saving. What chance have they? What on earth is the point of the radio announcer talking about the courage and fighting spirit of the Greeks when everyone knows that only air power counts?'

Most Londoners, however, hardly reacted at all. Peter Donald, the young pacifist from south London, whose ear for his neigh-

bours' conversation was uncanny, reported three slices of dialogue
on the day that Italy invaded Greece. Before reproducing them,
it is necessary to point out that one of the most popular couples
in Britain in 1940 was undoubtedly the Duke and Duchess of
Kent. The Duke was a brother of King George the Sixth; he was
serving in the RAF (and was to die in a flying accident the following year). The Duchess, beautiful, gay, worldly, was of Greek
nationality and was a great favourite of the British; they called
her husband 'the Duke' and they called George the Sixth 'the
King' but they almost all referred to the Duchess of Kent simply
as 'Marina'. This is Donald's report:

I came home to lunch and announced to Mrs R.* that Italy
and Greece were at war. She said: 'Oh, now that will settle
them.' I did not answer and she went on: 'Are *we* at war with
Italy?'

'Yes,' I replied, heavily. [Britain had been at war with Italy
for five months.]

She said: 'That's Mussolini's country, isn't it?'

'Yes, that's right.'

'And Greece is Marina's country, isn't it?'

'Yes.'

'That will please old Itler,' she said.

'Why do you think so?' I asked.

'Well, it will,' she said. 'I know that. And that will finish him.'

'Who?'

'Why, Mussolini,' she said.

'What do you think will happen now?' I asked.

'We shall smash them,' she said.

'Smash who?'

'All of them,' she said.

'A L L of them?'

'Yes,' she said. And then: 'They'll use up some petrol getting
to Shropshire.'

'Shropshire?'

'Yes, they're going there this morning.'

'What,' I said, 'Mussolini – going to Shropshire!'

'Naow. I'm talking about Mr and Mrs Blodwick across the
way. They're going to Shropshire today.'

* His landlady, 43, married to a postal worker.

'Oh,' I replied, weakly. 'I thought we were talking about the war.'

'So I was. That's why Mr and Mrs Blodwick are going to Shropshire.'

At that moment the siren sounded and Mrs R dashed off to the shelter.'

Presently her daughter, Brenda (pretty, 20, works in a shop) came in.

I said: 'Heard any war news this morning?'

'No, nothing at all,' she said.

'Nothing at all?'

'No,' she said. 'What's happened, is it over or something?'

'No. Italy's declared war on Greece.'

'Oh,' she said. 'That won't make any difference to us, will it?'

'It might,' I said.

She thought and then said: 'Why, we've had people in our shop all morning and no one's mentioned it.'

'Well,' I said, 'see how long you can go this afternoon before you mention it, and tell me what the first person says.'

'Okay,' she said.

Later, at tea, Brenda said: 'I waited three hours and no one mentioned Italy and Greece, so I mentioned it to the manager, and he said: "Oh that! I know. Greece is the country where Marina comes from, isn't it?" '

Mrs R.'s son, Tony, was home on leave. He was 21 and a gunner in the RAF.

I said to Tony:

'Italy's declared war on Greece. What do you think of it?'

'Oh, bugger the war!' he said. 'You will keep talking about it, won't you,' he said. 'I'm fed up! Can't you see I'm on leave, man? War, war, war, bombs, bombs, bombs, that's all anyone at home bloody well talks about!'

'Sorry,' I said.

3

It was a noisy winter for London, and a killing and miserable winter too. The capital was ripped and scarred everywhere now and no community had been spared. Every night the bombers came over and then the capital went dead. Not only the East End now but the other suburbs too locked themselves in for the night. There was nowhere else to go but the shelters.

Yet in the West End some sort of night life went on. The Savoy Hotel in the Strand and the Dorchester and Grosvenor House hotels in Park Lane had become clubs for politicians, pressmen and café society. A good deal of hard drinking went on in all of them while the bombs rained down, and some of the correspondents who covered the blitz on London did not move much more than a mile away from the Savoy during the height of the raids. They were quite right. They would have been running away had they done so. The Savoy was in the direct firing line. It was possible for a correspondent to cover the battle and interview the generals at the same time, for the Savoy was a favourite resort of Winston Churchill and members of the Cabinet.

There was entertainment of a kind. In a back street behind Piccadilly Circus the indefatigable showgirls of the Windmill Theatre were still prancing doggedly through their high-kicking routines, and behind them the tall showgirls were still posing with their breasts uncovered (except for the dust which fell all over them whenever a bomb dropped nearby). Once the Windmill had been the mecca of the middle-aged voyeur who paid for a close-up view of a motionless girl with her brassiere off. But now the Windmill girls had become a kind of a symbol of imperturbability under fire. Their pictures had gone out all over the world to messes, barracks and gunrooms, posing with tin hats and shovels as their only adornment. Their faces changed often (not because they were scared off by the bombing, but because they were called up into the Services) but in some way remained the same: fresh and young and earnest as they tried to keep up with the music against the crashing of the bombs. They were execrable dancers, but nobody really cared about that. The public, particularly the troops, loved them, just because they were there.

Most of the other West End theatres closed for a time at the height of the bombing, and then began to open again. Most shows went on with the performance in spite of the raids, simply putting up an announcement to say, 'an air raid is in progress' and then carrying on. Those who wanted to could leave the theatre and go to the shelters, but in fact few of them did.

'I remember one night,' said Harold Conway, who was a show-business writer in those days, 'I went with my wife Eileen to the

Apollo in Shaftesbury Avenue and the play was "Margin for Error" with Margaretta Scott. There was a big raid on all through the performance and at the end it was still going on. It was no use the audience trying to get home. So they all stayed on. Michael Redgrave was playing next door at the Globe in "Thunder Rock", and he and his company joined us. Between them, the two companies gave us what you might call socko entertainment until four in the morning. They sang. They told jokes. They had the audience join them in charades. They danced. It was marvellous fun. The audience responded wonderfully, of course. Most people who were sportsmen enough to go to the theatre in those days were bright people, of course, and they responded. On this particular occasion the all-clear went about 3.30 a.m. and people were so involved that they elected to go on – until it became clear that they were being discourteous to the cast, who needed to get some sleep before the performance next day.'

The two plays that made most impact in London in those days were 'Blithe Spirit' and 'Arsenic and Old Lace'.

'They were the best of a poor bunch,' Conway says. 'During the war there was an unwritten agreement between the managements and the Gallery First Nighters* that they would not boo the play, no matter how bad. This lowered the standard considerably, and any old rubbish went. But then, audiences were easy, too. They just wanted to forget the war for a bit.'

4

It was a night out in the West End that winter which finally changed Rosemary Black from a complacent young widow into a fighter.

There had been a lull in the bombing for almost twenty-four hours, and after a succession of claustrophobic nights in the shelter she decided that she would scream if she didn't get out. Her friend, Joy Bone, had been coming home day after day from the ambulance station with her hair and clothes covered in blood and a series of horrifying experiences with bomb-victims so much on her mind that she had felt compelled to unburden for hour after hour. Now Rosemary Black cut her short.

* An association of inveterate theatregoers.

'We've got to get out of here,' she said. 'You'll drive me mad
– and you'll drive yourself mad, too.'

She made her companion put on a smart black suit, saw the
children and the maids safely into the basement shelter, and then
set out for the West End. Mrs Bone thought it was ghoulish to
go around 'picking at London's sores', as she described it, but
Rosemary Black said firmly: 'I have to know.'

But when she saw what the Nazis had done to her beloved
London, gloom and misery began to steal over her. They walked
along a pavement littered with broken glass and then came into
Oxford Street, opposite the John Lewis store.

That night she wrote:

It was the most ghastly sight imaginable. I had no notion
that the empty, charred skeleton with its blackened walls and
gaping windows and rust-orange girders and its wax models
lying like corpses on the pavement could look so terrible and
forbidding. The pictures in the papers had given no idea of the
appalling reality. It was so horrifying a spectacle of tragedy and
waste that it reduced Mrs B. and myself to silence (which takes
some doing). We stood dumbly staring at it in a sort of sick
despair. I noticed that the few other "trippers" like ourselves
who had come to see it were affected in the same way. They too
fell silent, or if they spoke at all it would be in a hushed whisper,
as though in church; on their faces too was a look of awe and
fear.

They picked their way through the glass and rubble towards
Oxford Circus, where they stood on the lip of an enormous bomb
crater and stared at the wreckage everywhere.

Empty pavements and an empty silence through which the
few pedestrians seemed to hurry furtively. Empty grey air, yet
full of an oppressive feeling of desolation and despair. When
we left we agreed as one that it had been quite enough for us
and we didn't want to see any more horrors, and picking up our
driver we told him to take us quickly to the Café Royal, and sat
silently in the taxi in dumb despondency. But we couldn't get
away from it all. The western curve of Regent Street was
charred and pitted as high as the roof tops; and when we got
to the Café we found it shut. We knew it had been temporarily

closed some days ago but had supposed it had surely reopened by this date. It was a problem, now, to know where to go. Many of the restaurants must have closed for lack of custom for the streets were empty and dead. The Cumberland, which is always full and which we'd thought a certain last resort to fall back on, has been evacuated today owing to time-bombs. Pruniers is too far from bus and tube for us. The Aperitif, where we next turned, proved to be now open for lunch only. Eventually we landed up at the Ecu de France*, which actually turned out to be open and to have a few people in it. We sank dejectedly into chairs in the bar and ordered ourselves double champagne cocktails. It wasn't until I was three-quarters of the way through mine that the haunting picture of John Lewis' was erased from my mind.

It was the last winter that Britain was to know for many years when one could still go into a restaurant and gorge oneself on good food. Rationing had not yet begun to pinch. Restaurants were still free to serve a four-course meal, providing you could afford to pay for it, and there were still stocks of wines and liqueurs around. It was as if Rosemary Black sensed that this was the end of an epoch, and that things would never be the same again.

When they eventually came out into Piccadilly Circus, guns were booming, searchlights were threading the sky overhead, and there was 'an all too clear sound of bomber engines' in the sky. They had been hoping to catch a bus home, but while the raiders were overhead the buses were drawn up 'in a ghostly rank – policemen and wardens everywhere – a sense of haste and urgency and fear in the shuffle of many feet on the darkened pavements. . . .'

Half-way across Piccadilly Circus Rosemary Black flashed her torch for a moment to see where she was going.

'Put that light out!' came a sudden deep shout, and up loomed the shape of a policeman. She tried to put the torch out and, instead, it stuck. Frenzy! She stuck it in her pocket. The glow showed through. Meanwhile the policeman had reached them and was grasping them round the shoulders.

'Don't you know there's a war on!' he cried.

With rough hands he bundled them to the head of the stairs

* In Jermyn Street.

leading to the Underground and pushed them down. Rosemary Black lost her balance and fell down flat. She was still in a semi-daze when her companion helped her off the moving staircase and she came onto the platform of Piccadilly Station. And there she saw them.

> HORRIFIED by ghastly sights in Tubes. I'd gathered from the papers that people were sleeping there, but I thought from what was given out that they did so only in badly bombed areas – East End, Holborn, City. Also the pictures I'd seen of Tube sleepers showed only an odd half-dozen people or so lying in a vast expanse – it looked as if they had far more space and air than they'd have got elsewhere. Now, seeing every corridor and platform in every station all along the line crowded with people huddled together three-deep, I was too appalled for words. The misery of that vast wretched mass of humanity sleeping like worms in a packed tin – the heat and smell, the dirt, the endless crying of the poor bloody babies, the haggard white-faced women nursing their children against them, the children cramped and twitching in their airless, noisy sleep. Even a disused escalator was crowded with dumb, resigned humanity – why, if I wanted to torture my worst enemy, I could think of no better form of Procrustean bed for the purpose. And I saw a woman sleeping with her head on the bare platform, her face about an inch away from a great gob of spit. I was nearly crying. I felt so ashamed and disgusted to have eaten that huge, expensive meal, while here. . . .

Like some sort of Marie Antoinette, she rushed around the clustered platform handing out money from her handbag to the women and children. And then felt ashamed of herself. When she went home she went miserably to bed, thinking of all the suffering around her and of her own 'wholly undeserved' good luck.

> I sometimes feel I'd really be happier in a way – though, of course, miserable and raging too – if I were bombed out of house and home instead of always being 'one of the lucky ones' in this, as in every other way. Even so, though, I should never reach the depth of suffering in which thousands of my fellow citizens are now engulfed, because I'd still be well off. To lose my home and my possessions would still not be, for me, to lose

everything. God must surely have it in for me in my future life, that I, worthless that I am, am granted all this undeserved good fortune here and now.

Rosemary Black woke in a despairing mood next day, as though she had passed through a nightmare. And then the picture came back into her mind of Oxford Street and the vile reality of the women in the Underground.

That morning she pleaded again at the ambulance station to be taken on as a helper or a driver, but was firmly told that only qualified persons were being taken. She was offered a job as chauffeur to a high-up member of one of the fire services, but turned that down 'because he can well afford to drive himself or take taxis'. In frustration she altered the date on the back of her blood-card (she had given blood two days before) and went out to donate an extra transfusion. That would be at least something towards London's urgent needs.

It was while she was recovering at home from this with an extra-strong cup of tea – it would punch a hole in her tea ration, but she didn't care – that Mrs Bone rushed in, and she was in a rage.

One of the men ambulance drivers at their station had died in very unpleasant and tragic circumstances as a delayed result of exposure on duty, and Mrs B. was trying to arrange for his widow to get out of London for a week or so, to escape both the reminders of her loss and the blitz. She had phoned a woman she knew who was an obvious choice for a provider of refuge for the widow: plenty of money and servants, a peaceful district, a huge house which Mrs B. happened to know (on good authority from a neighbour) contained not one single 'refugee', though every other house in the neighbourhood was just about crowded out. But this woman always was a bitch – at least such is my opinion. She declared that it would be *most* difficult and inconvenient to take the widow in, as the house was already full to bursting with refugee friends. She *might* be able to think out some way of managing it – would have to think it over and see – the woman would go in the servants' hall, of course? Before she thought out things any further, could she have some details about the woman. What *class* was she, exactly?

Rosemary Black had never heard Mrs B. swear before, but she

heard her now. She came down to the drawing room stammering and incoherent with rage.

'My dear, I'm *bursting*. Can you imagine that at a time like this anyone could be so perfectly *bloody*? Servants' hall! Class! What does it matter? Damn her, damn her, damn her, I'll never speak to her again! Full house! All lies, she'd never do a thing to help a single soul and she won't do it now – heart like a stone!' She walked around the room shaking her hand above her shoulder. 'I'm simply bursting with rage. I'd like to hurt her. Bitch, yes, bitch!'

She swung round on Rosemary Black.

'Bitch!' she said, again, and then: 'Isn't there something worse I can call her? What's the worst name I can possibly use?'

Rosemary Black suggested the obvious.

Mrs B. said, 'Oh!' and looked shocked. But then she disappeared upstairs, and could be heard muttering the word over and over under her breath.

Next day Rosemary Black got up when the alarm rang at 6.15, ate a hurried breakfast, and started to make the rounds of various offices in London. Late the same afternoon she came back to the house in St John's Wood, kicked off her shoes and collapsed into a chair before the fire.

She was exhausted. But she had a job. Two days later she clocked in at an office in the Strand. Henceforward she would be a tea-and-sandwich dispenser on a YMCA Mobile Canteen. On her service-route card were only two words: *Bomb sites*.

5

On 3 December 1940, the authorities finally caught up with the young pacifist, Peter Donald in his lodgings in south-east London. He had deliberately failed to register for National Service, though his age group had long since been called up. Now a letter with a form in it flopped through the letter-box and Mrs R., his landlady handed it over to him. He deliberately did not tell her what was in it, despite the eager expression on her face. Later, at breakfast, her daughter, Brenda, said,

'It's the police, isn't it? They're on to you. Now you'll have to register as a conshie.'

The official letter contained a form formally asking him to state, in no more than 250 words, why he wished to register as a conscientious objector, and that afternoon he settled down to it. He wrote his objections in longhand and read them through afterwards and was rather proud of his effort. He wrote:

You will agree that war destroys life and property. You will agree that war mutilates men, women and children and animals alike. You will agree that war causes blindness, disease and insanity, and that during war immorality increases.

You will agree that war takes millions of the youngest and strongest men from the world, leaving weaklings, the infirm and the maimed to produce the next generation. You will agree that war causes men to kill and wound or to assist in killing and wounding each other when there is no hatred between them. It is obvious that they are only roused emotionally by speeches, stories, songs, parades, flags, etc., and above all by press, film and radio propaganda. Could each man speak the language of his so-called enemy, he would find that they had mutual interests including the desire to abolish all war.

You will agree that those who demand men to fight and to support war escape the horrors and death that they have imposed upon millions. It is because I too believe as you do that war creates these evils that I am a pacifist, for pacifism requires no lying, no distortion, no slaughter, no threats, and no economic loss, whereas war causes at least eight of the Ten Commandments to be broken and contributes nothing to the happiness of mankind.

I refuse to recognise any law supporting war. I maintain that the state has no moral right to order men to fight. I cannot conscientiously support war, either directly by actual physical combat or indirectly by making armaments or performing any work which is essential for the continuity of this war or any future war. I have been a member of the PPU* since the year of its foundation and have designed anti-war posters for the League of Nations Union and the No More War Movement. I support the abolition of the death penalty and am an anti-vivisectionist.

He signed it, put it in the envelope, and cycled to the post with
* Peace Pledge Union.

it. When he got back his landlady and Brenda were having tea in the kitchen.

'Now let them do their worst!' he said. Brenda said nothing. Mrs R. said, 'The war will be over by this spring.'

'What makes you think that?' he asked.

'Well, it will be,' she said. 'We are going to take the offensive.'

'How?'

'With all the men we've got, of course!' she said, sarcastically. 'How else do you think?'

'Yes, yes,' he said, impatiently, 'but what will they *do*?'

'Do? Why, drive the Germans out, of course!'

'Out of where?'

'Why,' she said, 'out of France and all the other places.'

He said, 'But to do that, France must be invaded.'

'Well, that's what we're going to do,' she said. 'Then there's the other way.'

'What other way?'

Brenda who had been listening in silence, chimed in, 'Yes, what other way? Go on, say!'

'With our Navy,' said Mrs R. 'We'll take the offensive.'

'Where?'

'Heavens, how do I know?' said Mrs R. 'Nobody knows nothing. They don't tell us nothing – no more than they do the Germans themselves. Yet you go on asking me as if I knew.'

'Well, now,' he remarked, 'are you sure they tell us nothing?'

'Of course. Nothing. No one knows!'

'Well, then, if *nobody* knows, how do *you* know that we are going to invade France?'

She hesitated and then said: 'It's in the papers.'

'Then they must know, surely – otherwise how did the information get there – and that indicates that someone knows something.'

Mrs R. considered this and then said, 'Well, *they* know, of course. I suppose Churchill must know. He's at the top.'

'But,' he said, 'Mr Churchill says the war is going to last until 1942 or 1943 and you said it would be over next spring.'

'Oh, that's what he *says*,' retorted Mrs R. 'But of course it will be over by the spring. It can't go on all the time. It would cost too much. Besides, the Germans have run out of ammunition. And we've smashed up all their planes, and they can't have many more left.'

Just then the sirens sounded, and Mrs R. departed hastily for the shelters.

Peter and Brenda were left alone in the house, but the girl's behaviour was strange. The raid was heavy but she stayed under her blankets on the floor, miserable but remote. Next day Peter Donald wrote in his diary:

'I will now touch upon another subject which you will find references to in other instalments of this diary. There you will see that I wrote that Brenda R. (aged 20) seemed to become very amorous whenever an air raid was in progress. Some complex functioning of the nervous physio-psycho systems, I conclude, and don't know enough about the matter to be definite.

Well, this condition has now ceased. Just in the same way that people have become accustomed to air raids and lost their fear, so she, having become hardened to the blitz, has lost this state of what I might term artificial or perverted sexual excitement.'

6

On the night of Donald Ketley's ninth birthday a large piece of shrapnel from an anti-aircraft gun came through the roof of his parents' house at Chadwell Heath, in East London. A heavy raid was going on at the time but Donald followed his father upstairs – he had gone up to inspect in case it was an incendiary bomb – and he retrieved the slice of torn metal from just beside the parental bed. It was still warm. Donald decided that it was a wonderful birthday present and added it to his collection of war souvenirs alongside a melted blob of metal from an incendiary bomb they had doused in their back yard last September, a strip of fuselage from a downed German bomber, and a signed picture of 'Ginger' Lacey, the RAF fighter ace who had destroyed the plane which had bombed Buckingham Palace.

Donald was enjoying the war, though he did not say too much about it. He knew his parents were not enjoying it, and he knew that there was much terror and suffering going on all around him. Sometimes in the air-raid shelter under the stairs he could hear his father and mother talking in whispers about the poor souls who had been bombed out of their homes. He remembered the morning when his father had come home unexpectedly from work. His face was white and his lips were trembling. Nowadays he worked as a clerk in a customs warehouse at Wapping, and when he arrived there that morning he had found the whole place ablaze from the bombing of the night before. The firemen were desperately trying to get to one of their comrades buried under a wall which had suddenly collapsed on top of him. (His father had gone back to the gutted warehouse a few days later to see if he could find any of his papers and office records, but all he had returned with were a pair of pliers, a drill and some wire-cutters. The fire had been at them and they were now so brittle that they were no good at all, so Donald had added them to his collection.)

By this time Donald had learned to distinguish bombs from guns, even in his sleep, and bombs always woke him up. He didn't mind the guns at all. Not so his parents. One night he remembered hearing his father grumbling about the noise, for there was an anti-aircraft unit in a park a few blocks away. Finally, when the noise was at its worst, he heard his father mutter, 'Oh, for God's sake shut up, and let them bomb us in peace!'

The Ketley family had slept under the stairs for the first couple of months, but then one morning they almost didn't wake up after the night's raid. The near-misses had broken a gas-pipe and the escaping gas had all but asphyxiated them. Thereafter they joined their neighbours, a middle-aged couple with a teenaged daughter, in their Anderson shelter in the back garden. In Chadwell Heath few people slept in public shelters – they were just far enough out of the East End to have small gardens and Anderson shelters dug into them. Some people were stubborn, of course, and neither used the public shelters nor Andersons but stayed in their beds. A neighbour of the Ketleys belonged in this category, and he was killed when the bed he was sleeping in was blown out of the house and through the roof of a house on the opposite side of the street. By blast. Blast did very strange things, Donald was discovering. He heard his mother talking one night about a relative of theirs who was killed in East Ham.

'And then the firemen got through the hole and there they found her,' his mother was whispering to her husband. 'You remember her. Really pretty, she was. There wasn't a mark on her.

But the blast had ripped every stitch of clothing off the poor soul, and she was dead.'

An Anderson shelter with six persons inside was pretty crowded, Donald remembered, but apart from being awakened by the general racket from time to time everyone managed to sleep. His father afterwards claimed that he had never felt better – it was rather like camping out. Certainly being in an Anderson was preferable to the public shelters. The Ketleys were forced to go to one on the night when they were evacuated because of an unexploded land-mine. There was a lull in the raid and they were all asleep when a voice from the alley behind cried out, 'You in there! All out, all out! There's a bomb!'

It was the air-raid warden. A land-mine had come down at the end of the street and the parachute had caught in a tree, so that the bomb remained swinging just above the ground. Donald gazed at it in wonder when he heard the warden say, 'Another six inches and this whole street would be flat by now.'

Since there was no certainty that the bomb would continue to hang there, like some fearful sword of Damocles, they were shuffled off to the public shelter in the park. It was the most uncomfortable night Donald Ketley could remember of the war. The shelter, a long concrete tunnel, was very cold and had nothing but wooden benches along the sides. About two inches of freezing water covered the floor. The Ketleys just sat there, feet tucked under them, waiting for morning. When morning came they went over to a friend's house, and were given some breakfast and a chance to thaw out. The friend's wife was still simmering with indignation over the events of the night's raid. She and her husband were keen gardeners and very proud of a small but lovingly cared-for greenhouse just behind their house.

In the middle of the night they had been awakened by a crashing of glass, and looking out of their Anderson they saw that a magnesium bomb had landed in the greenhouse. Bombs were dropping, but this was too much for the wife. She grabbed a sandbag outside the Anderson and raced for the greenhouse, where she effectively doused the flare with the sand.

'It's bad enough them bombing us,' she said, 'but how dare they try to wreck our greenhouse!'

The Ketleys were allowed back into their house the following afternoon, after the land-mine had been defused by a naval engineer. That was the nearest they had come so far to having the house destroyed. They had lost windows and pieces of roof from time to time, but that was all. Donald remembered going into his parents' bedroom one time after the window had gone and seeing all the splinters of glass embedded in the wall opposite the bedroom window. He had felt momentarily sick at the thought of what would have happened to his father and mother had they been in bed at the time.

But mostly he had no qualms. It was spectacular and noisy but never ever dull. And there was one good thing, too. Early in the blitz his school had been totally destroyed by a bomb. Donald had disliked the school intensely. He was shy and he was a poor student, and very unpopular with his teacher. He was therefore overjoyed to learn that the school was gone. Thereafter he went every day to his teacher's home to collect lessons, which he brought back next day for marking. In the next few months he changed from a poor to an excellent student – and he suspected that his teacher rather resented the change. But he didn't care. He was very happy, and he didn't mind if the blitz went on for ever.

'But if it stopped, Dad,' he said to Mr Ketley one day, 'what would Ginger Lacey and Al Deere and Johnnie Johnson do?* They wouldn't have any more Nazi bombers to shoot down!'

* Three of the most successful fighter pilots of the RAF.

9

ST PAUL'S IN PERIL

On the night of 29 December 1940, Winston Churchill was waiting to speak to President Franklin D. Roosevelt on the direct line to the White House when he learnt that St Paul's was on fire.

The 29 December raid was one of the most devastating of the entire blitz on London, not so much in loss of life but in the annihilation of some of the capital's most beautiful architectural treasures. Not the least tragic aspect of it was that it need not have been so destructive had London been prepared.

The Germans could hardly have picked a better time. Not only was it a Sunday night, and one between Christmas and New Year, when quite a few of the auxiliary services were taking holidays, but it was also a period of extremely low tides so that the water in the nearby Thames was abnormally low. The Nazi planes swept over at about seven o'clock in the evening and dropped basket after basket of incendiary bombs, with a smaller proportion of high explosives in between. The bombs spattered like hailstones upon the roofs of the ancient Guildhall and a score of old City churches, all of them full of old beams and highly inflammable. Within an hour the City was ablaze and the glow from the raging inferno could be seen from thirty miles away. Wave after wave of bombers came in to stoke it up.

The tragedy was this: for more than four months every house-holder in London had been dealing with incendiary bombs and had lost his fear of them. When Miss Vere Hodgson had heard one clattering down from the roof of her house she was out of the door as fast as her legs would carry her, spade in one hand, to scoop it up, bucket in the other to douse it out – or sand to smother it. Everyone knew how to put them out, quickly and efficiently.

The only trouble was that in the City on Sunday 29 December there was no one to deal with them. They landed on the roofs of churches and offices and warehouses and, once they started to burn, they kept on burning. The City of London had gone away for the week-end, and up on the roofs the small fires started, leaped across the narrow twisting streets, and ran through the area like any forest fire.

Even so, some of the most disastrous fires might have been saved had not the water run out. The fire services were on the scene within minutes of the raid, and were soon controlling the main blazes (though not the small fires eating their way in from the roofs at the back), but as more fires started and more incendiaries dropped from the sky, so did their supply of water diminish. They had established their pumps on the river Thames, and the Thames ran dry. Soon there were only gushes of muddy water coming through the pipes, and then they went flaccid.

The firemen stood by, forced to watch the old buildings burn to the ground, the steeples crash, the stained glass windows melt; and a series of fires that five or six hundred ordinary caretakers could have doused in a few minutes with a spade and stirrup pump soon engulfed the whole of the City.

Four months of blitz had not yet taught London that no building must ever be left unguarded from an attack from the sky, and now the nation was paying for its lack of vigilance with the loss of some of its greatest treasures.

But not St Paul's. From the start of the war, the Dean had established a regular watch there. The message had gone out to the world in the form that it had reached Winston Churchill: St Paul's Cathedral burns! It was the same message which reached the Very Reverend W. R. Matthews, the Dean of St Paul's, as he approached the precincts of the great Wren church shortly after the raid began. He discovered that it was not yet ablaze, though the great dome was threatened. A bomb, striking the dome perpendicular to its surface, had failed to penetrate and was lodged half-way through the outer shell.

There was no fire there yet, but the lead of the great shell was beginning to melt.

'It can't be long,' they told the Dean.

St Paul's was not one of the city churches which had been left unguarded, and the dome had been constantly patrolled all through the raid.

'We knew that once a fire got hold of the dome timbers it

would, at that high altitude, quickly be fanned into a roaring furnace,' wrote the Dean. 'Unless it could be stamped out at the very start the chances of the dome were very slender indeed.'

Practically every fireman in London was standing by ready to help, but their limp hoses, oozing mud from the nozzles, rendered them useless.

'All we can do now is pray,' said one of the vergers.

'Then do it standing up, and keep your stirrup pump handy!' replied the Dean, crisply.

By this time incendiaries had begun to fall upon the lower roofs, and were quickly seized upon by watching choirboys, sidesmen and vergers. All the buildings surrounding St Paul's were now in flames. The high wind carried sparks and blazing pieces of wood into the cathedral and they whirled about the great expanse under the dome like fireflies. It was an eerie scene, with the baleful fires licking at the stained-glass windows like hungry hounds. Crouched in one corner of the nave were about fifty men, women and children who had been driven by the fire out of a nearby shelter and had come to the cathedral for sanctuary. Dean Matthews wondered at one time whether to mobilize them for fire duties, but they seemed too stunned. Later he noticed that some of them had begun playing cards in the light from the flames and wondered whether to stop them doing such a thing in church. 'What absurd thoughts one has in times of strain!'

Up in the dome the lead continued to melt. Down in the street below Ed Murrow was already preparing a radio broadcast to the United States which would begin with the words, 'Tonight the bomber planes of the German Reich hit London where it hurts most: in her heart. And the church that meant most to Londoners is gone. St Paul's Cathedral, built by Sir Christopher Wren, her great dome towering over the capital of the Empire, is burning to the ground as I talk to you now.'

Only it was not. Because whether they were praying on their knees or standing up with stirrup pumps to hand, the silent pleas of the vergers of St Paul's seem to have been heard on the night of 29 December.

'Suddenly,' wrote the Dean, 'the crisis passed. The bomb fell outwards into the Stone Gallery and was easily put out. How difficult it is to write history! I have to confess that it is uncertain how the bomb came to fall. Was it by some artificial means or was it dislodged by its own weight? I incline to the latter opinion because, so far as I know, no member of the Watch claims to have had any part in producing the result. At any rate, the Cathedral was saved from one of its most perilous predicaments, whether by human means or by what we call "accident". In either case we thank God that our great church was spared at a moment when it looked almost hopeless.'

But the rest of the City of London was in ruins. A list of the churches and ancient buildings destroyed reads like a three-star guide in the Michelin. From Fleet Street to the Tower of London, whole areas had disappeared forever and piles of smoking rubble covered acres of what were once winding City streets. It was the Great Fire of London that need not have been, and at an angry Cabinet meeting on Monday 30 December Winston Churchill ordered that it should never happen again.

That day an Order in Council was issued. Henceforward it would be an offence to leave any building in London unoccupied both night and day. Fire spotters must always be on duty. Mr Herbert Morrison, the Minister of Home Security, told his department to draw up a regulation making a weekly round of fire-watching part of the duty of every adult citizen from now on.

No one grumbled about that. Most people felt guilty, as if it was their neglect which had brought havoc to the City. On New Year's Day Rosemary Black took a van from the YMCA headquarters in the Strand to the devastated City, where she was to bring warm cups of tea and pies to the firemen still dynamiting buildings and fighting the last fires. It was an icy cold day and the men were blue with cold, and utterly exhausted. Old buildings rocked in the wind and outside the wreck of Barking church someone had underlined in soot a Christmas message so that it now read, as it flapped in the wind: 'God rest you merry gentlemen, let *nothing* you dismay.'

At the end of five hours of picking her way through the ruins, Rosemary Black was suddenly overcome with rage at the whole business.

It is so terrible that because of sheer wanton neglect of the obvious precautions, millions of pounds' worth of damage should have been done, and hundreds of brave men's lives risked and lost: the loss of beautiful old buildings, tragic as it is, is of minor importance to a people who can look after them no better than this. Are they lunatics, these merchants and wharfingers and landlords, who abandon their invaluable property, unguarded, to the mercies of the night-raiders? Are they criminals, these vicars of historic churches, who are so quick to bewail irreparable damage after the event and pass round the hat for restoration funds – clamouring against the atrocities perpetrated by the ruthless Hun and yet caring so little to preserve their charges from going up in smoke?

And then she added:

But of course we ordinary citizens – nearly every one of us – are almost as much to blame. Ours is the guilt for the irresponsible apathy and heedlessness which made possible this lunatic negligence on the part of our elected rulers. How many of us ever troubled to think out clearly the position in regard to the danger of fires created by the existing set of fire regulations – their limitations, I mean? How many of us, if we had ever troubled to understand the position clearly in the first place, would have been public-spirited enough to agitate about it, and arouse general opinion in the matter? I know I shouldn't. Are we a nation of utter imbeciles? Really, it seems as though the anwers must be Yes, Yes, a thousand times Yes!

On her first free day after the raid, Miss Vere Hodgson took a bus as far as Ludgate Circus and then walked past St Paul's Cathedral into the blackened forest of the City. By the time she had gone a few hundred yards she was crying. She wrote in her diary that night:

I will never bother with Germans, or any other foreigners (except Greeks) ever again, Oh dear, what a way to celebrate the New Year.

IO

A QUEER LIFE

I

Miss Vere Hodgson sent a copy of her diary each week to all her relatives abroad, to keep them in touch with her life in wartime London. In the spring of 1941 she said in a covering letter to one of them:

> I hope you will not find it [the diary] too pessimistic and gloomy. Last night's experience was rather unnerving and quite frankly, my dear, I do not expect to survive the blitzkrieg. I'm not a bit brave, really. The only thing that can be said in my favour is that I've not run away. I'm the only representative of my family left in London. But it's a queer life.

In fact the bombing of London was no longer so intensive. There were days when there were no air-raid warnings at all, and these were somehow terribly difficult to bear. People found themselves getting irritable with each other, and one civil servant reported that his father interrupted his conversation with a friend at dinner by saying,

'For heaven's sake stop talking so loud, we'll never be able to hear the sirens!'

It was during these raid-less days that some of the more percipient Londoners began to suspect the difficulties that might lie ahead, when the raids slackened off but the war, with all its restrictions and regimentation, went on. There was something about the danger from the skies that kept the people together, firm against the enemy; and there were not only no squabbles while the bombs were falling but no worries about the future. Two or three days of quiet in London and people began to notice the inconveniences, the growing shortages of food, the poor news from abroad. As if aware of this, Winston Churchill spoke on the radio to the nation in February and he stressed the fact that the danger of invasion by Germany was not yet past. In fact it was. The Germans knew it, and Adolf Hitler had accepted the fact and

long since dispersed the invasion barges which had once concentrated on the Channel coast. Churchill himself knew it, for
already his Intelligence services were telling him of Hitler's plans
to attack Russia. But he considered the threat of invasion a red
flag with which to go on rallying the people, and he was reluctant
to put it down, especially when the raids showed signs of slackening.

Not that they disappeared for more than a day or so at a time
from the life of the average Londoner. London in the spring of
1941 was still one of the most dangerous cities in the world, and
the newly arrived American correspondent walking out for his
first stroll from the Savoy Hotel soon stopped smiling when he
saw in the shattered window of Gieves, the military outfitters,
bowler hats with the legend underneath: *Anti-shrapnel bowlers,
specially reinforced.* They were necessary. People went on dying
from shrapnel and from shells, all through that spring.

In January, Vere Hodgson wrote:

Today we hear from the Lambeth people that the raid was
down their way. A bomb fell on some workmen's flats near
Lambeth station. The bomb that fell on the Bank subway the
other night was a terrible affair. The blast threw many people
on to the live rails and they were electrocuted immediately. This
was from an eyewitness who came into our place this morning.
He also saw two children blown under an approaching train,
and a Jew crawled under the train and rescued them, at the
peril of his life.

A month later she was writing:

Last night's raid is described as having done 'considerable
damage', but one gathers that it was only one bomb. But today
I heard from an eyewitness that it was a new type of bomb and it
dropped on Hendon. It had a flare attached to it and it fell into
the High Street before the warning sounded. There were lots
of people about in the streets and so did not stand a chance.
It destroyed five streets and left devastation for three miles.
Large numbers of people killed and many injured, and hundreds
are homeless.

But later that day she walked from her rooms in Holland Park
to Hyde Park, near by, and wrote:

Tins of sand all around and many army lorries, but the Round

Pond is still round and the ducks and seagulls were basking in the first sun we've had this year. I haven't found any snowdrops yet, but I have heard they are out near the Peter Pan statue.

And then she added a note of a need that was a growing one in the minds of every Londoner that spring of 1941, a nagging need for a physical sweetness that was beginning to go out of their lives:

I'm just longing for some fruit but could not get any. I went out with the firm determination to spend a shilling per pound if necessary for apples, but to my horror there was not one in any shop in Notting Hill at any price whatsoever. The window seems to be full of turnips. Mrs Gray was so sorry later when she heard I was looking for an apple that she sent me up a Bramley, and although it was a cooking apple I ate it with great relish.

One of her fellow-workers, Mr Booker, had hated onions most of his life, 'but now he says that when once more we can get them he will eat one and enjoy it. I think we will all go in for onion binges when the war is over.'

For possibly the first time since war began, the rationing system instituted by Lord Woolton, the Food Minister, was beginning to squeeze, and Londoners were thinking with their stomachs.

Rosemary Black came home from a day driving her mobile canteen around the bomb sites to find a note awaiting her about the result of that day's shopping.

'Madam [the maid had written], there is no honey,
no sultanas, currants or raisins,
no mixed fruits,
no saccharine at present,
no spaghetti,
no sage,
no herrings, kippers or sprats (smoked or plain),
no matches at present,
no kindling wood,
no fat or dripping,
no tins of celery, tomato soup or salmon.
I have bought three pounds of parsnips.'

Mrs Bone was quite despondent about the home front situation

and said it was absolutely awful. She and Rosemary Black were
concerned to realise that their conversation together was increasingly devoted to various shortages of food, a subject to which it
invariably returned before long from any other topic.

One morning that spring, seeking inspiration for the week's
catering which she invariably arranged for her household, Rosemary Black took down for the first time for many months a booklet
which had been published just after rationing began in 1939.
It was called *A Kitchen Goes to War*, and it had been issued by the
world Ministry of Food to help housewives cope with wartime
shortages.

I remembered this vaguely as being a selection of poverty-
stricken sort of dishes of uninspiring drabness. [she wrote].
But very much to the contrary I was bewildered by a rich
lavishness and variety mostly quite unobtainable, and, in fact,
by present-day standards quite beyond one's wildest gastro-
nomic dreams. Can one ever have sighed over the limitations of
a diet in which could still be included stuffed onions, stuffed
tomatoes, onion soup, ragout of rabbit, or kedgeree of kidneys,
fish and leek pudding, prune roll, and such heights of luxury
as cream cheese and pineapple salad, cheese soufflé, rabbit
pudding with bacon and onion, topped with mousse made with
twopenny bars of chocolate, Cornish leekie pie, eggs baked in
potato cases with cream and cheese, sugarless water ice cream
made with two tablespoons of sweet condensed milk to each
gill of cream? Can this ever have been condemned to the category of economic wartime fare? Can one ever have seen even
the shadow of privation in a world containing such marvels?

Vere Hodgson went to the grocery in Notting Hill Gate for her
bacon ration one week in March.* She mentioned to the man

* Neither she nor other Londoners realised how lucky they were to get
it that week. The previous Friday afternoon Lord Woolton had received
five separate signals from the Admiralty reporting that food ships had
been sunk by German submarines while sailing in convoy across the
Atlantic. By an extraordinary coincidence, these five ships were largely
stocked with bacon. Woolton, determined to keep his pledge that the
ration would always be honoured, ordered all existing stocks taken out of
the warehouse and distributed at once. Two days later one bacon ship
limped into Liverpool and was immediately unloaded and its cargo
distributed. The ration was met – but only just.

behind the counter that it was rumoured cheese would soon be rationed and that then they would only get a square inch a week. Vere Hodgson loved cheese.

He got rid of all the other customers and then said 'wait a mo', [she wrote]. I waited and found being thrust into my bag with great secrecy and speed half a pound of cheese. When I went for my butter ration at the dairy I found I could get a quarter of a pound of cheese. I had no compunction in taking it. I went straight away and gave it to the Mercury café [where she often went for a meal in Notting Hill], where I knew they could not open tomorrow because they had no meat and only a morsel of cheese. I thought I was very lucky. My own piece was very good and I could not resist, as I got in, cutting a hunk and eating it then and there. I sympathise with Benn Gunn when he always dreams of toasted cheese in *Treasure Island*.

2

London was growing used to the sight of foreign soldiers on its streets, and all over the West End little clubs had mushroomed to cater for them. The bulk of the Polish army in exile was stationed in Scotland (where its dashing troopers were bowling over the girls in Edinburgh like ninepins), and the Dutch, Belgians, Scandinavians and French were in encampments spread over different parts of the country; but all of them had headquarters in London and abundant staffs with, it sometimes seemed, ample funds for entertaining. Their chieftains liked to forgather in the more fashionable West End restaurants and hotels, such as the Mirabelle, the Coq d'Or, the Ritz, the Connaught and Claridges, and it was not unusual on some days to see lunching simultaneously at the latter Moshe Shertok*, head of the Jewish Agency, General Sikorsky, leader of the Poles, Admiral Muselier of the Free French Navy, King Haakon of Norway, Colonel Passy† of Free French Intelligence, and Colonel Maurice Buckmaster of SOE.‡ They almost always occupied separate tables, eyeing each other with cold suspicion.

* Later Mr Moshe Sharrett.
† A *nom de guerre*. His real name was André Devavrin.
‡ Special Operations Executive, the British secret service operation for Europe.

The underlings generally preferred the back street clubs which had sprung up in Soho, where you could drink after hours and where, unlike the pubs these days, the liquor never seemed to run out, though it was expensive. Behind the bar you would find a tall redhead or a plump blonde with a man vaguely hovering in the background (he usually turned out to be a Polish or Belgian or Dutch sergeant; some of them became powerful in London's night-club world later). In front of the bar jostled a motley collection of foreign soldiers, some up from the camps, others back from mysterious missions in Europe, all of them with one or even two English girls by their sides. Foreign soldiers were very popular with London girls.

The favourite haunt of the Free French was Le Petit Club de France which was tucked away in a mews behind St James's Street, and numbered among its clientele some of the bravest men and some of the prettiest girls in London. It was presided over by an owlish blonde Welshwoman named Olwen Vaughn, who could handle an obstreperous drunk like a dose of soothing syrup and knew at a glance when a quarrel between two patriotic Frenchmen, one pro and the other anti de Gaulle, needed to be broken up before duels were challenged. She probably knew more about the operations of the French *action militaire* than anyone apart from Colonel Passy, its commander, for most operators who got back safely from a parachute mission into Occupied France made Le Petit Club their first port of call after handing in their reports, and often brought a bottle of pastis or a *boudin* sausage back from Paris so that Olwen could 'smell France again'. (Not that she needed to; the Club was always redolent with the un-mistakable scent of Caporal cigarettes.) There was little that she didn't know about what was going on among the Free French, and early in January 1941 she sensed that a feud at General de Gaulle's headquarters was rapidly coming to a head. A certain estrangement had been developing during the past few nights between members of the Free French Army and the Free French Navy; they stood at different ends of the bar and bowed with formal politeness to those who, only a week or two ago, had been bosom friends.

When young Robert Mengin, who belonged to neither side (for he was still resolutely anti de Gaulle), came into the club on New Year's Day and tried to bring a Navy lieutenant and an Army captain together over a celebration drink, he was met with muttered and confused refusals.

'What's happening here?' he asked. 'Everyone's acting as if the Navy's gone over to Vichy.'

'That,' said Olwen Vaughn, 'is probably the most unfortunate remark of the war.'

Indeed it was.

At Scotland Yard at that precise moment Special Branch officers were drawing up a warrant for the arrest of the Commander-in-Chief of the Free French Navy on a charge of conspiring to commit treason with agents of the Vichy Government.

Admiral Emile Henri Muselier was one of the earliest opponents of Pétain's decision to capitulate to the Germans in 1940. He had been against the Vichy Government right from the very beginning. At the moment when the aged Marshal Pétain appealed to all Frenchmen to accept defeat, Muselier was in Gibraltar with a squadron of his ships. He could have sailed them back to their base at Toulon or taken them to North Africa, but instead he talked to his officers and men and then announced that they were solidly resolved to go on fighting, and that his ships would rally to the side of the British. He had many friends in the British Navy and they roundly cheered him on his way when he left a little later to go to London to discuss the future of the Free French forces.

By that time General Charles de Gaulle had arrived in London and had issued his appeal for Frenchmen everywhere to join him. Nevertheless, most of Muselier's British friends presumed that once he got to London he would take over as leader of the Free French, for he was de Gaulle's senior both in rank and experience and, in fact, the most senior officer of all who had elected to reject defeat and carry on the war in exile.

The admiration which Muselier had won from British and French alike increased when he met de Gaulle at his new headquarters at Carlton House Terrace and made it immediately clear that he was not seeking the leadership. He told the touchy and suspicious General that he would willingly serve under him, and he became the first officer among the Free French to pin the double cross of Lorraine to his service jacket as a sign of his loyalty to the cause of Free France.

Olwen Vaughn and Robert Mengin were, however, not the only ones to notice in the weeks that followed that some members of de Gaulle's immediate entourage did not take kindly to the arrival of Admiral Muselier in their midst. Members of the General's intelligence service, which was then in the process of an intensive build-up, seemed particularly resentful of the Admiral's advent. It was a period when General de Gaulle was making the most strenuous efforts to persuade French men and women abroad that he was the incarnation of French resistance, and Robert Mengin was not the only one to find this arrogant and presumptuous. Though many thousands had rallied to the General's call, a surprisingly large number had not. They resented de Gaulle's use of the royal 'we' in all his statements to emphasise his superior status ('In the name of the French people and Empire, we, General de Gaulle, leader of the Free French'), and strenuously denied his claim that if they were not for him they must be for Vichy.

It was these Frenchmen in exile, suspicious of de Gaulle, of whom the General's cohorts at Carlton House Terrace were most afraid, for their antagonism might well undermine de Gaulle's claim to represent all Frenchmen who were still fighting. They were dangerous so long as they had an alternative fighter in exile to turn to. Admiral Muselier, for instance. He was much admired by the Free French Navy, the only arm of the Free French forces which was seeing any action at the moment. And if things went wrong for General de Gaulle, might they not begin to agitate for his replacement – by the Admiral?

So though Admiral Muselier gave no hint of disloyalty to his chosen leader and implicitly obeyed his every order, the inner ring of fanatic Gaullists continued to view him as a potential rival who must somehow be removed. They redoubled their efforts after an operation in September 1940 against the Vichy-held colony of Dakar by General de Gaulle's forces. This had been an absolute disaster. Dakar, with a splendidly equipped naval port on the West African coast, had treasures that General de Gaulle vitally needed to finance and fuel his Government in exile. It was the base for the great French battleship, *Richelieu*. Up-country, the gold bullion stores of the French, Polish and Belgian Governments were hidden after being flown from Paris. Here was a port which the British could use as an anti-submarine base for the war against the German U-boats which were annihilating the Allied convoys in the South Atlantic. And here was a base from which the British could halt any German attempt to push southwards into Africa from the French colonies and possessions in the north. The capture of Dakar would make de Gaulle a rich man, able to come to the bargaining table with Churchill and demand what he wanted instead of asking for favours. 'I can give you Dakar. This is what I must have in return.'

Only it hadn't worked out that way. The Governor of Dakar, though strenuously anti-German, had proved to be as equally anti de Gaulle. He would not rally when the General urged him to do so. When an Anglo-French force moved in, he opened fire. Three days later, the Allied forces retired and Dakar stayed in Vichy hands.

Now more than ever did de Gaulle's position seem to his cohorts to be threatened.

On 27 December fate (if that is what it can be called) played into their hands. They were able to go to General de Gaulle with evidence that Admiral Muselier was a traitor.

On New Year's Day, 1941, Mr Anthony Eden* telephoned General de Gaulle in Shropshire, where he had gone to spend a few days with his wife and son, and asked him if he could return to London immediately. It was an open line so that Eden did not say why he wanted the General back, but he did stress that it was urgent and that it concerned a Free French officer of distinguished rank. However, it was not until the following day, 2 January, that General de Gaulle decided to leave for London. By that time Admiral Muselier was under arrest. He had returned to London on the morning of 2 January after taking part in a Red Cross rally at Windsor and found two Scotland Yard Special Branch officers waiting on the doorstep of his home in Hallam Street, Knightsbridge. They told him he was under arrest, but would not or could not specify the charges.

Muselier went inside the house to change out of uniform and then, wearing his naval greatcoat against the cold, accompanied the officers to Scotland Yard. There he was given cups of tea, followed by lunch, with relays of officers watching him closely, and there he remained until the afternoon. He still had no idea why he was being held.

That afternoon General de Gaulle arrived in London from

* The then Foreign Secretary.

Shropshire and was driven at once to see Anthony Eden at the Foreign Office. It was a difficult moment for the British Foreign Secretary and his distress was visible. He was a great friend of France. He knew and admired Admiral Muselier. Yet he had to tell his chief, General de Gaulle, that Scotland Yard possessed evidence that Muselier was a traitor.

'I have an appalling thing to tell you,' Eden said. 'We seem to have the proof that Admiral Muselier is secretly in communication with the Vichy Government, that he tried to transmit to Darlan* the plan for the Dakar landing while it was being prepared, and that he was planning to send the *Surcouf*† over to him. The Prime Minister, having been told the facts, has given the order for the Admiral to be arrested, and it has been approved by the Cabinet. We needn't conceal what kind of an impression this terrible business will have upon us and upon you. But it was impossible for us not to act without delay.'

Eden then produced notes which appeared to have been written by General Rozoy on the notepaper of the French Consulate in London. General Rozoy had acted in London as chief French Air Force liaison officer with the RAF until the Franco-German armistice, when he had elected to return to France and join the Vichy Government. The French Consulate in London was still controlled by Vichy nominees. The notes, which purported to give details of Rozoy's dealings with Muselier (they also mentioned that he had been paid £2,000), were said to have been on their way to Vichy in the diplomatic bag of a South American courier when they were intercepted and turned over to British intelligence.

Now, as it subsequently turned out, anyone who studied the notes with anything like an expert eye would have seen at once that they were forgeries. General de Gaulle himself quotes Eden as saying, 'Après une minutieuse enquête, les autorités britanniques devaient, hélas! se convaincre de leur authenticité.'‡

But in fact the inquiries had by no means been meticulous. And it is surprising that General de Gaulle did not see at once that

---

* Admiral Darlan, Commander-in-Chief of the Vichy-controlled French Navy and one of Marshal Pétain's closest collaborators.
† A Free French submarine.
‡ After a meticulous inquiry, the British authorities, alas, are convinced of their authenticity.

the notes were forgeries, for there were several mistakes in the general usage of General Staff communications with which he might have been expected to be familiar. One must presume that he was still suffering from the effects of his rebuff at Dakar, for instead of the haughty choler which he usually displayed towards the British when one of his staff was called in question, he merely said that he must go away and think.

His departure from the Foreign Office without demanding Admiral Muselier's immediate release – and without threatening to sever relations between Free France and Britain, which is what Eden had feared – was taken as a signal by the Special Branch to go ahead with the arrest. Admiral Muselier was driven to Pentonville Prison and told to strip by the prison doctor, whose examination, the admiral was afterwards to say, was so meticulous that it reactivated a painful wound from World War One. When he protested that he was an admiral of France and should not be treated in such a way, the doctor curtly replied:

'If you were an admiral, you would not be here!'

He was still not told what charges had been levelled against him, merely that he had been arrested under a wartime regulation and that he could look forward to an indefinite period of imprisonment. By this time he had no doubt in his mind that he was the victim of an intrigue against him by his enemies among the French at Carlton Gardens.

While he sat and brooded in his cell, guests were assembling in the West End of London for a luncheon party. It was being given at Lancaster House by Mr Oliver Stanley, Secretary of State for War, for the commanders of the Allied nations, and the milling crowd of Belgian, Dutch, Czech, Polish, Norwegian, Greek and Yugoslav generals and admirals buzzed with speculation as the rumour swept through their ranks that 'the French have got a scandal on their hands'. But General de Gaulle gave no sign of being disturbed when he marched towards his place at the table, physically and mentally aloof from the lesser fry around him. A few minutes later he was followed by Admiral Muselier's chief of staff, Captain Moullec. No one had yet told Moullec what had happened to his chief. He stopped before the Admiral's place at the table, saw that a card had been hastily placed over the holder containing his name, and looked bewildered. A British officer hastened over to him and led him quietly away, explaining as he went. But everyone in the room had seen and they were now looking at de Gaulle. He stared grimly into the distance and took no notice.

That night, in Le Petit Club de France, there was a fight between a Free French major and a naval lieutenant that might have developed into an ugly brawl between the Army and Navy had not Olwen Vaughan intervened in time. The jeers were going around that the Free French Navy's leader was a spy.

It was not until 48 hours later that General de Gaulle at length made up his mind that the charges against Admiral Muselier were possibly false. He went to see Anthony Eden at the Foreign Office and tardily expressed his displeasure over the fact that his second-in-command had been unceremoniously flung into jail.

'Les documents sont ultra-suspects,' he said, 'tant par leur contexte que par leur source supposée. En tout cas, ce ne sont pas des preuves. Rien ne justifie l'outrageante arrestation d'un vice-amiral français. Celui-ci n'a, d'ailleurs, pas été entendu. Moi-même n'ai pas la possibilité de le voir. Tout cela est injustifiable. Pour l'instant, il faut, au minimum, que l'amiral Muselier sort de prison et soit traité honorablement jusqu'à ce que cette sombre histoire soit éclaircie.'*

Eden promised to do his best but maintained that the charge was such a serious one that for the moment Muselier must remain in jail. One might have expected that the General, now that he was convinced of the spuriousness of the documents, and therefore of the charges against his second-in-command, would have threatened a rupture with the British Government if the Admiral was not taken to more comfortable quarters. He must have been well aware that the British wanted at all costs to avoid an open quarrel with the Free French at this moment.

Instead, it was the British themselves who came to Muselier's aid. He had many warm friends in the Royal Navy and one of them, Admiral Dickens, went to see him at Pentonville. He was shocked by his conditions and by his state of health. (Muselier

---

* The documents are ultra-suspect, both in their context and their supposed source. In any case, there is no proof. Nothing justifies this outrageous arrest of an admiral of France. He has not even been heard. I myself have not been able to see him. This is quite insupportable. For the moment Admiral Muselier must, at least, be taken from prison and treated honourably until such time as this sombre affair can be cleared up.

was afterwards to claim that he was badly treated by his warders.) He shook hands warmly with the Admiral and promised to do something for him immediately; he was a man of his word and that afternoon he saw both the First Lord of the Admiralty, Lord Alexander, and the First Sea Lord, Admiral Sir Dudley Pound.

The following day Muselier was taken to guarded quarters at the Royal Naval College at Greenwich, and there he remained until 8 January. On that day he was driven to Scotland Yard and, for the first time, shown the documents which were supposed to be so incriminating. He took one look at them and said, 'But these are fakes. Bring in one of your French experts and he will agree with me.'

A French expert was already there. It did not take him more than a moment's examination to dub the five pages of notes 'forgeries, and clumsy ones at that'.

The same afternoon General de Gaulle called in General Sir Edward Spears and delivered an ultimatum to him. 'I told him that I would give the British Government twenty-four hours to release the Admiral and make suitable reparations, in default of which all relations between Free France and Great Britain would be broken off, no matter what the consequences.' In the opinion of most people concerned with the affair, the ultimatum had been a long time coming.

General Spears went with him to Scotland Yard where, in fact, Muselier was being released at that moment, with fulsome apologies. De Gaulle rushed up to him and embraced him, but Admiral Muselier all but repulsed him. His attitude was cold.

Next day there was a letter to Muselier from Eden apologising to him for his ordeal and saying that, 'His Majesty's Government have satisfied themselves that the documents, which first appeared to cast suspicion on you, are spurious.' It was followed by an invitation to dine with the Prime Minister and Mrs Churchill at 10 Downing Street at which more apologies were voiced. Then came a further invitation, to lunch with King George the Sixth at Buckingham Palace.

General de Gaulle watched these clumsy attempts by the British to make amends with a certain ill humour. 'The change of attitude on the part of the British and of the Admiral was so complete that it soon turned out to be excessive,' he wrote.

He blamed the British for having manufactured the charges against Muselier, and accused the British intelligence services of having recruited Frenchmen who had 'cooked up' the plot against Muselier. Muselier, on the other hand, remained convinced until his death in 1965 that the plot against him was hatched in Carlton Gardens among the Free French themselves. But the truth will probably never be known. One Free French officer who might have thrown some light on the mysterious affair was arrested by the French a few days after the Admiral's release and quietly taken out of Britain to a Free French colony in Africa, where he died in prison.

Relations between de Gaulle and Muselier became cool to glacial from now on, and they would deteriorate further in the months to come.

In fact, the only people to draw dividends from the whole sordid story were de Gaulle's security forces at Carlton Gardens. On 15 January, taking advantage of British embarrassment over the affair, General de Gaulle signed an accord with Anthony Eden giving the Free French on British territory jurisdiction over their forces and the right to set up their own military courts.

Henceforward, in such matters as the Muselier affair, General de Gaulle's investigators and tribunals would be left to handle the matter themselves, without any interference from the British.

3

On 29 April Winston Churchill broadcast to the nation to announce that Yugoslavia had fallen to the Germans and to hint that Greece would soon follow. Vere Hodgson listened to his words and thought that he sounded unutterably weary. She wrote in her diary that night:

He does love to give us good news, but there was nothing he could say but that there was worse to come. ... He sketched the fearful possibilities of Hitler extending into the Mediterranean, etc. He did not think we could do much about it. He did not explain lots of things we should like to know, but I suppose we shall know some day. First of all, if, as he said, it was inevitable that Yugoslavia should be defeated, why was he so elated the other day when he announced that they had declared for us? Then he never attempted to explain how the Germans got to Libya. Why did we not know they were coming?

You could almost hear her sigh as she paused between that and the next sentence, when she went on:

But he did not seem to mind his responsibilities and faced the future with equanimity. So we must do the same. If he cannot win through then no one can. It must be something within ourselves that is working against us.

London nowadays wore a gaunt and neglected look that was only partly relieved by the wild flowers beginning to sprout on the bomb-sites. Newcomers noticed that Londoners walked past their bombed buildings in the West End and Westminster and the City with an almost self-conscious refusal to look at them, rather in the way that the English don't stare at shabby beggars or cripples so as not to embarrass them (or themselves). It was as if they did not wish to hurt the feelings of the Houses of Parliament and the Guildhall and the Church of St James in Piccadilly by peering at them in their bombed-out misery.

One of the results of the war and the bombing was the restrictive effect it had had upon travel, so that citizens of one London borough had little if any knowledge of what had happened in another just across the river or the park. When they were forced to make a crosstown journey they were often surprised and shocked.

'I knew we'd had a rotten time,' they would say, 'but I didn't know it had happened to you too!'

One voluntary worker drove that spring through the City to the docks and found it difficult to put the cumulative shocks into words:

The further we penetrated into the City, down Mark Lane and past Crutched Friars, the more appalled we were by the perfectly tremendous extent, and degree, too, of the damage. Fire has razed this part of London. For every building that would have been wrecked by high explosive bombs there were twenty completely gutted, and there were acres of entire streets all done for together – barricaded and cut off from the outside world in their charred and smouldering death.

On to the docks, where it was a relief to be among ships and cranes and seagulls on a sunny morning, with the sun coming through the mist over London Bridge. But then more shocking sights too:

> Whole rows of three and four warehouses or factories along the waterfront all burnt out, or wrecked and silhouetted in a jagged, gaping unevenness against the milky sky. And of course the worst places of all were those where the casual eye perceived no damage at all, just emptiness; places where whole groups of huge tall buildings should have stood which had all been burned down to the waterline. There is, of course, nothing emotionally horrifying in the spectacle of ruined and gutted warehouses and wharves, as there is in dwelling houses in a like condition; but this first sight of the destruction among the docks gave me an awful shock, none the less. It really opened my eyes to the immense extent of the material damage that has been done.

Somehow, Londoners seemed to have lost the almost gay defiance with which they had faced the concentrated and brutal bombing of the previous autumn. The raids were not so frequent now, but the bruises they left on everyone's spirit somehow seemed to go deeper.

Towards the end of April 1941, Rosemary Black wrote:

> I found myself sinking deeper and deeper into a trough of depression, until at teatime I was positively maudlin. Perhaps fatigue has something to do with it, although I didn't feel tired in the least.

The West End as Evelyn Waugh and Cecil Beaton and Oliver Messel and Noel Coward had known it in the 1930s was now no more. The fashionable night club the Café de Paris had disappeared in a shower of blood and champagne the previous autumn, and in April its sister night-club, the Café Anglais, followed it into the dust. Quaglino's and the Aperitif had perished in the bombing of Jermyn Street along with Dunhill's and Fortnum and Mason's. If you went looking for entertainment now you went early, even to lunchtime concerts at the National Gallery (from which most of the pictures had been evacuated) and the crypt of St Martin's in the Fields. The appalling losses and the dislocation caused by the bombing were inducing a sort of numbing misery, especially as the casualty lists began to come closer to home and almost everyone knew a friend or a relative who had been maimed or killed or made homeless by the raids.

'It's always the best that goes, too, isn't it?' people would say.

A taxi driver described how the garage where he kept his cab had been heavily bombed. ' 'E [meaning Hitler] did my old cab in. But what upset us all was that 'e got the old chap 'oo was our washer. Been our washer there for years. Lovely old feller 'e was, too. Seems queer it 'ad to be someone like that to go.'

4

To the visitor from abroad, the West End of London that spring may have looked like a desolate waste of smashed buildings and shabby, tattered shops. But to the eye of an East Ender it was a world of gaiety full of tempting things.

Bill and Eileen Harriman and their son John came up West one Sunday in March and went to the Empire Cinema in Leicester Square to see *Gone With The Wind*. It was the first outing they had had since Linda's death in the bombing, and the fact that it dealt with the agonies and separations of war seemed to release pent-up emotions in all of them, and after a time Eileen was sobbing so much that people began turning round and they had to go out.

They wandered around the West End goggling at the tins of turtle soup in a fashionable store the fur coats in the shops in Bond Street, the colourful uniforms of foreign soldiers on the streets. They had tea of boiled beef, carrots and dumplings in Lyons Corner House in Piccadilly and marvelled at the plenitude around them.

There were still two worlds in London, Eileen Harriman decided; and she had no doubt which was the privileged one. The small flat which Bill had procured for them at the back of the factory in Aldgate was cleaner and airier than the old house in Canning Town, and the little Jewish children with whom John now went to school seemed to be cleaner than the ones in Star Road, and he no longer came home with nits in his hair. But they were surrounded by dreary wastes of bomb damage and broken down shops that never seemed to have enough food. She queued for hours every day to get the bare rations to which they were entitled, and there was nothing in the shops to supplement them –

and no cafés or restaurants to go to for a meal when your weekly quota was used up. She passed most of her own rations over to Bill and John, but they were still always hungry. So each morning she would set off on a tour of all the surrounding districts, tramping the streets for hours in the hope of picking up an odd orange or apple or a tin of goods on points.

It was bad enough to come back exhausted from the endless searching, but even worse to return empty-handed and have to face Bill's heavy sighs and John's reproachful: 'But Mum, I'm hungry.'

She looked in the West End shop windows and decided that here no one ever went hungry. There was always something you could get, to give variety to a meal. They went into Jackson's and bought curry powder and a tin of fruit and some tinned pilchards, none of which she had seen since before the war. And in the pub they went to in the Haymarket, the Bosun's Locker, they actually asked you what kind of drink you wanted, instead of saying, as they did at the Dragon in Aldgate: 'Only mild-and-bitter today, and the limit's a pint.'

As they were riding back home in the tube, John said:

'Dad, wouldn't it be wonderful if we lived in the West End?'

Bill patted his son's shoulder and didn't answer. He said good-bye to them at Aldgate Station, and hurried off to his weekly drill with the Home Guard, into whose ranks he had now been compulsorily enrolled.

Eileen and John walked back through the ugly gashed, empty streets.

The following day she was being registered for national service, which meant that she would soon be working in a factory. She had a sad feeling that the family was being split up.

All through the winter and spring of 1941 Rosemary Black drove a YMCA van through the bombed streets of London delivering tea and pies to the workers on the bomb sites, and her lively eye missed nothing of what was going on around her. By this time the capital was full of battalions of middle- and upper-middle-class women of the kind who always rally to England's aid when the nation is in danger. They were driving cars for generals, serving teas for soldiers, manning food trains for the homeless in the

Underground, solving problems for the sick and the poor and the helpless. They were brave, they were indefatigable and their hearts were warm. But there was no denying the fact that their outward appearance and manner were formidable, and rarely have angels of mercy come in less attractive guise.

Rosemary Black had been told from the beginning that she must regard herself only as a 'temporary' until she had 'won her wings, so to speak', and she meekly accepted the conditions, the hours and the arduousness of her routine. Her companions quite frankly daunted her. Most of the 'full-timers', as she called them, were youngish and conformed to a definite type.

Their class is right up to the county family level. Nearly everyone is tall above the average and remarkably hefty, even definitely large, not necessarily fat but broad and brawny. Perhaps this is something to do with the survival of the fittest. They are all heavily uniformed, of course, they all tend to drive their vans rather too fast and dashingly and make a great business of being clever with short cuts which in my opinion are often more swank than use. Owing to their seniority and experience and owing to the fact that they all know each other, they're inclined to treat the temporaries with casual scorn and throw their weight about.

She found herself resenting them and grew to dislike being sent out with them.

The older members of the heavyweight group fall into a sub-group of old trouts who are also heavily uniformed and are distinguished for their bossiness though this is not, in fact, justified by their efficiency. They are obsessed – can this be something to do with their age? – by the regulations as to the exact amount of sugar and milk to each mug of tea, the exact number of pieces to be got out of a slab of cut cake, and so on, to which no one else pays more than casual attention. I was with one of these horrors on the first day of my trials and she did nothing but nag me for being over-generous with both milk and sugar. ... [Then come] the betwixt and between group made up of drivers like myself, mostly youngish, who are ineligible for the county family heavyweight élite both on account of their inferior social standing and for their junior position, but who are more or less *débrouillard* in contrast to the dead-beats.

It was this type who pushed their way through the bombing to get tea to the firemen and the rescue squads at the height of the raids, who were up at dawn to bring tea to the demolition squads. For their bravery and persistence they received an occasional pat on the back from their ultra-aristocratic leader, Lady Dash, for whom Rosemary Black had nothing but praise, for under her fey manner she had drive and a sense of purpose and a formidable bravery. One morning at the end of an all-night raid, the drivers gathered in their canteen in the Strand for breakfast and were listening to the latest British defeats in the Mediterranean when Lady Dash joined them.

'Oh, dear, oh dear, what is one to do with oneself when the news is always so desperate?' she cried, in her booming voice. Then she looked round at her flock and added: 'Though I never have the slightest doubt but that we shall win in the end, so I suppose it is just a waste of time to worry.'

Rosemary Black reached out for another piece of toast, and then hesitated.

'Should I?' she asked no one in particular. 'I've had three already. I'll get as fat as a pig.'

'Oh, yes, do have it, dear,' said Lady Dash. 'With things so depressing you must take whatever enjoyment you can. I'm just going out to enjoy myself. Eat too much, sleep too much, drink too much. . . .'

While the others laughed, Rosemary Black looked across at the grey-haired, elderly woman. She had been out all night serving tea in the shelters. Not a hair was out of place, not a line on the face revealed the inner tiredness and despair she must be feeling.

They all knew how depressed and deflated this kind of work could make you, and it wasn't just because you saw death and destruction. You ran into hate and intolerance too. Most of the gangs now cleaning up the bombed buildings in London were an odd assortment of refugees, army rejects, ex-prisoners and other types who, for one reason or another, were not considered suitable material for the fighting forces. They were lumped together into units called Pioneers and they were given the dirtiest as well as some of the most dangerous jobs on the bomb sites. Most of the Pioneers were looked down upon – though with no justification whatsoever – by both civilians and military as the lower depths of the war effort. Their uniforms gave them no status with the armed forces and lost them the privileges of civil life. The contempt with which they were regarded was particularly strong towards those Pioneers who were registered conscientious objectors and had volunteered for work on the bomb sites.

'How can you bear to serve them?' a soldier's wife shouted at Rosemary Black one day. 'If I were in your place, I'd throw the tea in their faces.'

In fact, she found that the 'conshies' were usually the most amiable and thoughtful of her customers. At least they were never crushed like some of the craven refugee squads they served, who seemed to be treated like animals by the British NCOs in charge of them, and behaved like animals in consequence.

She wrote:

One gang had *the* most frightful bawling British NCO in charge of them, a real last-war sergeant type with a coiffe, a stentorian voice and a real, bully mentality. Every minute he was bawling at his men to hurry up. 'Hurry up there, don't take all day about it!' he would shout. 'Come on, get on with it, can't you, get on with it!' We were nearly demented as well as deaf from this incessant bawling. It made things more difficult for us, because it made the men more pushing and more whining than ever in their desperate haste, while we were nearly frantic at having to serve at such a fevered pace to keep up with this incessant nagging. . . . I was reminded of prisons, of snarling bullying warders endlessly nagging at their surly, stupefied convict gangs, driving them almost insane with their perpetual bawling. It was all beastly somehow, the pushing, whining, crouching refugee Pioneers shoving and shuffling like a herd of driven beasts in the pouring, chilly rain and the bawling bully boy metaphorically cracking his whip over them. There was an atmosphere at once of the cattle market and the concentration camp about it.

She was infuriated by the grumbling, querulous man and, as his compatriot, ashamed of him.

His petty bullying seemed more suitable for a Prussian official at Dachau than to the British Army. The whole thing depressed and disheartened us and made the work hard, anyhow, seem twice as tiring.

One of the great shortages in England now was sugar. Everybody missed it. The ration doled out to the YMCA mobile canteens was barely enough to flavour the cups of tea. But Rosemary Black had found a way. Early in May, she reported:

> Pouring with rain. We had a pleasant and uneventful day's work serving City fire sites, the General Post Office, demolition workers and Home Guard stations, etc. We were complimented at least half a dozen times on the quality of our tea. One North Country Pioneer said: 'It's the best cup of tea I've set eyes on since I left home,' and another said: 'Why don't you come round here more often, Miss? We could do with some more of your tea.' I think the provision of saccharine for the tea urns to compensate for the mean sugar allowance is my most successful piece of war work. *What did you do in the Great War, Mummy? Sneaked pills into the tea urns, darling.*

Britain had never forgotten that some of her most distinguished men had gone to prison during the First World War as conscientious objectors and had often been treated with contumely by the public and with great cruelty by their warders. It was a measure of the changed attitude towards pacifism that one of them, the Rt. Honourable Herbert Morrison, MP, was now a member of the War Cabinet with the vital job of Home Secretary and Minister of Home Security. No one was anxious to persecute conscientious objectors now, and provided they showed willingness to work on bomb sites, in hospitals or on the land, they could be reasonably sure of registration as a genuine objector and exemption from military service. Those who refused to co-operate in any way with the authorities could still be sent to gaol, but even for them the State moved with a great show of reluctance and seemed desperately anxious not to make a martyr of any young man, just because he was a pacifist.

The dilatoriness of the law in getting round to his case was, Peter Donald found, all but infuriating. He had failed to register for military service with his age group, and the law had not caught up with the omission until seven months later, when they sent him a registration form and asked for a statement. It had taken them another two months to digest this and summon him to an Appeals Tribunal in south-east London. Instead of attending,

Peter was determined to force them to take action against him. He had written to them just before the end of 1940:

> I have decided not to attend my tribunal on the 31st inst. I am enclosing a letter from my father and a copy of a letter from a friend. These letters will, I am sure, help you in your decision.
>
> I am not convinced that it is any more possible for a tribunal to judge a conscience than it was for Brother Juniper in Thornton Wilder's book, *Bridge of San Luiz Rey**, to reduce religion to an exact science. To my mind it is as impossible to measure a conscience as it is to calculate a degree of love, hate or faith. Because of this belief I refused last year to register as a CO. The Ministry of Labour required seven months to 'go to it' before they discovered my omission! The Ministry have described me as a Commercial Artist and an Industrial Designer. I am not at present engaged in either of these professions. I am an author. I claim that literature is essential for the culture and diversion of the community and for international goodwill and understanding. ... I have stated on the form [of registration] that I claim unconditional exemption. I will modify this by saying that the only condition I can accept is that I continue my present work. Should the tribunal not grant me either unconditional exemption or exemption under the condition I have named, I should be glad if your clerk would enter my name as one wishing to appeal. Looking forward to hearing of your decision, I remain etc.

As he posted the letter, he said to his landlady, Mrs R, 'I should like to see the faces of the worthy gentlemen when they read that over!'

'H'm!' she said.

'Now we must sit tight and wait. Such a lot of bloody rot – just because a man refuses to fight!'

'H'm,' said Mrs R, again.

'See you in quod,' said Brenda.

Only that was months ago, and he was still around.

'Still waiting!' he wrote in his diary in May, 1941. 'Twelve months have passed – all entangled with red tape!'

When he said good-bye to people and cycled away from them

---

* *I'll bet they've never heard of this book*, he wrote in his diary.

these days, he was in the habit of lifting his arm and giving the Nazi salute. They looked startled, but no one did anything about it, except a policeman who shouted to him:

' 'Ere, you! what d'you think you're doing, riding around one-handed? You watch it. You'll be breaking your neck!'

The last mass German bomber raid on London on the night of 10–11 May 1941 was a 'spite' raid ordered by Hitler to give London a last ordeal before he brought the Luftwaffe East for the attack on Russia. The raid involved 505 planes. They dropped 498 tons of high explosive and incendiary bombs and land-mines. The RAF's night-fighters now each equipped with their own radar sets, shot down fourteen enemy bombers for the loss of one of their own. 2,200 fires were started, including 9 officially classed as 'conflagrations', 20 as major fires, 37 as serious and the rest as medium. At one time 700 acres of London were burning, nearly twice the area covered by the Great Fire of London. Westminster Abbey was hit, as were Scotland Yard, St Paul's Cathedral, the City (again) and East and West Ham and Silvertown (of course); Cannon Street, Paddington, Waterloo, St Pancras, Euston, Liverpool Street, Blackfriars, and Victoria stations were out of action (in fact all mainline railway terminals except one); all bridges across the Thames were either cratered or blocked; the main telephone exchange was destroyed, so that telephone wires were cut off; and then there were the Londoners themselves.

That night 1,436 died (more people, as has been pointed out, than died in the San Francisco earthquake of 1906) and 1,800 were seriously injured.

But the raid did more than just kill and maim the people of London. It all but broke their spirit. When it finally came to an end shortly after dawn on the morning of 11 May and the sirens wailed over a blazing, smoking, devastated capital there were people in the streets openly weeping not from pain or weariness or fear, but from sheer downright despair. But most Londoners were too numbed to weep.

Not so Vere Hodgson.

Just heard the terrible news that Westminster Hall was hit last night, also the Abbey and the Houses of Parliament. [She wrote on 11 May]. They saved the roof to a large extent but some of it is gone. In the Abbey it is the lantern. They thought at first that Big Ben had crashed to the ground. I cannot comment on such disasters. I just feel grievously limp. I feel we must have sinned grievously to have such sacrifices demanded of us. ... There's bound to be further destruction, and there's not much satisfaction to hear of the treasures of our enemies being laid to waste in a similar manner. I don't wish it, but it is grievous not to be able to protect our own.

She turned the page and then wrote firmly:

I can see all our ancestors looking down at us reproachfully and saying: 'We gave it to you. You have not guarded it and handed it on as you received it. You have failed in your trust, even those of you who loved it best.'

But Rosemary Black, who was out in the middle of it in her mobile canteen, wrote of it differently:

The shine of headlights on water, gleaming oilskins and tin hats, a contrast of yellow highlights and deep shadows, and the grimy, haggard faces emerging out of the blackness at the counter. The apricot glowing beauty of light from a fire in Fetter Lane from which streams of sparks poured up into the peacock blueness of the evening. Evil pink and blue flickering tongues of flame from the hell-fire cellar of burning coke in the Temple. The shifting yet solid mass of humanity filling Fleet Street from side to side as a river in full flow fills its banks. Yet the really vivid impression of the night left on my mind after a lapse of some hours was the startlingly casual unemotional almost uncaring acceptance which struck me as the general reaction to this terrific smashing ... a shoulder-shrugging indifference compared with the grief and indignation aroused by last autumn's big blitzes and by the large City fires at the close of the year.

It was partly just case-hardening, she thought.

But also it is said that people who have lost their homes and possessions in the raids seem to experience a curious indifference, almost a feeling of relief and release through fulfilment of their worst fears and worries. I remember Mary telling me that after she had been bombed out of her flat with the loss of all her clothes and belongings, she had simply not cared about personal things ever since. ... Then too there is the human inability to take in more than a certain degree of calamity, which is God's merciful tempering of the wind to the shorn lamb.

For the next few days Londoners walked through their capital as if in a daze. Foreign observers noticed that though the weather was good, a fact which can make London in spring the most joyful place in the world, no one seemed to smile. Faces looked dead. Larry Rue, an American correspondent, saw two separate 'City gents' walking to their offices one morning in the regulation black coats and striped trousers, bowler hats on head, briefcases under arm, but stubble on their chins. There had been no raid to keep them up during the night. True, the 10 May onslaught had broken water mains and gas pipes and heating systems, but on most occasions that would not have prevented a City gent from shaving to go to his office. But suddenly people didn't seem to care.

'I began to get really worried for the first time,' Rue said. 'I began to realise to what deep depths of their being the 10 May raid had shocked and shaken the people of London. It was just one raid too much.'

All through the far-from-merry month of May the mood persisted. 'Oh, what's the use,' people everywhere were saying. If the sergeants-in-charge had bawled and nagged at their men working on the bomb sites before they were screaming at them in frenetic rage now, for the heart seemed to have gone out of their demolition work. They picked at the scarred London buildings like small boys picking at scabs. Most Cockneys sympathised with their apathy. What was the use of trying to clean up when everyone knew that the Jerries would be back again any night now to wreck and ruin London all over again?

And then, as two weeks, three weeks, a month went by without a serious raid, and night after night without even the wail of a siren, the zombie mood began to change to a kind of uneasy speculation.

'Something's up,' said a mate to Police Constable David Meade. They were having a farewell drink in Charley Brown's pub in

Limehouse. Next day Meade was off to report to the RAF.*
'You're well out of it, lad. Jerry's planning something, and you
can bet your life it'll be bloody painful.'

By the middle of June 1941, the general relief at the absence of
bombing still seemed too good to be true, and though everyone
luxuriated in the fact that whole nights could actually be spent
in sleeping, very few of them yet were going upstairs to their
beds. Every night the Underground station platforms were still
littered with the bodies of thousands of shelterers from the East
End.

And then, on 22 June 1941, the German Army invaded Russia.
The war had gone East. The pressure was off. BLITZ OVER, said
a headline in the *London Evening News*. MOSCOW'S TURN NOW.
Old women and invalids came out of the tunnels and the Underground for the first time for months and blinked in the unexpected
sunshine. Husbands and wives embraced with no fear of the in-
trusive and deflating siren. The creak of the marital beds was
almost audible all over London – though often, for war is still war,
they were wrong husbands and wives who were creaking them.

What joy it was to live in London and be safe again!

And then a strange thing happened. It was as if something had
gone out of their lives. Could it be true that Londoners, by July,
were actually beginning to miss the bombing, or rather the
camaraderie and excitement which it had brought into their
existence?

Chemists all over the capital reported that they were having a
run on sleeping tablets. 'It's so quiet at night now that people
get restless,' one of them said. Bus conductors and shopkeepers
reported that their customers were growing increasingly bad
tempered. An air-raid warden, a hero to his neighbours in April,
ruefully reported that one of them called him 'a bloody Nosey
Parker' in July.

The Government noticed the change, too. Now that their lives
were no longer in nightly danger, Londoners were beginning to
be aware once more of the inconveniences and the growing
shortages and discomforts of wartime.

* He left that month for Canada to train as a pilot, but later returned
to fly over Europe as rear-gunner in a bomber. He is now a school-teacher
in Cheshire, Connecticut, USA.

'Now I know the blitz is over,' said Arthur Ketley to his wife. 'People are beginning to grumble again.'

'What are we going to do about Donald's clothes now we've got clothes rationing?' asked Mrs Ketley. 'He either grows out of them or wears them out in weeks. We'll *never* manage on the coupons we're entitled to.'

'See what I mean?' said Mr Ketley, winking at Donald.

EXTRACTS FROM THE DIARY OF MISS VERE HODGSON, SOCIAL WORKER, HOLLAND PARK, LONDON W.14.
1941

Sunday 23 June. There is great news. It seems that Germany has invaded Russia, and now we will see what *they* will do about it. They have not been too nice to us in the past, but now we have to be friends and help one another. . . . Tonight I heard Mr Churchill talking about it on the radio. He says we have now reached the fourth climacteric of the war. The first was a year ago when France fell prostrate under the German hammer and we had to face the storm alone. The second was when the Royal Air Force beat the Hun raiders out of the daylight sky, and thus warded off the Nazi invasion of our island. The third turning point was when the President and Congress of the United States passed the Lease-Lend enactment, devoting nearly 2,000 millions sterling of the wealth of America to help us defend our liberties and their own. The fourth was the entry of Russia into the war. He called Hitler a bloodthirsty gutter-snipe and said we should support Russia as much as they wanted us to.

2 July. I cannot weep for the Russians as I did for the Greeks because they have had plenty of time to prepare for this fight, and if they are not ready it is nobody's fault but their own. Also they have been so secretive and only looked after themselves. They have not shown any vision about what might happen to them, and I can watch this duel with a kind of detachment. Though I know that if the Russians are overcome, our day will be on us with a vengeance. But somehow I think that Stalin is more of a match for Hitler than any of us. He looks such an unpleasant kind of individual.

15 July. Churchill told us to expect a resumption of the air raids in the autumn but said we would be better prepared, and that the shelters would be heated, etc.

18 July. I forgot to mention that I was heavily told off by the Kensington Salvage Council for throwing away a crust of mouldy bread, and therefore wasting food. Mrs Gray, my landlady, has no arrangement for storing old food for the salvage collectors [who use it as pig-food, etc.] and the charwoman put it in the tub, where someone poking around found it. It seems rather hard that I should be the one singled out, since I have several times nearly poisoned my friends Barishnikov and Miss Hillyard in using up my stores of ancient food. I am one of the most economical people, but having been far from well lately, I was afraid to eat the food. But anyway I hope they drop on the real offenders.

14-21 July. I was moved nearly to tears tonight by a postscript [a Sunday night programme on the BBC] by Mr Harry Hopkins [President Roosevelt's special envoy]. . . . He said America would not let Britain go hungry, but would get food through to her no matter how the U-boat war developed at sea. Dorothy Thompson [US war correspondent in London] spoke this week. She compared England to a gigantic Noah's Ark riding the storm with examples of every species aboard.

14 September. There are magnificent apples in the shops at ninepence a pound. I bought a whole pound and felt like wolfing the lot, but instead Auntie Nell and I made blackberry and apple jam on Saturday with the sugar I saved out of my ration. The shops are cheering up a bit. There are tomatoes – not hidden behind the counters or anywhere, but on view. Plums, too. Lord Woolton [the Food Minister] says that if we are bombed again he will increase our rations to keep us going.

16 November. We shall soon need suitcases to carry around our ration books. Milk is now the big problem. We are to have two pints a week for each adult.

28 November. My first egg for a fortnight turned out to be bad. How annoying. Just as milk rationing came in. It is the one thing we have felt most, other than the shortage of fruit. It rather dishes any attempt at hospitality. Tea scarce, no milk to put in it. The cat is being introduced to a milk and water diet. He takes it very hard and looks at us as if we were crazed and feeble-minded. Fish is very difficult to get. Mrs McKay managed to get me a bit of cod, and I made a kedgeree from a tin of salmon I managed to get on points; it was very good. It needs a lot of points to get a tin of salmon and I can't get another for at least a fortnight. Sardines are seven points and baked beans four points.*

4 December. Powdered milk has appeared in the shops today. I bought ninepenny-worth with great avidity. It does not sound very nice but it is a stand-by in case you have a friend, for you can mix two tea-spoons with your tea. They only allow us one tin a month. I shall be glad when the cows are working full-time again. I am all in favour of cows, more than I ever was. Pears have been seen in some shops, I hear, but at three shillings each.

9 December. AMERICA IS IN THE WAR! ! ! And we are at war with Japan. And the whole world is in it. There have been air-raid warnings in San Francisco, and though I do not wish anyone to be bombed, a little wholesome shaking up is good for people who contemplated with equanimity the sufferings of others, just as we did the Czechs, and only woke up when we came within the orbit of the enemy. ... We looked up our map of the Pacific for Hawaii and Pearl Harbor. Poor dear people, in those islands of bliss and sunshine – and fruit drinks. They must have had an unpleasant Sunday afternoon, and I expect now that there will be a slump in jazz all over America. It's amazing how serious even the most frivolous become after an air raid. Will the year now approaching see the end in sight?

* A points system for canned goods had been established by the Ministry of Food in 1941 to prevent them being bought up by the better off when they became scarce. It was points rather than money which from now on decided whether you could buy salmon, bully beef, beans or canned fruit, and each person got the same number of points.

PART THREE

A PAIN IN
THE HEART

II

A BLEAK YEAR

I

Charles Snow came back to London from a trip to Dublin, in neutral Ireland, with a horrid feeling that the worst moments of the war were about to confront his fellow-countrymen. It was February 1942. Singapore had fallen to the Japanese. The US Pacific Fleet was out of action as a result of the attack on Pearl Harbor. The Russian Government had removed itself to Kuibishev and its armies were battling desperately to keep the Germans out of Moscow.

True, the mass air raids on London were over, and no one could be more relieved about that than he was. For a couple of weeks he had been savouring in Dublin the bliss of peacetime existence: of being able to walk through lighted streets instead of stumbling through them in a black-out; of eating as much meat and butter and drinking as much whisky and wine as his stomach could take (which, in truth, was very little, English rationing having severely diminished his capacity).* The great joy was to know that not even a siren would sound, let alone a bomb drop during the night.

But in London people slept uneasily through the bombless hours, as if the rumblings of disaster beyond their shores nagged at their minds. There was a general feeling of disquiet and dissatisfaction around, Snow found. Life at home had become dull and drab and restricted, and the gloom and boredom were not helped by a wickedly cold winter and spring plus a desperate shortage of coal and coke for heating.

---

* Snow made regular visits to Ireland during the war to recruit scientists for work on military projects in England. 'It was one of the oddities of the situation', he said. 'The Southern Irish, whose Government was determinedly neutral, took a much more active part on Britain's side than did the Northern Irish, who were in the war with us. We had thousands of Southern Irish soldiers fighting for us, of course, but we had scores of scientists too. There were many quite good ones at Trinity College, Dublin, for instance who were passionately eager to work for us. I was dining in Trinity the night Singapore fell, and there were as many drawn faces that night among the Irish as there would have been in London.'

237

London that spring was a city of strange contrasts. Some parts of it had now been deserted by their inhabitants and whole streets of gaping, crumbling houses were left to stray cats, rats and house-sparrows. Poor wretched Silvertown had been so badly damaged by bombs that all attempts to repair it had been abandoned. The last few stubborn old people had been forcibly re-located, and the Army moved in with guns and bazookas, and Silvertown had now become a battleground for training troops in street warfare. Those inner and outer suburbs of the capital which had been less damaged by the blitz nevertheless became places of the dead after darkness had fallen. People retired to their beds because of the cold and the frequent cuts in electrical supplies, and stayed there until morning, when the harassing day began again. Observers began to report an increasing drop in civilian morale among the middle-aged, for whom the zest seemed to have gone out of life. On the other hand, younger people were surging into the West End of London in a search for the variety in food, drink and amusement that they could no longer get in their own boroughs, and every place of entertainment was full. There was no lack of spice to the fun that was to be had, for Piccadilly and its surrounding streets had had an influx of females in the past few weeks: scores of young girls, escaping compulsory work in factories or conscription into the women's services, had come swarming into the West End in search of male company and the money that went with it.

Most Londoners were only half-aware of the change that was coming over their city, but it hit newcomers like a pain in the heart. One woman who came to London from Dorset to seek a war job early in 1942 recorded her impressions in a diary she kept on her visit, and it has its poignant moments:

22 February. Very cold. But many people go out at night and the West End on a Saturday night is packed to overflowing. Hotels, restaurants and amusement parks, pubs, snack bars and the streets around Piccadilly, in spite of icy winds. Queues for cinemas, long queues for cheap dine-and-dance places, etc.

25 February. Long queues for tinned fruits, which have just come on the market on points. I got the best, most expensive kinds. News is as abominably bad as ever. Churchill admits big shipping losses. Went home by Tube, Piccadilly to Swiss Cottage. What a lot of drunks! On the whole more women than men, and more servicemen than civilians. Not many people sleeping in the Tubes now.

1 March. Cold weather persists. People seem depressed, bad news, bad weather, the usual outbreak of colds and flu. Notice in the cloakroom of a smart restaurant:

> Visitors are requested not to take SOAP or TOILET ROLLS as in that case we may have to discontinue supplies.*

Another notice near the stove of an office:

DON'T STEAL THE MATCHES – THEY'RE TOO HARD TO GET.

Outbreak of stealing everywhere. The rich steal now and are hard to keep up with. For a long time restaurant owners and shopkeepers associated good clothes with honesty. Now that things rather than money are short, their problems increase, and the ban on wrapping paper of course makes things harder on the shops.

7 March. Snowing. Longest cold spell for centuries. Propaganda from the Government urging women into war jobs is having its effect, and many, especially young ones, are beginning to look harassed and worried if they don't happen to be doing strenuous jobs. What a different London from last year, when people were keyed up by raids and threats, and filled with recklessness, very gay and smart. Now they're bored, very concerned with food and what they can get in the way of food, very many drunk late in the evening, especially young boys and girls in the Services. Civilian women not so smart, a distinct feeling of depression, disillusionment, and above all boredom in the air. Curious how little emotional response there is to our desperate position overseas – the Japanese successes, the Hong Kong atrocities published today, the Indian situation, these things are just mentioned and passed over.

21 March. Shopped for bacon. There were two men at the counter and a queue at one as the other had only just appeared. I asked him for my bacon and he served me. A woman in the queue said didn't I know that this was the bacon queue. The man tried to soothe her as much as he could. People now have a

* Soap rationing had recently been instituted.

239

queue mentality and don't believe anything can be had without queuing for it.

25 March. Had a meal at which we were served chicken (very rare), and fruit (tinned). My companion said: "This would cost hundreds of points." Points are the new measure of wealth, not money.

29 March. Sun out. Bright clothes come out and city no longer looks like a city at war. Bright red fashionable colour for women. *But people rarely smile.* No soap in men's West End rest rooms now. Thousands of young women around West End picking up soldiers.

5 April. Fortnum and Mason's serves tea out of unmatched cups. We ordered tea and the waiter took the order and then said: "And now I'll *try* and find you some cups." Eventually came back with unmatching ones.

6 April. You can't leave anything hanging about. Particularly milk outside the door, or flowers in your window box.

Along Piccadilly the ladies come out about 5.30 and there is a great deal of jockeying for position. Some of them really *are* lovely – real *poules de luxe*, and what strikes one is not only quality but quantity. There's hardly room in Old Burlington Street and Cork Street and Burlington Gardens for everyone to get places. Typical uniform: two-piece costume, black kid gloves and very sheer silk stockings. They must have saved up many pairs before they became unobtainable, or do their sailor friends bring them in from USA?

In March 1942 Mass–Observation asked its observers to give their opinions of Winston Churchill as a leader and were startled by the result. The man who was still regarded throughout the world as the saviour of Britain and the undisputed and sacrosanct director of the war effort seemed to be suffering from a somewhat tarnished reputation. The ringing sound of his oratory which had rallied the people during the Battle of Britain and the blitz now sounded hollow in the ears of many of his people. A forty-year-old married accountant wrote:

I think Winston Churchill is over-rated. Probably he has appealed to the public in England and America by his vigorous oratory, but that, though impressive, is not everything. Certainly he is not the man to build up a lasting peace.

A solicitor let him down a little more lightly by writing:

My own opinion seems to be shared by most of the middle classes, and it is that Winston Churchill is a capable leader and certainly the best man in the country for the job. Some doubts seem to be felt by the working classes who seem to feel that they have not got his sympathy and that there is something autocratic in his attitude. Although I think this criticism is to some extent justified, this is less important in wartime than qualities of leadership. As a leader he is outstanding.

But that expression of opinion was far less general than one from a London clerk, who wrote:

I feel that it is time he went. After all, the only connection in which one thinks of Churchill now is with regard to high strategy, whatever that may be. High strategy stinks to high heaven. If Churchill is responsible he should get out. This view I have confirmed by quite a few people. His speeches are no longer listened to.

And a fitter in Dalston, East London, wrote:

I feel that Winston Churchill, though a fine man, is not doing enough to make people believe in him. His speeches hold promise of action which never comes and people are beginning to notice this. Of people I asked, they said: 'Not so good as he was' and 'Should be replaced by a younger man' and 'I don't know what he's up to?'

These cross-sections of public thinking were passed on to 10 Downing Street and drawn to Winston Churchill's attention, and they cannot be said to have improved his temper. It was a period of the war when those who were his closest observers, even those who were his greatest admirers, felt that he was at his worst: short-sighted, selfish, dictatorial and stubborn. They were also surprised to discover that he who took praise so well reacted so badly to criticism. He had glowed under the praise lavished upon him for winning the Battle of Britain, but he glowered when his Government was condemned for losing the battles of Greece and Cyrenaica and Malaya. A popular daily newspaper (*Daily Mirror*) which dared to suggest that his Cabinet was composed of incompetent yes-men and that his admirals and generals were poor specimens of their kind was threatened with instantaneous suppression under a wartime regulation for publishing, 'with reckless indifference to the national interest and to the prejudicial effect on the war effort ... scurrilous misrepresentations, distorted and exaggerated statements and irresponsible generalisations'.

Yet in the corridors of power in Whitehall it was generally accepted that the *Daily Mirror*'s criticism had been mild compared with what was really going on. The newspaper had only blamed the Government for the disasters and setbacks of the past few months, but in Whitehall and Westminster they were much more specific. It was Churchill himself whom they were criticizing. It was due to his personal decision that British troops had been pulled out of the Western Desert in Egypt to fight in Greece, with the result that Greece was now lost and Cairo and the Suez Canal threatened. It was Churchill himself who had insisted on the dispatch to the Far East, against the strong advice of his best Admiral, of the two great battleships, *Prince of Wales* and *Repulse*, without the necessary air cover to protect them. Japanese bombers had promptly sent them to the bottom.* It was Churchill who allowed the British Navy to be directed through the great crises of 1939–42 by a First Sea Lord at the Admiralty who was suffering from a tumour on the brain, was known to his colleagues as 'poor old Pound', and went to sleep during vital conferences. He was Admiral Sir Dudley Pound and in the lobbies of Parliament and at the Admiralty they whispered that he stayed in his job only because he would never argue with Churchill and consented to the Prime Minister's habit of falsifying (upwards) the number of German U-boats sunk in the Atlantic.†

No one who watched Churchill tearing through the corridors of the House of Commons, cigar clamped in his mouth, face red and scowling, cutting a swath through the members like a clipper in full sail, could help but admire his tremendous energy and dogged spirit. But there were many who believed in 1942 that too little of his collaborators' strength was engaged in managing the destinies of the nation, and that by turning it into a one-man-war he was in danger of losing it for Britain.

* Ironically enough, the man who so strongly fought Churchill to prevent them going commanded the squadron when they were attacked and went down with his ships. He was Admiral Tom Phillips.

† Admiral Sir Dudley Pound retired on the grounds of ill-health in 1943 and died in October of that year from a brain-tumour.

It is an indication of his fall from grace in the eyes of his fellow Tories about this time that 'Chips' Channon refers to him in his diary as 'His Obese Highness'. He also touches on the topic that was now a regular gossip item in the House of Commons and in Whitehall: Churchill's increasing reliance upon the advice of his chief scientific adviser, the cold, ruthless, arrogant Professor Lindemann, now ennobled under the title of Lord Cherwell, but known to most MPs, because of his German antecedents, as 'Baron Berlin'.

Lindemann's influence upon the Prime Minister was so strong and so influential that even a particularly obtuse Tory Member of Parliament, Sir Waldron Smithers, made a slighting reference to it during Question Time in the House. Later he was in the smoking room of the House of Commons when Churchill, in a bellicose mood, strode in.

Suddenly, [wrote Channon] the Prime Minister saw Smithers and rose, and bellowing at him like an infuriated bull, roared: 'Why in Hell did you ask that Question? Don't you know that he (Lord Cherwell) is one of my oldest and greatest friends?'

Indeed he was. And, so far as Britain was concerned, a dangerous one.

2

In the mind of Professor Lindemann there was no doubt that there was only one way to win the war, and that was to bomb the German people out of house and home and kill so many of them that the rest would scream for mercy. He had spent his formative years in Germany and believed he knew the character of the German through and through.* It was the crack in civilian morale which had brought about the defeat of the German armies in the First World War, and it would be the ordinary German's suffering and despair behind the lines rather than the German soldier's defeat on the battlefield which would lose them the Second World War, Lindemann insisted.

This was a moment in the war when the Allies must make up

* F. A. Lindemann (Lord Cherwell) was, in fact, born in Sidmouth, Devon, of a German-Alsatian father and American mother. He went to school in Germany.

their minds what strategy must be followed in the West which would best help the embattled Russian armies to hold and eventually annihilate Germany's armed forces. Much would depend upon how Winston Churchill was thinking, for once he was persuaded of a policy he could quickly bulldoze his Cabinet and his General Staff into agreeing with it. After which their recommendation would be conveyed to President Roosevelt, who would pass it on to the US Chiefs of Staff as the combined wisdom of the war-experienced British. So half the battle of getting Churchill's ideas accepted by the American generals would already have been won.

But what were Churchill's ideas in 1942?

Charles Snow remembers that in every West End Club and at every policy meeting he attended in those days the argument was always the same: Should there be a Second Front Now against Germany (meaning a landing by the Allies in France) or Should We Bomb Them into the Ground?

The proponents of a Second Front Now were the vociferous ones, and they were not just the Communists jumping on to the war-wagon now that Russia was involved. The British public had become besotted with the Russian Army, not unnaturally, perhaps, since they were the only troops fighting the Germans and actually holding their own against them. Ivan Maisky, the Russian Ambassador, was cheered and besieged for his autograph when he passed in the streets. Public meetings, though often sponsored by Communist front organisations, nevertheless drew tens of thousands of non-political Britons who raised their hands and cheered their heads off when the speakers on the platforms demanded a Second Front in the West to take the pressure off the gallant Red comrades.

The British public had some support in high places, too, in their enthusiasm for immediate aid to Russia. The energetic and irrepressible Lord Beaverbrook, after a triumphant wartime career as the man who kept the RAF supplied with fighter-planes during the Battle of Britain, had gone to Russia to talk to Stalin and had come back a fervent admirer of the Russian Armies and a convinced advocate of a Second Front in the West. He came back to urge it upon his friend, Winston Churchill. But the Prime Minister was already giving his ear to Lindemann.

Beaverbrook's advocacy of a second front wasn't as wishy-washy as that of some of the wild Reds and pro-Reds running around London at the time [said Snow]. He had talked it out with experts. His idea was that all other campaigns except the single-purpose one of invading France and hitting the Germans there should be abandoned. Out with the sideshows like Africa and the Balkans. But of course what he was advocating was a complete change of policy. Instead of building bombers [in 1942] we would have had to change to building landing craft. The big bomber was already taking up an awful lot of our industrial resources and those of the United States, but at that time the change might have been made – and certainly there were plenty of people in America who were all for it. General George Marshall, for instance. His judgement was ultimately better than Churchill's and far ahead of General Brooke, the Chief of the Imperial General Staff, whose judgement, particularly about Russia, was abysmal. Beaverbrook found a ready market for his advocacy of a second front among the Americans. They wanted to go in quickly too. Unfortunately, they were out-argued by Churchill.*

For Churchill was convinced that his friend Lord Cherwell was right, and that bombing was the way to win the war. To the Prime Minister, always conscious of the disastrous slaughter at Gallipoli in the First World War (a disaster for which he had been blamed), a second front meant not only the expenditure of vast numbers of landing craft but of vast numbers of troops as well, and that he was not prepared to contemplate in 1942.

On 30 March, 1942, Lindemann produced a report for the Cabinet in which he advocated the heavy, continuous stratetic bombing of Germany as the cardinal measure of military policy between 1942–3. Charles Snow wrote of it:

It described in quantitative terms the effect on Germany of a British bombing offensive in the next eighteen months (approximately March 1942–September 1943). The paper laid down a strategic policy. The bombing must be directed essentially

---

* Lord Snow in a note to the author writes, 'It is important to stress that, with the best will in the world, and granted that production had been shifted from bombers to tank landing craft, there could not have been an invasion until the summer of 1943. This might have shortened the war by nine months to a year.'

against German working class houses. Middle-class houses have too much space around them and so are bound to waste bombs; factories and 'military objectives' had long since been forgotten, except in official bulletins, since they were much too difficult to find and hit. The paper claimed that – given a total concentration of effort on the production and use of bombing aircraft – it would be possible, in all the larger towns of Germany (that is, those with more than 50,000 inhabitants), to destroy 50 per cent of all houses.

There were no scientists in the Cabinet and therefore, when Lindemann circulated a Paper, there was no one capable of arguing with him on the points he raised. Like Churchill, everyone accepted his suggestions as gospel.

This time, however, the Paper, instead of being confined to Cabinet eyes only, was seen by other top scientists. These included Sir Henry Tizard, Lindemann's rival, and a number of Tizard supporters, among them Professors P. M. S. Blackett and J. D. Bernal, both of them experts on aerial and naval warfare. Charles Snow heard about it from them. It is typical of the times in which they were living that none of them voiced their objection to Lindemann's Paper because it advocated genocide. ('What will people of the future think of us?' Snow wrote later. 'Will they say, as Roger Williams said of some of the Massachusetts Indians, that we were wolves with the minds of men? Will they think that we resigned our humanity? They will have the right.') They did not even put forward the argument that the German blitzing of London had already proved the ineffectiveness of strategic bombing. Morale had never been higher in London than during those nights when the death-dealing rain came tumbling down, and had sunk to a low ebb now that the bombers no longer came over.

'It was not Lindemann's ruthlessness that worried us most,' said Snow, 'it was his calculations.'

Sir Henry Tizard concentrated his keen scientific brain on Lindemann's paper and quickly proceeded to demolish it. He came to the conclusion and proved it with facts and figures beyond doubt that Lindemann's estimate of the number of houses the Allied strategic bombing could destroy was five times too high. Meantime, Professor Blackett was studying the Paper too, and he produced a further devastating rebuttal, showing that Lindemann's estimate of the destruction by a strategic offensive was not five but six times too high.

The combined reports of these two wise and eminent men dropped upon Whitehall like the bombs they were arguing against. Air Marshal Sir Charles Portal, Chief of the Air Staff, read them through and said 'But if what these two say is true, the bombing offensive wouldn't be worthwhile.'

This raised a further problem. If strategic bombing was not worthwhile, what were they going to do with all those bombers now rolling off the assembly lines?*

'We should have to find a different strategy, both for production and for the use of elite troops,' said Snow. And that would play into the hands of those who advocated a Second Front Now.

Charles Snow has been moving in the corridors of power since he was a young man, but of the impact of Tizard's report on Whitehall, on Lindemann and on Churchill he says:

> I do not think that, in secret politics, I have ever seen a minority view so unpopular. Bombing had become a matter of faith. I sometimes used to wonder whether my administrative colleagues, who were clever and detached and normally the least likely group of men to be swept away by any faith, would have acquiesced in this one, as on the whole they did, if they had had even an elementary knowledge of statistics.

It would probably have made no difference. Lindemann had the ear of the Prime Minister, and he was saying what Churchill and his air advisers wanted to hear: that this was the cheap way to win the war, by bombing German cities into rubble and hammering the civilian population into the ground.

Lindemann did not forgive Tizard's latest (and, as it turned out, last) attempt to demonstrate the arrogant stupidity of his rival's scientific ideas. He made it clear to all the Service ministries that there was no room for the two of them in the war effort, which meant inevitably that Tizard must go – for Lindemann was to Churchill what Sir Horace Wilson had once been to Neville Chamberlain, only he was more ruthless with his rivals.

'The minority view was not only defeated, but squashed,' commented Charles Snow. 'The atmosphere was more hysterical than

---

* 'Use them to bomb U-boats and motor torpedo boats and help to keep British supply lines open at sea,' said Tizard.

is usual in English official life; it had the faint but just perceptible smell of a witch hunt.'

To Churchill, Tizard's opposition to bombing made him a defeatist (for Churchill never got around to reading his reasoned statement against it). He could have no further say in the direction of the war effort, and even his closest friends advised him to retire from the scene. He opted for an academic life at Oxford.

It was not easy [wrote Snow], for a man as tough and brave as men are made, and a good deal prouder than most of us, to be called a defeatist. It was even less easy to be shut out of scientific deliberations, or to be invited to them on condition that he did not volunteer an opinion. It is astonishing in retrospect that he should have been offered such humiliation. I do not think there has been a comparable example in England this century.

The humiliation was Tizard's but the loss was the people's.

If he had been granted a fair share of the scientific direction between 1940 and 1943, the war might have ended a bit earlier and with less cost.*

Churchill had made the decision. When General Marshall arrived with his staff from America and earnestly advocated an opening of a Second Front in 1942, he belligerently jutted his jaw and vigorously shook his head.

Lindemann, sitting at his side, said, 'It's no use. You are arguing against the casualties on the Somme.'†

From then on, the bomber fleets of the RAF and the USAAF roared across England night and day on their way to Germany to smash the houses of the working-class people.

'Raze the people's houses! How's that for a statement of postwar aims?' exclaimed Tizard, bitterly.

He had described Lindemann's estimate of the strategic bombing programme's results as five times too high. Blackett had said they were six times too high. The US Strategic Bombing Survey

---

* 'My comments were written some years after the events,' says Snow in a note to the author, 'though I should not wish to alter any of them. They are a reflection of what was thought at the time.'

† One of the more disastrous campaigns of the First World War.

conducted after the war discovered that Lindemann's forecasts had been no less than ten times too high.

Yet it didn't really need all these experts to prove the ineffectiveness of strategic bombing. Any Londoner, walking among his ruins, could have told the Government that it didn't work.

The meetings went on. All over London and the rest of Britain the slogans were chalked on the walls. But there would be no Second Front Now in 1942. The Allies were too busy making bombers, and sending them out every night for Hamburg and Cologne.

'It is a sickening business,' Vere Hodgson wrote. 'But I am glad the Germans know what evil they have let loose upon the world.'

3

Donald Ketley was bored.

'Nothing ever happens,' he complained to his mother one day in 1942. 'Has the war stopped, Mum?'

He knew it hadn't, of course. Otherwise they wouldn't have instituted sweet rationing, which is what they did that summer, so that now he had to take his ration-book every time he bought a bar of chocolate or a bag of liquorice all-sorts. But now that they no longer got bombed every night, now that he and his pals no longer went out hunting for German parachutists, the excitement seemed to have gone out of everything. You couldn't even have fun at school any more. There wasn't enough paper to make darts, pencils were taken away and locked up after lessons because they were so scarce, and teacher quite often ran out of chalk for the blackboard. The only highlight of the academic year had been the discovery among them of a boy with scabies and a girl with nits in her hair.* They had all had their hair cropped close to their heads, and Donald had a fine time pretending to be a German general called Von Votzisname, until his hair grew again.

What he couldn't understand was why his parents still insisted on sleeping every night in the shelter, when it was quite obvious

* One of the by-products of the blitz and the evacuation of the East End slums was the spread of these infestations among British schoolchildren.

that the Jerries had given up bombing, and that it was our turn now. They now had what was called a Morrison shelter,* a channel steel framework about seven feet long, two-and-a-half feet wide and five feet high, with an armour-plated top and steel mesh all round the sides. His father had installed it inside the living room and each night they all crawled into it. It was like sleeping in a cage.

Donald disliked it, especially when it wasn't necessary, but when he asked them why he couldn't sleep in bed, his mother said, 'You never know. You can't trust those Nazis.'

Every night, as he lay in the cage, Donald could hear the planes of the RAF roaring overhead on their way to bomb Germany. It gave him a delicious feeling of both security and pleasure, but he was not so sure that his parents felt the same way.

'It makes me feel sick in my stomach,' he heard his mother say one night. 'All those bombs falling on people.'

'You can't say they haven't asked for it,' said his father. There was a pause and Donald heard him sigh. 'All the same, I don't like it,' he said, at last.

Lying there, Donald would sometimes hear his parents talking quietly to themselves about the war and how it was affecting themselves and their neighbours. The daughter of one of their neighbours, a dressmaker and designer, had been called up and was now working in a munitions factory, and hating every moment of it.

'What can you expect?' said Mrs Ketley. 'At least what she was doing before was creative. Now all she does all day long is turn out thousands of little brass stampings, it's soul destroying. She doesn't even know what they're for, and no one tells her. No wonder she's bored.'

Mr Ketley said, 'She should have done what Millie down the road did.' He lowered his voice to a whisper. 'Got herself in the pudding club. That's what they're all doing now if they don't want to be called up – register and then go out with their young man and get pregnant.'

'Or something worse,' said Mrs Ketley. 'It's dreadful the amount of VD going around. I hear it's driving the MOs in the Army frantic. Can't cope with it. It's terrible, all this immorality.'

'What can you expect when there's a war on?' said Mr Ketley.

'All the politicians can talk about is the brave new world we're going to have when it's all over. I think they're bluffing. They

* Named after the Home Secretary, Mr Herbert Morrison.

don't want it now any more than they did before the war. They're just talking to keep the people quiet.'

It was Mrs Ketley's turn to sigh this time.

'What *am* I going to give you to eat tomorrow,' she said.

That was the trouble, Donald noticed. Most women looked worried these days, he found, and it was always the same thing that was troubling them: how to feed and clothe their families.

The war must have been particularly hard on women in London [he recalled, in a note to the author]. The combined strain of never knowing whether my father was going to come home and the great strain of getting food certainly showed in my mother. She would be gone for hours searching around for some fruit or titbit to add spice to the monotony, and time and again I remember her apologizing that this was all she had been able to find, feeling guilty for something completely beyond her control. I think food was more difficult to come by in London than in the rest of the country. There was one period when the only thing we seemed to be able to get was sprats, a minute fish about half the size of a sardine. When the US started to send us dried eggs, milk and Spam it was an unbelievable luxury.

He added:

By and large, people just went about their daily business as best they could because there was nothing else to do.

One night his father came home and said, 'Now it looks as if we're going to lose Egypt, too. Tobruk's gone'.

'Oh dear,' said Mrs Ketley. 'We don't seem to be having much luck this year, do we?' Then she brightened. 'Never mind. We've got a treat for supper. Mr Roberts [the shopkeeper on the corner] let me have three oranges that were going bad, and I've managed to save more than half of them. We're having orange and apple salad!'

'But I ate the apples, Mum,' said Donald.

'Not the cores, you didn't,' she said, laughing.

4

The news that Tobruk, the British bastion in the Western Desert, had been taken by German troops under Rommel hit Britain like a blow in the face. With people's spirits at such a low ebb, it could not have come at a worse time. In London reactions ranged from the sorrowful to the indignant.

Vere Hodgson, who had always been one of Winston Churchill's most fervid supporters, was downcast when she heard that he was in America [for a conference with President Roosevelt at the White House] and could not defend himself against the attacks now being made upon him both in Parliament and the Press. She wrote of the news:

> It really is humiliating, and so discouraging to the Russians, who are still holding out at Sebastopol. ... Mr Attlee [the Deputy Prime Minister] read a statement in the House today from General Auchinleck [C-in-C, Middle East] which seemed to consist almost entirely of the word *unfortunately*. *Unfortunately* the enemy did not seem to understand what was expected of him and failed to fall in with our plans. As Miss Moyes says, it makes you see red, pink and heliotrope. I squirm beneath the bed-clothes and grind my teeth with rage. If we can't do better than this, we don't deserve to keep the Empire.

It was mid-summer's eve, but neither that nor the good weather which suddenly wafted in scented zephyrs across London alleviated the general gloom. In Rosemary Black's case, her mental condition was not helped by a sudden attack of rheumatism which seems to have been brought on by poor diet and some bad teeth. As luck would have it, her two children were home from school and in quarantine as a result of an outbreak of measles. She crawled out of bed each day in considerable pain and groaned as the noise of children at play came from below.

> Poor brats, I've simply loathed their noise and chatter and the endless little activities, unnoticed ordinarily, that their presence involves, and I've been avoiding their company like the plague, poor darlings.

At first the news from the Middle East left her remote and disinterested.

On 11 June, she wrote:

> The war seems to be going badly for us now in the Middle East. Odd, as according to all the reports we have been starting the season so well out there and had air superiority. My dentist

said that the very fact of holding Rommel up all this time was success for us,* but everyone else seems very depressed. I can't care much: I happen not to know anyone in Libya at the moment, so it all seems remote.

She went on to complain that the price of peas had gone up to two shillings and ninepence a pound, that melons were on sale at two pounds ten shillings each, peaches at eight shillings and sixpence, and all the strawberries (normally plentiful at this time of the year) had disappeared from the shops.

I hope to heaven the milk shortage won't get too acute again. As for the fish, which always seems to be more or less decayed these days by the time it reaches the shops, I am completely sickened by the everlasting stink of it. I'm sure I shall never again want to touch it myself, nor can I conceive how anybody who has handled and smelt the flabby muck can ever go on cooking and eating it. The other day R. came back from shopping in high feather because she had got half a dozen herrings, but as soon as they'd been in the warmth of the kitchen for fifteen minutes or so they began to smell so appalling that I couldn't face keeping them about even for the cats, and shoved them in the boiler at once, holding my nose. It seems terrible that men should risk their lives in order that disgusting muck like this should be on sale.

But by 16 June her mind was right back on what was happening in the Middle East, and now her thoughts reflected the dismay she heard all around her:

The position in Libya suddenly seems rather bad. Mrs Bone said she thought it a great pity we couldn't hire Rommel for six weeks or so just to get our side going, as otherwise we didn't seem able to do any good. Well, anyhow I suppose [Generals] Ritchie and Auchinleck will shortly be kicked out in disgrace in succession to [General] Cunningham. Where will we go for honey then? Who will fall heir to the short period of publicity? Who'd be a general in the British Army?

A week later, like most of her fellow Londoners, she was in full

* General (later Field Marshal) Erwin Rommel had lately arrived in Libya with a mobile German army specially trained and equipped for desert warfare.

cry against a bungling Government and incompetent generals.

23 June. Front page news space halved between lamentations over Tobruk and chit-chat about Churchill, who, it is announced, is at present in the U S conferring with Roosevelt all over again.* It really does seem a remarkable coincidence that he should again manage to be out of the country, doing himself well too, no doubt, just at the moment when things take a peculiarly nasty turn. I expect he'll manage yet again to shuffle out of the 'explanation' which is already being demanded . . .

It is a measure of how Churchill's stock was falling that she was writing a few days later:

The news of Churchill's being in USA seems to have given rise to a fine crop of rumours. B. said one of her 'dailies' told her that 'everyone was saying he was selling England to America'. Several of the tradespeople supposed that, in this case as before, he'd seen disaster coming and got out in time, hoping to avoid the worst anger of the people. One particularly wild tale I heard via Ruth alleged him to be a fifth columnist, though if he were it's still not clear why he should have gone to Roosevelt.

She added:

One thing, I think he'll have a big reckoning to face on his return, and that this time he'll really have to face it. The whole tone of articles, letters and editorials is infinitely more determined and demanding than before, and much harder set against Churchill as Minister of Defence and Secret Session King. I should think his stock can never have sunk so low before. I must say I myself felt pretty disgusted with him when I saw a photograph of him enjoying himself at the White House again. If only he'd keep those great gross cigars out of his face once in a way, I'd feel better about him – though he's still far from being the man to talk about tightening one's belt.

Rosemary Black was right. A reckoning was facing Winston Churchill on his return. On 24 June a Tory member of the House, Sir John Wardlaw-Milne, put down a motion of censure against

* They had met at the beginning of the year.

the Government over its conduct of the war, and made it clear that the chief target of his criticism was the Prime Minister. The same day Churchill flew back from the United States to face his accusers.

It was a grim moment for Britain, and everywhere in London people sensed the rising tension. In the Western Desert the Eighth Army was in full flight before the tanks and armoured cars of Rommel's Afrika Korps. In Cairo the generals at Middle East Headquarters were burning their secret papers. Alexandria, Cairo and the Suez Canal were threatened, and not since the days of the Battle of Britain had the Empire been in greater peril.

Wardlaw-Milne met Churchill in the lobby of the House shortly after his return and offered to withdraw his motion, in view of the gravity of the situation.

'Refused!' said Churchill, his face red, jaw jutting.

He was determined to fight back against his critics, but he was aware that it would be a savage and brutal battle. Nor would it be a victory for him if he merely got a majority of members voting for him after the debate. The Party Whips could always round up enough Members to give him that. Chamberlain had had a majority of eighty during the crucial debate in 1940, but it had not saved him. It would not save Churchill now. He needed not only the votes of the House but the hearty support of it, too. And for that he would need every drop of eloquence and persuasiveness he could muster, and he would need friends on both sides of the House to back him up.

Could he, for instance, count on Emmanuel Shinwell to rally the Labour Party members to his side? Shinwell was a warm friend and a poisonous enemy. He was an eloquent Scottish-Jew with a tongue like a cobra.

Churchill's Parliamentary Private Secretary, Brigadier George Harvie-Watt, went scurrying round to see him, but handled the interview badly.

'The Chief has a lot of worry just now,' he said. 'He doesn't deserve to be annoyed by attacks in the House. You mustn't forget the Prime Minister has great military gifts. His ancestor was the Duke of Marlborough.'

'If military genius can be handed down like that,' Shinwell replied, sourly, 'then I should be a good critic. My ancestor was Moses.'

Nonetheless, he made it clear he would be on Churchill's side, but with reservations.*

Where would the Prime Minister find a powerful and convincing voice on the other side of the House, among the Tories? Who would speak up for him and sound not like an obedient Party hack but a genuine support, resonant, clear and convincing?

The great debate that would settle Winston Churchill's fate was set for 1 July.

For twenty-four hours before that men and women from all over London took time off from their jobs, or got leave from their gun-sites, to listen to it. Great crowds queued up for seats in Westminster Hall, where the House now assembled, and those who could not get in stayed in the streets to watch. It was as if all London were listening in.

Twenty members from both the main parties in the House had put their names down to speak in the debate. Winston Churchill went through them on the night of 30 June, trying to pick out friend from foe, the dullard from the dangerous. His thick finger stopped down the list when it came to the name: Boothby, Robert.

Robert Boothby had once been his private secretary and his friend. But they had parted in anger and they had not spoken since 1940, when Boothby had gone into the wilderness.

Boothby was a young man of words. He spoke with force and strength and conviction.

But how would he speak tomorrow in the debate that could seal Churchill's fate: as the friend he once was, or the enemy he might now have become?

5

Flight Lieutenant Robert Boothby, MP, came up to London on the morning of 1 July from his bomber station in Suffolk. He had been working since before dawn checking-in the exhausted pilots and crews of the bombers which had been over Germany the previous night, and in his mind he still carried a picture of those strained young faces and bloodshot eyes. To walk into the dining room of the House of Commons and see once more the smooth, complacent faces of his fellow MPs was a contrast that filled him with revulsion. Not for the first time he looked around him and

* In the event, he abstained.

thought what a shoddy lot they were, these men who were supposed to represent the people in the tribunal of the nation. Thanks to an electoral truce for the duration of the war, they knew they were safe. There would be no general election until Germany was defeated, and until then they would remain members of the most exclusive club in the world, with all the perks and privileges that such membership bestowed upon them.

Yet as he saw it they were the same bunch who had (with a few notable exceptions) applauded Neville Chamberlain for appeasing Hitler, who had hissed and booed Churchill for advocating a policy of standing up to Germany, who had only accepted him as their Prime Minister during the Battle of Britain because invasion threatened, because they were afraid and he seemed to be the only man capable of rallying the people behind him. They hated him because they knew he despised them, and they would not hesitate to kick him the moment they thought he was down. Now their moment seemed to have come. The disasters were piling up and the people were no longer hailing Winston as their great saviour. The man who had led them through the Battle of Britain was now the man who was losing the Battle for Egypt and the war at sea. What better opportunity could there be to deal their hated leader a really damaging blow?

Bob Boothby sipped his drink and considered his own feelings about the Prime Minister. Winston had hurt him badly and he still felt the pain of the humiliations of 1940. One word from him could have saved Boothby's parliamentary career by pointing out quite how unjust (and how trivial) the charges against him had been. He had not spoken. Worse than that, he had refused Boothby the personal interview that he had felt their friendship deserved, and had sent him no word of sympathy during months of political exile made more miserable by the death of his beloved father.

There was no doubt that the old man had behaved churlishly* and it was hard to forgive him. There was no doubt, too, in Boothby's mind that war had turned Churchill into an irascible dictator who was trying to do too much; he interfered with his generals and his admirals; he bullied his Cabinet and ruthlessly rode down his Ministers. He could be a stubborn and, sometimes,

---

* 'He had a streak of cruelty in his nature,' says Boothby in a note to the author.

even a stupid old man and he had made some glaring errors in his direction of the war.

But compared with the pygmies with whom he was surrounded, he was a super giant. If he went, who could take his place? For Boothby had no illusions about what would happen if the coming debate went wrong. The men who had put down the motion of censure maintained that all they wished to do was curtail the Prime Minister's powers and save him from himself by preventing him from doing too much. They merely wished, they said, to make him give up the post of Minister of Defence and confine himself to the premiership. But that was nonsense. Such a vote, if it succeeded, would emasculate Churchill, and he was no man to accept the post of a political eunuch. If the support of his policy was not forthcoming, he would resign. And Boothby knew what that could mean. The heart would go out of the nation, and Britain could lose the war.

So what choice was there but to rally round the old man, damn and blast his stubborn old guts?

He stared across the crowded dining room as he was ruminating in this fashion and suddenly saw someone waving at him from a discreet corner table. It was Winston Churchill, beckoning him to come over. He got up and made his way to him, and it did not fail to cross his mind that this would be the first occasion that the old man had deigned to talk to him for over a year. And only now, he thought, because he's in trouble. . . .

Churchill seemed quite unaware of the fact that there was any coldness between them. He looked straight into Boothby's eyes and said bluntly, 'Are you in favour of the Government?'

'Of course,' said Boothby. 'There is no alternative.'

Churchill: 'Are you in favour of me?'

Boothby: 'Yes – although you have done me great harm.'

The old man ignored this. Instead, he said, 'Will you speak for us this afternoon?'

'Yes,' said Boothby.

He nodded, rose to his feet, and they walked together to the Speaker of the House of Commons, Captain Fitzroy, to whom Churchill indicated that Boothby would be speaking for the Government. Afterwards they went into the smoking room, where large whiskies were brought to the table. Churchill raised his glass and so did his companions.

'To the Pegasus wings of Bob's oratory,' said Winston Churchill.

Chips Channon wrote in his diary on 1 July, 1942:

'John Wardlaw-Milne moved his much-publicised Vote of Censure in strong and convincing language today and I watched the front bench squirm with annoyance. Winston looked harassed and everyone was emotional and uneasy. I thought it all rather horrible. Wardlaw-Milne held the House well, he was fair, calm and dignified, and he was listened to with respect.'

This was true, until he made a ludicrous mistake. Wardlaw-Milne was a man of imposing appearance and impressive voice, but everyone but his best friends considered him something of a pompous ass, and were surprised that he had marshalled his attack against Churchill's administration so ably. But suddenly, having roundly condemned the Prime Minister for choosing such inept military commanders in the field, he made the mistake of telling the House the name of the man whom Churchill should have chosen to lead the troops into battle.

He ringingly proclaimed the name of the Duke of Gloucester.

Now this is no place to go into the merits or qualifications of King George the Sixth's younger brother, except to mention that he had never heard a shot fired in anger. The idea that he should be made Commander-in-Chief of the British Army made the House first catch its breath in embarrassment and then burst into hoots of laughter.

'For a full minute the buzz goes round, "But the man must be an ass,"' Harold Nicolson, MP, recorded. 'Milne pulls himself together and recaptures the attention of the House, but his idiotic suggestion has shaken the validity of his position and his influence is shattered.'

Chips Channon saw 'Winston's face light up, as if a lamp had been lit within him, and he smiled genially.'

It was not all over as simply as that. There were other more able and wounding attacks to come, but Wardlaw-Milne's gave Boothby, when he rose to speak, just the opportunity he had been waiting for. His great organ voice poured scorn upon the gaffe critics who dared to suggest that the Government was incompetent in its strategy and in its choice of the men to lead the troops into battle, when all they could suggest as an alternative were impossible goals and incompetent men to carry them out. It was a speech

exactly fitting to the mood of the House, with just the right leaven-
ing of criticism of his own (*why were so many young British lives
being wasted bombing Germany, when they should be pounding the
enemy's ports in the Mediterranean?*) to make it clear that he was
not absolving Churchill from all blame, but with savagely funny
thrusts at the lumbering bulls who were daring to charge such a
toreador as Churchill. The old man sat there, glowering at first,
then smiling and even laughing out loud at the sallies. When
Boothby sat down a new opponent rose to attack the Prime
Minister, but Churchill did not even stay to listen. He knew that
the originator of the Vote of Censure had been destroyed, and he
could handle the rest himself.

That he did next day, in a jut-jawed, challenging speech which
angrily brushed aside all criticism and boldly (and unfairly) dared
the House to dismiss him. By now he knew that they would
no longer have the courage even to challenge his powers. The
rebellion was crushed. The dissidents were in full retreat.

When the vote came, it was 476 to 25 in Winston Churchill's
favour, and the announcement of it brought him a great ovation
in the House. It was all over. There would never be such a con-
certed and potentially dangerous effort to get rid of Winston
Churchill again until after the war.

Three days later Churchill flew out to Egypt, where he sacked all
his desert generals and appointed Generals Sir Harold Alexander
and Bernard Montgomery to take their place. The last act of the sacked Commander-in-Chief, General Claud Auchinleck, was to stop
Rommel and the Afrika Korps at a desert ridge called El Alamein.

Churchill was well aware of the part Robert Boothby had
played in his victory in the House of Commons, and just before he
flew to Egypt he sent him a telegram expressing his thanks.

But that was all. So far as the Prime Minister was concerned, he
had done his job and he could now go back to the political wilderness from which he had temporarily emerged. He did not speak to
Boothby again until two years later, and then it was in a fit of
blazing temper.

Diaries
   2 September 1942. I saw this morning the American troops

parade through the City of London. They made a fine show, and the most noticeable thing about this parade was the silence of their marching, due to the rubber-heeled shoes. The American Marines certainly looked all very much like the type they have been made out to be, thanks to the pictures. But I must say that the physical standard was not at all good, at least not as I expected. For height they are not a patch on the Australians or New Zealanders. *(From the diary of L.N.A., works manager.)*

2 September 1942. A procession took place this morning, when a contingent of American troops and Marines marched to the Guildhall for lunch with the Lord Mayor and various celebrities. They looked very smart despite the fact that they wore rubber-soled shoes, and London gave them a very friendly reception, but I did miss the tramp of marching feet.
(From the diary of K.M.T., secretary and canteen worker.)

9 October 1942. John, by no means pro-American in the ordinary way, is the only person I've come across yet with anything but curses for the Americans over here. It is really extraordinary what a passion of dislike everyone seems to feel for them. I suppose their pay, so enormously higher than that of our own fighting men, is at the bottom of it: that and the amount of time off they get and their double rations plus, and in general the vast superiority of their clothing and feeding allowances and their accommodation. Then stories like B.'s of the local billeting officer who went from house to house on the very first day of the fuel target scheme* inquiring whether each had central heating, as, of course, Americans could only be billeted in centrally-heated houses! Things like K.'s boy-friend saying he by God hated England, he was so goddamned bored in the damn place, he just wished the blitzes would start over again as it would be *some* excitement. Even with John it's not a matter of any liking, but merely the conscientious refusal to give way to dislike because he feels that to do so is playing Hitler's game. As it is, of course – but how can one help resenting the full-fed, candy-pampered, gum-chewing swagger of our invaders?
(From the diary of Mrs Rosemary Black, widow.)

---

* A Government rationing project to cut down the consumption of coal and coke in the home.

12

THE INVADERS

The Americans had been around for quite some time, but it was not until the summer of 1942 that ordinary Londoners became aware of their presence. It was some time in August that a friend of Vere Hodgson's named Mrs Turner, whom she had been showing Tyburn Tree in Hyde Park, suddenly said:

'But it's Sunday afternoon! Let's go and see the Americans – this is the day they play baseball in the park.'

Sure enough, there they were, three teams of tall young men going through the ritual of their national game, to the amused curiosity of Miss Hodgson. She wrote:

> We took two chairs and sat down to watch them. It is a sort of glorified rounders, though I expect they would not want us to call it that. Many of the players wear strong rubber gloves. The ball, which though made of rubber seems to be very heavy, gives quite a wonk when it hits the gloves. They were splendid at catching but the bat is the very funniest thing. It is long and round and it seems very difficult to hit anything with it. Only occasionally did they hit the ball. The players kept shouting to each other terms of encouragement in what seemed to be a foreign language. I don't think we play cricket in such a noisy way.

'The Yanks' were still sufficiently a novelty to stir up a crowd of curious Londoners, but already they were established in discreet offices all over the West End of London, and late at night in the smoking room of 10 Downing Street, or down below in the Hole in the Wall, or in a small house merely marked with the name 'Tube Alloys' in Old Queen Street, the distinctive sound of transatlantic accents could be heard. The Americans were in conference with the British to concert their war efforts, and there were plans afoot.

Unfortunately, the Allies were not by any means agreed over which plans to employ.

262

People like General George Marshall came to London about
this time [said Charles Snow], and made a tremendous impression on most of us. He thought like Beaverbrook and all the
others who believed in a second front in North West Europe.
He and his delegation had come over from America eager to
wipe out the humiliation of Pearl Harbor and the setbacks in the
Pacific. He wanted to do something positive, and do it soon, in
north-west Europe that would materially help the Russians
fighting so doggedly in the East. Almost immediately he ran up
against, as Beaverbrook had run up against, people like Brooke,
who was anti-Russian to the point that his military evalua-
tion of them was entirely absurd.* Brooke was always wondering
when the Russians were going to collapse, especially in 1942,
and saw no reason for linking Allied operations with what was
happening in Russia.

Every kind of pressure was being put upon the Americans to
curb their impatience and their military ambitions, and to dampen
their enthusiasm for the Russian army's achievements.
'Many seemed to imagine that Russia had only come into the
war for our benefit,' Brooke wrote. And of General Marshall, whom
he thought 'a very dangerous man while being a very charming
one', he expressed the view that he was urging action against
France only because he wished to keep his troops out of the hands
of his two most ambitious rivals in the Pacific, Admiral King and
General Macarthur.
'To counter these moves Marshall,' he wrote, 'has started the
European offensive plan and is going one hundred per cent all out
on it. It is a clever move which fits in with present political opinion
and the desire to help Russia. It is popular with all military men
who are fretting for an offensive policy. But, and this is a very
large "but", his plan does not go beyond landing on the far coast
[of France]. Whether we are to play baccarat or chemin de fer at
Le Touquet is not stipulated.'
When Marshall flew back to America with the President's en-
voy, Harry Hopkins, aften ten days of conferences with Brooke,
Lindemann and Churchill, they took with them an agreement that
planning should start at once for a 'build-up of American military
and air forces in Britain for a major cross-Channel offensive in

* General Sir Alan Brooke was Chief of the Imperial General Staff.

1943 and for a possible emergency landing in 1942'.

But the British had no intention of sending their troops into France so soon. Sir Arthur Bryant, biographer and confidant of General Sir Alan Brooke, summed up the London conversations in 1942 in these words:

> Nor had [Brooke] and his colleagues committed themselves to a cross-Channel operation in 1942 or even in 1943 but merely to the desirability of launching one if, and only if, conditions at the time made its success seem probable. What, in effect, the British Chiefs of Staff had agreed to do was to start preparing plans, in conjunction with the US, for an invasion of Europe whenever it became a practical operation, and to *welcome in the meantime the maximum concentration of American military and air strength in England – the place where it would be most valuable, whether Russia held out and made an invasion of the Continent possible or whether she collapsed and left Hitler once more free to attempt an invasion of England.**

Since that time the convoys had been regularly making their way across the Atlantic carrying troops, ground crews, tanks and planes. At first their staging post was Northern Ireland, but soon barracks, encampments and airfields all over Britain were flying the Stars and Stripes, while every tot in the vicinity was chewing gum or sucking Hershey bars. It would not be long before the first discreet GIs on leave, with strict instructions to 'play it quietly', were filtering into London, silk stockings in their pockets, cigarette packs under their arms.

Perhaps the first to feel the peculiar impact of British life was a certain US general who flew in during the spring of 1942 on a reconnaissance trip from Washington. He spent the week deep in conferences with the American Ambassador, John G. Winant, the American naval representative, Admiral Harold Stark, and his British opposite numbers. When Sunday came they took a break from work, and the General was asked what he would like to see.

'I've always wanted to have a look at Windsor Castle,' he said.

It was arranged that Lord Wigram, the custodian, should show

* My italics. Turn of the Tide Collins, 1957

the General and a companion around the royal castle. Wigram did not tell the Americans that Sunday was normally the royal family's own day at the Castle and that visitors were generally barred. Instead, he asked George the Sixth's permission to make the tour, and the King promised to stay out of the way while it was going on.

But it was one Sunday in May when the sun was shining and the gardens of the great castle were at their best, and the King and Queen could not resist it. They went down after lunch from their apartments to a favourite corner of the gardens. They were sunning themselves there and reading the Sunday newspapers when they heard the sound of an American voice asking about the flowers and Wigram replying.

George the Sixth looked at Elizabeth, and decided without words that a meeting might be embarrassing. They nipped across to a hedge, in a great flurry. The General, his companion and their guide came round the corner just in time to see the royal couple, on their hands and knees, scrambling under the hedge.

'Good God,' said the General, 'who on earth is that?'

'I am afraid I have to confess,' replied Lord Wigram, 'that those are the rear views of Their Majesties King George the Sixth and Queen Elizabeth of England.'

'Well, well,' said the General, 'if it isn't just like Sundays at home when unexpected visitors turn up.'

That night George the Sixth said to Wigram:

'I'm sorry we were in the garden when you were showing your American around today. We forgot all about it. Didn't want to embarrass them, you know, by being there – but I think we got out just in time.'

'You didn't, sir,' said Wigram. 'The General saw you.'

'Did he, now?' said the King. 'Ah well, I don't suppose we'll ever have a chance to explain. Who was he?'

'A lieutenant-general from Washington,' said Wigram, 'named Dwight D. Eisenhower.'

2

Towards the end of August in 1942 Mrs Sally Thomas appeared before the magistrates at a London police court on a charge of neglecting her three children. After evidence had been given by Sally's landlady and a representative of the Royal Society for the Prevention of Cruelty to Children, the probation officer was called and asked to give a report.

'I have talked to Sally at great length,' she said, 'and I would ask the magistrates to consider very sympathetically all the circumstances which have led up to her appearance here today. At the outbreak of war her husband was sent to the Middle East, leaving her alone to care for three very young children on what, I am sure, the Bench will agree is the not very generous marriage allowance from the Army. She was evacuated to the Midlands in September, 1939, and there unfortunately had a liaison with the husband of the woman upon whom she and her children were billeted. When this was discovered, she was thrown out of the house and returned to London. It was there that she discovered she was pregnant. Sally tells me (and I believe her) that she bitterly regretted having been unfaithful to her husband, that it was only one isolated lapse when she was feeling especially lonely, and she was naturally horrified when she discovered that she was going to have the man's child.'

She paused, and looked up at the two women and the man on the magistrates' bench. Their faces were stony and forbidding.

'She did her best to arrange for her unborn child to be adopted, but it was pointed out to her that even though the child might not be his, her husband must give his permission. Then (and she considers it a piece of good fortune) she was involved in the bomb incident on Marble Arch Station, as a result of which she had a miscarriage. When she recovered, she came back to her children determined not to stray again. Unfortunately, her mother-in-law collected some of her belongings from the hospital and found the adoption papers inside, and found out what had happened. Very unwisely and perhaps cruelly, you might think, she informed her son of what had happened. He has since written to say that he will have nothing more to do with Sally and is anxious for a divorce.'

Another pause. One of the women magistrates said,

'Is there much more of this, Miss Winter?'

'No, your honours. But Sally took her husband's rejection very badly. She was and still is unbalanced from her experiences in the bombing. She began drinking and frequenting bad company, going to clubs and mixing with foreign soldiers. She admits she neglected the children. But she assures me she is eager to turn over a new leaf. If you will take a lenient view of her lapse, she promises to get a part-time job and swears that she will not neglect the children again.'

She sat down.

'Thank you,' said the chairman of the bench. He leaned over and consulted first with one and then with the other woman magistrate. Once or twice they looked across at Sally Thomas, a pale, pretty girl in a light summer dress. Then the chairman cleared his throat.

'This is a very unedifying story,' he began, and then proceeded to launch into an attack upon the falling moral standards of the country. Men were dying in foreign lands while their womenfolk at home ... the West End was becoming a festering sore of immorality ... too much illegitimacy ... women betraying their trust ... it was necessary to think of the welfare of the children first.

The upshot of his speech was that Mrs Sally Thomas was bound over to be of good behaviour, and should report regularly to the probation officer and the Army Welfare Officer. In the meantime, the children would be sent to a home.

Everybody looked across at Sally Thomas, expecting some sort of an outburst. She said nothing at all, but on her face was a look of utter despair.

As she came out of court, a young man in a dark blue suit came quickly towards her and took hold of her hand.

'Ah, those old bastards!' he said. 'What did I tell you?'

He slipped his arm around her waist.

'What you need is a drink,' he said.

They walked around the corner to where a car was parked and climbed into it and drove away.

3

In the bar of le Petit Club de France in the mews behind St James's Street rumour had it that General de Gaulle and his erstwhile rival, Admiral Muselier, were fighting again, and that this time it would be a fight to the death.

When Robert Mengin came in for a drink in the evening these days (he was now writing and broadcasting in French for the BBC) he noticed that Free French naval and Army types were once more forgathering at opposite ends of the bar, and bosom friends who happened to wear different uniforms were no longer speaking to each other. He knew how they must be feeling. His own wife was a passionate supporter of General de Gaulle and so was his brother-in-law, and they could not understand Mengin's suspicion of the General's motives and dislike of his methods. It did not exactly make for harmonious family relationships.

Like most Frenchmen in London in 1942, Mengin was well aware that de Gaulle's headquarters at Carlton Gardens was less a centre of military operations than a hot-bed of intrigue. The acrid smell of suspicion was almost tangible in the nostrils as you walked down its corridors towards the General's rooms.

It was the most frustrating period of de Gaulle's London operation. Nothing was going right for him. Recruitment into the Free French forces had fallen far below expectations, to such an extent that Winston Churchill was rumoured to be regretting ever having accepted de Gaulle as the incarnation of French resistance. Too many now suspected that the General was fighting more for personal power than for the liberation of France from the Germans. For instance he had told those who had sworn their personal allegiance to him that they would never be asked to fight against their own countrymen, yet so far the only engagements in which the Free French had been involved were against the Vichy French in Dakar and Syria.

It was a period when strange rumours were whispered among the French in London about the activities of de Gaulle's secret services. He had won from the British the right to run his own intelligence operation, his own courts, even his own prisons. They were operated by men whose standards were not perhaps as high as those of Scotland Yard and the Old Bailey. Duke Street, where one of the more notorious 'investigation bureaus' had its headquarters in the heart of Mayfair, was rumoured to be the centre from which anti-Gaullists were consigned to a prison-camp outside London where conditions were dire.

Mengin was lucky. He had powerful friends and a pro-Gaullist wife. Otherwise, his critics at Carlton Gardens and Duke Street might not have been content just to spit at the mention of his name and call him a *salaud*.

Amid the disappointment among the British (and even more among the Americans) over the Free French, one branch of it continued to be exempt from criticism. De Gaulle knew it and it did not please him. The Free French Navy under Admiral Muselier was at sea and fighting the Germans, pounding the convoy beat across the Atlantic with their British naval comrades, battling U-boats and the Luftwaffe on the Arctic supply routes to Russia, and winning admiration everywhere for their skill, tenacity and bravery. General de Gaulle is a great man and he has never resented it when he has had to listen to praise heaped upon one of his subordinates, as it was upon Muselier.

But in the tricky times of 1942 he could not be sure that Muselier was a subordinate. In fact he need have had no fear of the Admiral, who had sworn an oath of allegiance and never thought of betraying it; but the intriguers at Carlton Gardens would have it otherwise. Muselier was not to be trusted, they whispered. He was too close to the British. He wanted power for himself.

That was one thing de Gaulle was determined he would never cede to him. If France was to be saved, de Gaulle had long since told himself, he was the only man capable of achieving it, and he would ruthlessly remove anyone who threatened his position as France's man of destiny. Did Muselier so threaten him? He could not be sure.

Just before the end of 1941 General de Gaulle, looking around for an opportunity of expanding the control of Free France, stared at his map and saw the islands of St Pierre and Miquelon. These two tiny islands not many miles south of Newfoundland had been French for two hundred years. Their inhabitants were said to be enthusiastically pro-Free French but their governor was pro-Vichy. Moreover, there was a radio station on Miquelon which regularly broadcast weather reports and these could well be useful to German U-boats operating in the Atlantic against Allied convoys.

These facts General de Gaulle conveyed to Winston Churchill when he sought him out and told him that he proposed to liberate the islands in the name of Free France. Fine, the Prime Minister replied, but first the Canadian and United States Governments must be informed and their permission secured, for the islands were in their defensive orbit.

To the fury of de Gaulle, the reply arrived from Washington a few days later and it was a terse ban on the operation. It seemed that the United States had a tacit agreement with Admiral Robert, who commanded the French fleet in the Caribbean. Both Robert and his ships still paid allegiance to Vichy France, but they had promised the Americans to stay at anchor in Martinique and take no part in the war so long as Robert and Vichy were recognised as the rulers of France's islands in the Western hemisphere. St Pierre and Miquelon were part of that pledge.

Now this is where versions differ and the documentation is missing. Winston Churchill always maintained that strongly approving of the American embargo as he did, he extracted a promise from de Gaulle that he would immediately forget about the expedition to St Pierre and Miquelon. On the other hand, de Gaulle called in Admiral Muselier (who had already been apprised of the operation and had undertaken to lead it) and told him that Winston Churchill had agreed that the liberation of the islands should go ahead. But, de Gaulle went on, because Churchill did not wish the Americans to know that he was ignoring their embargo the operation must take place in the greatest secrecy and no one must know where Muselier and his ships were going.

Muselier set sail with three Free French corvettes from Scotland in November 1941 and after a perilous journey* reached the St Lawrence River on 9 December. By that time the attack on Pearl Harbour had taken place and America was in the war, and so far as Admiral Muselier was concerned that changed everything. Even General de Gaulle could no longer ignore America's feelings.

Leaving his second-in-command, Captain Louis Heron de Villefosse in charge of the squadron, he went to Ottawa to consult the US representative. On Washington's instructions, that representative told Muselier:

'It is of vital importance that the Free French should cancel at once any operation against St Pierre and Miquelon. There are urgent reasons for this which I cannot go into. But the US Government would be seriously embarrassed by any Free French assault on the islands.†

Muselier was disappointed and immediately cabled de Gaulle in

* The corvettes were only 1,000 tons in displacement and the Atlantic gales were particularly fierce that winter.

† The State Department was not only worrying about the pro-Vichy Admiral Robert and his ships in the Carribean, but also the pro-Vichy Navy in North Africa. In the event of an Allied landing in French North Africa they did not wish to have a resentful French Navy opposing them. Appeasing Vichy was very much a part of American policy at this time.

London asking that the operation be postponed pending further negotiations with the Americans. At the same time, Anthony Eden, the British Foreign Secretary, called in de Gaulle and after a long conversation extracted (or believed he had) a definite promise, as Churchill had done previously, that the operation would be called off. At least he cabled the Americans that he had seen de Gaulle who agreed 'that the proposed action should not, repeat not, now be undertaken.'

That was not, however, the way General de Gaulle interpreted the conversation. By this time he had heard rumours that the Canadians were about to occupy the two islands and he was determined to forestall them.* Accordingly, he cabled Muselier:

WE HAVE, AS YOU REQUESTED, CONSULTED THE BRITISH AND AMERICAN GOVERNMENTS. WE ARE INFORMED RELIABLY THAT THE CANADIANS INTEND THEMSELVES TO DESTROY THE WIRELESS STATION OF SAINT PIERRE AND MIQUELON. UNDER THESE CIRCUMSTANCES I COMMAND YOU TO RALLY SAINT PIERRE AND MIQUELON BY YOUR OWN MEANS AND WITHOUT SAYING ANYTHING TO FOREIGNERS. I ASSUME THE ENTIRE RESPONSIBILITY FOR THIS OPERATION, WHICH HAS BECOME INDISPENSABLE IN ORDER FOR FRANCE TO RETAIN HER POSSESSIONS. SIGNED: GENERAL DE GAULLE.

This was jolting enough, but it was followed shortly afterwards by another cable. This one came from Muselier's chief of staff, Captain Moullec, and it said:

FOREIGN OFFICE INFORMS US THAT THE PRESIDENT OF THE UNITED STATES IS CATEGORICALLY OPPOSED TO THE SCHEDULED OPERATION. SIGNED: MOULLEC.

What was the unfortunate Admiral to do? If he refused to go on with the operation he would be disobeying his Commander-in-Chief, General de Gaulle, to whom he had sworn allegiance. On the other hand, if he went ahead in secrecy with the liberation of the islands, all the confidence and goodwill which he had built up between the Free French Navy and the Allies would be shattered. They would never be trusted again.

The Admiral reluctantly decided that he could not go back on his word. He would obey the orders of General de Gaulle. But

* The Canadians did have that idea about this time but were dissuaded by the British Government from carrying it out.

once he had obeyed them, he would return to London and resign.

Admiral Emile Henri Muselier was an honourable man. That, as it turned out, was the tragedy.

On Christmas Eve the French squadron, now accompanied by the Free French submarine *Surcouf*, arrived off St Pierre and the first batch of sailors went ashore. There was no resistance. Next day a plebiscite was held and Muselier was able to inform de Gaulle that all but 2 per cent of the population had rallied to the Free French. De Gaulle cabled back:

PLEASE TELL THE POPULATION OF THE ISLE OF SAINT PIERRE AND MIQUELON, SO DEAR AND SO FAITHFUL TO FRANCE, HOW JOYFUL THE NATION FEELS TO SEE THEM LIBERATED. SAINT PIERRE AND MIQUELON WILL BRAVELY TAKE UP ONCE MORE WITH US AND WITH OUR BRAVE ALLIES THE FIGHT FOR THE LIBERATION OF THE HOME-LAND AND THE FREEDOM OF THE WORLD.

TO YOU PERSONALLY I ADDRESS, IN MY NAME AND THAT OF THE NATIONAL COMMITTEE, MY HEARTFELT FELICITATIONS FOR THE WAY IN WHICH YOU HAVE REALISED THIS WINNING OVER WITH SUCH ORDER AND DIGNITY. VIVE LA FRANCE! SIGNED: CHARLES DE GAULLE.

But if de Gaulle was pleased, the British were not. Churchill found himself having to apologise personally to Roosevelt (he was on a visit to Washington at the time) for having deceived him, for he had assured the President that de Gaulle had given him his word that he would not take the islands.

Roosevelt shrugged his shoulders. He had always disliked de Gaulle.

'You see,' he said, 'I was not wrong about him.'

As for the State Department, they were furious. The action of the Free French, they maintained, had upset all their plans for winning over the French fleet and the French possessions in North Africa to the Allied cause without a fight.* Cordell Hull, the Secretary of State, was so angry that he committed the error of referring to 'the so-called Free French' in a statement condemning

---

* In fact it made no difference whatsoever. The Vichy Navy and the French possessions in North Africa had no intention of siding with the Allies until they were sure they were going to win.

the operation, a pejorative description of a brave group of exiles for which even anti-Gaullists found it hard to forgive him.

The scene moves forward to 1942 and back to London. Winston Churchill was home again from Washington. He summoned de Gaulle to see him at 10 Downing Street. He did not tell the General that one melancholy result of the St Pierre and Miquelon affair was that President Roosevelt had decided that henceforth the Free French would be told nothing of the Allies' future plans, and that General de Gaulle would not be accepted as the leader of France until the French people as a whole had indicated their acceptance of him. In this decision Churchill had reluctantly concurred, but he kept it to himself.

He glowered at the tall Frenchman standing so cool and unconcerned before him and proceeded to rebuke him for having gone back on his word, for having upset his own relations with Roosevelt by having misrepresented him, and for an overall breach of trust.

De Gaulle was unrepentant. He had already cabled his representative in Washington to tell the State Department:

SAINT PIERRE AND MIQUELON HAVE BEEN FRENCH TERRITORIES FOR CENTURIES AND ARE PEOPLED EXCLUSIVELY BY FRENCHMEN. TAKING POSSESSION OF THESE ISLANDS IS A MATTER CONCERNING THE FRENCH AND NO ONE ELSE. . . .

But, as Churchill quickly made clear to him, the Americans refused to see it that way. He had only with difficulty succeeded in persuading Roosevelt not to send in a force of US Marines to throw the Free French out of the islands. Instead he had compromised by agreeing to the stationing of a joint American-Canadian representation on the islands to direct their affairs. At first de Gaulle angrily refused to accept the arrangement, but later agreed provided that the arrangement should be kept secret. He was crisply told that the US could not agree to this suggestion.

It was an extremely ruffled General de Gaulle who emerged from the unhappy meeting. Nonetheless, this did not prevent him from cabling a happier account of the conversation with Churchill to Admiral Muselier than in fact appears to have taken place.

This, at least, seemed to be the case when it was compared with the British version of the same conversation. Muselier's Chief of Staff in London, Captain Moullec, had some extremely good contacts in Whitehall and it was from one of these that he got hold of the British transcript, and was appalled when he realized how much it differed from de Gaulle's own. He at once cabled his chief in a code known only to the two of them:

HAVING HAD OPPORTUNITY TO EXAMINE THE OFFICIAL MINUTES OF THE CHURCHILL–DE GAULLE MEETING ON 22 JANUARY ... I MUST INFORM YOU THAT THE ATMOSPHERE DURING THE CONVERSATIONS WAS HEAVILY CHARGED. IN THIS LIGHT TELEGRAMS 2821 AND 2849 FROM THE GENERAL REVEAL GRAVE MISREPRESENTATIONS. ...

Admiral Muselier arrived back in London on the last day of February, 1942, and was greeted by General de Gaulle with a warm embrace. They drove together to the Admiral's lodgings at the Hyde Park Hotel. Three days later a meeting was called by de Gaulle of the Free French National Committee at Carlton Gardens to discuss the St Pierre and Miquelon affair. Since Muselier was both a member of the National Committee as well as the leader of the expedition, he had a double reason for being present. No one, least of all de Gaulle, suspected that he had come to the meeting with a hand-grenade fizzling in his pocket.

The members of the Committee sat around the great table in the Clock Room at Carlton Gardens and happily listened to Muselier's account, strictly factual and operational, of the landing in the islands, deliberately avoiding any reference to the political events which had preceded and followed it. The General seemed relieved that he had done so, and smiling, said, 'This operation was handled perfectly.'

But then he made an error. He went on, 'So you see, messieurs, how right I was in ordering the liberation in spite of the opinion of our Allies.'

Admiral Muselier broke in, 'I took great pains not to discuss the affair from the point of view of foreign policy,' he said. 'But since you yourself have raised the subject, I wish to state emphatically that I do not share your opinion.'

De Gaulle tried to wave him aside. 'Let us talk about that aspect at a later date,' he said, shortly.

'No, General,' said Muselier, 'with your permission we will discuss it now. I wish to declare here and now that on two occasions during the operation St Pierre–Miquelon I was not told the truth: for example, in the matter of the promise made to the

Americans that the operation would not take place without their previous agreement, a promise made in your name, General.'

De Gaulle made as if to rise to his feet, but the Admiral persisted: 'On 22 January you had an interview with Churchill and Eden. You did not send me the official minutes of this meeting as prepared by the Foreign Office. On the contrary, I received an account over your signature, Sir, and it did not agree at all with the Foreign Office version.'

He went on for some time after that, blaming the General for all that had happened. Finally, he said, 'I find it no longer possible to continue working with this committee. I herewith resign as National Commissioner.'

By this time General de Gaulle had stubbed out his last cigarette and was regarding the excited and emotional sailor with the cool regard of a scientist examining a bug.

'I ask you to reconsider your decision,' he said, at last.

'I refuse to reconsider,' replied Muselier.

De Gaulle nodded. 'Very well, I ask you to send me your resignation in writing.'

'It will be with you this afternoon,' said the Admiral.

That afternoon he dispatched a letter to de Gaulle at Carlton Gardens formally resigning from the Free French National Committee. Not only did the General accept it. Next day, 4 March 1942, he also stripped Admiral Muselier of his post as Commander-in-Chief of the Free French Navy.

'Do you know what's happened?' asked A. V. Alexander, First Lord of the Admiralty, of Churchill that night. 'De Gaulle has sacked Muselier. He can't do this! Muselier built up the Free French fleet. It wouldn't exist without him. It won't go on existing without him. We've got to have him back. De Gaulle must rescind his decision.'

But General de Gaulle would not rescind his decision.

On 10 March at six in the evening Charles de Gaulle arrived at Westminster House, headquarters of the Free French Navy in London. He had asked Muselier's friends in the Royal Navy to keep the latter away, for he had a delicate task in hand. He proposed to interview every officer member of the headquarters staff personally, to find out which were dedicated Muselier-men – and therefore dangerous – and which were prepared to give de Gaulle their personal and unswerving allegiance.

The officers had gathered in the main hall to await the General. He faced them with a grave expression on his face and said, 'Messieurs, I am General de Gaulle. You are officers of the Free French Navy. Respect will be paid where it should be paid, and, most particularly to Admiral Muselier.'

As he was saying these words there was a sound from the back of the hall and Admiral Muselier entered.

'General, you have sent for all the officers of the Navy,' he said. 'I am an officer of the Navy, and here I am.'

De Gaulle stared at him in cold silence, then held out his hand. 'Welcome,' he said. Then speaking over his head to the others, he went on, 'I wish to see each officer individually, and I will begin with the most junior.'

He strode off towards one of the offices, but turned in surprise when he discovered that Admiral Muselier was following him.

'My wish is to see each officer alone,' he said, coldly.

Muselier: 'General, in no French military organisation is it customary to interrogate officers other than in the presence of their commanding officer.'

De Gaulle: 'Admiral, you are committing a breach of military discipline.'

Muselier: 'No, General, but I know that certain of my officers are rather excited* and I would not wish any of them to put themselves in the wrong.'

De Gaulle was now rigid with anger. He kept repeating: 'A breach of military discipline.' Finally he turned and started for the door.

'Under the circumstances,' he said, 'the only thing I can do is withdraw. But messieurs,' he went on, addressing the watching officers, 'rest assured that what must be done will be done.'

Then he was gone.

Anthony Eden, the Foreign Secretary, was in his office on the morning of 11 March 1942, when his secretary came through and laid a note on his desk.

'I think you should read this at once,' he said.

The Foreign Secretary ran his eyes over the note before him and

---

* Many of them were threatening to resign if Muselier went.

then read it again, to make sure what he was seeing was actually there.

'Good God,' he said. Then: 'Get me the Prime Minister. I must talk to him at once.'

Soon the news was all around Whitehall.

'Do you know what de Gaulle has done now?' said A. V. Alexander, the First Lord of the Admiralty to one of his aides. 'He's arrested the Commander-in-Chief of the Free French Navy – and sentenced him to thirty days' imprisonment in the Tower of London!'

4

For most Londoners it was the worst time of the war because it was the dreariest. The heart seemed to have gone out of the great city. There were no victories to cheer the people on and not even bombing to spur them into defiance. No one was starving but rationing had reduced the national diet to a drab, starchy minimum that sustained life but lowered the spirits and sapped everyone's energy. Most people were pasty-faced and always yawning, increasingly subject to coughs and colds and stomach troubles – and tired, always tired. The buildings looked drab, for they had not been painted for nearly four years, and the civilians in the streets were shabby, for now everything which had not completely disappeared from the shops was rationed and available only with coupons or points: clothes, shoes and underwear took too many coupons for most people to buy them, and frayed shirts and torn vests were worn until they no longer hung together.

The neighbourliness which had been born during the blitz seemed to have died out again, and people appeared to be filled with envy and resentment. They watched each other in the shops to see that no one got a milligram more meat on their ration than anyone else. They bickered in the queues. The civilians envied the military their lack of worries over clothes and food and grumbled over their apparent idleness. It was the women's services which came in for the bitterest criticism, particularly the girls of the ATS (the women's section of the Army). It is true that at weekends now the West End seemed to be full of girls in uniform, often the worse for drink, and alarming stories floated around about their filthy language and their even filthier habits, about the increasing number of pregnancies among them and the growing amount of venereal disease. People seemed to have forgotten that it was the ATS which had helped man the anti-aircraft guns all through the blitz with great bravery; and they conveniently forgot that if thousands of girls were now in uniform, that was not necessarily through choice. Ernest Bevin, the Minister of Labour, had made service compulsory for both sexes by now, and all women were liable either for work in the factories or the Services. Since the Army needed most women they inevitably had gathered in what the soldiers now referred to as 'some real scrubbers'. The other two Services could afford to be more selective and the girls of the WAAF (Women's Auxiliary Air Force) and WRNS (Women's Royal Naval Service) were consequently held in higher public esteem.*

The civilians resented the Army's easy rations, clothes and perks, the Army resented the RAF's easy-going ways, and all the services resented the pay and privileges and sexual successes of the increasingly ubiquitous Dominion and American troops.

But it was the civilians who were the depressed class in London that autumn of 1942. They went about their ordinary jobs in the scarred and grimy city, eyeing the uniforms all around them, well aware that the capital was now a notoriously gay Mecca for all troops on leave, and they felt like spectres at the feast. For the majority of them there was no let-up and no light. The years of the war stretched ahead and it seemed that there would never be an end to them.

On 3 September 1942, Vere Hodgson wrote:

We enter the fourth year of war today. How well I remember the day when Mr Hillyard rang up Miss Moyes [her boss] three years ago and said that the Germans had invaded Poland and we must get the blackout ready for the night. It does not seem to have gone according to plan except for our rationing, which is exceedingly good. We expected to be bombed and we have been. Today we all bought Union Jacks in the street. At 11 a.m. Miss Moyes assembled us and we listened to the broadcast service from Westminster Abbey.

But after that it was back to the daily grind of listening to hard

---

* Though there were public references to their lack of morals, too. 'Up with the lark and to bed with a Wren,' was a current joke.

luck tales from servicemen's wives, helping out the factory girl who had got herself pregnant by the married foreman, shopping for the rationing of not only herself but the old and infirm of Holland Park and Notting Hill. Vere Hodgson was lucky, and she obviously had a way with her. She rarely met with the rudeness and trickery in the shops about which so many Londoners were now beginning to complain. She wrote that autumn:

> Struggled to get an onion. I tried the old Pole's shop but he had none so I went across to Mr Buy Best, where I sometimes shop. The manager had only a few and those were booked. I agreed very humbly that of course other people had a prior claim, as I was not a regular customer. I bought a pound of carrots and wandered around the shop, still thinking of those onions. Then I purchased a stick of celery. I could see an idea was germinating in the man's mind, so I lingered on. Finally I won without saying more. A voice behind me murmured, 'If you only want an onion for flavouring, I will let you have one.' I poured blessings on his head and walked away. It was a victory indeed.

Next day she wrote:

> Horses are to have ration books. I wonder when they will issue them for cats. They say nothing about donkeys.

Rosemary Black was beginning to find life something of a strain, and that October she allowed herself what was, for her, an unusual outburst of grumbling about her domestic difficulties.

> Tea-cloths and towels are suddenly put on clothing rations. No extra allowance, needless to say. Hell! I'd just decided last week that I really must get a new stock of tea-cloths – *if only* I'd taken action at once instead of procrastinating in my usual feeble way. I shall simply *have* to get new clothes soon, too, in spite of rationing. The laundry, to which I was reduced to sending them by pressure of work and rheumatism and lack of suitable soap has turned mine into the condition of Doctor Johnson's net. Present arrangements really are hard on that section of the community whose members happen to be housewives or mothers. Surely there is a good case for giving us some sort of extra coupon allowance? First of all, various household polishes and cleaners are put on 'points' – perhaps the muscular effort these

goods save is supposed to be equivalent to their value in 'points' food! Then a mother will almost inevitably be faced by the inexorable growth of her children into spending most of her own clothes coupons on her family to supplement their own. And now this final blow of the towels and tea-cloths! I had looked forward, now that the brown clothing coupons are valid at last, to getting a few garments, badly needed, for myself: shoes, stockings and winter underwear above all. But now, with L. growing like a beanpole and new tea-cloths an unavoidable necessity, it looks as though I must give up all idea of ever being able to get anything for my own personal use. Luckily I'm one of the few who don't give a damn about clothes, but if I don't crave to be smart I still should like to be warm!

Rosemary Black continued to feel guilty because, she felt, she was luckier than most people in wartime London.

I have a chronic feeling of guilt. Having a hired car to take the children to school each morning – not having to struggle there with them in crowded Tubes makes the whole difference to my life, and no doubt to the lives of the other two mothers whose children fill up the car, too, but even so I can't help feeling uncomfortably that any arrangement so agreeable must be wickedly wasteful and wrong. *Giving human food to the cat:* though I'm not convinced that any fish sold during the past six months is fit for human consumption, and anyway I'd like to know who doesn't. *The fuel economy.* What with having no living-in maid and making an effort, I've cut the house fuel consumption by over 50 per cent, but still, alas, without approaching the exiguous allowance of my fuel target, which recks nothing of the height and coldness of my rooms, the dampness of the house, or the hopelessly furred-up pipes, to say nothing of my rheumatism!

She had tried, she really had tried, she told herself, and she would go on trying.

But I have a chronically guilty conscience about hot water, on which I admit I find it impossible to cut down. *Spending too much money on my own pleasure.* Of course I'm saving money, by way of the gradual elimination of more and more expenses, wages, clothes, luxury goods of all kinds, but I'm dismally aware none the less that I'm still spending more than I ought – on drinks, expensive fruit, etc. when there is any, restaurant meals, books – and nothing at all that I can help on the war effort. *The state of the dustbins.* I simply cannot get K. or Mrs G. to co-operate in the slightest degree in regard to salvage. Their idea is to stuff anything that will burn into the boiler including perfectly clean paper, rags and all the rest of it. . . . I've even gone so far as to stick up a diagram saying which dustbin is for tins and which for ash or refuse, and where paper and bones are to go, but no good. The same old muddle goes on and makes me feel most ineffective that I can't carry reforms through, and most unpatriotic.

It was too depressing for words, and she was finding her bad conscience demoralising.

It makes one feel set apart from the 'home front' war effort, and therefore thoroughly browned off by it – and also that I might as well be hung for a sheep as a lamb, so to speak, whenever the choice presents itself. Why not burn a crust or show a light or turn the second bar of the electric stove on, when I'm all wrong on so many counts already.

And compared with the bulk of London's population, Rosemary Black *was* privileged. She was a 'good customer' at her local stores, always ready to buy the more expensive trifles and tit-bits, and was therefore never forgotten when there were a few extra grams of butter or ounces of meat left over. She knew nothing of the queuing in shops, of the rudeness of shopkeepers, and of the self-satisfied way in which some of them 'delight in telling you that there will be no more of this or that until after the war', as one office worker put it.

These were the doldrums of the war. It was when people behaved their worst towards each other and when there was no excitement to alleviate the misery, the sameness, the boredom, the bitchiness and the spite.

'I had terrible trouble this morning,' reported a young woman named Grace North. She was a scientific worker who had lived through some of the worst moments of the blitz in the East End, but was now 'tensed up and unsettled'. She added: 'Trust me to get involved in other people's troubles.'

Grace North's friend was in trouble with her butcher, and had been for some time.

Yesterday it came to a head. For one thing she's never allowed to have any choice – she gets just a dollop of meat handed out to her. If she dares to ask for anything different, this pig of a man snaps at her. For instance, he insisted that she should have pork again this week, making it the third time in succession, whereas he had other meat in the shop, but not for her. Also he never weighs the meat in front of her, just hands her a parcel for which she pays cap in hand like a beggar almost. Another thing, unless she tells him in the morning whether she will be calling for the meat on Friday or Saturday he tells her when she calls for it that it is shut away in the refrigerator and he can't let her have it. Yesterday ... she felt she should collect the meat and part cook it, as she is going out. It would mean carrying the wretched chop around with her until late at night. She took a few minutes off from work yesterday to arrange to go round to the shop at ten past four in the afternoon, and he refused to let her have it as it was in the safe. She was furious as it would mean her not having any meat at all, but he didn't care.

The girl had been too fed up to go in again and was prepared to sacrifice her ration for the week, but Miss North offered to go in her place.

So I went into the shop this morning and said I had come for Miss M's meat ration. He at once handed me a parcel wrapped up in a newspaper. I said: 'What is that?' He said, in a cocky, take-it-or-leave-it sort of voice: 'It's pork.' I said: 'How much per pound is it?' He said: 'Two shillings.' Then he seemed to hesitate and stutter and then asked why I wanted to know. I said: 'Never mind, you'll soon find out.' I've long had the suspicion that he has overcharged her but he would probably have got away with it if he had kept a civil tongue in his head. I said: 'I thought loin of pork was one and eightpence a pound.' He said: 'This is a chop. Mrs S (his wife) will tell you the price of it.' Mrs S. looked at the register and said: 'One and sixpence' and I paid her with a shilling and sixpence. I then turned to the butcher and said: 'I wonder what Lord Woolton would think of shopkeepers like you who make things as difficult as you can for people in business.' He and his wife both got into a rage and told me to get out of the shop. I said I was going to find out if he was entitled to withhold a customer's meat at four in the afternoon when he had it on the premises. Also I said if there was anything wrong with the weight and price of the meat he would hear about it.

This redoubtable young woman then marched across to the nearest post office and had the small packet of meat weighed. It weighed just under twelve ounces in the newspaper,* and that was about right at two shillings a pound, but Miss North telephoned the local Food Office and discovered that the prevailing price for pork was one shilling and tenpence – so that he had over-charged by threepence.

The local Food Officer was on to it like a shot, and an enforcement officer cycled round to see us immediately. He took the chop round to the shop and asked the butcher to weigh it, and it weighed only eleven ounces unwrapped. But the butcher said he had only charged me one and threepence, making it right. The officer came round and told us and asked us whether we would come round and challenge the man. I went round with him and asked the man why he said he had charged one and three when I had paid him one and six. He absolutely denied it, and I said: 'Can you absolutely look me in the face and say you only charged me one and three?'
'Yes.'
I said: 'How much a pound did you tell me it was?'
He said: 'One and tenpence.'
I turned to the officer and I said: 'That is a lie.'
The butcher bridled. 'Don't you call me a liar.'
I said: 'I will because you are a liar.'
'The officer then asked to see the register, which was written in pencil and quite clearly had been deleted, and the figure three written over it, not even done carefully, so the man is stupid as well as dishonest and disobliging. The butcher denied that he had altered it, and the officer said:
'Don't you call *me* a liar. Already you are accusing Miss North of robbing her friend of threepence. I believe her and I don't believe you.'

* This was the meat ration for one person for a week.

He then wrote down the particulars ... and said I would be doing a public service if I attend as a witness if the Food people decide to prosecute. ... Oh dear, my friend and I hope other people in the office will not hear of it as it makes us seem viragos to take a man to court for threepence. But it's the principle. ... He has bullied my friend for months and she's a gentle sort. ... Anyway, we have no option. Born under Mars, born under Mars!

But rationing and shortages brought moments to British households of sheer pleasurable bliss that they would never experience in the days of peace and plenty.

A friend of Vere Hodgson reported:

I had a new laid egg sent to me from the country for breakfast. First new laid egg I've had for five months. Have given away to a delicate child both my ration eggs during this period. There was an agony of indecision over how to cook it: fried with bacon, omelette, scrambled? Decided that boiling it made it more – *more*. How delicious it tasted as I rolled it round and round my mouth. ... A friend of mine when she gets an egg can't bring herself to break the shell, with the result that two have gone bad on her and stank to high heaven when she at last went to use them.

And Grace North reported on the family which had spent the bulk of its precious 'points' on a tin of Bartlett's pears which had just been released to the shops. The mother opened them for tea that evening for the family and then said to them:

'Now we mustn't talk. Just concentrate on the pears and get the utmost out of them.'

Which moved Miss North to ask, 'Are we showing deprivation symptoms? Or are we gluttons?'

In fact, Londoners were simply in need of a little excitement in their lives and a little sweetness in their stomachs.

5

Obviously, General de Gaulle could not be allowed to get away with it. On that Winston Churchill was determined. What he was demanding was that the British do his dirty work for him. He had quarrelled with the Commander-in-Chief of the Free French Navy, Admiral Muselier, and wanted him out of the way. Because he had disobeyed orders, de Gaulle said. *Insubordination*, he had called it in his note to the British Government, and had continued:

'A penalty of thirty days' fortress arrest is imposed on Admiral Muselier.'

Aside from the fact that you couldn't do such a thing to such a gallant and distinguished officer, it was simply too much for de Gaulle to demand that the British immediately take the matter in hand and carry off Muselier to the Tower of London. The British Navy would never forgive a British government for involving themselves in such a mean and sordid affair. They knew Muselier as the only Admiral in the whole of the French Navy who had volunteered to go on fighting after the defeat of France. Though of senior rank to de Gaulle, he had willingly put himself under the General's rank in the interests of French resistance. He had organised the Free French Navy. He had served with great bravery at sea. He had already been humiliated once by being hauled off to jail on a fake espionage charge. It mustn't be allowed to happen to him again – just because of a shabby family quarrel.

It was pointed out to the Prime Minister, however, that under the terms of the agreement which he had signed with de Gaulle on 15 January 1941, the General had every right to expect the British Government to act on his behalf. The agreement had given him full jurisdiction and discretion over the fate of all Free Frenchmen, and Muselier was certainly one of them.

No. Winston Churchill decided that agreement or no agreement, he could not do it. When he had given General de Gaulle his powers, it was not for such petty spitefulnesses as this.

He told his liaison officers with the Free French to get out of the obligation somehow. He could not save Admiral Muselier from dismissal – that much was certain. If he did so, de Gaulle would publicly announce that the British Government had broken its pledge, and the British public would never hold with that. They were passionate supporters of General de Gaulle.

It was arranged instead that Muselier should retire 'on sick leave' to a house in a London suburb and have nothing further to do with the Free French Navy.* General de Gaulle protested, but

* He remained inactive until the liberation of French North Africa, when he rejoined the French Navy.

was quietly told that the Prime Minister was adamant and would not be moved, and he decided not to make a public issue of it.

But it was the beginning of the end of friendly relations between Winston Churchill and Charles de Gaulle. When, later that year, the British decided to take over the Vichy-controlled island of Madagascar in the Indian Ocean, to prevent it falling into the hands of the Japanese, Churchill neither informed de Gaulle of the operation in advance nor did he utilise Free French troops or ships. They would only cause unnecessary fratricidal strife by getting into a fight with the Vichy forces on the island. De Gaulle stomped his way into Downing Street to complain vehemently, and, according to his own memoirs, this is what happened:

> Mr Churchill then attacked me in a bitter and highly emotional tone. When I pointed out that the establishment of a British-controlled administration on Madagascar would be an interference with the rights of France, he exclaimed furiously: 'You claim to be France! You are not France! I do not recognise you as France!'

De Gaulle's reply to that was, 'If, in your eyes, I am not the representative of France, why and with what right are you dealing with me concerning her world-wide interests?'

Churchill could do nothing but remain furiously silent. It was true. He had recognised de Gaulle and he could not now go back on it. But in the next few months he tried to, and was to discover that when it came to political in-fighting, Charles de Gaulle was more than a match for him.

The moment Admiral Muselier vanished into retirement, General de Gaulle moved swiftly, and the purge began. All naval officers in the Free French fleet were summoned for personal interviews with the General, and were reminded of their oath of allegiance to Free France and to General de Gaulle in person. If they wished to go on serving at sea, there was no choice for them. By the terms of the agreement Churchill had signed, no member of the French armed services could transfer to the forces of any of the Allies; and any officer who refused to recognize the new situation in the Free French Navy would face court martial. And this time, de Gaulle made it clear, it was the French who would handle the punishment of recalcitrant officers.

These threats did not prevent Captain Heron de Villefosse from making his position clear. He had been Muselier's second-in-command on the St Pierre and Miquelon operation, and had been left behind to take command in the islands afterwards. From there, when he heard of his chief's humiliation he cabled:

KINDLY TRANSMIT THE FOLLOWING TO ADMIRAL MUSELIER: LEARNING THAT YOU ARE OBLIGED TO TAKE A REST, I WISH TO SEND YOU IN MY NAME PERSONALLY AND IN THAT OF ALL OFFICERS ON SAINT PIERRE OUR MOST AFFECTIONATE GOOD WISHES, IN THE HOPE THAT YOU WILL SOON BE ABLE TO RESUME YOUR POST AT THE HEAD OF THE FREE FRENCH NAVAL FORCES. IN OUR EYES, YOU ARE STILL THE MAN WHO SAVED THE HONOUR OF FRANCE IN THE DARKEST PERIOD OF ITS HISTORY. YOUR NAME AND YOUR EXAMPLE ARE INSEPARABLE FROM THE ENSIGN BEARING THE CROSS OF LORRAINE WHICH, BY YOUR ORDERS, WILL CONTINUE TO FLY OVER WARSHIPS OF FREE FRANCE. RESPECTFULLY, VILLEFOSSE.

Muselier never got the message, but Villefosse received a reply:

FOR CAPTAIN DE VILLEFOSSE, TO BE DECODED BY HIM: HAND OVER YOUR COMMAND TO THE NEXT SENIOR OFFICER ON SAINT PIERRE AND RETURN TO LONDON IMMEDIATELY. INSUBORDINATION. GENERAL DE GAULLE.

The captain returned to London and there refused to renew his pledge of allegiance to de Gaulle. He was not pressed to do so. He was not court-martialled. Why is not quite certain. Perhaps his close association with Muselier made the Free French decide to be cautious with him. But he was forced to shed his uniform. He could not go on fighting at sea, for the British Navy, which would have willingly done so, were unable to take him. He found himself odd jobs in London instead as a translator and broadcaster in French for the BBC.

Others were not so lucky. Insubordination was becoming a favourite word in Free French circles.

13

WOMEN'S WOES

I

In August 1942, the Russians were still fighting desperately at Stalingrad but looked as if they might, at any moment, be overwhelmed. The British not only felt gloomy about the outcome of the great struggle but guilty, too, because Allied armies were not fighting in Western Europe to take the pressure off their comrades in the East.

That same month, six thousand Allied Commando troops (mostly Canadians) attempted a landing at Dieppe and were driven back with a loss of 2,000 men killed, wounded or taken prisoner. The raid was a 'fiasco',* more as a result of delays and poor planning than of German toughness. The only people in any way satisfied by the raid were those advisers of Winston Churchill, like Lindemann and Sir Alan Brooke, who thought it would prove to the Americans once and for all that a second front across the Channel was unthinkable for at least another year.

For women one of the most irritating things about that summer was a sudden shortage of hair-grips and sanitary towels. Most women were now wearing head-scarfs to keep their hair out of their work, but there were occasions when they liked to take them off and show the colour of their tresses. The prevailing topic amongst most women was compulsory registration of female labour, and, in many cases, how to dodge it. It was remarkable how many women suddenly discovered invalid mothers and fathers needing their constant care, and how many young married women – and single women too, of course – found themselves pregnant within a week or two of registration. The bulk of Britain's women responded readily enough to the call, but they resented how often they were taken out of admittedly unessential work and compulsorily directed into even more ineffective occupations; and their loudest grumbles were reserved for the members of their own sex in the Labour Exchanges who had the power to decide into which

* General Eisenhower's word.

288

jobs they should go and wielded it with such bureaucratic lack of feeling. It was reported in the newspapers that one young woman slapped the face of an official who told her, 'Don't argue with me. You're our property now.'

There was much sympathy for her when she was fined for assault. But there was no sympathy at all for the girls who swarmed into London to go on the streets or into the shady clubs rather than face the call-up. It was about this time that police and female red-caps (military police) began regular checks in Piccadilly and its environs to round up deserters from the female forces and the munitions factories.

With plenty of women on the loose (in more senses than one), with British, American and Dominion troops cramming the streets in search of leave-time entertainment, London experienced a mounting epidemic of black-marketeering and thieving. There were silk-stockings, lipsticks, butter and meat to be bought in the back streets of Soho, but naturally the bulk of London's population did not have the wherewithal to buy them. It was, in any case, the achievement of the Government that though rations were low and dull, at least the system allowed a basic diet for everyone and there was no danger of starvation. On the Continent and in Russia they were shooting people who were found dealing in the black market where the shortages were desperate and men, women and children were dying of starvation because black marketeers had cornered what food was going.

In Britain there was never any need for such dire penalties. No matter how many food vans and meat carcases were hijacked by gangs in London and the provinces, the ration was always met. It was on the luxuries: cigarettes, drink, silk stockings, clothing and petrol coupons that the black marketeers battened.

It wasn't that the people of London were starving that autumn, they were just weary and downhearted.

'I'm fed up with the ceaseless gamble of living,' a woman complained to a questioner. 'There's no let-up anywhere. I leave off work to carry bricks, so to speak. I never get enough sleep.'

But there was one commodity needed in London now which no black marketeer could keep up with, and that was sex. London had by this time become a gigantic staging post, and it was bursting with troops (particularly American troops) waiting for the day when they would be called upon to fight and die. In the meantime, what most of them needed – and needed like a drug – was women.

After only a few days of responding to their needs Sally Thomas discovered that they had plenty to give in return. Or at least the Americans had, and it was on the Americans that she concentrated from now on. They had brought with them from the United States all those little things that had once been the stuff of everyday life, but were now long-forgotten luxuries: fountain pens, wrist watches, cigarette lighters as well as whole cartons of cigarettes and bottles of whisky and gin. They were the new millionaires, thanks to the PX they had set up in Grosvenor Square: and when they left you to go back to their depots you found gifts of clothing coupons and tinned food and silk stockings on your mantel shelf as well as money.

One night a shy young sergeant from New Jersey, made bold by drink, insisted that the stockings he had brought were particularly special and giggled like a naughty schoolboy as he helped her put them on. They were fantastically sheer and yet somehow more durable than silk, and she kept walking around in them, but otherwise naked, staring in narcissistic awe at herself in the mirror.

'But what kind of silk is it?' she asked the sergeant.

'But that's it, honey,' he said. 'This isn't silk at all. It's a new kind of fibre we've invented. It's called nylon.'

He was a technical sergeant in one of the photographic units and he launched into a detailed account of the process which she ignored. Next day all her friends looked in envy and admiration at her slim legs in their attractive new sheaths, and the word spread among the girls to ask their American friends to bring them nylon.

Most of the girls flocking into London now were incredibly young, bored schoolgirls from the Midlands and Wales, teenagers dodging the call-up into the Services and factories, deserters from the ATS and the WAAFs. The majority ended up in the West End and their favourite places for picking up soldiers were the pavements around Rainbow Corner, the chief recreation centre in the West End for US troops on leave. After darkness, in the blackout, the pavements were a seething mass of girls and men grabbing at each other, shrieking, shouting, laughing and then pairing off and leaving for a Soho club or a bomb site in a back street.

Thanks to Joey, Sally Thomas never found it necessary to

pound the beat along Piccadilly. He had picked her up in a pub in Chelsea one night, and, it being the day she had heard that Jimmy wanted a divorce, she was in no mood to say no when he asked her back to his flat. After the court had taken away her children, she moved in with him. It was he who took her along to the big hotels like the Mayfair, the Dorchester, the Park Lane and drank with her in the bar until a likely customer turned up. One always did. The hotels got a special quota of drinks and they were always full of officers and US NCOs, on leave. The moment one of them responded to Sally's laugh or smile, Joey would excuse himself and not come back.

Two months later, Sally Thomas had more money than she had ever dreamed of, and was seeing a side of London that she did not know existed. Joey was not like most men she had heard about who lived on women's earnings. He was kind and easy-going. He only took half her money, and let her keep all the gifts except clothing coupons. In the daytime, while she slept, he went off into Soho, where he played endless gambling games with groups of his fellow deserters (he had walked out of Catterick Army Depot in 1939, after two days drilling on the square, and had never been back since). At the weekend, he went with her to the greyhound races at the White City and always seemed to know at least one winner. He even came with her to the two foster homes where they had farmed out her children – until she gave up the visits, figuring that it made all of them too unhappy.

One Saturday, however, when she and Joey were leaving the White City a couple of military policemen suddenly moved in on them and asked them for their identity cards. Joey showed no sign of panic. He had long since equipped himself with false papers. Unfortunately, by one of those odd coincidences, he had run up against just the wrong MP.

'Haven't I seen you somewhere before?' he said, peering at him. 'Yes, by God, I have. Catterick, wasn't it, Joey?'

That night and the next, Sally Thomas stayed away from Joey's apartment, in case the police were there; but the night after that, in the Panama Club in Knightsbridge, she met a woman who said she was the owner of the apartment, and suggested that Sally take over the lease. When Sally said it was too big and the rent might be beyond her, the woman gestured to a girl on the dance floor who was going through the routine of a lackadaisical strip-tease.

'That kid's looking for somewhere to live,' she said. 'She'll share the place with you.'

The striptease dancer was billed as 'Georgina Grayson' but her real name was Elizabeth Marina Jones. She was also a soldier's wife. It was a name that would become notorious in Britain later.

2

On 24 October 1942 the Eighth Army under the command of General Bernard L. Montgomery launched the attack upon Rommel's Afrika Korps in Libya that was to become known as the Battle of El Alamein. During its most decisive moment, just as the twenty-mile front artillery barrage lifted and the armoured corps began their advance, Winston Churchill was at dinner at Buckingham Palace with the King and Queen and their guest of honour, Mrs Eleanor Roosevelt, wife of the American President.* He was a gloomy and uncommunicative guest for most of the meal until the moment when he was called away to the telephone. He returned with a beam on his round red face. The Germans had broken and were on the run. The Eighth Army was advancing on what was to prove its greatest victory.

'We open a second front! Oh, yes, we do!' wrote one commentator. 'Libya will be our second front.'

By that time Rommel's forces had begun their retreat, first into Libya and then into Tunisia, the great convoys carrying Allied forces under General Eisenhower were on their way to a landing at the other end of the Mediterranean, and operation TORCH had begun. The great squeeze of the Axis forces in Africa was under way.

Eisenhower's forces had as their objective the occupation of France's possessions in North Africa: Algeria, Tunisia and Morocco, all of which were in the hands of Marshal Pétain's puppet administration in Vichy. They hoped to achieve the occupation without having to fight the Vichy French armies on the spot, and President Roosevelt had calculated that they stood a far better chance of doing so if General de Gaulle and the Free French were not associated with the operation. He had insisted (with Churchill's not so reluctant concurrence) that not only were the Free French

---

* They ate a frugal, rationed meal, Mrs Roosevelt afterwards recalled, but off ceremonial gold plates.

forces to be kept out but that General de Gaulle was not to be told about it until operations had begun. He had recently renamed his troops the Fighting French but at five a.m. on the day of the landing he was awakened in London and told that this was one operation the Fighting French would have no part in. According to one source,* his first reaction was to say angrily,

'Eh bien! I hope the Vichy clique will throw them back into the sea.'

But that night he broadcast over the BBC to give his full support to the landing and ask all Frenchmen in North Africa to lay down their arms or join up with the Allied forces. That was before he realised that Eisenhower had taken with him to North Africa a French general who was much senior in rank to de Gaulle. He was General Georges Giraud, who had escaped from prison in France, and with Allied approval he now proclaimed himself Commander-in-Chief of all the French forces in North Africa. It was a grave threat to de Gaulle's claim to speak for France, for Giraud would command an army almost ten times the force under de Gaulle. On 11 November, de Gaulle called a meeting of his followers in the Albert Hall in London (hundreds of pro-Gaullist Britons tried to get in too), ostensibly to celebrate Armistice but principally to make his position clear. He proclaimed:

Today is Armistice Day, and it is also the day to celebrate the spirit of Fighting France. From the Fighting French alone will liberation come. In truth, every day France makes a plebiscite in favour of Fighting France. It is towards Fighting France that the nation turns. It is from Fighting France and from Fighting France alone that she expects the direction of her struggle. Therefore we suffer no one to come and divide our country's war effort by any of these so-called parallel enterprises.†

From somewhere in the hall a retired French general named Eon rose and read an appeal to de Gaulle, pointing out that Giraud was his senior, commanded ten times as many men, and therefore had the right to command the French from now on. He asked de Gaulle to rally to Giraud and put himself under his command. He was immediately seized by irate Gaullists and roughly escorted from the hall.

* J. R. Tournoux, *Pétain and de Gaulle*, Heinemann, 1966.
† Charles de Gaulle, *Memoirs*, Weidenfeld and Nicolson, 1960.

General de Gaulle had made his position clear. No one, no matter what his rank, was going to oust him from his role as the saviour of France. It was a warning both to ambitious officers in the French forces and to any Allied heads of State who might be tempted to sponsor them. It was an attitude of which the British public heartily approved.

On 29 November, Vere Hodgson wrote:

De Gaulle had lunch with our Prime Minister today. I do hope they understood one another. I have much admiration for de Gaulle and when he has done all the hard work I don't want to see him pushed out. I heard his clarion voice on the wireless the other day – he is most thrilling. I can well believe what it meant to France when they first heard him in 1940 calling to them.

She had no real need to worry. General de Gaulle was soon demonstrating that he knew how to look after himself and the Fighting French.

In January 1943 the Germans inside Stalingrad collapsed before the Russian armies and surrendered. Other victories followed. They were by no means decisive, but they gave Adolf Hitler his biggest setback of the war, and they were a cause for great rejoicing in Britain.

From the BBC in London went a haunting song to the German people whose words and tones so caught the ear of the British public that a translation was made. It was called 'The Ballad of the German Soldier's Bride and it went:

> 'And what did he send you, my bonny lass,
>   From Paris, the city of light?
> From Paris he sent me a silken dress,
>   A dream caress of a silken dress
> From Paris, the city of light.
> And what did he send you, my bonny lass
>   From the deep, deep Russian snows?
> From Russia he sent me my widow's weeds,
>   From the funeral feast my widow's weeds
> From the deep, deep Russian snows.'

The words were written by the anti-Hitler emigré, Bertholt Brecht.

But though Russia's successes heartened them, news from other Army fronts continued to depress weary Londoners.

The operation in North Africa had fallen far behind schedule. The Eighth Army was not moving fast enough from the East. In the West, Vichy trickery in Tunisia had enabled the Germans to establish themselves there and begin fighting back. The Americans, in their first major encounter with the Afrika Korps in the Battle of Kasserine Pass, got their noses severely bloodied, and lost the Pass.

Far from clearing North Africa and the Mediterranean before the end of 1942, as they had hoped, the Allies would need several months to overcome Rommel and his armies. In the meantime, the bulk of the Allied armies in the West and the ships to supply them were still stuck in the Mediterranean and in Africa when they should have been preparing for the invasion of Europe.

14

SCALDED CATS

I

They were known in the newspapers as 'scalded cat raids' because the bombers (usually Messerschmitt 110s or Focke-Wulffs) came in at rooftop level under the radar screen in formations of four or six, dropped their bombs on their targets, and streaked for home.

The first ones attacked London on 17 January 1943 and the sirens wailed for the first time for several months. Several raids followed, but there was no rush for the shelters.

'We became quite adept at diving for cover, though,' Donald Ketley said.

On 20 January, six bombers slipped under the radar net and were over East London before the sirens could sound the alert or the barrage balloons be raised. Their bombs hit a school at Lewisham just as 150 children and their teachers were assembling for lunch in the main hall. The heavy building crashed in on top of them and buried them in a mountain of rubble. It was a disaster which aroused feelings of sorrow and anger in the East End of London which were stronger than anything they had felt during the blitz. Forty children died and forty were injured plus six teachers, and Londoners cringed at the descriptions and pictures of frantic parents digging with their bare hands in the piles of masonry in the hopes of uncovering a missing child. Ten thousand people turned up for the burial ceremony on 27 January.

There was another appalling disaster in London on 3 March, and this one too hit the East End very hard. Its impact was not quite so widespread because news of it was censored out of the newspapers, but word of mouth spread it quickly across the capital and roused feelings of great horror. The raids had become so regular by this time that many people had begun taking to the shelters again, and on 3 March their arrival coincided with the evening rush-hour traffic as well as the sounding of the sirens. At Bethnal Green Underground Station a vast crowd swarmed down the stairway to the platform beneath the surface, a mixture of men, women and children, home-going workers and shelterers. Suddenly, at the top of the stairs, a woman carrying a baby was jostled by an old man and slipped and fell. She collapsed into the people in front of her, and they tripped in turn. Soon other people fell. Those down below, hearing the sound of screaming and shouting, rushed on and fell themselves, or turned and tried to struggle up to the surface.

It took several minutes to build up, survivors said afterwards, and then the mass of struggling, screaming, panic-stricken humanity fell upon each other and collapsed down the stairs like a human avalanche into a quivering heap below. 178 people died from suffocation. Up above, the German raiders killed four.

Save for the school bombing, in fact, the 'scalded cats' did far less killing and wounding than shrapnel from the anti-aircraft guns and rockets which London now turned against them.*

Many people have been killed by our shrapnel in the past few days [wrote Vere Hodgson that January]. The wardens begged people to go inside, and on Wednesday, during the daylight raid, people were pushed into Marks and Spencers in Oxford Street and made to stay there, as the Hyde Park guns were in full cry. In the park itself the wardens were hastily opening the trench shelters. A friend from our office was there airing a dog, and when the warning sounded everyone scattered. She was in conversation with an old lady who refused to budge. The noise of the guns was really terrific and my friend, Mrs Winnal, was really frightened, but she didn't care to leave the old lady alone. They were near Queen Victoria's statue. Poor old Queen. I wonder what she would have said if she had been alive.

Charles Snow asked:

How did Londoners feel in the early days of 1943? I think those in the know were afraid of the future, afraid that we were still in danger of losing the war. Even the Americans, who had come to Britain full of optimism, were disillusioned. They were nursing the bruises they had taken from the Germans in Tunisia and beginning to realize what sort of a military machine they were facing. They knew that we couldn't match the Germans unless we had an overwhelming superiority in material.

* Though one isolated bomb on a Hammersmith dance-hall later in the year did kill three hundred young people.

He added:

And, of course, the more percipient realized that the fate of all
of us was being decided not in North Africa or over Germany
itself, despite our vast bombing raids, but on the battlefields in
Russia. But so far as the ordinary Londoners were concerned, I
would say that their feelings were about equally divided between
what they were going to eat today and what was going to happen
in Britain tomorrow. It's important to remember how idealistic
everyone was in those days, despite the rigours and the pressures
of war. Winston Churchill forgot it, or wouldn't believe it, and
look what happened to him.

Early in February the House of Commons held a debate on what
had become known as the Beveridge Plan. It was a blueprint
drawn up by a committee headed by an economist and sociologist
named Sir William Beveridge for the building of the post-war
world in Britain, and it set out in some detail plans for what subsequently became known as the Welfare State. It proposed schemes
for education, health service and pensions that would look after
the ordinary Briton from the cradle to the grave, and its civilized
and egalitarian ideas for bridging the gap between rich and poor
caught the imagination of the British public. If this is what Britain
was fighting for, they were all for it.

It was with great reluctance that the Government consented to
discuss the Beveridge Plan at all, and then only because Labour
Party members of the Cabinet, egged on by their rank and file,
insisted. It so happened that Winston Churchill took no part in
the debate, for he had caught pneumonia in North Africa after
meeting President Roosevelt there and was seriously ill. His views,
however, were pretty widely known and they were shared by most
of the Tory rank-and-file members of Parliament: that this was a
blue-print for Utopia, far too costly to implement, and, in any
case, premature.

'Let's win the war first and talk about the welfare state afterwards,' was the burden of the Tory speeches. When the debate
came to the vote only 119 members, out of a House of over 600,
voted for the plan, and they were nearly all members of the Labour
Party.

It was a serious misreading of the mood of the British people
thus to push the Beveridge Plan to one side so curtly, and civilians

and soldiers alike mentally marked it up against the Tories. Parliament had once more voted to prolong itself in being, and there would be no general election until the war was over. But people did not forget.

On 14 February, Grace North wrote:

I am seething over the Beveridge debate, just seething. The same old gang right out of the Ark. Wish Bevin and Co. [the Labour Ministers] would resign and damn the consequences. Just as important to win a victory here by establishing the principle that the welfare of the people is the first charge on the nation's resources as it is to win the war. Who cares whether we win the war or not if we are going to be saddled with these ninny-hammers [the Tories]. I wanna kill 'em.

Two days later, after the vote, she wrote:

Only 119 against the Government on Beveridge. Mr Churchill's indisposition was very timely from one point of view, but what an opportunity was lost! How his name might have gone down in history as one of the truly great if he had defied the Tories and come out for the Beveridge scheme. He could do what no other British statesman could do at this juncture. All this talk about cutting our coat according to our cloth my foot! If the war were to last another ten years we should find means of financing it, by hook or by crook. Only when it's a question of raising the standard of life of the people does this niggling cutting-of-coat crop up. What a world!

One can almost hear her sigh as she went on:

Yet it's a glorious day. Real spring. Feel nostalgic and unsettled. One's mind is never at leisure nowadays. I go down the road on a bus four times a day and have been told that the japonica along it is in bloom, yet I have never seen it. What with the stuff over the bus windows and being tensed up inside wondering whether I shall succeed in getting my foot inside a shop before they let the shutters down, or catch trains, etc. ... More retreats in Tunisia. Feel apprehensive. When, oh when are we going to starting winning this bloody war?

Vere Hodgson too was finding it hard to keep cheerful. She

wasn't surprised that Winston Churchill was ill. Everyone she knew seemed to be ill.

To her relations in Rhodesia, she wrote:

I think it's the diet. Everyone is overtired with all these years of blackout and domestic difficulties.

Every Sunday, as always, she would lie late abed and read about the state of the war in her favourite newspaper (the *Observer*, though she also took the *Sunday Express* now that her favourite commentator, J. L. Garvin had transferred to it), and then up to bath, dress and away to explore London to see what the war had done to it during the week.

I came along Tottenham Court Road today and couldn't help noticing how quiet it was. It was like a country town, an occasional bus, a taxi here and there, but practically nothing on the streets. I believe Cairo has all the traffic nowadays. Our roads are wonderfully peaceful, no noise, it's heavenly.

In mid-March she went out to see what was happening to the great campaign to raise money for the war, a Government-sponsored propaganda effort called Wings for Victory week. That night she wrote into her diary a vivid picture of what the West End of London looked like in the fourth year of the war.

Truly, Piccadilly is a thrilling place to walk along. All the uniforms of the United Nations jostle you along the pavements, and since there is no traffic hardly you can walk right round the Circus. Some of the soldiers label themselves POLAND or CANADA but there are lots of them with just emblems on their shoulders. Such varied faces and manners. Girls too in their Service costumes by the hundred. Very few fashionably dressed women, because all the pretty ones are in uniform.'

She went on to Trafalgar Square, where a big bomber had been parked, a veteran of the raids on Germany.

Such crowds of people. Men selling flags and baubles. Music playing and some soldiers in a jeep going round and round the square. I edged my way in and saw the big bomber O for Orange, a Lancaster. It was perched high up and looked very aristocratic. The crowd was constantly moving, so I slithered into the centre of things. Presently I found some firemen selling odd stamps to put on the bomber, so I bought one and with great satisfaction stuck it on. Then I worked my way to the fountain where some air cadets were shouting and enjoying themselves. I found they were trying to raise one million pennies to try and buy a Typhoon [fighter plane] for Westminster. They paddled around in a rubber dinghy such as wrecked airmen use and you threw pennies to them. Other lads were in rubbers wading about in search of pennies which had gone into the pool. I forbore to give them this trouble but put my threepence into a bag which came round.'

Like the rest of the crowd, she gaped at a man holding up two precious lemons which, he said, had been brought back on a convoy from Gibraltar. They were to be auctioned off for the war effort in a theatre that evening.

2

It seemed that the feelings of the average Londoner towards the foreigners in their midst went in inverse ratio to the numbers of them around. The less there were of a certain nationality, the more they appeared to like them. A Mass N Observation survey in 1943 about Britain's allies and Londoners' reactions to them came out this way.

Attitude towards the Dutch

Favourable	73%
Half and Half	4%
Unfavourable	5%
Vague	18%

Attitude towards the Czechs

Favourable	64%
Half and Half	12%
Unfavourable	2%
Vague	22%

Attitude towards the Fighting French

Favourable	52%
Half and Half	32%
Unfavourable	11%
Vague	5%

Attitude towards the Poles

Favourable   27%
Half and Half   39%
Unfavourable   17%
Vague   17%

Attitude towards the Americans

Favourable   33%
Half and Half   44%
Unfavourable   21%
Vague   2%

The Poles and the Americans had more of their troops in Britain (and more of them were visible in London on leave) than all the other Allies put together. The lukewarm attitude towards the Poles may be explained by the fact that they were a dashing body of men and, so far as many an English male was concerned, far too charming and gallant. Their success with women had been considerable. But there was also the factor that the attitude of the Poles towards Russia was almost overwhelmingly hostile, and the British resented this. So far as they were concerned, the Russians were winning the war for them at this moment.

The curious thing about the Londoners' feelings towards the Americans was that practically everyone in London, male and female alike, now seemed to have a friend in the US Forces, and showed him off proudly to everyone, but was always criticising the Americans as a whole. Kathleen T., a secretary who worked at nights in the New Zealand Club in the Strand, put in her report:

> We were very busy tonight. Talked to an American sailor. He is a nice-looking lad who will get on well here. He had such nice manners. I think we can divide the Americans up into two distinct groups. Some have dreadful manners and are rude and uncouth. Yet the rest – and these are most of them – have most charming manners. It is a pity the other, unpleasant ones are agreed upon to be typical.

It was a period of the war when Americans were pouring into London in hordes every weekend on leave and looking for fun and relaxation, and guests and hosts were eyeing each other with a wary suspicion. The surprises in store for them were not always pleasant. A survey of British feelings towards the American forces took a cross section of the people and asked two questions. They obtained these answers:

What Are Your Main Reasons for Liking Americans?
Enterprise
Energy
Generosity
Friendliness
Fighting qualities
Technical Efficiency
Intelligence
Adaptability

What Are Your Main Reasons for Disliking Americans?
Boastfulness
Immaturity
Material and commercial preoccupation
Morals
Accent
Conversational superficiality
Intolerance
Ostentation
Attitude to Negroes
Habit of chewing gum
Overpaid

At the same time a cross section of the US Forces visiting London were asked for their opinions of their English hosts, and almost at once they mentioned the 'lower moral standards' of women in the capital. Most of them, however, made haste to point out that it was women with the lowest morals who were likely to consort with foreign soldiers, and that the West End of London was hardly typical of the rest of England. But on other aspects of London life they could be forthright.

An American soldier:
Well, I'll be frank with you. I was here in 1937 and the difference in London today is terrific. I mean the difference in the tradesmen, most of all. They used to be proud of their businesses, proud of their craftsmanship, proud of what they were selling. They were much too proud to do you down. That's all gone.

They're all on the snatch now. They don't care. I don't care for the attitude of the shopkeepers, the hotel-keepers, the taxi-drivers towards us Americans – they're all as indifferent as hell and apt to do the living lights out of you. The English still think themselves the top dog everywhere.

An American sailor:

One thing struck me a lot. Your civilians are pretty decent about helping out about money, about the exchange. One of the times one of our boys couldn't figure it out about your money some civilians stopped and helped out, and they've never done one of them a dirty deal yet. But they're slow in giving change in the shops and the shopkeepers are surly. They don't seem to want to serve you. You'd think they wanted to keep their stocks to themselves.

An American airman:

I think sex morals here are very low, and our boys take advantage of it. I don't think they respect the women for it. I know it's the worst women who pick up soldiers in any country, but our boys don't see it that way. . . . But I don't think you English should blame our boys for being wild. Of course we're wild. We're 3,000 miles from home for the first time in our lives. It's the chance of a lifetime. It's just the same when a British ship docks in a foreign port. They go wild just the same as us.

For most Britons now coming into contact with American troops what seems to have made the most impact at the time was the deep gulf existing between white and coloured members of the US Forces. The increasing evidence of discrimination against black soldiers by their white comrades did much to influence the reaction of Londoners to the Americans in their midst.

The previous autumn (on 2 October 1942) *The Times* had published a letter which had become a talking point in many a British home. It read as follows:

Sir, I am the manager of a snack bar in Oxford, and have had a rather unfortunate state of affairs, which is beginning to exist in this country, very forcibly brought to my notice. The other night a coloured United States soldier came into our establishment and very diffidently presented me with an open letter from his commanding officer explaining that 'Pte —— is a soldier in the US Army and it is necessary that he sometimes has a meal out, which he has, on occasions, found difficult to obtain. I would be grateful if you would look after him.'

Naturally we 'looked after' him to the best of our ability, but I could not help feeling ashamed that in a country where even stray dogs are 'looked after' by special societies, a citizen of the world, who is fighting the world's battle for freedom and equality should have found it necessary to place himself in this humiliating position. Had there been the slightest objection from the other customers I should not have had any hesitation in asking them all to leave.

I should like to feel that everybody shared my views, as England's reputation for hospitality is in danger of being questioned. Incidentally, the gentleman in question showed his gratitude by a donation of just twice the amount of his bill in the poor box. (Signed) D. Davie-Distin.'

Thereafter, a wave of warmth towards the black Americans and a coolness towards the whites who treated them shabbily seemed to spread over England. Kathleen T. noticed the increasing frequency with which the colour question emerged during conversations with Americans. She writes:

Had an interesting conversation with an American tonight. We discussed the colour question. He said he had no idea of the feeling here before he arrived in England, he had naturally presumed that we had the same ideas as the Americans. He said that until he got to England he had never seen a white girl dancing with a coloured boy, and he didn't like it and that if he married an English girl he would take very good care to investigate her family tree so that he would not find himself the proud father of a black baby. I pointed out that I thought this was far more likely to occur in America, there being so many more black people in that country than there are here. My American friend then said that in America they never intermarried except in the slums and I told him (with no authority to back up my statement) that although intermarriage of this sort was quite rare in England, it too was usually in the slums of some of our ports. Eileen, who had been listening to the whole conversation with amusement, said that anyway it did not follow that because a girl danced with a coloured American, babies would follow, but the

American said 'Why not?' and added 'If the girls go around with the coloured boys, surely they intend to marry them,' and this really made us laugh, he was so serious about it all, and really thought that they were after marriage, and he didn't believe that a girl might dance with one of the coloured soldiers in order to show him that we didn't ostracize them here, and his final comment was 'Don't worry, the coloured boys will soon take advantage of this tolerance and you will feel the same way as we do.' This conversation was just typical of many I have had recently with those Americans who are willing to talk seriously about the problem.'

A few months later she was writing:

We had an unpleasantness here [in the club] this evening when a young American Negro came in and walked up to the bar to be served. All the Americans there turned away or made loud insulting remarks to him. We were furious and I served him and was rather hurt when he said 'Is it all right for me to come in here?' Anyway, a moment later a New Zealand officer came up and stood next to him and after a few moments the Negro asked him, very humbly, if he wouldn't have a drink with him. We were pleased to see the officer accept and they talked and drank for about half an hour. It showed the Americans up, but they weren't a bit ashamed of their behaviour. We didn't hide our feelings.

It was about this time that Mass–Observation did a survey of American troops and discrimination. Forty-three per cent of those Britons questioned had at some time or another met American black soldiers. Men met black troops almost three times as much as women. Both sexes were asked the question (which admittedly sounds somewhat loaded): 'Do you think the treatment of American Negroes is just?' The answers were:

	Male	Female
Just	13%	10%
Unjust	45%	34%
Treatment Improving	4%	1%
Not Our Affair	10%	7%
No Opinion	28%	48%

Not that Londoners were immune from prejudice as far as coloured troops were concerned. A Mrs May Hopkins wrote to Mass-Observation in May 1943, to report a conversation she had heard in a fish queue, between a man (retired colonel type) and a women (with the 'right' accent):

WOMAN: Look, there's a black soldier. No, he's an *officer!*

MAN: Can't be.

WOMAN: Yes, it is. American probably. No, I think he's French. Senegalese, I expect. Well (*with contempt*) they can keep him.

MAN: By jove, yes! Mind you, these fellows fight well and they're good fellows in their way, providing they know their place.

WOMAN: I was talking to some American boys the other day and I said to them: 'How do you manage when these fellows get back home? Is there any difference?' and they said: 'Well, they know their place. They know they're' (*and she turned her thumb down*), 'and we're' (*and she turned it up*).

MAN: (*with enthusiasm*) That's it. The utter rot you hear talked nowadays. As if they were our equals, as if they could be.

Mrs Hopkins ended her report with the words:

'I left the fish queue in order not to say something rude or hit the speakers.'

3

Wherever he went in Whitehall in the early days of July 1943, Charles Snow could hear the whispers about Italy. The Allies had mopped up the German Armies in North Africa at last and were about to land in Sicily, but first the 'negotiators' were at work trying to do a deal with Italy and there were emissaries all over the place furtively tempting Mussolini's cohorts to desert him and take Italy out of the war.

'I thought at the time that they were going about it in an extra-ordinarily flat-footed way,' Snow said, 'and I don't think history has proved me wrong. In any case, at that moment Italy, as far as

I and informed onlookers like myself were concerned, hardly seemed to matter. It was just a sideshow and the fate of the war was being settled 1,500 miles away near Kharkov, in Russia.'

For Snow and the little group of top scientists with whom he was spending most of his hours now, the first half of 1943 had not been by any means as depressing as for most Londoners, for they had news – which, for safety reasons, the public could not share – which considerably enlivened their spirits.

For over a year Snow had been haunted not only by the fear that Britain would lose the war but by a spectre even more terrifying: the atomic bomb with which the Germans might win it. He said:

> We had no idea how the Germans had mishandled their research into atomic weapons. We couldn't guess that Adolf Hitler wouldn't have a scientist near him, or even someone who understood scientific developments, with the possible exception of Speer. So that no one could get to him and persuade him to back the research and provide the resources that would be necessary to prove that an atomic bomb was possible. But we didn't know that. And there was always the feeling, even when everything was going all right for us, that there might be this horror in the background. We none of us expected that, so far as atomic research was concerned, the Germans were so bad.

And then in the spring of 1943 news had come from Germany that gave them strong hope that the Nazis would never produce an atomic bomb, not even if the war lasted another five years.* Whereas an Anglo-American atomic bomb was a year away from production.

Intelligence in wartime can never be entirely trusted. Nevertheless, this was heartening news indeed. But for Snow (who heard this news at second hand) there was a crucial trial of strength to be watched and its outcome awaited before he could really rejoice.

* The news reached them from, among others, Professor Niels Bohr, the Danish atomic scientist, who got a message through to London by a microdot concealed in the hollow handle of a doorkey which the Underground smuggled out of Denmark. Professor Bohr and his wife were also smuggled out of Nazi-occupied Denmark in the autumn of 1943 and helped to build the Allied atomic bomb. The Nazis never really knew what they had lost.

When everyone else in London hung around their radios or snatched up the newspapers on 11 July to read about the Anglo-American
landings in Sicily, Snow was searching the ticker tapes for news
from Russia. The battle of the Kursk Salient had begun north of
Kharkov on July 5, and it was the biggest and most savage German
assault of the war.* The front was over 200 miles long and thousands of guns, tanks and planes were involved. The German Army
lost nearly 600 tanks in the first day, but went on butting and bash-
ing its head against the armoured Red defences for ten more days
before the blood and the pain were too much. On 15 July the
great German retreat westwards began and Russia had inflicted
the most decisive defeat upon an invading enemy since Napoleon's
retreat from Moscow.

'I don't think Alan Brooke or any of the other people on the
general staff in London had any idea that it had been the decisive
battle of the war,' Snow said. 'All they were interested in was
Sicily and what the Italians would do in Rome. But compared with
this, it didn't matter. In Russia the Germans had launched their
greatest offensive, and it had been thrown back. If this was the
utmost they could do – and it was – then it was clearly the end.
We couldn't possibly lose the war now.'

He came home to his flat that night and turned on the news. Yes,
there it was. Buried well below the reports from Sicily was the
announcement of a German withdrawal around Kursk. Charles
Snow sat down to write a note to a girlfriend, for he felt that he
must write to someone.

'Dearest,' he wrote, 'this is it. This is the end. No, I don't mean
between you and me . . .'

He went into his kitchen to look for a drink, but could find
nothing.

'It was very difficult to get drunk in wartime,' he said, 'but I felt
I must go out and find a pub and do the best I could.'

He went out to a pub behind Dolphin Square and managed to
obtain a couple of drinks, then went on and had two more, and
then on again. Around closing time, when he was feeling very
merry, a couple of friends came over and joined him. Noting the
warm glow of happiness suffusing his normally owlish features,
one of them asked:

* And almost certainly the biggest land battle in history.

'And what might you be celebrating, Charles?'
'Victory!' he said.
'Where? Sicily?'
'No,' he said, shaking his head hard. 'Kursk. The Kursk Salient.'
They looked at him as if he must be mad.

4

Tea, that perennial English stand-by, was rarer (and even more rationed) than gold by 1943, and Rosemary Black, who had once drunk it hot and strong enough to stand a spoon in at every hour of the day, now preferred coffee, or at least convinced herself that she did. But what about her friends?

B. and John rang up for the night, [she wrote.] B., being rather a tea-drinker and always having been a most generous host to me with rationed commodities, I was dismayed to find that I'd let myself run out of tea. ... However, my Wine Society order having been delivered a few days ago, I then had the idea of sending K. to the J.s with the suggestion of trading a half bottle of whisky for a pound of tea – at which J. apparently simply leapt. Presently I began to get conscience-stricken, feeling a pound altogether too much tea to have accepted in return for a mere half bottle of whisky. After all, it's a 4-week ration. But just then J. phoned in a state to say was it really all right, she couldn't help feeling they were profiting madly on the exchange, and so forth! It seems that both parties are equally satisfied.

The 'scalded cat raids' affected her badly, particularly as they went on and on all through the spring and summer. Repeated attacks of rheumatism had left her ill-equipped to face up to the new bombing. The noise was the worst thing about them, even though she knew that it came from the increasing strength of the anti-aircraft defences and the new types of rocket guns, and not from Nazi bombs. 'Each burst of shellfire seemed to thunder and shake the house as only big bombs did in the good old days.' She crouched miserably on the floor of her draughty basement shelter (which now had no heat to keep it comfortable) and tried to soothe her two children, who, now that they were older, seemed to have become nervous in a way that they never were before. And then there was her rheumatism.

What with one thing and another, I was more shaken than I ever remember being. Both physically and mentally I felt completely incapable of rising to meet any emergency which might occur. Frankly, I was completely limp with terror, and after the all-clear had gone I felt too weak and shaken to so much as turn over in bed. I don't feel I can *possibly* face up to a renewal of the blitz, if this horror is what the future holds in store for us.

She felt suicidally depressed and apprehensive all next day, and derived no comfort from the fact that 'no one else seems to have worried much over the raids which scared the daylights out of me.' Asked by her friend Mrs Bone whether she was keeping up her reports to Mass-Observation, she replied, waspishly,

I used to feel that Mass-Observation, by enabling an increased knowledge of 'the will of the people' by the people's representatives and rulers to be known, was making a real contribution to democracy, and that by working for M-O one was, consequently, playing some part, however small, in improving the democratic system. Nowadays, like Gallio, I care for none of these things. Democracy seems pretty well blown to hell, and really the man-in-the-street's ideas are so bloody silly (no wonder, since they're formed by newspapers and irresponsible advertisements) that I feel this is just as well. How can democracy be any good anyway until a decent and universal system of education makes government of, by, for the people something else than government of, by, for ignorant prejudiced fools? Until such a decent system of education comes into being, to attempt to improve democracy is to ornament a house built without foundations. Anyway, I just don't give a damn.

But even her bad case of nerves could not last too long, and with spring her mood changed:

A lovely day. Things certainly do seem brighter when birds are singing and buds bursting, and the yellow crocuses in front of the kitchen window opening out into quite a good patch of colour in the sun. A great stroke of luck today: the greengrocer let me have a jar of greengages and promised some prunes later on in the week. Supper with the P.s and Mrs B. over the canal. They had provided a most terrific blow-out – actual shell eggs and bacon (two rashers, moreover) and tinned apricots. . . . To my consternation they then put the frying pan in the sink to be washed up, just as it was, with a good half inch of priceless bacon fat congealing in it. Later P. fell upstairs carrying a full pint bottle of milk of which three quarters spilt – mostly over her. This to me was worse than the burning of a £5 note.

It was a time when people dreamed at nights not of wealth or handsome lovers or of castles in Spain, and not even of peace, but of food.

5

14 July 1943 was warm and sunny in London. For the Fighting French it was Bastille Day, and they and their friends danced to the music of a concertina in the mews outside Le Petit Club de France in St James's until well after midnight. One Fighting Frenchman who did not join them was General Charles de Gaulle. He was fighting for his future, and, he believed, the future of France.

Relations between the leader of the Fighting French and the leaders of the Western Allies had by this time reached their lowest ebb. Winston Churchill was now seeing him as little as possible, because he found de Gaulle's arrogant attitude increasingly difficult to stomach, and he had difficulty in keeping his temper with him. Though he had once been the General's most enthusiastic supporter, he was by this time bitterly regretting he had ever recognised him as the leader of the French.

'After all we have done for him,' he once said to his son, Randolph, 'he has the impudence not only to be ungrateful, but to make it plain that he dislikes everything that I stand for.'

He had already cabled President Roosevelt, who shared his dislike of de Gaulle, to say that 'I agree with you that no confidence can be placed in de Gaulle's friendship for the Allies'. In his war memoirs, Churchill was subsequently to claim that he understood why the General acted as he did.

'He had to be rude to the British to prove to French eyes that

312

he was not a British puppet,' he wrote. 'He certainly carried out this policy with perseverance.'

The truth is, however, that he found de Gaulle impossibly rude, arrogant, importunate and monomaniacally ambitious, and like an English king and a turbulent priest, he must often have wished aloud that someone would rid him of his unruly and unpleasant protégé.

If he did, then someone at the Special Branch of Scotland Yard must have heard him, because it was about this time that the file on General de Gaulle was sent to 10 Downing Street for his perusal. There was material in it to involve the General in quite a public scandal. Or so its compilers suggested.

President Roosevelt had no doubt whatsoever that the Allies should rid themselves of Charles de Gaulle. He could not stand the General's high-handedness, but it was not so much his personal arrogance which he disliked as his insistence that France must be treated on exactly the same basis of equality as the United States and Britain. That was no part of his plan. *Time* Magazine reported in July that Roosevelt was supporting General Giraud as the leader of the French, mainly because he was a weaker and more amenable character, and that Washington was full of inspired stories attacking the motives and personality of General de Gaulle.

'Pet reporters of the State Department and the White House,' reported *Time*, 'were called in and given confidential tips. . . . Wrote Harold Callender in the *New York Times*: "In the opinion of high American officials General de Gaulle is less interested in helping to win the war than in advancing his personal political fortunes."'

What was the reason for the campaign? asked *Time*:

Why is the President so set against de Gaulle? Why all the inspired anti-de Gaulle stories? No matter how unlovable a personality, de Gaulle is still, to most living Frenchmen, the symbol of French resistance. What is the President's case against him? The President's case appeared be this: he is convinced that the solution of European problems will be much easier if its basic lines are established by the three big powers – the United States, Great Britain and Russia. The President wants to assure all European powers, great and small, full independence and freedom. But he believes that they need not all be consulted; their voices would complicate a solution or even make it impossible. For that reason Mr Roosevelt would prefer to have France absent when those solutions are worked out – in short, not only no de Gaulle but no Giraud.

On Bastille Day 1943, Franklin D. Roosevelt sent a cable to Winston Churchill in London. The exact text has not been (and is not likely to be) released by either country, but its purport was: BELIEVE YOU HAVE A GOOD CASE FOR ARRESTING AND SACKING DE GAULLE. URGE YOU TO DO SO.*

Charles de Gaulle had resolved, after his experiences with Admiral Muselier, that never again would he let the British authorities be involved in the domestic affairs of the Fighting French forces. Henceforward, he ordered, all arrests and punishment of members of the forces in England would be carried out by the Fighting French themselves; and with this aim in view, he agreed to the immediate expansion of the Fighting French intelligence organisation under its commander, Colonel Passy (otherwise Devavrin). This was known as the BCRA (*Bureau Central de Renseignements et d'Action*) and shortly after the Muselier affair it established its headquarters in a multi-storeyed house in Duke Street, Mayfair, and a prison camp near the Free French barracks at Camberley in Surrey. No details of what went on at either establishment were furnished to the British, but soon the Special Branch at Scotland Yard was tipped off by the SOE (Special Operations Executive, a British intelligence branch) that they really ought to look into the activities of the BCRA. A discreet surveillance was begun from that moment on, and some disturbing reports began to emerge.

Duke Street, it emerged, was not only the headquarters of the BCRA but also its chief interrogation centre. Stories appeared in the press to the effect that some of the French officers operating there used methods of interrogation which included maltreatment

---

* On 19 July 1943 *Time* Magazine reported: 'From sources as unimpeachable as those which fostered the anti-de Gaulle stories had come many definite reports that Franklin Roosevelt even had won over Churchill to the sacking of General de Gaulle. Twice, it was said on high authority, Franklin Roosevelt had cabled Winston Churchill actually suggesting the arrest of de Gaulle. Churchill refused.'

and torture. These reports continued for some time and culminated in the Affaire Dufour.

Lieutenant Dufour, it appeared, was a young and gallant member of the French Army who had been wounded in his abdomen in France in 1940. Upon his recovery he joined the French Resistance as an operator for British Intelligence inside France, and his enterprise and daring had won him high praise from his superiors in London. When the Gestapo began to close in upon him, he was ordered to England and was smuggled across the French frontier first to Spain and then via Gibraltar to London.

He immediately expressed the wish to volunteer for the Fighting French Forces and duly presented himself to General de Gaulle at Carlton Gardens. He signed the controversial oath of allegiance and put on his uniform and proudly walked out into the streets of London, happy, free, eager to carry on the fight.

Accounts of what happened next diverge. The account given by Dufour himself was that he did not remain free for long. Shortly after his induction, Lieutenant Dufour was asked to report to BCRA headquarters in Duke Street, where two Fighting French intelligence officers were awaiting him. He most willingly gave them the information they asked of him regarding his operations against the Nazis in France, but when he was thereupon urged to give full details of all the British agents with whom he had worked in France, the names of his contacts both in France and in London, and details of the codes he had used, he immediately pointed out that he had sworn an oath of secrecy to the British and could not possibly break it without their prior permission.

'I will leave now and go and ask them,' he said.

'That will not be necessary,' one of the intelligence officers said. 'You will tell us anyway. You are now a member of the Fighting French Forces. As your superior officer, I order you to give me the details for which I ask.'

'I cannot break my oath to the British,' said Dufour.

'You can and you will,' the intelligence officer said.

In the next four days Dufour relates that he was alternatively coaxed, bullied and beaten. He was struck repeatedly with a steel rod, particularly in the region of the wound in his kidneys. At one point a girlfriend whose acquaintance he had made since his arrival in London was picked up at her home and brought to Duke Street, where she was slapped and threatened in front of Dufour. But still, the account goes on, he would not break and tell the BCRA what they wanted from him.

Eventually Dufour was brought before a Fighting French court martial on a charge (which he denied) of 'assuming a rank and title he did not possess namely the rank of Lieutenant and the title of Chevalier de la Légion d'Honneur'. He was found guilty on this charge and was sent to Camberley prison camp. With the aid of his friends, he succeeded in escaping at the end of 1942, and was immediately posted as a deserter by the Fighting French.

De Gaulle's version of the affair differs considerably from that of Dufour. According to the Fighting French leader the whole thing was set up by British Intelligence as an intrigue calculated to discredit both de Gaulle himself and the Fighting French Forces. Dufour was put up to make allegations against the Fighting French, which were completely unfounded, and was simply being used by British Intelligence.

In any event the details of Dufour's allegations were drawn up in a dossier which was forwarded to Winston Churchill, and in July 1943 a memorandum containing a damning indictment of General de Gaulle's attitude, antipathy towards Britain and America, and his methods with his own countrymen began to be circulated in certain select circles in London. It was said to have been personally approved by the Prime Minister himself. The word was that Churchill now agreed with Roosevelt that de Gaulle must go.

On 22 July 1943 Robert Boothby rose in the House of Commons to ask a question, and since most of the members had seen it beforehand they crowded into the Chamber to hear the Prime Minister's answer. Boothby had, by this time, transferred his hero worship from his own Prime Minister, who had, admittedly, treated him shabbily, to Charles de Gaulle, whom he considered the apotheosis of statemanship and heroism. He was infuriated by the rumours and sly gossip about him which were circulating in London. He asked the Prime Minister whether he was aware that a memorandum was circulating in London containing the most odious accusations against General de Gaulle, and what steps was he taking to put an end to the spreading of such shocking lies?

To his astonishment and to an audible gasp from other members of the House, Churchill replied that a memorandum such as the honourable member had mentioned had indeed been circulated, that he took complete responsibility for it, but that he could only discuss the nature of its contents if the House went into secret session. Such a session would be arranged in the near future.

The moment of truth, it seemed, had come. Churchill was ready to tell all. And if he told all, he would undoubtedly ask the House to back him in taking action against the turbulent French leader. And that would mean the sack for de Gaulle – or at least withdrawal of Allied support and subsidy for him.

No word of the scandal appeared in British newspapers, for they were under censorship, but as MPs awaited the vital secret session wild rumours suddenly began to circulate in the corridors that the quarrel was going to break into the open, and that the place where it would be settled was not in Parliament but in the law courts. For Dufour had gone to his solicitors, and had asked them to take action in the courts against General de Gaulle, Colonel Passy and four others for mistreatment and false imprisonment.

Now it was Winston Churchill's turn to feel harassed. Immediately after making his statement in the House about de Gaulle he had been assailed by doubts. Even though the general was a thorn in his side, was he justified in extracting him so ruthlessly and casting him aside? Moreover, was it politically wise? General de Gaulle was the darling of the British public. They cheered him wherever he went. They would not thank the Prime Minister now if, after lauding him so long, he suddenly revealed him as a trickster, a fascist and anti-British to boot. So he had let the days pass and the secret session was not called, and when MPs asked about it they were fobbed off with excuses.

But what was he to do now? He could not stop the processes of the English law. If Dufour insisted on going on with his action, the fat really would be on the fire, and de Gaulle was not the only one who might get burned.

And then the Foreign Office had an inspiration. Pierre Vienot, Fighting French representative in London, was called to the Foreign Office and handed a note about Dufour's proposed legal action. Dufour had, explained the note,

... Put into the hands of the British courts a complaint about maltreatment against several French officers and against their leader, General de Gaulle. Because of the separation of powers, which in England is absolute, the British Government cannot prevent justice from taking its course. Furthermore, General de Gaulle does not have diplomatic immunity in our country. Perhaps the General could settle the matter by friendly agreement with Dufour? Otherwise, he will be implicated in the trial. We must urge General de Gaulle to attach serious importance to this matter, for a conviction is likely, and would constitute an occasion for disagreeable publicity, particularly in the United States press, with regard to the methods and procedures of Fighting France.*

In other words, buy off Dufour. And, Winston Churchill might have added, for God's sake do it quickly.

What happened next is the subject of conflicting reports. One version is that Dufour consented to withdraw his action on payment to him of substantial damages. On the other hand General de Gaulle insists that he refused to agree to any such terms.

De Gaulle writes in his *Memoirs* that the matter was disposed of altogether differently because, fortuitously, the British Intelligence Services found themselves with an 'affair' on their hands, also involving a Free French officer. Only this time the accusations were against them.

At the beginning of 1943, he relates, a Free Frenchman called Stephan Manier had returned to England from Accra on the orders of the Fighting French, having honourably fulfilled his duties. On his return British Intelligence seized him and confined him for questioning. While he was confined, he died – probably from malaria. His son, however, was not satisfied with British explanations and wanted to pursue the matter of his father's death. He announced his intention of taking action in the French Courts against the officers of British Intelligence and possibly against Winston Churchill himself. From the Fighting French point of view, his announcement could not have come at a better moment.

What is quite certain is that neither case ever reached the courts, the secret session was never held, and that autumn General de Gaulle ousted his rival, General Giraud. and became undisputed Head of the Fighting French.

With the British public, he was more popular than ever. Whenever his lofty figure was seen in London there were scattered

* Charles de Gaulle, *Memoirs*, Weidenfeld and Nicolson, 1960.

cheers and a rush of autograph hunters. 'Good old Charley!' the Cockneys cried.

Winston Churchill had other names for him, and they would become even more colourful in the months to come.

6

Early in December 1943, a row blew up in Parliament and the newspapers when Sir Oswald Mosley, leader of the British Union of Fascists, was released from gaol. He had been detained under Regulation 18b since 1940, but in the last twelve months had been allowed to share two cells with his wife in Holloway Prison. Now he was being let out, the Home Secretary (Herbert Morrison) announced, because he was suffering from phlebitis. Public reaction to the announcement was almost uniformly hostile in London, and there were cheers when Communist Party orators called for a strike to protest the release and shouted:

'Why don't they let the bastard die in gaol?'

Dolly James read the news of Mosley's release in her morning paper and almost at once a smell, the lovely aroma, of rich red wine haunted her nostrils. She had never seen Mosley herself in Holloway, for the married Fascists had been given a wing over on the far side of the prison where they lived a cosy communal life flapping their hands and kowtowing to the Fuehrer. But one day, after a 'big nob from the Government', as the wardress called him, had been in to see Mosley – for the British Fascist still had many friends in high places – she saw the woman who now acted as 'batwoman' to the Leader and his wife coming along with a tray in her hand and two dirty plates and mugs on it. She was bringing back the Mosleys' midday meal to be washed up, and as she passed Dolly smelled it. It was a moment of great despair when she would have given her all for a drink, a great whacking alcoholic drink, and then this wave of scent washed up her nose. *By God*, she told herself, *the so-and-sos have actually had wine with their lunch, would you believe it?* It was as much as she could do not to burst into tears in the agony of envy and frustration.

But she did not grudge the Mosleys their freedom. It was hard not to feel sympathy for anyone who had suffered the rigours and humiliations of Regulation 18b, even a Fascist. What were people squawking about? If they wanted to keep him locked up, why

319

didn't they put him on trial and charge him with something? But what would they charge him with? Wanting Hitler and National Socialism to win the war? All right, it was a reprehensible wish if they could prove he cherished it, but was it to stop people from thinking reprehensible thoughts that this war was being fought?

'Pardon me for being rude,' said Dolly James, 'But may I ask what we are fighting this war for, anyway? Will someone please tell me. Or do I sound bitter?'

But she said the words into her mirror in the privacy of her room. Having convinced the authorities at last that falling in love with a Nazi didn't make her a National Socialist, she had managed to get out of Holloway. She didn't want to go back again for spreading gloom and despondency by speaking her stray thoughts in public.

She couldn't help smiling wryly, though, when she read in her paper that 'Sir Oswald and Lady Mosley were driven away from Holloway by a friend after their release. Sir Oswald will stay with friends in the country to recuperate from his illness and his prison experiences.'

The only person Dolly had met when she came out of Holloway was a pale man with glittery eyes in a sleek, tight suit. He was waiting for his girl friend, just finishing a stretch for rifling the pockets of a soldier-client, and those eyes burned with eager fire when he saw Dolly.

'You're a pretty girl,' he had said. 'Got a job to go to, my dear?'

'No,' she said.

'I can put you in the way of lots of money,' he said. 'And a good time, too. There's lots of lolly around in London these days.'

'And lots of people like you, too,' Dolly had said. And then she repeated a phrase which she had learned in Holloway, and even he looked shocked when he heard it from such tender-looking lips.

It meant 'push off', and he had pushed off.

There had been no resting in the country for Dolly after *her* prison experiences. Her ex-husband had found a room for her in Marylebone and paid the rent on it for three months, and she was grateful to him. Then she got a job as a secretary-typist to a small, fat, asthmatic man in Soho who was making a small fortune (which he did not share with her) buying up second-hand jewellery and selling it to the big stores. He paid her in cash and she had to lie about it at the Labour Exchange, so she had been 'directed' to do twenty-four hours' work a week at a factory in Camden Town making camouflage nets. The rope played such havoc with her hands that she could hardly type the following morning, and she had taken to going around in gloves to conceal the weals on her palms and fingers. But she got by, and for the time being she shunned company. She did not even go near her old pub, the Gluepot, just in case she ran into former friends. She didn't think she could face them, yet.

For her Christmas meal that year she had an omelette made from three black market eggs and a quarter of a bottle of whisky. She wondered what Sir Oswald and Lady Mosley were having.

There had, of course, always been a grey market in the odd extra cutlet or chicken wing or pound of butter, but it was not really until 1943-4 that a black market of any importance sprang up in London – and even then it was never big enough to cause the Government or the police any serious concern. Commander Reginald Smith's diary of the war years in K Division, which covered a vast tract of Eastern London, makes references to many other crimes but does not mention a single case of black marketeering.

'Of course there was thieving in the docks,' he said. 'Carcases of meat and crates of tinned fruit disappeared and were sold somewhere at inflated prices. But such petty thefts have always been a fact of life in the docks, and the war didn't particularly change any habits.'

Most of London's black market was centred in Soho, for this was the gathering place of troops on leave, deserters on the run, girls dodging the call-up. The troops (particularly the Americans) had plenty to sell, such as cigarettes, surplus rations and nylon stockings. The deserters with whom they mostly traded, had services to offer in return of various kinds, including the girls. They were also the receivers of surplus or stolen petrol coupons and clothing coupons, and it was in these that the liveliest black market trade was conducted. No black marketeer in London ever got rich selling meat or butter or eggs, but he made a considerable fortune flogging coupons that would buy fuel or clothes. Private motoring had been banned and even motorists with priority rations never had enough; and unlike men and women in the Services, civilians had to have coupons for every article of clothing from suits and shirts to nightgowns and knickers.

'The last thing I must record in my diary is very *serious*,' wrote Vere Hodgson on 18 June 1944. 'I have lost my best satin nightdress, my best silk underskirts and a dress. . . . They are just the things people steal nowadays.'

You could buy anything from a fur coat to eider-downs and blankets on the black market in Soho by 1944, or the coupons for purchasing them in the shops. By paying double the controlled price, you could get steaks and butter. Some of the deserters used their stolen petrol coupons for forays into the country, where they pillaged unoccupied houses of curtains and furniture and pictures, and these were sold off for tidy sums in the back bedrooms of Soho to men who paid in cash. It was one way the buyers had of concealing from the Government the excess profits many of them were making out of the war.

But whereas, in all other warring countries, everyone at one time or another was involved in the black market, in Britain, and even in the nation's capital, only the very few ever dabbled in it.

'Why should you need a black market, anyway,' one refugee from occupied Europe said in 1944 after a week in London, 'when you don't even have to ration bread?'

In Europe, bread was a valuable black market commodity, and you paid high prices for edible loaves.

The official histories of the wartime rationing system give credit to the law-abiding qualities of the British people for the small amount of black marketeering. The reason may also be that no one was ever desperately in need. You could be hungry in wartime London. But it was impossible to starve.

EXTRACT FROM THE DIARY OF MISS VERE HODGSON, SOCIAL WORKER.

Sunday, 19 December 1943. So we are near to another Christmas of war. This is the fifth, and we are pretty well on our beam ends as far as Christmas fare is concerned. Though we all have enough to eat, there is no chance of turkey, chicken or goose, or even the despised rabbit. If we can get a little mutton that is the best we can hope for.

There are a few Christmas puddings around but not many. However, I managed to get one. This is marvellous because many people have not been able to get any at all. There are shops with three Christmas puddings and 800 registered customers.

The most worrying event of the week has been the illness of Mr Churchill. He has been taken with pneumonia.*

The shops are full of expensive goods which only munition workers can afford, but no decorations anywhere. The best I've heard are what American soldiers have done for children somewhere. They've given them a great dinner and a Christmas tree and Father Christmas arriving in a Flying Fortress. I've seen very little in the shops except for one wet Saturday morning when I scoured the West End for gents' socks, not utility or wool, and of the prewar length. I found them at last, and I hope they will give satisfaction. Otherwise I give the shops a wide berth.

Won't it be lovely if this time next year there is no black-out. The only worry for us now is coal. It seems as if it is going to be a hard winter, though we have had no snow. There have been a great number of deaths from flu this week and thousands are down with it. In fact, they've had to put off the few passenger trains there are because the drivers and signals-men are down with flu. I hope they run one for me on Thursday [to her home in Birmingham]. It seems the epidemic has now spread all over Europe, and it is like the plague, though a quicker and less unsightly death.

Well, a happy Christmas to all my readers, and also a New Year without the shadow of air raids on our beloved island!

---

* He had been taken ill after the Teheran Conference with Roosevelt and Stalin and was recuperating at Marrakesh.

PART FOUR

LIGHT AT LAST

15

THE RUN UP

It needed fresh eyes to see London as it was at the beginning of
1944, for the eyes of Londoners themselves were strained from
four and a quarter years of war and they had become apathetically
unconscious of the way they and their capital looked now. London
was an old Mother Courage of a town, sagging, seedy, knocked
about, dirty, rheum in her eyes, her face pock-marked, lined and
furrowed with pain, suffering and deprivation.

But if you had asked a Cockney what London was really like
now, you wouldn't have got much of an answer beyond: 'Oh,
jogging along, you know, weathering through.' Time had erased
peacetime memories with which to compare it, and the great city
had learned to live and come to terms with queues and shortages
and shabby clothes, with over-crowded transport, with under-
heated rooms, with the blackout,* with the dull, nagging feeling
even immediately after meals that one's appetite had not been
satisfied. Charles Snow found himself, during one of his visits
to Dublin, walking down Gresham Street in the bright lights of the
Irish capital sucking on a bar of rather execrable local chocolate
and feeling that man could hardly ask for anything better in life.
He brought back the menu from the Gresham Hotel and showed
it to his girl friend, who promptly burst into tears.

But most Londoners had lost the power to know what they were
missing, and what had gone out of the life of London town. It
needed the Americans, now swarming in from across the Atlantic,
to see the capital with eyes afresh. One of them who saw it clear
and saw it true was a young man from South Orange, New Jersey,
named Charles Gillen.

Private First Class Charles Gillen had come over to Europe
with the 28th Infantry Division in the autumn of 1943 but it
was not until January 1944 that he got his first furlough. It was

* It had become what was called a 'dim-out' now, but this was only a
minor amelioration of the darkness.

eight days, long enough to allow him to travel up to London from his camp at Tenby, in Pembrokeshire in Wales. It was to be a journey he was to remember all his life. He writes of it now as if it were yesterday.

A US Army lorry dropped him, that January morning outside a large house in Hans Crescent, in Belgravia, where most of the great rows of Regency houses had by now been either bombed out or taken over as clubs and billets for Allied troops in London. This one was manned by the formidable women of the WVS (Women's Voluntary Service) and they gave Charles Gillen his first look at the English class system.

> The place was largely managed by women volunteers of the upper middle class [he remembers], and by one or two titled ladies, and was staffed by working class girls, and the cold and to me rather contemptuous manner in which the former spoke to the latter was quite fascinating because I was used to the belligerently egalitarian attitudes of the States.

He had been instructed that he should take his meals at the Hans Crescent billet because of the tight food situation, and he had been given ration chits; but that would mean breaking into his journeys around London twice a day. Instead, he either went hungry or made the acquaintance of Lyons restaurants, pubs, fish-and-chip shops and Chinese cafés, and ate starchily but happily.

> London was my first experience of a foreign city, and it enthralled me with its ubiquitous reminders of its literary greatness: I made a pilgrimage to Keats's house in Hampstead, and visited the literary shrines of Chelsea, and saw Arnold Bennett's house in Cadogan Square close by my billet, and had many other reminders of literary greatness in the London County Council's plaques. London's long history jumped out at a newcomer everywhere, and I made trips to St Paul's, the Tower (which was closed), the Inns of Court (open), got lost repeatedly in the City but found my way around quite handily in Mayfair, and, of course, went to the House of Commons. The Commons was then *hors de combat*, and oddly enough the thing about the place that intrigued me most was the sight of the empty terrace – you see, I had read several times of the swank of having 'tea on the Terrace'.

He was aware that his wide-eyed appreciation of London and
his enthralment at its sights and sounds was not always shared
by his fellow G Is. At any moment now, as far as they knew, they
would be on their way out and across the Channel to butt their
heads against Hitler's Fortress Europa, and their mood was eat,
drink and be merry for tomorrow. . . . Gillen remembers:

They travelled in packs, and seemed to head straight for the
flesh market in Piccadilly Circus, or tried to get drunk on the
weak, warm beer (whisky was practically unobtainable) or to
have a black market meal of steak and eggs, and they shunned
the 'Limeys', regarding them distastefully and disdainfully.
This dislike was heartily reciprocated by the English, particularly as the American soldiery was paid on a far more lavish
scale than the average Englishman: when a London taxi was
hailed simultaneously by an English civilian and an American
soldier, the cab driver invariably stopped for the American because he knew he could charge any rate he liked (Americans
seemed to consider it infra dig to know about British coinage)
and that he would be given a lordly tip into the bargain. The
boxes in the theatres (to my observation) were almost always
filled with American soldiers, usually champing on dead cigars
and always exuding an ineffable boredom, while the English in
the stalls regarded them resentfully.

January was comparatively warm in London that year and
Gillen travelled avidly around London, mostly on the tops of
buses.

Since American soldiers seldom ventured beyond Central
London I was often the subject of the curiosity of the 'clip-
pies', the women conductors of wartime. I went to Wimbledon
and Limehouse, Dulwich and Hampstead, Putney and Shepherd's Bush. Everywhere the scenes were somehow what I had
expected of them from my reading about London: Lilliputian,
or grim, or ornate, and I often felt the 'shock of recognition'.
The neighbourhoods away from the centre were not nearly so
crowded as they are today. There were not many men of military
age about, and the women were mostly obviously housewives
out shopping. The general feeling was one of uncrowdedness.
There was comparatively little motor traffic, just the buses and

329

taxis, few civilian cars. There was a prevalent drabness, too – the austerity of wartime, a lack of colour and the gaiety of new shop-fronts and no street lighting helped to produce this effect. Everywhere the air raids had knocked out houses and big buildings which had not been replaced, producing a gap-toothed effect.

The days of the blitz were long since over, but the scalded-cat raids were still on, and practically every night of Charles Gillen's leave the air-raid warnings went, the searchlights flicked on out of the blackout, and the great barrage of guns and rockets opened up. One night, just as he was going down into Knightsbridge Underground station the great ring of anti-aircraft guns in Hyde Park opened up just behind him.

They seemed to be firing some sort of rocket-propelled missile because one felt one's body lifting upwards with every round fired; it was a most curious sensation. A little crowd gathered in the area of the station in the hopes of observing something of the action skywards, but the clouds were impenetrable, although the noise was thrilling enough. Just next to me was a couple who seemed to be viewing the spectacle against their better judgement. 'You know,' said the man to the woman, 'this is the way that fifty people were killed in a raid on Battersea – gawking up when a stick of bombs fell on 'em.' I shuddered slightly at the picture this conjured up and then, a few seconds later, I heard a low whistling sound above me. The noise grew rapidly louder; the little crowd of Englishmen around me affected indifference and did not budge, so that I could not possibly be the one to run to shelter. As the screech grew louder I began to tremble and in the crescendo of sound of the last few seconds I was certain that my time had come. Then something hollowly metallic, like a length of pipe, struck the street about a block away, and bounded around with a loud jangling. Apparently I had heard part of an anti-aircraft round returning to earth. I was shaken, petrified, but no one around me had turned a hair.

Nearly every night he went to the theatre, which was just different enough from Broadway in physical surroundings, production and general pacing to be fascinating to him. Buskers still plied their trade outside the theatre, entertaining the queues with music or songs or acrobatics, and this he found most exotic. Among the plays he saw was Emlyn Williams' *Druid's Nest* and from there he went on to the Windmill, where the girls were still indefatigably kicking their legs and the nudes were still valiantly breasting the flood of male stares from the stalls below. Gillen preferred New York burlesque, if truth be told, but there was one revue which set him enthusing because its star was a comedian named Sid Field. He won the hearts of every GI in the audience by doing a side-splitting skit of a brash American Air Force officer, a type from whom everyone was suffering in those days.

One night I went to the Haymarket to see *Love for Love* with Gielgud and (I think) Ralph Richardson. It was a very fine thing, and played with a gloss one seldom saw in New York. About half-way through two large signs on either side of the proscenium arch suddenly lit up. 'ALERT' they read, meaning that the Luftwaffe was visiting somewhere in the London area. The audience ignored the lit-up signs; the play's cast ignored the signs; and I, in American uniform, could not possibly get up and conspicuously seek shelter in the face of such sang-froid, although the rumblings of the ack-ack were now quite close. It was an impressive show of English coolness and phlegm.

When the theatres came out, he usually headed for Piccadilly Circus.

The Circus, particularly that part of it around the foot of Glasshouse Street and the foot of Coventry Street, then reminded me of nothing so much as the Third Circle of Hell. You must picture it as almost completely blacked out, although one was allowed to use a torch with an anaemic bulb and a blue-coated lens. These weak little things cast a sickly dribble of bluish light that had no effect whatever on the inky night. Packed along the sidewalks of the Circus, in what seemed to be thousands, were prostitutes of every age, shape and size, although one couldn't be sure of individual looks because the pitiful torches revealed very little even when swept upwards closely from toes to head, a procedure most potential customers seemed to be using. One was solicited every few steps, sometimes in the baldest words, sometimes in more genteel phrases

331

like: 'Want to come home with me, love?' One curious thing was this: there were a lot of Continental accents among the English ones, and I had the puzzled thought: Did the whores escape from Europe just to cash in on the Golconda in Piccadilly Circus?'

It was the picture of Piccadilly by day and night which Charles Gillen carried away with him at the end of his eight days' furlough.

Uniforms of all the Allied services abounded, a good many new to me, but I was really captivated by the get-up of the British Women's Land Army – brownish jodhpurs stuck into swagger knee-length boots, and a wild sort of Australian big-brimmed hat. I had to inquire as to just what the hell these girls were supposed to be, and after I had been enlightened by one of them I tried to imagine them in this get-up ministering to potatoes, swedes and cabbages.

The predominating uniforms around, though, were American. The Yanks seemed to just swamp the centre of London then, most of them on leave like me, I suppose, but reinforced by the thousands stationed in the 'Little America' around Grosvenor Square or the many other American military establishments around London. I could well sympathise with the natives' resentments and fears in the face of this flood.

But the time was not far away when suddenly the streets of London would empty of this flood, and the transatlantic cry of 'taxi!' would be as rare around Berkeley Square as the song of the nightingale.

And then the natives would miss them.

2

London had no respite from German air raids that spring and although, in weight and frequency, they were nothing like the brutal and unrelenting attacks which the RAF and the USAF were now making against German cities, Londoners found them wearing on their nerves and tempers.* Not many people were

* What German bombs lacked in size they made up in fiendish ingenuity. Worst to deal with was the so-called butterfly bomb which came down in showers and was timed to detonate on impact, by time-fuse, or on

killed or injured, but the alerts were of long duration, the anti-
aircraft barrage was ferocious, and Whitehall, the City and the
House of Commons took yet another round of punishment that
shattered the last windows and tore bigger holes in the walls.

I walked past Westminster Abbey [wrote Vere Hodgson on
Sunday, 5 March], and the less said about that the better. It
will soon be all right again as an army of men were working on
it. I did not try to go to St James's as I believe it is rather
nasty. I see that Mr Partridge [who owned a well-known picture
gallery] tried to get into his treasures when the firemen were
pouring water on the place, had an altercation with the police,
and has been fined £75. I am very sorry for him because it must
be agonising to think that your Rembrandts are being soused
with water and you cannot get in to save them.

But it was hard to guess, on that or most other Sunday mornings
of spring 1944, that only a few hours before thousands of lengths
of lethal steel had been flying over London's housetops and that a
great battle had been raging in the skies overhead. The streets
were full of pedestrians airing their dogs and soldiers up on leave
from the camps. The air was beginning to be balmy with the
smell of spring. In Hyde Park, at Speakers' Corner, the same
crowds hung around the same orators preaching doom or
revolution or far-out religion.

'What are we fighting for?' cried a speaker.

'Spam!' replied someone in the crowd.

'Who are the two greatest men in the world?' asked another
orator.

'Flanagan and Allen,' said the voice in the crowd.

It took so very little to cheer people up. In March enough citrus
fruit had arrived in Britain for a special issue to be made to shops
in London.

There are lemons about! [wrote Vere Hodgson]. I've had an
orgy of pancakes. We haven't had them for years. There are
oranges, but I haven't got any yet.

But a couple of weeks later everyone in London seemed to have

---

contact. It was extremely difficult to defuse and bomb-squads called it
'the Beast'. A big shower of them could tie up a whole district for days.

found them, and like the cherry stones of 1941, orange peel now lay in the gutters of Oxford Street and Leicester Square to demonstrate the change in the national diet. But it continued to be frugal.

The meat ration lasts for three evening meals [Vere Hodgson wrote to her cousin in Rhodesia]. I don't think anyone can make it go further, whatever you have. This covers Saturday, Sunday and Monday. Tuesday and Wednesday I have a handful of rice or macaroni dogged up in some way with curry or cheese. But the cheese ration is so small now that there is rarely any left. Thursday I have an order with the dairy for a pound of sausages. These do for Thursday, Friday and Saturday lunch. They do not however taste much of sausage. I understand they are nearly all soya bean flour and the flavour is nothing much. However they look like sausages and we pretend they are. Of course a little fish would help a lot but there are always long queues for it and my dinner hour is only one hour and I never have time to wait. But you see, we manage and we are not hungry.

On 1 April the Government announced that all coastal areas along the Channel facing France would henceforward be prohibited areas. Only people living in coastal resorts and the coastal fringe would now be allowed in. Police and military police manned the main-line stations and boarded south-bound trains to check the identity of travellers.

On 17 April, a young buyer in a munitions factory noticed a strange thing when he came up to London.

I have suddenly noticed the *absence* of American servicemen both in buses and the Underground. None of them to be seen in the streets, either. I have quite missed them, being used to seeing many of them in the course of the day.

Speculation about the second front had been the conversational gambit in every pub and restaurant in London for some time. Everybody had a guess about the date and a theory about the landing, and in every group there was always some chairborne belligerent who ended up the argument by saying, 'I don't understand what we're waiting for. Why don't we just barge in on them and batter our way through to Berlin. That's what the Russians are doing, aren't they?'

But suddenly a restraint seemed to fall upon the armchair strategists, as if the knowledge the invasion of Europe might really be coming at long last caused them to face up to the horrid reality of what it might mean.

The second front talk buzzes [wrote one woman to Mass-Observation from her home in west London]. Some hope that the present bombing offensive is designed if possible to avoid a really bloody second front. Most think it will be a blood bath.

Captain Harry Butcher, naval Aide to General Eisenhower, wrote in his diary just about this time (21 March):
The target date for OVERLORD* is 31 May 1944. Will the Channel run red with blood?'
Vere Hodgson wrote:

What I must remark upon is the beauty of the spring in London just now. I suppose it has always been just as beautiful, but it is such a joy to us this year after five years of war that I notice it especially. There are such a lot of lovely prunus trees all in full flower and a wild cherry on the opposite side of the road. It seems like a wedding every time I pass. The plane trees are a golden green just now and my chestnut has all its candles out and the lilacs are coming on fast. It is the best time for London. As I pass the park on the bus, the beauty of the trees is overpowering. They look like the shades of the blessed. . . . The second front is busily preparing but it is not launched.

3

All Charles Snow's closest friends were now deeply engaged in preparations for D-Day and two of them, Professors P. M. S. Blackett and J. D. Bernal, were directly attached to SHAEF.†
'By this time Blackett's researches had brought to light an item

---

* Code name for the invasion of Europe. Harry C. Butcher, *Three Years with Eisenhower*, Heinemann, 1946.
† Supreme Headquarters, Allied Forces in Europe.

about France,' Snow said. 'He had discovered that it was several feet further away from England than we thought it was, and that would make important differences to our landing plans.'

Bernal had always been a fervid member of the Communist Party and had refused anything but passive help to Britain so long as the Soviet Union was neutral in the war. But now he was one of the most invaluable members of the invasion team, full of brilliant ideas and a mine of information about the conditions which the invasion force would be likely to encounter. No one remembered that he was a card-carrying Communist any more; no one, that is, except the Security branch.

One morning early in 1944 the telephone rang in Snow's office in Tothill Mansions. It was Professor Bernal speaking.

'Bernal wanted a former colleague of his – let's call him Williams – to be attached to him very rapidly. This chap was an expert on solid structures, like beaches, and Bernal needed him for the D-Day preparations. It so happened that Williams was working at something of fairly high priority in another Government department, and I knew it was going to be difficult. But I worked at it, and after some pressure I managed to get Williams released and posted to Bernal. And I thought no more about it.'

But about six weeks later, Snow's telephone rang again and this time it was Bernal's chief at SHAEF, a famous admiral. He was very angry.

'What the bloody hell do you mean,' he said, 'not getting Williams transferred to Bernal as he requested?'

'Sorry,' said Snow, 'I thought it had been arranged.'

'It has not been arranged,' said the admiral. 'Will you look into it? And don't take too long about it,' he added. 'If you don't get cracking today, I'm going to take it up with the PM tomorrow.'

Snow promised to do his best and put down the telephone. He was puzzled. And then suddenly the reason for the delay hit him.

'I picked up the telephone and rang up the chap who was in charge of security at Supreme Headquarters, and I told him to come over and see me without delay.'

When the security officer arrived, Snow said, 'I've just been told from high up that Williams hasn't been allowed to join Bernal at Supreme Headquarters. I want to know why.'

The security man hesitated.

'Look,' said Snow, 'this matter is going to Winston Churchill

tomorrow, so you'd better come clean with me. It's about
Williams' security clearance, I suppose?'

The security man nodded, glumly.

'What's wrong with him? What have you got against him?'
asked Snow.

Once more the man hesitated. 'I couldn't possibly tell even
you,' he said.

Snow drew a deep breath. 'Look, man,' he said, 'I've told you
already that this matter is going to the PM tomorrow. Bernal has
asked for Williams and what Bernal wants he both needs and gets.
If the PM hears we are standing in his way, all our heads will roll.
Now tell me. What's the black mark against Williams?'

'Well,' said the security man, 'it's like this. We've discovered
that before the war Williams used to work very closely with a
notorious Communist.'

'And who was the notorious Communist?' asked Snow.

'Bernal,' said the security man, sheepishly.

Snow, Bernal, Blackett and their friends walked around London
all that spring with a nasty sensation of prickling on the back of
their necks, and every time they heard an aeroplane pass overhead
they would look up with a screwing of eyes and an intense concern. Those acquaintances who remembered Snow's anxieties
during the height of the blitz immediately put his edginess down
to nerves. 'He's getting bomb happy again,' they said.

It wasn't that, however, which was causing the boffins and the
War Cabinet and Eisenhower and his invasion staff at SHAEF
to begin looking over their shoulders during the lovely spring days
and nights of April and May, 1944. They knew what Londoners
didn't: that at any moment Hitler's secret weapons, pilotless
planes and rockets, might come winging in to spread death and
destruction among them.

'It wasn't so bad for the generals and the Cabinet ministers,'
said Snow, 'because although they knew the menace that was
threatening London they were able to talk about it among themselves. We who lived the lives of ordinary Londoners and moved
around with ordinary people could not. It was a curious feeling
being with friends in a pub at night. They would begin to talk
about the invasion, they would voice their apprehensions about

the slaughter which might soon be facing our troops – and of their own guilt in being safe in London when it happened. And one couldn't succumb to the temptation and say: "Don't feel guilty. You will be in a hell of a dangerous place yourself any moment now. London might be as bad as the beaches." '*

For those who possessed the troubling secret the itchy question was: which would arrive first, the Allied armies on the beaches of Normandy or Adolf Hitler's secret weapon on the people of London?

4

When would the invasion begin? Everyone was asking the question now. People laid bets in the pubs. Factories ran sweepstakes on the exact time and date. There was no doubt in anyone's mind in London now that it had to be a matter of days rather than weeks. All day and all night, in the warm May sunshine or the cool night, the bombers flew low over the rooftops on their way to smash and gouge at the railway communication centres in France and Germany. The coastal areas to the south of London were now locked tight against civilian intruders. Foreign diplomats had been officially informed that until further notice they could neither travel in and out of the United Kingdom nor send messages to their governments in code.

The only American troops left in London were chair-borne types with no desire to eat, drink and be merry because of what might happen tomorrow. The boys with fires in their bellies had gone south for a rendezvous with the invasion barges, and the 'Piccadilly Commandos' were not the only ones in London who would miss them. The great city went about its daily business that spring with its mind on other things. And it waited.

5

Charles de Gaulle was in Algiers and he was in a state of cold anger with Winston Churchill. The ban on the transmission of

* 'Even when the Vis arrived we could not tell people what they were,' says Snow in a note to the author. 'It was somewhat irritating to hear acquaintances cheering because they thought we were bringing aircraft down in flames.'

diplomatic messages in code from London had been extended to include the representatives of Fighting France, and, not without reason, he considered that a deliberate insult to himself and his organisation. Was he not an ally? Was he not to be trusted?

The truth is, so far as Churchill and Roosevelt were concerned, he was not. Their relations with the Free French leader had reached their lowest point. They now considered him not only arrogant and unco-operative but unreliable as well. The President, in particular, felt so strongly about him that in the days before the invasion he would not willingly have trusted him with the name of his third cousin. He had already told Eisenhower that when D-Day came he would be welcome to use all the French soldiers he could get – except de Gaulle. He was to be kept out of it.

On 24 May the House of Commons held a debate on Foreign affairs and Winston Churchill made the main speech of the day. Soon the lobbies and the smoking room were loud with comment on the Prime Minister's words. To everyone's surprise he had warmly praised Franco's Spain for its neutrality in the war, and had spoken of France and of General de Gaulle with a coldness which had practically frozen the House. The friends of the general among the members were either furious or distressed, not least Robert Boothby, who considered Churchill's cavalier treatment of the French leader to be little short of scandalous. But it was Harold Nicolson who rose to reply to the Prime Minister and he said: 'It seems to me and many Frenchmen that the United States Government, with His Majesty's Government in their train, instead of helping the French and welcoming them, lose no opportunity of administering any snub which ingenuity can devise and ill-manners perpetrate. I hope that the Foreign Secretary [who was due to speak after him] will go further than the negative and even ungracious statement made on this subject by the Prime Minister. It is most unwise, most weak and most ill-informed of the United States Government to refuse to accord any special recognition to the [de Gaulle] National Committee and Provisional Government. I am convinced that this is a grave error of policy.'

Whether this rebuke hit home or not, Churchill realised that he may have gone too far in making his dislike of de Gaulle so publicly plain. On 3 June he sent his own aircraft to Algiers to bring General de Gaulle back to London, and the following day the General joined him on the special train which was drawn up in a siding near Portsmouth. Here Churchill and several of his ministers, including Anthony Eden and Ernest Bevin, were waiting for the invasion to begin.*

The meeting began badly and ended worse. When de Gaulle came into Churchill's presence he found the South African premier, Field Marshal Smuts, with him. Smuts a few months previously had delivered a much publicised speech in which he had called France a 'third-rate power' and suggested her only chance in the post-war world was for her to join the British Commonwealth. De Gaulle refused to shake his hand.

Soon Churchill and the General were quarrelling bitterly, much to the embarrassment of the other Englishmen present. Churchill was urging de Gaulle to bend a little, to go to America and talk to Roosevelt, to make concessions in order to secure America's support for his administration. De Gaulle was haughtily insisting that he didn't care what the Americans did or said, because he was France and all Frenchmen would recognise him as such. He launched into a bitter attack on American policy towards France, and of its insults towards him.

'How do you expect us to come to terms on this basis?' he asked.

'And you! How do you expect that Britain should take a position separate from that of the United States?' Churchill blazed back. He drew in an angry breath and then said words that de Gaulle would always remember, words that would colour Anglo-French relations in the postwar world so long as de Gaulle was in power.

'We are going to liberate Europe,' said Churchill, 'but it is because the Americans are in agreement with us that we do so. This is something you ought to know: each time we have to choose between Europe and the open sea, we shall always choose the open sea. Each time I have to choose between you and Roosevelt, I shall always choose Roosevelt.'

He glared at the frigid Frenchman and then turned away.

Invasion was only a matter of hours away, but no one suggested that de Gaulle should remain with Churchill and the others and see the great armada set off for France. He went back to London that evening.

* Eisenhower's headquarters was nearby.

6

Chief Inspector Reginald Smith was called to Scotland Yard from his office in the East End in mid-May and told the approximate date of D-Day, but he didn't really need to be told how imminent it was. For several weeks now thousands of men had been working against the clock on the great green flats called Hackney Marshes, building something called Mulberry Harbours. The marshes were below the level of the River Thames, on which they abutted, and when the time came breaches would be cut in the banks and the floating harbours launched and sent on their way to France. The need for them was so urgent that the work went on day and night, and no one was allowed to stop for air raids.

Ships and landing craft started assembling in the Royal Group of docks all through May, and by the end of the month every landing stage and inlet was jammed with them. Then the convoys began coming in, bringing the troops by their thousands. Most of Canning Town had fallen down as a result of the blitz, and what few houses were left had been knocked about by the street-fighting school which had been established there and in Silvertown. Tents were erected in the ruins and barbed wire rolled around the perimeters of the camps. Over Whit week-end (28–30 May 1944,) one of the biggest contingents of troops arrived from Scotland and the North of England, and these were shepherded into West Ham football stadium. As in all the other camps, barbed wire fences were set up and sentries posted, and the troops cut off from the civilian world outside.

That was how the trouble began.

On 1 June the troops inside the stadium were divided up into groups and addressed in turn by their commanding officer. They were told that they would be going to France 'any day now' and given a rough idea of the nature of their task and the area of their landing. They were afterwards allowed to come forward in groups to study maps of the Ouistreham beaches in Normandy where their tank landing craft would soon be taking them. Then they were told to queue up before their supply sergeants, and were issued, and signed for, their first payment in French money, for use when they got to the other side.* Some of the NCOs were

* These 'invasion francs' were the subject of a bitter quarrel between

issued with escape kits which showed routes through France to the Spanish frontier, in case they found themselves trapped behind the enemy lines, together with various intriguing articles and information put together for their use by the Intelligence services. After which they assembled in mid-field and were addressed by an Army chaplain, and his gloomy tone of voice and even gloomier forecast of the 'perils that lie ahead of all of us' drove the soldiers off the field in the direction of the canteens in search of a soothing drink and a smoke.

By seven in the evening the beer had run out and there was not a cigarette to be had in the stadium. Angry soldiers who approached the supply sergeants had it pointed out to them, in no uncertain terms, that this was Whit week-end and the NAAFI depots were closed. No one thought of ordering up emergency supplies.

So, with the prospect of a dry and worrying week-end before them, several scores of D-Day soldiers did the logical thing. They crept past the sentries and crawled under the barbed wire. They snipped their way through it. They climbed on each other's shoulders and leaped over it. Some of them, who knew the ground and had smuggled themselves into it to see the game as kids, now tunnelled their way out of it in search of a beer. Soon every pub in the vicinity was filled with British troops clamouring for drinks and smokes and even offering to pay for it in French francs, which the landlords were taking in as souvenirs.

Inspector Smith was looking over three German air force men at Wanstead police station when the news reached him. The Nazi fliers had been shot down in a raid on the marshes and were being very truculent. They not only refused to answer questions, as was their right, but they were deliberately baiting the British with what would happen to them when the invasion began, *if* it began. Smith had to control himself from punching the most insolent one on the nose, and realised that he was nervy and anxious. When his office at last reached him and told him what had happened at West Ham Stadium, his first reaction was to think:

'My God, this could wreck the invasion!'

---

the US forces, who had printed them and decided their rate of worth, and General de Gaulle, whose views had not been consulted.

It couldn't do that. But it could put invaluable information into the hands of a spy if the troops were allowed to go on roaming around the East End pubs. God knows what they would start saying if they got drunk – and drunk was what they seemed bent on getting.

'But what could we do?' he said. 'By this time everybody from Montgomery down was telling us to get the soldiers back inside the stadium. My office had already been on the job and the bulk of the AWOLs had gone back quietly. Only about thirty remained, but they were carousing in pubs as widely apart as Limehouse and Canning Town and were in no mood to respond to the orders of the military and civilian police who had been sent to round them up. Their attitude was that if they were going to die on the beaches tomorrow, they might as well get drunk on the streets of London tonight and no snotty policeman was going to tell them otherwise. The army was all for getting tough and strong-arming them back to the stadium, but in the circumstances that seemed to me to be the height of unwisdom. It would cause bitterness through the camp just when spirits needed to be high.'

And then, in Canning Town police station, Smith found the man who did the trick for him. He was an old retired police sergeant who had come back into the force as a volunteer for the duration of the war. He had sons of his own in the Forces. He had been used to dealing with people in trouble all his life and was known to have a heart of gold, and also a way with him.

'If you'll just give me a truck and a driver, sir,' the sergeant said, 'I think I can get the boys back for you. No rough stuff, either.'

It was decided to try him. He departed on what he was afterwards to describe as the 'longest pub crawl of my life'. He went methodically from pub to pub. When he found troops forgathered and raucously singing together he joined them, sang with them, drank with them, listened to them, and then sweet-talked them back to the stadium.

It is a measure of his achievement that by five o'clock next morning not only had he got them all back, but there were six more soldiers in the stadium than there were before the thirsty invasion troops decided to make a break for it. A half-dozen ordinary soldiers not concerned with the invasion had fallen for the old sergeant's persuasive line and decided to come too.

They had to be held in custody until after the D-Day barges were scraping the beaches of Normandy. So did a couple of East End pub keepers. But they were allowed to keep the 'invasion francs' with which they had been paid when they were released.

7

A full-dress meeting of the Cabinet Committee was held in the Hole in the Ground a few days before D-Day and anybody who had anything to do with the Intelligence services and had been involved in the invasion preparations was summoned to attend. In turn the heads of the different branches read out reports from their agents inside Occupied Europe, but there were no surprises until Rear Admiral Edmund Rushbrooke rose to his feet. Rushbrooke was Director of Naval Intelligence at the Admiralty and on this occasion a young assistant, Ian Fleming, sat at one side, while on the other was one of his brightest female aides, Joan St George Saunders. Both of them had difficulty in keeping the suppressed excitement out of their expressions.

For what Rushbrooke had to reveal was startling information indeed. As he explained to the committee, everybody knew that in the neutral capital of Lisbon there was a certain Czechoslovak whose code-name was Radek and who was a spy for the Germans.

'Oh, Radek!' said someone along the table. 'No one pays any attention to him!'

Indeed they didn't – neither the German masters who paid him nor the British counter-intelligence services in Lisbon who intercepted and read his messages to the Abwehr in Berlin. For he never seemed to get anything right. He moved around the foreign colonies in Lisbon and was always to be seen at the right (and even the wrong) parties, but what he put into his secret cables was purest trash. Everybody in London had long since decided that the Germans only kept Radek on because he had a relative somewhere in the Abwehr organisation. They must certainly by now have learned to discount anything he reported.

'Which brings me to my report,' said Admiral Rushbrooke.

He then proceeded to read to the Cabinet Committee the breakdown from Naval Intelligence's agent in Lisbon of Radek's latest cable to his masters. And as he read, a stillness fell over the room that was tense and brittle. For what Radek's cable purported to set out was the date of the Allied landings in France and the nature of the invasion. He said: 1. The Allied forces would make a feint attack in the region of the Pas de Calais but that their main landings would be in Normandy, in the neighbourhood of the Ouistreham beaches ('where King Henry the Fifth and his English Army landed'); 2. The invasion would almost certainly occur between the dates of 4 June and 7 June 1944, because that was the only time when the tides would be right; and 3. Airborne forces would be used to secure the two flanks of the invasion area, probably dropping on the Orne River and Canal to the East and the Cherbourg Peninsula to the west.

Through the consternated silence which followed Rushbrooke's reading, someone said, 'My God, the only thing he's forgotten are the Mulberry harbours!'

'Well, gentlemen, what do we do?'

Ian Fleming said, 'We can hardly call off the invasion, can we? Or change it around.'

Joan Saunders said, 'Radek's been wrong so many times before that Canaris is bound to think he's wrong again. I don't think he'll even bother to pass it on to Hitler.'

Everybody round the table nodded, vigorously. In the circumstances, it was the only thing to do.*

'There's just one thing, though,' Joan Saunders added. 'Don't you think we ought to put Mr Radek out of harm's way? Just in case he gets things right a second time?'

They looked at her as if she had suggested something terribly ungentlemanly.

8

The six weeks leading up to D-Day 1944 were among the happiest of Dolly James's life, mainly because she fell in love again.

One night in mid-April, sick of sitting around in her bed-sitter, sick of her own company, too fidgety to face going to a cinema, unwilling to go into a pub where she wasn't known, she decided to face it and went back to the pub of her pre-18b days, the Glue-pot. She had not felt up to risking snubs from the landlord and her old friends since coming out of prison, but now the need to see a

* Joan Saunders was right. Radek's report was ignored.

familiar face, even if its expression was hostile, drove her towards Mortimer Street.

She need not have worried. The landlord greeted her as if she had never been away with a broad smile and a gin-and-tonic. Dylan Thomas, his red lips breasting the foam of a large beer, dashed down his glass and rushed forward with a great shout.

'Dolly, my love, my beautiful, my fairy's child!' he cried, folding her in his arms. '*What* have those brutes been doing to you?'

He drew her into a throng of people round the bar, musicians, painters, soldiers, British, American, Canadians. When the pub closed they all moved to someone's apartment in a mews behind Broadcasting House, and apparently this was a usual procedure, because they had all brought some kind of bottle of beer or spirits along with them; and the drinking went on amid fumes of smoke and torrents of talk all through the night. No one mentioned the war. Everyone pressed drinks upon her and put their arms around her, and somehow it was warm and affectionate rather than lascivious when they squeezed or embraced her. And through the increasing haze the face of one man kept swimming in and out, looking owlishly concerned at her, making sure she was never without a drink or a cigarette . . . and next morning, when she awoke in a strange but enormously comfortable bed, it was to find his face bending over her, smiling this time, but still owlish.

'I had to bring you here,' he said. 'I didn't know where you lived, and I thought you needed a little help. Here, drink this.'

He handed her a fizzing alka-seltzer, and though she didn't need it, because she never suffered from hangovers, she found herself drinking it and staring at him over the glass. When she put it down she felt under the bedsheets, and found that she was still in her pants and brassière.

He was a war correspondent. He told her that he had just come back from Italy, where he had been reporting with General Mark Clark's Fifth Army, and was now 'waiting for a new assignment'. Later when she went to one of the cupboards for her dress, she saw his uniform hanging there with the insignia of a paratrooper on the shoulder just below the war correspondent flash, but he just shrugged his shoulders when she asked about it.

'It was just one of those things I fell into when I got drunk,' he said.

Over breakfast of a luxury she hadn't experienced for a long time (tomato juice, eggs and tinned bacon, lots of toast and butter and American coffee) she decided that she liked him a lot. So much so that she thought she had better tell him about herself before someone else did it for her. So she told him. About 18b. About Holloway. About the German.

'Actually, I know all about it,' he said. 'But I'm glad you told me yourself. I can't tell you how sorry I am that these terrible things should have happened to you. It isn't fair. It's a bloody horrible world – especially for women.'

He reached over and took her hand, and then suddenly she was crying and he was embracing her; and it seemed logical afterwards that they should go to bed and make love. They made love again and again. Oh, how they made love.

But in between, they did everything together. It was simple enough to get leave of absence from her rag-trade boss. He didn't mind as long as she promised to come back and so long as he didn't have to pay her. But the net-making chore was more difficult. But he solved it by finding a doctor friend who produced a medical certificate giving her a month's health leave.

They wandered round London hand in hand, through the spring sunshine. They sat on the grass at Lords in the frizzling sunshine and watched the cricket. He put on his uniform and waved a pass and took her down to forbidden Brighton, where the seashore was covered with tank traps and minefields and barbed wire, but where the restaurants were full of fresh fish and there seemed to be no scarcity at all of food or drink. They went to concerts. They dined at the Ritz and the Savoy and the Berkeley and the Dorchester and she was introduced to Duff Cooper and Ambassador Winant and Boothby and Edward Murrow. They danced to Carroll Gibbons and his orchestra and then retired to watch in pop-eyed admiration as a quartet of two slim US sailors and their equally slim WAAC partners performed the latest dance from America, the jitter bug.

The days went by so fast that April went and May and then June was upon them. Still they never talked about the war. The only time it had come up was when she had asked him what was his next assignment likely to be, and he had replied, 'Some boring story with the RAF, I expect.'

Early in June he received an enormous quota of clothing coupons from his friends at the War Office. There were more of them than the average British family got in a year, and they were more precious than money. He had already provided her with six pairs of nylon stockings he had somehow obtained from his American friends. Now he took her on a round of the shops, buying her frocks and costumes and everything she needed to restock her faded and frayed and shabby wardrobe.

But it wasn't the clothes she loved. It was him. And she loved him most when she was wearing no clothes whatsoever.

One morning the telephone rang. It must have been 4 June and dawn had only just broken, and Dolly had only just fallen into a heavy sleep. She barely felt him move away from her and go into the other room to answer it. She slept heavily on.

It must have been about an hour later that she rolled over and felt for him, and there was no one there. She listened for sounds in the bathroom, and there were none. She got up to look, and when she got into the next room she saw the note propped up on the telephone.

Darling Dolly [it said], I didn't want to wake you but I had to go. Thank you, my love, for everything. Please stay in the flat for as long as you like. The lease runs until the end of the month.

Underneath the note was his emergency ration book and the rest of his clothing coupons.

Three days later she read his story of the Allied parachute landing in Normandy. But she never saw him again. He never came back to her. It was a long time before she could bring herself to use the clothing coupons.

PART FIVE

THE WORST TIME – AND THE BEST

16

MEMORANDA

L. N. A., to Mass-Observation:

6 June 1944. At 7 o'clock this morning I switched on the wireless
and then I heard what sounded to me like the beginning of
our great invasion of the Continent, but I wasn't sure. During
the hours of darkness we had been much disturbed by the
constant drone of our bombers, and with the coming of first
light this increased in intensity. It is not often I see Mosquito
bombers, but they were travelling to the unknown horizon in
great numbers. I wondered why.

I did not think much about the subject until coming to the
office I again switched on the wireless and heard the Belgian
Prime Minister speaking to his country in French, and he was
telling them not to take any hasty action, but to await events.
Then I knew that the great day had arrived. Later of course
followed the official communiqué which gave the greatest news
the world has ever known: the free nations of the world, coming
from England, had landed in France to liberate their countries.
All my work today has seemed so unimportant and inconsequen-
tial: the petty telephone calls from irate customers about
delivery of goods, the attendance at a meeting to hear yet another
person talk about postwar planning, and so on. The fact that
up to the present I am not taking part in this momentous affair
is particularly irksome, and I have a feeling of suppressed
frustration. . . .

In my carriage this morning was a woman talking to a friend
about her son who had recently been killed at sea. She did not
(as the papers would say) feel proud of him, she only said:
'There is an emptiness with me all the time, for Gerald will
not come back.' This 'emptiness' will soon be multiplied a
thousand-fold, for great victories and banner-waving successes
are not without cost. I have no faith, and never have had, in a
rapid Nazi collapse. Germans do not show fight and then run

away. All through the war they have fought to the bitter end and they will again.

6 June 1944. I turned on the 8 a.m. news on Tuesday morning and pricked up my ears as I heard the man say with a voice of suppressed excitement that the Germans were fighting invasion barges in the Channel. I didn't think they would speak like that on our wireless if there were not something in it, so I took it as certain. Later people came in to say that Eisenhower had spoken on the radio to say that the invasion was on. We listened to every scrap of news all day. At nine o'clock when the King was to speak we were all agog. His speech was nice and sincere and, just like him, he brought the Queen in a lot and told us all to pray.

It is one man's vision which has brought this about. In those awful days Mr Churchill was the only one who could see the comeback, and knew that if only we could hold on we had the power to beat them . . . Let not future ages forget it.

Vere Hodgson, social worker.

6 June 1944. The King spoke at 10 p.m. tonight about the invasion. He began: 'Four years . . .' and then there was a terrible pause during which one could almost see the poor devil struggling to articulate the word, and then he got it out: '. . . ago.' He got better as he went on, but why *do* they make him do it.*

George Bramwell, teacher.

6 June 1944. I go down to the House, arriving there about ten to twelve. When I enter the Chamber, I find a buzz of conversation going on. Questions had ended unexpectedly early and people were just sitting there chatting, waiting for Winston. It was an unusual scene. He entered the Chamber at three minutes to twelve. He looked as white as a sheet. The house noticed this at once, and we feared that he was about to announce some terrible disaster. He is called immediately, and places two separate fids of typescript on the table. He begins with the first, which is about Rome.† Alexander gets a really tremendous cheer. He ends with

* King George the Sixth suffered from a bad stammer.
    † Allied troops, under the overall command of Field Marshal Alexander, had entered Rome on June 5.

352

the words: 'This great and timely operation,' stressing the word 'timely' with a rise of the voice and that familiar bending of the two knees. He then picks up his other fid of notes and begins: 'I have also to announce to the House that during the night and early hours of this morning, the first of a series of landings in force upon the Continent of Europe has taken place. . . .' The House listens in hushed awe. He speaks for only seven minutes and then Greenwood follows with a few words. We then pass to the Colonial Office estimates in the Committee of Supply.

Harold Nicolson, MP

17

THE LAST STRAW

I

The weather was terrible in the days after D-Day and everyone in London, slopping through the rain, gazing up at the dark clouds, was depressed. They pictured the men fighting their way through the Normandy mud under the fire from Rommel's guns and tanks, without the air cover of which they had been deprived by the low clouds. In fact, everything was going well, and the Germans never at any moment showed themselves capable of driving the liberating armies back into the sea.

Londoners were itchy and nervous, nevertheless. They had been long schooled to expect Allied setbacks and swift German ripostes, and they could not believe that all could possibly be going well.

'Just you wait,' they were saying in the pubs. ''E'll 'it back. 'E won't take it lying darn, 'Itler won't.'

But except for those in the know, few Londoners guessed that the reprisals, when they came, would not be against the troops in Normandy but against themselves.

Harold Nicolson, MP, thought that General Charles de Gaulle was in a most agreeable mood in the days after invasion of France. His fellow MP, Robert Boothby, was far from agreeing with him. He found de Gaulle an angry and unhappy man, and believed the General had good reason for feeling as he did.

Nicolson dined with de Gaulle on 9 June 1944, and asked him about the war. He replied that he thought it was going well.

'Ça va très bien – au delà de nos espérances,' he said. 'C'est la dernière année de la guerre. La guerre sera finie avant Noël.'*

But later in the evening, when Nicolson asked him to make a grand gesture and bring part of his Government-in-exile to

* 'It goes well – beyond our hopes. This is the last year of the war. The war will be over before Christmas.'

354

London (it had been established in Algiers) he refused and launched into an attack against Eisenhower and the Americans. He was going back to North Africa, he said, and wanted no more of London.

Robert Boothby, on the other hand, knew that de Gaulle's dearest wish was not to return to Algiers at this moment but to cross the Channel and set foot in his native France, to be part of the struggle for liberation which was now going on. He thought it outrageous that an edict from President Roosevelt (willingly accepted by Winston Churchill) should prevent him from doing so. What right had the Americans to insist that de Gaulle did not represent France, that his presence there would 'muddy the waters', when there was every indication from the liberated areas that de Gaulle was the man most Frenchmen and women were now waiting to see?

Boothby decided that it was not good enough. He went around his colleagues in the House of Commons canvassing their opinions and came to the conclusion that most of them agreed with him. To put a wall around France against Charles de Gaulle was an outrageous interference with his rights as a Frenchman. Something should be done about it.

Churchill was mysteriously absent from London and so, when Boothby approached the Government leaders to express his dissatisfaction, he was fobbed off with such remarks from the Party whips as: 'The Yanks don't want him there, and that's it, old boy.' Or, 'Winston knows best, and Winston doesn't want him in France.'

Irked by the unimaginative tactics of the Government spokesmen, Boothby decided to draw up a list of names of members who would support him in a motion which he proposed to put before the House. It would recommend that General Charles de Gaulle, Head of the Provisional French Government, Commander-in-Chief of the Forces of Fighting France, should be allowed to set foot at once in his native France to join other Frenchmen fighting to liberate their country from the Nazi yoke. He collected sixty names but had no real intention of putting the proposal down as a serious motion until he heard why Winston Churchill was not available.

He had gone on a trip to the Normandy beach-head with the Chief of the Imperial General Staff, Field Marshal Sir Alan Brooke.

But what particularly infuriated Boothby and his friends was the fact that Churchill had taken with him Field Marshal Smuts, the South African leader who had sneered at France a few weeks back. To have preferred him as a companion on the voyage to the leader of the Fighting French seemed to be a calculated insult to de Gaulle and to the Frenchmen he represented.

Boothby went at once to the Speaker of the House and got permission, rarely given, to move the adjournment of the House 'on a definite matter of urgent public importance'.

As he sat in the Commons, waiting to be called, Boothby heard that Winston Churchill was back in London. Not only that, the Old Man was on his way to the House. Someone had dared to wake him from his afternoon siesta to tell him about Boothby's motion, and he was coming to do something about it.

Those members who saw him will always remember Winston Churchill's face that afternoon. It was strained and black with anger. Legs slightly apart, like a sailor on the deck of a rocking ship, he marched into the House and moved along the Opposition benches until he reached Boothby's seat, and there he stood over the young Scot.

'You will withdraw your motion!' he said, in a loud voice.

Everyone in the House was watching them.

'I will withdraw it if you will allow the General to go to France,' Boothby replied. 'Not unless.'

For a moment it seemed as if Churchill was going to lose control of himself. His face went purple with fury. He lifted his arm and clenched his fist, as if he were about to bring it down with a slam on Boothby's head.

'Oh God, no!' someone said.

The old man went rigid, and then, but very slowly, dropped his arm to his side. In a quieter voice, he said, 'There are political reasons why he cannot go. But you will withdraw your motion, just the same. Otherwise I shall move that the House go into secret session, and then I will tell the House why de Gaulle cannot go.'

Boothby said: 'In that case, I must withdraw my motion. Its only motive is to ensure that the matter is debated in public.'

'Yes,' said Churchill, 'and that I will not allow. So withdraw it.'

He turned and stalked out of the Chamber. Boothby sat there, unconscious of the buzz of talk all around him. He reflected that he had never seen Winston Churchill so near to losing control.

It has gone on too long, he thought. *It is breaking too many men. It is time this war came to an end.*

He got up and went out to let the Speaker and his friends know that he was withdrawing his motion. He was shattered by the memory of Churchill's blind fury. 'Bob, that man does not like you, and you must face it', said David Kirkwood, a fellow MP.

But twenty-four hours later, word reached de Gaulle that the ban on his movements had been withdrawn. He left for France in a Fighting French destroyer and on 14 June 1944, set foot on French soil for the first time since the collapse of his country.

2

At 2.35 on the morning of 16 June 1944, the air-raid sirens wailed over Banstead Common, on the southern outskirts of London, and John Eaves rolled over on his side, groaned, and tiptoed out of bed so as not to disturb his wife. But she had been awakened too.

'Don't forget your helmet, dear,' she said.

He dressed, put on his tin hat, and went out into the cool blue darkness and padded down the road towards the ARP post where he was a warden. As he walked, he noticed a small glow in the eastern sky streaking towards him at a slightly downwards angle. Ah, he thought, a Nazi plane on fire. The engine coughed and spluttered and then suddenly ceased, and the glow of the flames disappeared. Good, the damn thing is coming down. A few seconds later there was a fearful explosion. Bombs on board, Eaves decided. He had reached the post by this time and instructed the warden on duty to send a 'crashed aircraft' report to Control, and then he telephoned the fire brigade. With two other wardens he set out for the scene of the crash, all taking spades with them in case there was a German airman in the machine who might prove obstreperous.

But when they reached the crater there was nothing much to see: a shallow bowl of spilled earth, a few bits of wreckage, three long curious bits of metal, but no Germans. It was a stretch of open field so there were no civilian casualties.

Eaves was puzzled. He phoned the Home Guard and told them to look out, for a German pilot and his crew must be wandering around somewhere. Then he went back to the ARP post, peering suspiciously at passing pedestrians en route in case they should be Germans in disguise. But once he was back at the post, real trouble began. He wrote later:

'More and more of these 'crashed aircraft' came over, and it began to dawn on our feeble intelligence that we were faced with something entirely new. I called out every available man and woman and settled down to deal with the new menace. We made a hurried search at the post for information about these things and any instructions, but couldn't find much of value. True, we had a few meagre details but very little. All the time these instruments of destruction were skidding across the sky and coming down and then blowing up. The mid-day paper then told us what it was. Incidentally, the speed is announced as 200 miles per hour. What rot. At least 400 miles per hour would be nearer. It was a blow when the alert was still on at 6.30 a.m. but I had to go off to work, and so left fresh wardens to deal with the remainder of the raid.

This is something we definitely hadn't bargained for, but no doubt our defences will soon find the answer.

P.S. I have forgotten all about our invasion of France.

When Eaves first realised that Hitler's secret weapon had begun to hit London at last, he was alarmed. 'I don't mind admitting that for a moment my knees shook and I was scared stiff,' he said.

But in a way, he was relieved, and so were most other Londoners when they realised that this asthmatic crate eructating across the sky was the devastating weapon that would bring them to their knees. At first, that is. There were jokes on the radio about them and ruder ones in the pubs. The newspapers first of all called them Robot Bombs, then The Robots and then Doodlebugs, and finally settled for the German name, V1. Ruder citizens called them the Farting Furies.

At this time most of them were fired on London from launching sites hidden in the ground in the Pas de Calais in Northern France, and as they trundled across Kent and Sussex towards the capital (the route became known as Bomb Alley) RAF fighter planes and anti-aircraft guns did their best to explode them in the air. Their success in doing so was not spectacular, and the bulk of them got through. And yes, they were exciting at first, even though they kept on coming through the day and the night.

Today I have really seen one [wrote Vere Hodgson on 7 July 1944]. It was in this wise. As I got the meat at the butcher's the alert went. I walked back to the flat, deposited my goods, and, as I could hear nothing, I walked down to the Sanctuary [the social centre where she worked]. Half-way down the road I heard a thrum-thrum but as it was a long way off I didn't pay much attention. However, a platinum blonde on the other side of the road lifted her head from reading a letter and called out to me: 'Can you see it?' I said: 'No,' so she said: 'Come over here.' I crossed and sure enough right over our heads was a horrible black thing. It seemed three inches over our heads. It gave me quite a turn. The platinum blonde pursued her way unperturbed, still reading her letter.

But after ten days of almost continual alerts and the strain of keeping an ear cocked for a strange sound in the sky, the nerves of most Londoners changed for the worse. Those who could afford it started to leave London again for the West Country, as they had done during the blitz. Those who stayed behind began flocking to the Underground shelters. Conditions down there were better this time: small cubicles had been rigged up, and playrooms for children, as well as regular canteens with tea and hot food.

Life is one long air raid [wrote Vere Hodgson]. Things go bump in the night and frequently for most of the day. I sleep on the ground floor of the office now. The doodlebugs keep coming and one listens fascinated as they pass over one's roof, praying that they will go on but feeling a wretched cad because you know that means they will explode on someone else. No sleep at all. As a result, I feel pretty cheap today.

She set down a list of buildings which had been hit by the Vis. The Regent Palace Hotel, in Piccadilly Circus. Selfridges, in Oxford Street. Barker's stores in Kensington. And innumerable places in the East End, where, as usual, most of the Vis had been crashing down.

A Canadian soldier came in the other day [Vere Hodgson went on]. He saw a bad one last week. A doodlebug came down just beside Adastral House [the Air Ministry] in Aldwych. As he turned the corner, the Canadian saw it come down and half a dozen WAAFs [Women's Air Force Auxiliaries] who had been working on the top floor and had put their heads out of the windows to see the beastly thing had been drawn out by the blast, and bodies flew through the air. They were killed on the pavement, whereas if they had thrown themselves on the floor they would have been all right. Those who stayed inside were unhurt.

It was summer and examination time in London's schools.

I feel so awfully sorry and sad for children having to take their exams in these conditions, sitting in air-raid shelters all night and unable to concentrate the night before they take their papers. Poor kids. Rotten.

The atmosphere of London had changed now. The excitement over D-Day had disappeared, and when people talked about the operations in France it was to say: 'Why the hell doesn't Monty get on with it? What's he waiting for?'

British troops under Montgomery were being held up on the left flank of the invasion, and did not seem to be able to break the German lines defending the Pas de Calais. And the Pas de Calais was where every Londoner wanted the Allies to be, so that the launching pads of the Vis could be captured and destroyed.

Theatres stayed open, though the placard with ALERT on it was now permanently placed on the stage. The chorus line at the Windmill Theatre still went through their indefatigable routines and the nudes still posed with what imperturbability they could muster; and the customers still thought they were marvellous. Even some of the Americans. A USAAF pilot named Major Carl Greenstein came down to London on leave with pilot, co-pilot and the rest of his crew about this time and they went through the whole routine of buzz bombs (which really shook them), Piccadilly Commandos ('dogs'), back-street Soho Clubs (where the hooch set them vomiting before they could get their hands on the hostesses), but it was the Windmill show which stayed in their memories. 'The girls were real pretty – *all* of them,' Greenstein remembered.

But for the Londoners who lived and worked in the great capital the time was one of irritability, terrible tiredness, and great apprehension. There was very little of the camaraderie of the blitz around now. People snapped at each other and jumped queues or jostled each other in the streets. They were always staring up at the skies and flinching at odd noises, and visitors noticed that a great many of them could be seen talking to themselves as they walked along the streets.

Everyone had one great fear: that one of the monsters from the sky would come down and kill them now, just when the end of the war was in sight. It was a fate too awful to contemplate, but contemplate it they did. They were all exhausted by it.

3

On 19 June 1944, Mrs Sally Thomas was charged at Bow Street Magistrates' Court in London with 'receiving clothing coupons, petrol coupons, cigarettes, liquor and other uncustomed goods, knowing them to be stolen'.

Joey had somehow got out of the military prison to which he had been consigned and come back to London. He had tried to move back into his old apartment and take over his old protégée, but had been dissuaded by Sally's current boy friend, a supply sergeant in the US Army. He had retired to nurse his wounds and his resentment, and an anonymous 'tip' to the police had followed. They had raided the flat in Lexham Gardens and taken Sally into custody after finding a stock of goods from the US Army PX.

The probation officer read out Sally's history, and the old story of the neglected children and the miscarriage and the bombing and the 'temptations of London for a young and pretty girl' were rigmaroled once more for the benefit of the magistrates. But Sally Thomas knew that she hadn't a chance. She had been dressed in her smartest clothes when the policemen took her in, and she had the look of possessing all the things that were now beyond the reach of ordinary drab, depressed Londoners: lipstick, nylon stockings, expensive shoes and an elaborate hair style.

The magistrate talked about putting a stop to 'illicit activities' and 'immoral goings-on, particularly with foreign soldiers' that were turning London into a 'city of shame'. It was all good headline stuff, and Sally knew she was for it.

There was a slight rustle of applause from people in the court when she was sentenced to twelve months' imprisonment.

But in a way, she was lucky. The next day the apartment in

Lexham Gardens was hit by a flying bomb. Elizabeth Marina Jones, who was also living at Lexham Gardens, had been doing her strip-tease act at a club in Carnaby Street when the raid happened, but now she decided that London was becoming too hot for her. She left to go home to Neath, South Wales, taking with her the stock of canned goods, cigarettes and nylons that were her personal trophies from her stay in London. She was luckier than Sally Thomas. When Welsh police asked her how she had got them, she told them they were gifts from 'my friends in the US Army' and they left it at that.

She stayed in Wales for six weeks, and then boredom drove her back to the big city. This time it would be she who would end up in court, but on much graver charges than living on the favours of US troops.

4

For the Ketley family in their home on the edge of the East End of London the V1s came as a complete surprise. They were all in the Morrison shelter in their living room one night when Donald's mother woke them and said something strange had happened. Mr Ketley told his wife she had been having a nightmare, but then, suddenly, they heard an aeroplane pass low over the house and its engine suddenly stopped. Shortly afterwards came the explosion.

The Ketleys found the V1s much harder to bear than the blitz because they never knew what they were going to do.

You would be lying there at night and hear the characteristic throbbing of the engine [Donald recalls]. If the thing stopped then the thing might come down right then and there, or it might glide down to some place a mile away. I remember one whose engine cut out right over our house – we could hear it gliding – a strange noise almost like the beating of a large bird's wings. We lay rigid, hardly breathing, but it continued to glide and perhaps a minute later we heard the muffled boom as it hit the ground .

During the daytime, unless the cloud ceiling was very low, you could see the bombs coming over Chadwell Heath. Donald recalled:

People ignored them, unless they were coming directly towards them. We were at a pub one evening which was next to a transit camp for US troops. Now and then a V1 would come over a mile or so to the north or south. When this happened, the troops, who had just arrived from the US, would make a wild dash into the shelters across the street. Everybody else thought this was hilarious.

His father was working, by this time, in the Royal Victoria Docks in East London, and this was a prime target for the new weapons because it was from the Pool of London that most of the supplies for the armies in France were now being shipped. The docks were crammed with shipping. So far as the official statements went, the secret weapon was an instrument of terror only, sent over simply to drive Londoners to distraction while killing as many of them as possible. But though a large number of them continued to land on the ordinary civilian centres of the capital,* the Germans were guiding many of them towards the docks and doing great damage there. In a space of four weeks no less than 139 V1s landed in the Royal Docks Group target zone. A sharpshooter could hardly have asked for a better score.

From his office window, Mr Ketley could look down on a railway yard that was normally full of munitions trains. He worked constantly with one ear cocked for V1s. On one occasion he heard one and stepped out of the office to see it coming right towards him. He began running towards the shelter, which was in the basement of a warehouse, with a feeling that the flying bomb was chasing him.

He made it just as the V1 exploded but fell down the stairs, breaking his ankle. The V1 hit a munitions train but, miraculously, only struck the last few cars which contained not explosives but food. However, they were aflame and the fire was creeping along the carriages towards the shells and explosives when a dock policeman dashed out and uncoupled them, and the rest of the train drew away to safety.

Several ships were sunk in those summer weeks of the flying bombs. In September came the rockets. One of the first homed in on the Royal Group of docks and couldn't have picked out a more useful target to hit. It smashed down on the bascule bridge which connected East Ham and Canning Town with North Woolwich.

* Just as RAF and USAAF bombs were pattern-bombing workers' houses in the great German cities.

There were few casualties because there were few people and houses around, but the destruction of the bridge locked inside the docks a vast number of ships loaded with heavy equipment for Normandy.

For the next forty-eight hours, while rockets continued to come down, Royal Engineers struggled with the tangled mass of steel which clogged up the passageway leading from the docks to the river and the sea. They worked with oxy-acetylene cutters throughout the night to chop up the clutter of steel and drag it clear of the channel, while the loaded convoy fussed to get out and the commanders in France screamed for their supplies. Three days later they were on their way.

Charles Snow hadn't minded the V1s ('You could always dive beneath a table or something like that') but he loathed the rockets which began to descend in the autumn of 1944. Donald Ketley agreed with him. Snow said:

> The rockets frightened me much more than the others. Quite unrealistically, in fact. As you know, if one had been hit by a rocket one wouldn't have known anything about it. Most people took them more calmly than I did. This was purely subjective. They hadn't a big enough warhead to be really dangerous, but somehow the idea that fate was above one without one knowing anything about it – that I found disturbing.

Donald Ketley had long since lost the feeling that the war was nothing but a great lark, but it was only when the rockets began coming over that he became aware of the risk and possibility of death.

> Before that, I always felt that one could get into a shelter when a raid started or a V1 was coming, and the chances of getting killed were small; in fact, non-existent from a boy's point of view. With the V2s there was no question of getting into a shelter. If they were near enough you could hear them enter the upper atmosphere but that was probably no more than a few seconds before they hit the ground. So all you could do was attempt to ignore them. Probably the worst damage to our house was done by a V2 which hit the railway near Chadwell

Heath station one Saturday morning. Fortunately the rocket fell behind an embankment. I was in the kitchen facing the railway. The embankment caused the blast to be diverted upwards so that only the upper part of the house was damaged, except for the wall between the kitchen and the living room, which cracked right through (in those days they made internal walls of brick rather than cardboard). It was the only structural damage the house ever suffered. Fortunately for me the kitchen windows held – they were covered with this glued-on net which was enormously effective.

Mr Ketley had a favourite rocket story. He passed a house one morning on the way to work where a V2 had just landed. The warhead had not exploded and the thing had buried itself upright in the garden. The man of the house was standing, open-mouthed, in his doorway staring in amazement at this enormous, gleaming tower which had suddenly appeared in his yard.

But there was another rocket story that was not so pleasant. One evening he ran to try and catch a bus and just missed it as it departed for the docks. He took the next one that came along, and, a mile on the way, was halted by a pile-up of traffic. A V2 had dropped beside the road and among other things had completely destroyed the bus he had just missed taking.

The Ketleys found the V2s eerie and unsettling and depressing. Like all other Londoners, his parents were tired out, sick of the war, wondering whether it would ever end, growing old with worry and the exhausting round of everyday wartime living.

'Do you realise,' said Mrs Ketley, one day, 'that our Donald is thirteen years old and he's never flown a kite.'

It was true. In their part of London, at least, kite-flying was prohibited as part of the defence regulations.

One Sunday that autumn the family went walking up onto the plateau above Chigwell and looked back upon the great black-and-grey mass that was London, with the silver thread of the river Thames winding in between. It was a quiet, still day. It was also a day when the Germans were beefing up their rocket attacks upon the capital, and the Ketleys must have heard more than twenty as they landed with puffs of smoke and flame all over the landscape. Donald remembers:

'You could hear the explosions, now close, now far, now

somewhere in between, like muffled drums. Before, one had felt always like a participant in a battle, but the lack of anti-aircraft fire or the sight of fighter planes during the V2 period gave them an air of invincibility. People became more on edge, more irritable than they had been before – in part this was because the war had been going on so long, but I think it was also in the nature of the V2s. They were cosmic terrors.

Mr Ketley held his son and his wife by the hand as they looked down on the great grey field before them and listened to the muffled drums.

'You know,' said Mr Ketley, at last, 'if the Germans had had those things in 1940, I think we might have cracked.'

5

Slowly, but oh so slowly, the war was being won. Paris was liberated. The French without much hesitation acclaimed General Charles de Gaulle as their leader, and America and Britain had no option but to accept him as such. Past quarrels were pushed under the diplomatic carpet; but they were not forgotten, and, so far as Charles de Gaulle was concerned, they were not forgiven.

The Russians slogged on into Poland and into the Balkans. The British at last captured the V1 sites in the Pas de Calais area, but both flying bombs and rockets kept on coming over from Holland and from inside Germany. There was to be no respite yet for the people of London. At the height of the summer they had been dying at the rate of 130 a day, and 168,000 of their houses were being damaged by the Nazi terror weapons. Now the slaughter began to slacken off but by night and day the ugly menaces still came trundling over London or swooping out of the sky, and though the bangs were less frequent life for everyone in London was no less fraught.

But yes, the war was ending. In September the Government announced that the Home Guard would stand down. There was a final parade in Hyde Park at which King George the Sixth took the salute, and then the part-time soldiers sadly put away their rifles, looked sentimentally at the broom-handles and muskets with which they had prepared to defend the island kingdom in 1940, and went back to their offices and factories. For many of them, things would never be quite the same again.

That autumn, too, the black-out was officially changed to a dim-out. The lights did not immediately spring up and bathe the great city in midnight sunshine. But it meant that black-out curtains did not have to be pinned up so rigidly in the evenings, and that some measure of pale illumination could be thrown onto the drab broken buildings and chipped pavements of London. Soldiers on leave and in search of fun in the West End could now actually see the painted faces of the Piccadilly Commandos without shining a torch on them. It did not seem to cause any slackening in the pairings off.

Not everybody welcomed the end of the black-out, surprisingly enough. Alice McLean, a young member of the ATS (the women's branch of the Army) heard nothing but grumbles at her depot in Kensington. On 8 November 1944 she wrote:

Lighting conditions along Knightsbridge and Kensington Road are such that the Albert Hall is now surrounded by light after being surrounded by gloom for all these years. The stretch of pavement from the corner to the door of our billet is shining bright and completely deserted. Ever since the ATS descended upon this quiet Kensington backwater at the beginning of the war countless swains of all nationalities have bidden a fond farewell to their khaki-clad Juliets along this strip of pavement. Now the lights have gone up along this paradise, and the couples will be forced to seek some less public rendezvous for their goodnight kisses. Among many of the girls in my unit the lifting of the black-out at this particular spot is most unpopular, and they say so with feeling.

18

THE END?

General de Gaulle had forecast that the war would be over by Christmas, but of course it was not. Instead, the Germans counter-attacked in the Ardennes and the Battle of the Bulge began.

No one in London was particularly surprised that the war dragged on. It had lasted so long now that they were finding it impossible to imagine an existence without it. Christmas 1944 was marked by a killing cold which covered the streets with frozen snow and numbed the spirit. Disillusionment and hopelessness were spectres at Christmas dinner all over the capital, and though most households managed to get hold of some sort of chicken or rabbit for the feast there wasn't much else to go with it. The Christmas extras announced by the Ministry of Food were confined to an extra half a pound of margarine and half a pound of sugar. No tinned fruits. No reduction of points on the purchase of the rarer foods. No oranges. No lemons. And many pubs, which had taken to closing early anyway because of lack of booze, used Christmas as an excuse to close all day.

There was no doubt that this was the most miserable Christmas of the war. All the fine hopes of the summer, when the Allied armies had landed in London, had faded. And with them, the spirit seemed suddenly to go out of Londoners. Five years of lowering diet, bombing, defeats and humiliations, conscription, the increasing regimentation and dim degradation of life in a great city in wartime seemed to have sapped the strength and optimism of seven million Cockneys.

One reporter for Mass-Observation reported on 22 December, 1944:

My landlady said, 'I've never heard as much grumbling as I've heard this year.' Her husband: 'You can't wonder at it. This is the worst Christmas we've had. I think so many people were counting on the war being over that it's fallen flat now. People are sick of the war. You can stand it so long but there comes a time when you can't stand any more.'

They were not just sick of the war, they were sick of everyone connected with it, and that included Winston Churchill. It was a time when all over the country there were signs of discontent with the Government in power and a surging feeling that it must be changed.

'No one should have been surprised about that,' Robert Boothby said. 'These were the same old MPs who had been elected before the war began. Every six months from the date when Parliament should have been prorogued they had voted themselves extensions of power. They may have chosen to forget themselves that they were the same squalid lot who had appeased with Chamberlain and fawned before Hitler, but the people hadn't. Now that the war was coming to an end, they wanted them out.'

As for Churchill, it was not that he was tarred with the same brush. His fighting spirit was still admired everywhere. But so far as the people were concerned, he was an old Tory taskmaster who could lead them in war but never learn the civilised ways of the kind of peace of which they were dreaming. They looked forward to a world where there would be no more war, no more unemployment, no more exploitation, to what they were increasingly calling the welfare state. They sensed that Churchill was looking not forward but backward to the kind of privileged world he had known all his life. They resented it when he warned that a welfare state could not just be created; that it must be worked for and paid for.

Just before Christmas the Labour Party held its annual conference and its leaders, Attlee, Bevin, Morrison (all members of Churchill's Coalition Cabinet), found themselves harried by the rank-and-file and told to get ready for the political battle to come. The sooner the Coalition was ended and a general election called the better, in the opinion of the ordinary members of the Party. Attlee stiffly told them that there must be no thought of a break in the Coalition until the war was well and truly won.

The Tories were restive too, and they did not have the same compunction about breaking up the Coalition. Already the Party managers were working on a plan for an election the moment the war with Germany was over. They would then ride to victory on the shoulders of Winston Churchill, the man who had won the war. Even the worst of the appeasers hoped to get back into Parliament so long as they could hold on to Winston's coat tails.

If the Tory managers had only read the reports that were flowing into Mass-Observation at this time, they might have realised that it was not going to be quite that simple. The first trickles were already visible of the anti-Tory tide that would soon engulf even Winston Churchill.

The people were determined on a change in the coming days of peace.

19

PERMISSION TO GRUMBLE

I

For London the first few weeks of 1945 were hard to bear. It was, as Vere Hodgson put it, 'thunderingly cold' and since gas and electricity were in desperately short supply there was little they could do to get the ache out of their bones. Every day over the radio and in the newspapers came the sounds and descriptions of new conquests and more Nazi retreats, but so long as a German remained with a gun in his hand, it seemed, the war in Europe would go on and London's own ordeal would continue. Vere Hodgson wrote:

> Just as all these wonderful sounds were coming over the air, behold I heard a rocket bomb drop in the distance. It was a long way away but it was there to remind us that there are still some very unpleasant things about and that THE WAR IS NOT OVER.

It was particularly hard for her, because her doughty and beloved Aunt Nell, who had stayed alive just to hear that the hated Hitler was beaten, was dying in hospital. She went to see her on 1 February and was allowed into the ward.

> She looked very, very ill and grey. They said she was in great pain. I kissed her and she opened her eyes. I told her that the Russian Army was rushing for Berlin, and the old spirit flashed out in her joy. But she was too tired to talk.

Two weeks later she was dead, and Vere Hodgson wept. On 18 February she wrote:

> We are pushing the Germans from our side, and the Russians from the other. It is like a giant nut-cracker. But it is all a long time and I had prayed earnestly that dear Auntie would survive to the Peace. We had planned such a party. She and I. We were going to put on our best frocks and drink the health of England

and Mr Churchill in great style. But now that little party will never take place.

While they waited for peace to come, small achievements had to make life bearable. An issue of oranges helped to appease the desperate need for sweetness and change in the stodgy diet.

Other than the war news, which many a Londoner only glanced at nowadays, the big story was a murder trial. A girl from South Wales had come up to London to dodge the call-up and had joined the Piccadilly Commandos in search of easy money and a good time. She had picked up an American GI deserter and they had carried out a series of petty robberies and frauds culminating in the murder of a taxi driver for the few pounds in his wallet. Sally Thomas shivered as she read reports of the trial. For the girl was Marina Jones, with whom she had shared a flat in Lexham Gardens, before they sent her off to jail. *Well*, she told herself wryly, *at least you haven't murdered anyone.**

The case produced a rash of articles about war-time morals, good-time girls, the rise in illegitimate births and venereal disease. One school headmistress wrote in Mass-Observation giving details of 40 girls or boys at her school whose mothers were having affairs with soldiers or had had illegitimate children.

> I talked about it to our school nurse, [she wrote,] and she said: 'You're telling me! Every week we have a policeman searching our pre-natal records to see if they can discover who abandoned a newborn baby in a ditch or in a pond, or tried to dispose of the effects of an abortion.

But there was always one thing that was calculated to rouse Londoners from their gloom, and that was the weather. They had become more than ever conscious of it during the war, because when the moon was shining they could see in the black-out, when it was dry they didn't have to bother about the holes in their shoddy utility shoes and the patches in their raincoats, when it was warm they did not have to shiver because of lack of rationed

---

* Private Karl Gustav Hulten, 22, an American paratrooper of Boston, Mass. was found guilty of murder, sentenced to death and subsequently hanged. His girlfriend, Mrs Elizabeth Marina Jones, 18, was sentenced to life imprisonment.

coal, gas and electricity. All winter they had stumbled because clouds covered the moon, splashed through rain and suffered through spells of biting cold. But suddenly, as it can only in England, the weather changed and the mood with it.

There are many things to say, [reported Vere Hodgson on Palm Sunday, 25 March 1945.] First of all The Weather. It has been marvellous all week. Never can we remember such a March, and we shall PAY later on. Yesterday was the hottest day in London in March for half a century. The sun blazed down from a cloudless blue. I went out without a coat and even then was too warm. It was glorious. Now it has clouded over, but I do hope it won't affect the armies.

It did not. The stirring in Londoners' blood may have come not just from the weather but from a precognitive realisation that at long last the ordeal was coming to an end. On 25 March a rocket had dropped on what was described in an official British communiqué as 'waste ground in southern England.' The waste ground was, in fact, Hyde Park and the rocket hit just wide of Speakers' Corner and took down most of the remaining windows in the houses and hotels of Park Lane.

The following day a rocket demolished the Whitfield Tabernacle in Tottenham Court Road. No one realised it at the time, but it was, in fact, the last rocket (or bomb, for that matter) on London.

2

'NO BOMBS ... ain't it lovely?' reported Vere Hodgson on 11 April 1945.

The ordeal was over. There would be no more white nights of waiting for the cumulative swish of high explosive, the sudden cough of the engine of the jalopy in the sky, the whunk of a rocket hitting one's neighbour's house. But still how could anyone tell that it was over, that it wasn't just a lull, that Hitler didn't have another engine of terror waiting to strike?

Nevertheless, anyone walking the streets of the capital in those lightening spring days could almost feel the smile opening on the face of London.

'Well, what sort of a night did you have last night, Mrs Murgatroyd?'

'Slept like a log, love. And in my own bed too. It's hard to believe, ain't it? Haven't snuggled up to me old man in our own double bed since 1940, straight we haven't.'

'Hope you didn't get up to any mischief, Mrs Murgatroyd.'

'Why, Mr Brown! Didn't you know there was a war on?'

3

On 12 April 1945 President Franklin D. Roosevelt died, and no American can guess how broken-hearted the British were to hear the news. It is the voter in his own country who sees the politician in his own statesmen. Churchill was always a Tory to the British but they never thought of Roosevelt as a Democrat. He was a world statesman, a liberator, a man they had hoped would be in the forefront when they marched into the brave new postwar world. His death, before he could see the victory he had helped to organise, hurt them deeply.

'I don't think I have ever seen London quite so devastated by an event,' said Charles Snow. 'Even my old landlady was crying. The Underground was full of tearful faces – far more than if Winston had died, I'm sure.'

Vere Hodgson wrote:

It's a black day for all of us. What a shock it was when I hopped out of bed and found the *Daily Telegraph* all in black and the terrible announcement. Then I heard a bit of the wireless and really I shed tears, because it will make it harder for Mr Churchill. They got on so well and I am afraid Stalin is a hard nut to crack and a very different mentality. .... Anyway, thank you, Mr Roosevelt for all the help you gave us, and the way you helped us in those dark and lonely days of 1940.

The House of Commons adjourned for the day on 13 April, the first time it had ever adjourned over the death of a foreign statesman. All over London the people walked around as if they had suffered a death in the family.

As, they felt, they had.

4

So far as Londoners were concerned, 7 May 1945, was the messiest day of the Second World War. They knew that the war was over but nobody would make it official, and no one quite knew what to do.

From somewhere in their cellars most of the big stores had dug out a vast collection of the flags of all nations. The streets of the West End of London were suddenly alive with street traders selling paper hats and favours, and rattles and whistles of a kind which hadn't been seen since 1939. Everybody knew that Hitler and Goebbels were dead and, somewhere on Luneburg Heath, German generals had signed an armistice with General Montgomery. The scene was set for the signature of unconditional surrender at General Eisenhower's headquarters in Rheims.

But the English are a formal people. They do not like to celebrate something, even a victory, until it is official. And Peace was not official yet. There had been no Announcement.

VE DAY MAY BE TOMORROW the newspaper headlines said, but nobody could be certain.

So the crowds began converging on London in preparation for the end-of-war celebration and simply hung around.

An unexcited expectancy was the dominant mood, [a Mass-Observation survey reported,] coupled with the usual uncertainty and confusion. The knowledge that the dates, and perhaps also the length, of their VE holidays depended on the official announcement was probably most important of all in maintaining people's interest in the matter.* The official announcement was, after all, a technical matter. Everyone knew that the European war in actual practice was an affair of the past, and all that remained now was, it was hoped, the experiencing of some dramatic moment when the transition from official war to official peace might be felt and recognised.

That day people went to work uncertain whether the next day would be a holiday or not. Everyone was confused. The newspaper headlines continued to say GERMANY SURRENDERS but, as a bus conductress said, 'It's neither one thing nor the other, is it?'

The pubs were full and the pub-keepers suddenly seemed to have found extra supplies of drink from somewhere. But attempts

* The Government had promised to make the official end of the war with Germany a paid holiday.

to start mass celebrations were discouraged. A Cockney group who started to dance to the tune of *Knees Up Mother Brown* in Trafalgar Square were looked at as if they were dancing on a grave, and soon became self-conscious and stopped.

But next day it was official. 'The war is over,' announced Vere Hodgson. 'Churchill says so.'

That afternoon a vast river of Londoners flowed down the Strand and the Mall and through Trafalgar Square into Whitehall, where it had been announced that the Prime Minister would speak. At 3 p.m. the great bell of Big Ben struck and over loudspeakers came a voice to tell them that Churchill was coming.

He came out alone onto a balcony of the Ministry of Works and looked down upon the pulsating sea of people below him. A great cheer rose up, and then a sudden and heart-aching silence. There had been no silence quite like it for more than five years. Vere Hodgson remembered:

> People hung onto every word he said. When he told them that as from midnight hostilities would cease, there were loud cheers and a waving of hats and flags; and then a louder cheer when he said: 'The German war is therefore at an end.' People began to cry and laugh and cheer at the same time. Mention of Eisenhower's name and 'our Russian comrades' started more clapping. He ended his speech with 'Advance Britannia,' and the buglers of the Scots Guards sounded the ceremonial cease fire. Then the band struck up the National Anthem and looking round I saw everyone, young and old, civilians and soldiers, singing with such reverence that the anthem sounded like a sacred hymn.

5

There were, of course, the wildest kind of celebrations all over London. Now, when people danced *Knees Up Mother Brown* and *The Lambeth Walk* in the streets, everybody joined in. A British sailor, an American GI and a Pole did a striptease in Piccadilly Circus. A young blonde did likewise in the fountains of Trafalgar Square, and was much more popular. A US paratrooper, his face covered with lipstick, passed along Oxford Street thrusting his cheek towards every passing pretty girl and saying: 'Please, add to my collection.'

They did. Nobody said no to anybody in London on 8 May 1945.

But there were many who eschewed the crowds and tried to be on their own with their families. Young John Harriman had gone off to school to take part in the celebrations, but Bill and Eileen stayed at home and listened to Winston Churchill on the radio.

'Thank God it's all over, Bill,' Eileen said. They looked at the picture of their daughter, Linda, on the mantel-shelf, and she began to cry.

Henry 'Chips' Channon was where everyone expected him to be on such an auspicious day: at the Ritz Hotel. It was 'beflagged and decorated: everyone kissed me, Mrs Keppel, the Duchess of Rutland and Violet Trefusis all seized me alternatively.'

George Hitchin was happily in bed with Arlene, his new wife, for 8 May was the day chosen, quite fortuitously, by London bus drivers to go on strike for better pay and working hours.

Sally Thomas was also in bed, fast asleep, in her new flat in Shepherd's Market; she would need all the rest she could get, for VE Day was going to prove a tiring day for members of her profession. Still, as she often told herself these days, it was better than jail.

6

On VE night the Ketley family left their home at Chadwell Heath and walked through the fields to a pub at Chigwell. Mr and Mrs Ketley went inside to get their drinks, leaving young Donald in the garden. He remembers it so well. There were a lot of people in the pub, a beautiful old hostelry dating back to Charles I. Donald recalls:

It was not a rejoicing crowd. Rather one had the sense of people relaxing, getting their breath back after having run a long, long way. Two RAF trucks drove into the parking lot and disgorged a group of aircrew and WAAFs who laughed and horsed around as they went into the pub. I watched them and felt very happy. Towards the end of the war, the thing that had really bothered me was that I'd get killed before I'd ever had a girl. Like everybody else that night, I could think about the normal pleasures of life again.

Below him, in a pattern of shimmering light that was suddenly brighter than the stars above, a London newly released from the black-out lay before him. It glowed and sparkled. He stared at it, fascinated. For the first time in his life, he realised that London in peacetime was a City of Light.

And so it all ends, [wrote Vere Hodgson,] and the long nightmare I have recorded in these pages is over. Our great city is sadly broken and her wounds are dire, but she lives. All we can say is THANK GOD, and I can get along to St Paul's or Westminster Abbey or somewhere like that and tell him so. I shall go and represent Auntie Nell who, I know, would have gone to one of them, and give thanks for all the family for this great deliverance. As Mr Hillyard says, we have been spared the worst in this country. We have not had to take part in a Resistance Movement and see German soldiers marching through our streets. We have not starved. We have not been herded into gas ovens. We have seen our beloved London stand up and take it.

She left a space in her diary, and then she wrote:

I see that Parliament's first act after the end of the war in Europe has been to rescind the Bill making it a punishable offence to spread gloom and despondency. So great was our danger in certain years that we were forbidden to look miserable. Now we can be as unhappy as we please. Freedom is returning.

EPILOGUE

On 5 July 1945 the British public went to the polls in the first general election in Britain for ten years. The Tories were convinced that they would ride to victory in the slipstream of Winston Churchill's glory. Even the Labour Party leaders did not think they had any hope of winning in face of Churchill's overwhelming prestige.

Neither side, in fact, had any inkling of the way the minds of the mass of the British people were turning.* They were looking forward to a brave new world of peace and light in which an old belligerent like Winston Churchill could not, they considered, play any part. He was all right for war, but they had no place for him in the peace they envisioned. So he was dismissed. (Unfortunately, they could not dismiss Joseph Stalin at the same time.)

To the amazement of both parties, Labour was voted into power by 393 seats to the Tories' 213. Clement Attlee took Churchill's place at the head of the British Government and went to Potsdam to deal with Stalin and Truman in the first great conference of the post-war world. A new era had begun. It would not be as pink and warm and promising as British voters hoped.

Winston Churchill, the old warrior, retired to lick his wounds. But when his friends suggested that he was a victim of base ingratitude, he shook his head. He would not have such a charge levelled against his beloved fellow-Britons. Ingratitude?

'Oh, no,' he said, 'I wouldn't call it that. They have had a very hard time.'

* Though there were clear indications. Mass-Observation reports, for instance, clearly showed the trend away from Churchill and the Tories.

APPENDIX

ABOUT MASS-OBSERVATION

During the 1930s I made several scientific expeditions on behalf of the British Museum, the Royal Society, the Royal Geographical Society and other learned bodies – to the Arctic and St Kilda, Borneo and the Western Pacific. During two years in the New Hebrides, Melanesia, I had occasion to live among people who were still eating each other. The Big Nambas of Malekula proved to be as pleasant as, and no more difficult to live with than the English, Irish and Welsh of whom I had previous experience. And it was slowly borne in upon me that while anthropologists were being generously financed to go all over the world studying so-called primitive peoples, no one at that time was making comparable studies of ourselves.

When the expedition was over, therefore, I determined to return to study the cannibals of Britain. This led me, more or less by chance, to a cotton town, Bolton in Lancashire, where with the help of other interested volunteers (including Woodrow Wyatt, Humphrey Spender, John Sommerfield, Bill Naughton, Julian Trevelyan, William Coldstream, William Empson, Tom Driberg), methods of studying this complex society were devised and developed along somewhat original lines.

Quite separately, the poet Charles Madge – then a *Daily Mirror* reporter, now Professor of Sociology at Birmingham University – was approaching the same situation by a rather more literary method, aided by a lively group of friends, including the late Humphrey Jennings and Stuart Legge as documentary film makers; David Gascoyne, Ruthven Todd and Charles's wife Kathleen as poets. From the industrial north, a more objective-aimed approach; from London in the south, a literary and documentary one, including the important idea of recruiting a nation-wide panel to report upon their own everyday lives and all that went on around them. We joined forces, north and south, as Mass-Observation.

This double-pronged attack developed into an affair of national proportions. Mass-Observation became famous, perhaps the first of the techniques directly to study ordinary behaviour and (among other things) public opinion which attracted general interest. Our 1939 Penguin Special *Britain* confirmed this effect.

Unfortunately, the Second World War stopped the continuing progress of our big project in Bolton ('Worktown'). On the other hand, the Panel of Voluntary Mass-Observers, as well as the techniques for full-time investigation which we had considerably refined, proved of high value to governmental and other bodies, when deployed upon the multiple problems of Britain at war. At this stage, Charles Madge's interests took him elsewhere. I continued to run the organisation until I went into the Army late in 1942 when others carried on until I returned in 1946. As I then decided to live in South-East Asia, M-O became a Limited Liability Company in 1949.

All the material collected from 1937–49 was passed to me under a 1949 agreement. It is presently on loan to the University of Sussex with a view to organising it as a significant archive of the '30s and '40s. The Vice-Chancellor, Professor Asa Briggs, is keenly encouraging this enterprise. Leonard Mosley is one of several far-seeing writers who have recently made use of the material for writing about the past. Each of them has found it contains information and insights for this period not available anywhere else in Britain, and perhaps anywhere else in the world? Mr Mosley has particularly appreciated its value, as shown in his generous foreword.

After more than two decades in South-East Asia it is strange to return with a fresh eye to this old story. It is easier, also, with this far perspective, to try and assess the M-O achievement of those distant days. By looking, listening, observing, *without asking questions*, we set out to revolutionise sociology and even – in my youthfully naïve view – to seek some sort of new philosophy based on a better understanding of human relationships in modern society. In our 1938 book *First Year's Work by M-O* I put it like this:

> Tom Harrisson believes that Mass–Observation, by laying open to doubt all existing philosophies of life as possibly incomplete, yet by refusing to neglect the significance of any of them, may make a new synthesis. This may lead to something less fierce, more understanding and permanent, than the present miserable conflicts of dogmatic faiths in race, politics, religion. The whole study should cause us to reassess our inflated opinions of our progress and culture, altering our judgements on others accordingly. We must find the range of mass agreement and variation, the LCM and HCF of man, between which lies his practical potentialities.

Of course, the effort really changed nothing, either in society or sociology! If anything, both are in worse shape now than they were 33 years ago. In fact, it is a real shock, after living in Borneo so long, to find that many of the things that seemed to us 'wrong' in society in the thirties are equally if not more wrong in the seventies. It is also surprising to find that almost no research thinking is being done along these lines. Superficial devices for measuring public opinion and an obsession with statistical method for social research of basic problems dominate all else. These in effect help top people to evade and *certainly not to face* the breakdown in communications within democratic societies here and all over the world.

So, not too ashamed of past naïvety and weathered with malarial age, at least one can believe that it was worth doing that work those years ago, if it can prove helpful for others now and in the future – seeking accurately to reflect the past and get below the surface of political speech or newspaper column. At the same time, it remains disturbingly in mind that what we rashly set out to try and do with M-O as a research *method* and tool in 1937 may even now be worth up-dating and reviving presently, to fill the continuing aching voids of social ignorance today.

M-O Archive,   Tom Harrisson
c/o Vice-Chancellor,   July 1970
University of Sussex

INDEX

absenteeism, 170
AFS (Auxiliary Fire Service), 12, 55, 150
air-borne troops, 52, 345, 346, 348
Aircraft Production, Ministry of, 62
airfields, bombed, 90–1
air-raid shelters: in streets, 10, 136; none in West Ham, 128; different types of, 135–6, 250; percentage of people spending night in, 136, 170; *see also* underground railways
air-raid sirens (3 and 4 Sept. 1939), 17–18
air-raid wardens, 12, 55, 357–8; in West Ham, 128–9
air raids: (24–5 June 1940), 69–72; (7 Sept. 1940), 106–22; (winter 1940–41), 122–98; (29 Dec. 1940), 199–203; (10–11 May 1941), 227–9; 'scalded cat', 296–7, 330, 332–3
'alarm and despondency', 53, 54, 378
Aldwych Underground station, entertainments in, 167
Alexander, A. V., First Lord of the Admiralty, 216, 275
Alexander, General Sir Harold, 260, 352
Algiers, de Gaulle's government in, 338, 355
ambulance stations, 12
ambulance workers, 149, 150; *see*

also 'Bone, Mrs'
Amery, Leopold, MP, 3, 36, 37–8
Anderson, Sir John, Home Secretary, 81–2, 84
Anderson air-raid shelters, 135–6, 196, 197
anti-aircraft guns, 107, 115, 171; casualties from fire of, 143n, 171, 205, 297, 330; radar for, 180; noise of, 196, 310, 330; women with, 278
Arandora Star, S.S., sunk with internees aboard, 80n
Ardennes, German counter-attack in, 368
ARP (Air-Raid Precautions), 12, 81, 145, 150, 162
Asquith, Lady, 174
Atlee, Clement, leader of Labour Party, 37, 40, 80; deputy Prime Minister, 252, 369; Prime Minister (1945), 379
atom bomb, 63, 308
ATS (Auxiliary Territorial Service), 11, 277, 290, 367
Auchinleck, General Claud, C.-in-C., Middle East, 252, 253, 260

bacon: loss of ships loaded with, 207n; queuing for, 239
Balfour, Harold, Minister for Air, 172
Balham Underground station, bombed and flooded, 166
barrage balloons, 9–10, 75

385

Hulten, Private K. G., of Boston, Mass., sentenced for murder, 372n
Hungerford Bridge, unexploded landmine on, 165
Hurricane aeroplanes, 74, 90, 105, 107
Hyde Park: anti-aircraft guns in, 330; Speakers' Corner in, 333; V2 falls in, 373

illegitimate births, 372
Imperial Defence Committee, on prospects of air raids, 12
incendiary bombs, on the City (29 Dec. 1940), 199–201
influenza, 323
Information, Ministry of, 132, 134, 139
internment under Regulation 18b, 58–9, 61–9, 79–80
invasion of England: Hitler's plans for, 90, 93; said to be imminent, 104, 105; directions to public about, 112–13; Churchill on, 133, 204
invasion of Europe, see second front, D-Day
Ireland, 237, 327
Isle of Man, internees in, 80n
Italy, 183, 184, 307

Jackson, F. W., deputy chief of London Fire Service, 100–101
'James, Dolly': internment of, 61–68, 69; and Mosley, 319–20; in six weeks before D-Day, 345–8
Japan, 233
Jews, 56–7, 60
Jones, Elizabeth Marina, strip-tease actress, 292, 362; sentenced for murder, 372

Keitel, General, 79

Kennedy, Joseph P., US Ambassador, 35, 77
Kent, Duke and Duchess of, 174, 184
Ketley family, Chadwell Heath: (on 3 Sept. 1939), 21–2; (on 7 Sept. 1940), 112–15; (during winter 1940–41), 195; (in 1942), 249–51; in 'scalded cat' air raids, 296; and V1s and V2s, 362, 364–5; at end of war, 377–8
Keyes, Admiral Sir Roger, MP, in debate on Norway (1940), 36–7
King, Admiral, USN, 263
Kirkwood, David, MP, 357
kite-flying, forbidden, 365
Kursk salient, decisive battle of (1943), 308, 309, 310

Labour Party, returned to power (1945), 379
Labour Party Conference (Dec. 1944), 369
Lacey, Sergeant-Pilot J. H. ('Ginger'), shoots down bomber over Westminster, 134n, 195
Lambeth, bombed, 205
Lancaster bomber, on show in Trafalgar Square, 300–301
landmines, 158–65, 197
Langham Hotel, bombed, 158
Lease-Lend, 231
lemons, 301, 333
Lewisham, school bombed at, 296
Libya, 218, 292
Limehouse Causeway, 1, 18
Lindemann, Prof. F. M. (Lord Cherwell), 243, 288; and radar, 180–3; and bombing of Germany, 245–9
Lisbon, spy in, 344–5
Local Defence Volunteers, 55; see further Home Guard

'London can take it', 170

MacArthur, General, 263
McLean, Alice, of ATS, on end of black-out, 367
Madagascar, taken over by British from Vichy control, 286
magnetic mines, 158
Maillaud, Pierre, of French news-agency in London, 45, 49; and de Gaulle, 49, 50
Maisky, Ivan, Russian Ambas-sador, 244
Manchester, bombed, 141
Manier, Stephan, Free French officer, dies in British prison, 318
Marble Arch Underground sta-tion, bombed, 169–70, 266
Margate, snap poll on Hitler's intentions taken at (1939), 8–9
Margesson, David, MP, Govern-ment Whip (1939), 16–17
Marshall, General George (US), 245, 248, 263
Marylebone, bombed, 148
Mass-Observation, xii, 311, 381–383; on air raids, 69–72, 73–4, 122–6; with Cockney regiment, 132–3; on Greece, 183–5; on Churchill, 240–41; on attitude to foreigners, 302; on treat-ment of American Negroes, 306; on landing in Europe, 335; in last winter of war, 368, 370; and election (1945), 379
Matthews, W. R., Dean of St Paul's, 113, 156, 200–201, 201–202
Maud Committee, 63
Meade, P. C. David: (3 Sept. 1939), 1–2; (4 Sept. 1939), 17–18; (7 Sept. 1940), 97–9, 109–110; (May 1941), 229; in RAF, 230

meat, ration of, 283, 334
Mengin, Robert, attaché at French Embassy in London, 45, 47, 48; and de Gaulle, 49, 50–51, 86–9, 209–10, 211; broadcasts for BBC, 267
Messerschmitt aeroplanes, 90, 107; (109s), 74, 106; (110s), 106, 296
milk: rationing of, 232; powdered, 233
Miribel, Elizabeth de, French typist, 47
Montgomery, General Bernard, 260, 292, 360, 375
Moore, Henry, 32-4; and Under-ground shelters, 136–41
Morrison, Herbert: chairman of LCC, 11–13, 40; Home Sec-retary and Minister of Home Security, 202, 225, 319, 369
Morrison air-raid shelters, 250
Mosley, Sir Oswald: interned, 68, 69; released (1943), 319
Mosquito bombers, 351
Moullec, Capt., chief of staff to Admiral Muselier, 214, 271, 273
Mulberry Harbours, at Hackney Marshes, 157n, 341
Murrow, Ed, 201
Muselier, Admiral, in command of Free French Navy, 208, 210, 211; charges against, 212–17; and de Gaulle, 267, 269, 273–7, 285

National Gallery, concerts in, 219
Negroes in US forces, 304–7
news correspondents, in Savoy Hotel, 174, 175
'Nichols, Robert,' armaments worker, 135, 173
Nicolson, Harold, MP, 3, 17, 36, 43, 259, 339; on D-Day, 352–3;

Wardlaw-Milne, Sir John, MP, 254, 255, 259
water-shortage, for fire services (29 Dec. 1940), 199, 200
Watson-Watt, Sir Robert, inventor of radar, 61, 181
weather, 372-3
weather forecasts, banned, 53
Wedgwood, Josiah, 42
Weininger, Richard, Jew from Czechoslovakia, internment of, 57-9, 79-80, 82-6
Welfare State, 298
West End, 131, 171-2, 219-21; crowded (1942), 238; cosmopolitan (1943, 1944), 300, 332
West Ham: Council of, 127-8, 131n; taken over by government, 131n
West Ham stadium, 103-4, 113; break-out from D-Day camp in, 341-3
Western Desert, 242, 255
Westminster Hall, bombed, 227
Whitehall: Hole in the Ground beneath, 76, 105, 115, 344; parts of, evacuated while land-mine is dealt with, 165
Whitfield Tabernacle, last V2

falls on, 373
Wigram, Lord, 265
Wilson, Sir Horace, 14
Winant, John G., US Ambassador, 264, 347
Windmill Theatre, 186, 331, 360
Windsor Castle, Eisenhower at, 265
women, conscription of, 221, 238, 250, 278, 288
Women's Land Army, 332
Wontner, Hugh, Managing Director, Savoy Hotel, 175
Wood, Sir Kingsley, Minister for Air, 10; Chancellor of the Exchequer, 85
Woolton, Lord, at Ministry of Food, 56, 206, 207n, 232
Woolwich Arsenal, bombed, 107, 118
Wright, Flight-Lieut. Robert, at Fighter Command, 104
WRNS (Women's Royal Naval Service), 278
WVS (Women's Voluntary Services), 144-5, 328

Yugoslavia, fall of, 217